EDINBURGH
EDUCATION AND SOCIETY
SERIES

General Editor: Colin Bell

EDUCATION AND OPPORTUNITY IN VICTORIAN SCOTLAND

Schools & Universities

by
R. D. ANDERSON

EDINBURGH UNIVERSITY PRESS

© R.D. Anderson 1983

First published by Oxford University Press, 1983
Reprinted in paperback, with corrections, in 1989,
by Edinburgh University Press
22 George Square, Edinburgh

Printed and bound in Great Britain
by Billing & Sons Limited
Worcester

British Library Cataloguing in
  Publication Data
Anderson, R.D.
Education and opportunity in Victorian
Scotland: schools and universities
  1. Education—Scotland—History—19th century
  I. Title
370′.9411   LA652
ISBN 0 85224 617x (pbk)

PREFACE

This book is the work of a European historian with an interest in the comparative history of education rather than of one whose starting-point is Scotland, but I hope that it will do something to rescue from neglect a theme of great interest and importance for recent Scottish history. My original intention was to write on the history of the Scottish universities, but I soon found that this could not be understood without looking also at secondary education and at the parish schools which were the distinctive feature of the Scottish system. This led me to write institutional and social rather than cultural history, and not to discuss directly the contribution of the universities, and indeed the schools, to the intellectual life of the nation. Perhaps this was just as well, for this involves so many fields of activity —science, medicine, religion, law, philosophy—that polymathic abilities are needed to do it justice. Even so, I am conscious that the book says less than it might about what actually went on in the classroom and about the transmission of values and ideas which was the ultimate purpose of education.

The first aim of the book is to give a clear account of the general history of secondary and university education between the 1820s and 1914, showing how the different institutions and the structural relationships between them developed. This necessarily involves dealing with much general legislative and administrative history, but no attempt is made to give full coverage to elementary or to technical education. The theme of 'opportunity' relates chiefly to the chances of access to higher education, and hence to the question of how 'democratic' Scottish education really was. Such statistical material as exists —and it is far more abundant for Scotland than for England— is analysed in order to examine the social consequences of educational changes. Another aim is to put the origins of these changes into their social and political context and to stress— in contrast to the bland, consensual tone in which educational history is too often written—how conflicts of interest and class shaped the evolution of Scotland's educational institutions.

The avoidance of nineteenth- and twentieth-century history

by historians of Scotland is often complained of, but it is especially striking to anyone familiar with French historical scholarship. No region of France has the kind of national identity claimed by Scotland, yet there are few regions of France about whose social and political history we do not know more in the nineteenth century than about Scotland's. It is not just that educational history is neglected in Scotland—though it is—but that the educational historian is handicapped by the lack of an accepted framework of interpretation into which to fit his contribution. The Scottish working class and the Scottish agrarian community are beginning to find their historians, but the history of the middle class is still largely unwritten, as is the history of the great Scottish cities. If we knew as much about nineteenth-century Glasgow and Edinburgh as we know about Bordeaux or Lille, my task would have been easier. As it is, some of my general conclusions are necessarily tentative, and my references to the 'middle class' may often be found irritatingly vague. What I have tried to do, however, is to provide an interpretative framework of my own against which others may test their research, and if my book stimulates scholarship which proves me wrong I shall not complain.

The sources for this subject are abundant, but the historian's path through them is smoothed by Dr James Craigie's indispensable *Bibliography of Scottish education*. I have been able to draw on the admirable resources of the Scottish Record Office, the National Library of Scotland, and Edinburgh University Library, and I am grateful to their staffs for their courtesy and efficiency. In consulting the records of the universities, I have benefited from the help and advice of Mr Colin McLaren, University Archivist at Aberdeen, Mr R. N. Smart, Keeper of Manuscripts at St. Andrews, and Mr Michael Moss and Dr Irene O'Brien of Glasgow University Archives. I have also been assisted financially by the Travel and Research Committee of Edinburgh University.

Many friends and colleagues have given me information, advice, and encouragement. They include Paul Addison, Gordon Brown, John Brown, Angus Calder, Terry Cole, Owen Dudley Edwards, Nigel Griffiths, Christopher Harvie, Andrew McPherson, Nicholas Phillipson, and Donald Withrington. Any errors of fact or interpretation are, of course, my own.

CONTENTS

ABBREVIATIONS

ATSS	Association of Teachers in the Secondary Schools of Scotland
AU	Aberdeen University
EIS	Educational Institute of Scotland
EN	*Educational News*
EU	Edinburgh University
GC	General Council
GU	Glasgow University
3 Hansard	*Parliamentary Debates,* 3rd [etc.] series
HC	House of Commons
HL	House of Lords
NLS	National Library of Scotland
PP	Parliamentary Papers (House of Commons series)
SED	Scotch Education Department
SRO	Scottish Record Office
St. AU	St. Andrews University

All books cited are published in London unless otherwise shown.

1.
THE SCOTTISH TRADITION

National educational systems, directed by the state, are one of the characteristic creations of the nineteenth century, linked in the western world with the process of industrialization, the rise of political democracy, and the development of 'mass society'. This was as true of Scotland as of any country, and most features of Scottish education today are the product of the late nineteenth and early twentieth centuries. But in Scotland there was an advanced and distinctive educational tradition which could be traced back to the Reformation, and nineteenth-century Scots considered it to be both a point of superiority over England and a guarantee of Scotland's social and cultural autonomy within the Union. The belief that Scottish education was peculiarly 'democratic', and that it helped to sustain certain correspondingly democratic features of Scottish life, formed a powerful historical myth, using that word to indicate not something false, but an idealization and distillation of a complex reality, a belief which influences history by interacting with other forces and pressures, ruling out some developments as inconsistent with the national tradition, and shaping the form in which the institutions inherited from the past are allowed to change.

This democratic myth became, and has remained, a central part both of the Scottish sense of nationhood and of the image which others have formed of the Scots. In the history of European nationalism, education often had a vital role in transmitting, or helping to revive, national languages and cultures. In Scotland this was not the case—indeed, the schools became notorious for their neglect of Scottish literature and history. Instead it was the institutional forms of the educational system, and their articulation with each other, which were seen as the distinctive heritage to be preserved against alien influences and unsympathetic reforms. From this point of view, four distinct aspects of the 'myth' may be identified. First there was the

ideal of 'universality', of a school system which would put
religious education and the elements of literacy within reach of
the whole population through the provision of a school in every
parish. Second, there was the role of the school in affording
opportunities to the 'lad of parts': poverty should be no barrier
to talent, and individuals from whatever background should be
able to climb the educational ladder. Third, the school was
seen as a place where all social classes rubbed shoulders. This
was perhaps the aspect of the myth where sentiment and reality
were furthest apart: the classes might mix in rural schools, but
their segregation was well established in the towns, and social
differentiation was the keynote of educational change in the
nineteenth century. The defence of the democratic tradition
came to mean insisting that at least schools should not be one-
class institutions, and that in particular Scotland should avoid
the rigid identification of elementary education with the needs
of the poor which was imposed in England.

The fourth aspect of the tradition was that the three parts of
the educational system—parish schools in the countryside,
burgh schools in the towns, and the universities—should be
seen as forming a national system, with no social barriers
between them, and that since this system served the community as a whole it should be established by law, supported
from public funds, and supervised by the authorities of Church
and state. Parish schoolmasters, teachers in burgh schools and
university professors were all in a sense public officials, paid a
fixed salary which they supplemented by charging fees for their
services. In this, of course, there was a marked contrast
between Scotland and England, where the idea of a national
system hardly existed, and where there was great reluctance to
extend state action to the educational field; when it came, it
was at first confined to the elementary sphere, and for middle-
class education the doctrines of *laissez-faire* prevailed until the
end of the century. This gave rise to problems, for legislation
on Scottish education depended on the British Parliament,
which tended to follow English ideas on state action and class
differentiation. But England was the odd man out in Europe,
and Scots could feel more sympathy with the continental tradition of state support for secondary schools and universities.

The Church was the agency entrusted with education in the

past, and there was clearly a link between the ethos of Calvin-
ism and Scottish respect for intellectuality and individual
achievement. Historians of Scottish education rightly see its
founding charter in the document of 1560 known as the First
Book of Discipline, which outlined a national system of schools
and put special emphasis on helping the poor through scholarships and on the benefit which the community as well as the
individual derived from a wide recruitment to the professions
—medicine and law as well as the ministry. The proposals of
1560 envisaged three types of school below the level of the
universities, but they were not put into effect at the time, and
when the expansion of education was seriously undertaken in
the seventeenth century it concentrated on the provision of a
school in every parish. These efforts culminated in an Act of
1696 which, with some amendments in 1803 and later years,
remained the basis of Scottish educational legislation down to
1872. The 'heritors' in each parish (the substantial landowners)
were obliged to maintain a school, open to boys and girls alike,
and to appoint a salaried schoolmaster. The funds were provided by a rate on landed property, the minister exercised
day-to-day supervision, and the presbyteries of the Church
inspected the schools and tested the teachers' religious and
scholarly qualifications. The teachers were expected to teach the
Church's 'Shorter Catechism', but their main business was to
teach reading and writing to all; moreover, parish schoolmasters were expected to be able to teach Latin, so that they
could prepare boys for the universities where a demand existed.
Thus although education was neither free nor compulsory, it
was in principle within reach of all.

The parish-school legislation did not apply to towns, and
although by custom all burghs were expected to maintain a
burgh school, these often hardly rose above the level of a parish
school, and only in the largest towns did burgh schools give an
education of a mainly secondary type. This underdevelopment
of secondary education encouraged the most distinctive feature
of Scottish education, the direct relationship between the parish
schools and the universities. The parish schoolmaster taught the
so-called 'university subjects'—Latin, mathematics, and
perhaps Greek—and the universities came down to meet the
parish schools by admitting boys at fifteen or even younger and

by providing elementary instruction in the 'junior classes' which began the college course. Some Latin was essential for university entry, but the Greek junior class began with the alphabet. For boys with talent but no resources, bursaries for university study were quite widely available, and many of the men thus educated returned as schoolmasters to carry on this educational cycle which bypassed altogether the urban schools. Functions which in other countries were reserved for secondary schools were in Scotland performed both by the parish schools and by the universities themselves, many of whose students were very young. But some were older, for one consequence of the system was that the universities were open to anyone who could scrape together a little Latin and mathematics, and this included men who decided to change course in adult life. The student body was a diverse one, and the universities were not hedged off by the kind of social barriers which made Oxford and Cambridge places of privilege. Their customs, indeed, recognized that many students would combine university attendance with work of some kind, or would need to earn their living in the summer, for the university session ran only from late October to Easter.

The 'parochial tradition', to adopt a convenient shorthand term for the link between universities and parish schools,[1] was especially adapted to the training of ministers and schoolmasters, and students aiming at these careers largely populated the arts faculties. The two careers, indeed, were not sharply differentiated, for many parish schoolmasters were men who had not attended university long enough to qualify for the ministry, or who had done so but were still waiting for a parish. Teachers were a good deal worse paid than the clergy, but for many men teaching was only a temporary stage, and the teacher could himself enjoy a status which had no equivalent in England, where at the beginning of the nineteenth century teaching was still a refuge for those who had failed in other occupations. In village society, the minister and the schoolmaster, linked through their university experience with the culture of the landed class and the upper bourgeoisie, could work

---

[1] Adopted from L. J. Saunders, *Scottish democracy 1815-1840* (Edinburgh, 1950). This remains the best description of education in this period, now supplemented by T. C. Smout, *A history of the Scottish people 1560-1830* (paperback edn., n.p., 1972).

together to diffuse intellectual and moral values and promote social cohesion.

For the parochial tradition was best adapted to the needs of a rural society. When communications were difficult in a thinly-populated country, it made sense to give a rudimentary secondary education in a large number of schools, and the parish school was a convenience for the rural middle class. In the old Scotland, social distances had been relatively short below the gentry level: farmers, artisans, shopkeepers, and lesser professional men could make similar demands on education and share a common culture based on their religious life. But with industrialization and urbanization—the percentage of the population living in towns rose from 21 in 1801 to 39 in 1861 and 58 in 1901[2]—strains appeared. The towns contained both a growing mass of semi-skilled and unskilled workers for whom education beyond the basics did not seem a pressing need, and an expanding and multi-layered middle class with new professional and practical needs. This middle class required more formal qualifications in a society which was becoming more complex and more achievement-oriented, but it also valued education for reasons of status. It was a means of acquiring the traditional culture which lent dignity to new wealth, a badge of class identity and a mark of differentiation from the classes below, and a way of ensuring that the social hierarchy was reproduced in the next generation. Secondary education best served status needs when it was a distinct sector with strictly controlled entry, and most nineteenth-century educational systems were of a 'dualist' kind with separate 'bourgeois' and 'popular' schools: on the continent this dualism was formalized in state-run systems, and in England the operation of the free market and the restriction of state aid to schools for the labouring classes had much the same effect. In Scotland, the process of social differentiation was well under way in the cities in the eighteenth century, and the parochial tradition of combining elementary and secondary education in the same school seemed to have no particular value in urban conditions. In the early nineteenth century, the middle class still made much use

[2] M. Flinn (ed.), *Scottish population history from the 17th century to the 1930s* (Cambridge, 1977), p. 313 (towns over 5,000).

of private tuition and small private schools, but the trend was towards larger and more formally-organized schools of a 'collegiate' type. The burgh schools were there to form the nucleus of a system of middle-class day schools, Scottish opinion was not hostile to state support in this field, and the middle class had all the more freedom of action because the Scottish upper class's educational interests now lay largely in England. From the 1820s onwards, middle-class pressures lay behind a movement for reforming and improving secondary schools, but (it will be argued) the strength of the democratic myth eventually operated to counteract them, and by the end of the century political conflict over the shape of the school system led to a settlement which kept secondary schooling relatively open and accessible. Moreover, where social and geographical conditions were favourable, the parish schools or developments from them still had a part to play. Rural and small-town communities survived alongside the new urban society, and they retained an important and increasingly sentimentalized role in the national psyche.

The extent to which the parochial tradition was really working in the nineteenth century will be investigated in Chapter 4, but the mechanisms of mobility can be illustrated through a few life stories. Perhaps the best known is that of Carlyle, whose devout family, small farmers in Dumfriesshire, sent him from the village school to the grammar school at Annan with the ministry as the ultimate goal. In 1809, at the age of thirteen, Carlyle walked to Edinburgh to enter on the classic life of the impoverished student, living in lodgings, sending his laundry home by the carrier and receiving supplies of oatmeal in return, and making what sense he could of the lectures. Like James Mill before him, and many others, Carlyle eventually abandoned the planned clerical career and launched himself on the literary world.[3] But this was only one pattern, for men from poor backgrounds often went to the university as adults rather than directly from school. There was, for example, Alexander

---

[3] J. A. Froude, *Thomas Carlyle. A history of the first forty years of his life, 1795-1835* (New York, 1882), pp. 11 ff., 16-18, 113 ff., 136.

Murray, a Galloway man who rose from shepherd-boy to professor of Hebrew. Murray hardly attended school at all, but taught himself Hebrew, Latin and Greek while tending his sheep, and got intermittent work teaching the children of local families. He owed much to the encouragement of local clergymen, and was eventually found a bursary at Edinburgh University, which he entered at the age of eighteen in 1793. He was to serve as a parish minister for several years before being appointed to the chair.[4] A less exalted rural exemplar was Alexander Gray, born in Aberdeenshire in 1822, who by the age of twenty was celebrated as a champion ploughman. At twenty-two, he went back to school, studied at the university, and ended his days as a rural clergyman.[5]

England too had its university professors of humble origins, and there are parallels between Murray's career and those of Joseph Wright (b. 1855) who began work at the age of six as a Bradford wool-sorter and became professor of Comparative Philology at Oxford, or Samuel Lee (d. 1852), a carpenter who became professor of Hebrew at Cambridge.[6] Yet these men are forgotten, while Murray became something of a legend, and a monument to him still broods over the hills where he studied his books.[7] Such cases contributed to the idealization of the parochial tradition, though the school had actually done little for Murray; it was often more important for imparting a basic literacy which bore fruit later in life, or for help which the schoolmaster might give to older men privately, than as a direct means of preparing for the university. Besides, the chances of getting on in this way were very haphazard, and depended much on local conditions, on individual initiative, and on patronage and encouragement—patronage from the minister who helped to find a bursary and pulled strings at the university, or from the landowner who might give generously to help a local boy; encouragement from the schoolmaster who

[4] J. Reith, *The life and writings of Rev. Alex. Murray* (Dumfries, 1903), pp. 5-36.

[5] I. Carter, *Farmlife in Northeast Scotland 1840-1914. The poor man's country* (Edinburgh, 1979), p. 112.

[6] J. F. C. Harrison, *Learning and living 1790-1960* (1961), pp. 46-7; D. Vincent, *Bread, knowledge and freedom. A Study of nineteenth-century working class autobiography* (1981), p. 147.

[7] Erected in 1834-5, but the inscription was added to in 1877—exactly when the parochial tradition was felt to be under most threat: Reith, op. cit., pp. 138-9.

identified intellectual promise, or from the uncles and cousins who dug into their pockets to allow one member of the family to shed reflected glory on the rest.

In the towns, similar encouragement could come from the milieu of the artisan community, self-educated and serious-minded, which was one of the products of widespread literacy. Alexander Bain, for example, the son of an Aberdeen weaver, left school at eleven, because his parents could not afford to keep him on, and from thirteen to eighteen worked at the loom while educating himself. With some like-minded friends, he revived the Aberdeen Mechanics' Institute and profited from its library and from a 'mutual instruction class' based on it. Bain was eventually taken up by a local clergyman, who coached him in Latin and interested the university professors in his case. He was given a free place at Aberdeen Grammar School for a few months to complete his preparation, and after that a bursary at Marischal College (one of the two universities in Aberdeen). Thus when Bain went to the university at the age of eighteen, it was as an adult with experience of work and life. After a career spent partly in teaching and partly in the London literary world, he returned to Aberdeen in 1860 as professor of Logic.[8]

It is generally thought today that by the end of the eighteenth century the network of parish schools in the Lowlands was reasonably effective, and that literacy was at a high level.[9] When the ability to write a signature was first measured, after the civil registration of marriages was introduced in 1855, Scotland had a literacy rate of 89 per cent for men and 77 per cent for women, compared with 70 and 59 per cent for England and Wales in the same year.[10] In the majority of Lowland counties male literacy was over 90 per cent, the exceptions being the industrializing counties of the West; literacy was high in some Highland counties like Argyll, but low in the western

---

[8] A. Bain, *Autobiography* (1904), pp. 5-8, 13-16, 26-32.

[9] Smout, op. cit., pp. 421 ff.

[10] C. M. Cipolla, *Literacy and development in the West* (Harmondsworth, 1969), pp. 122-3. The county figures, relating to the ten years 1861-70, are from *Census of Scotland, 1871*, Vol. II (PP 1873, lxxiii), p. clxix.

Highlands and Islands—65 per cent for men in Ross-shire, 64 per cent in Inverness. Poverty, remoteness, demographic crisis and the language barrier helped to explain Highland backwardness, but in general the pattern of literacy reflected the strengths and weaknesses of the parish schools. In the Highlands the parishes were very large and the population scattered, but even in the Lowlands the parishes were ill-adapted as units of administration, with boundaries inherited from the medieval past. The law only required one school to be maintained in each parish (with some exceptions sanctioned in Acts of 1803 and 1838), and there was no real mechanism for expanding public provision when new industrial settlements grew up. In many areas in the West the parish school was totally swamped, and in the burghs there was also only one school established by law; in small burghs the burgh school would be very similar to a parish school, but in larger ones it would normally be devoted to middle-class needs.

The parochial tradition came nearest to its ideal form in the North-East, the region dominated by Aberdeen, where the schools had a symbiotic relationship with the city's two universities, King's College and Marischal College. The cultivation of the 'university subjects' in the North-East was encouraged by the local social structure—there were many small farmers in this region who were prosperous enought to afford school fees, but whose sons needed to look to the towns or the professions for their future—and by the unusually large number of bursaries at the Aberdeen universities, mostly awarded by open competition, which extended interest in higher education downwards from the farmers to labourers and rural artisans. The annual bursary competition was the target to which the schoolmasters directed their most promising boys, and it became a part of local folklore. Since the examination was based almost entirely on Latin prose composition, it had the effect of keeping the classics somewhat artificially alive, and of diverting to the university and the professions boys who in other parts of Scotland might have studied some more modern subject and found an outlet in commerce.

Most of the schoolmasters were themselves Aberdeen graduates, and from the 1830s their quality was maintained by an important charitable endowment, the Dick bequest. James

Dick was a West India merchant from Forres, who left his money 'to elevate the literary character of the Parochial Schoolmasters and Schools' in the counties of Aberdeen, Banff, and Moray. The trust gave a substantial supplement to the salaries of schoolmasters who passed its special examinations, and its inspector—between 1856 and 1890 the leading Scottish educationist, S. S. Laurie—ensured that the schools kept up to the mark. In the North-East, therefore, the university-qualified schoolmaster survived in strength, and the importance of university preparation was itself an attraction, allowing the teacher some relief from the drudgery of elementary teaching through keeping his scholarship alive and the pleasure of working with one or two enthusiastic pupils.

Elsewhere in Scotland, the parish schoolmaster was usually equipped to teach Latin, but did not necessarily find any takers for it. Besides, the parish schools were now outnumbered by other types of school, provided both by the churches and by private enterprise. Much of the church effort went into the Highlands, but in the Lowlands many 'private adventure' schools appeared, some of the 'dame school' type, but others opened by men who could offer the more advanced subjects and charge higher fees. In the 1820s, the Church moved into the field of urban education, opening 'sessional schools' in Edinburgh and Glasgow, and later in other towns. These were supported by individual congregations, and made some effort to reach the standards of the parish schools. This movement was accelerated by the Disruption of 1843, when the Free Church broke away from the Church of Scotland. The Free Church had to provide for schoolmasters who were ejected from their posts for joining it, and it tried to compete with the Established Church by creating a complete range of church-related institutions. The Free Church schools were modelled on the parish schools, and established a reputation for quality; there were even some Free Church 'grammar schools' which competed with the burgh schools, notably at Inverness, Campbeltown, Hamilton, and Arbroath. By the 1860s, out of 4,450 schools in rural Scotland only 916 were parish schools in the strict sense, but 617 of the remainder were connected with the Free Church.[11]

[11] *Argyll Comm. 2nd Rep.*, p. 24. (Abbreviated forms are used for official publications which are listed in the Bibliography.)

Thus as Scotland became more urbanized, a clear division appeared between two types of school. On one hand were the parish schools and those modelled on them—the better sessional and Free Church schools, superior private schools; in these, Latin and other higher subjects would be on offer to a minority. On the other were purely elementary schools— rural schools away from the parish centre, charity schools founded for the poor, private schools in which the teacher scraped a living by charging fees within reach of the working class. The expansion of such schools created a need for a new type of trained teacher, one with more modest qualifications and salary expectations than the parish schoolmaster, who was himself in increasingly short supply. As long as the clerical profession was overcrowded, and as long as other career openings were scarce, the supply of graduate teachers could be kept up; but these conditions were disappearing. The denominational competition which followed the Disruption mopped up much clerical unemployment, and economic expansion was creating opportunities more attractive than elementary teaching. As late as 1865, Laurie reported that nine-tenths of the teachers aided by the Dick bequest saw teaching only as a stepping-stone to the ministry, but that showed how the bequest allowed the survival of conditions which elsewhere were vanishing. To provide teachers for the elementary schools, the government introduced the pupil-teacher system in 1846, in Scotland as in England. This paid children to stay on at school as pupil-teachers, and if they passed the necessary examination they could go on to one of the 'normal colleges' which had been founded in Edinburgh and Glasgow in the 1830s, and which were duplicated by the Free Church after 1843. Intellectual standards in these colleges were hardly on the university level, the emphasis being on the standard school subjects and the rather mechanical teaching methods of the day. But they undoubtedly turned out efficient teachers, who soon began to compete with university graduates for the better posts; this competition, and the problem of relations between the training colleges and the universities, gave rise to some complex disputes.

It was the challenge of the big cities, above all, which forced the defenders of the parochial tradition to redefine it. The clergy were the most eloquent of those defenders, and none was more eloquent than the Evangelical leader Thomas Chalmers. During his experimental ministry at St. Johns, in the east end of Glasgow, Chalmers established two schools of the sessional type, in which—as in the system of voluntary poor relief which he applied simultaneously—he attempted to transfer the social relationships of a rural parish to an urban context. At the opening of these schools in 1820, he urged the rich to send their children to study alongside the poor, praising the 'indiscriminate mingling of the children of all ranks and degrees in society' which he had experienced in the parish schools of his youth. By such an arrangement, 'The ties of kindliness will be multiplied between the wealthy and the labouring classes of our city, ... and instead of rude encroachment on the one side, and the pride of a distant and disdainful jealousy on the other, will there be a community more humanized by the circulation of a mutual good-will, and of which the extreme parties will be more mellowed into one as the intercourse of advanced life is thus softened by the touching remembrances of boyhood.'[12] The same faith in the effects of a shared schooling was held by another minister with experience of the Glasgow slums, George Lewis, whose *Scotland a half-educated nation* (1834) focused attention on the problems of urban growth. 'We look in vain, in the large towns of Scotland,' he complained, 'for those kindly feelings between all classes, which arose in the parish schools of Scotland, and were cherished in her parish churches, sweetening the intercourse, and strengthening the bands, of society.' Like Chalmers, Lewis was a strong advocate of state action, and called for a national system embracing all classes, so that 'the children of rich and poor, brought up at the same school, may ever after cherish kind feelings towards each other, and society in town and country may recover that kinder tone, which it is fast losing, from the present state of our churches and schools'.[13]

[12] W. Hanna, *Memoirs of the life and writings of Thomas Chalmers* (Edinburgh, 1849-52), ii. 240-4.
[13] [G. Lewis], *Scotland a half-educated nation* (Glasgow, 1834), pp. 43, 55.

Chalmers, a political conservative anxious to reassure his bourgeois subscribers, stressed that his aim was not to kindle a 'diseased ambition' among the workers, or to overturn the natural inequalities of society, but rather to 'turn an ignorant operative into a learned operative'. Education was the birthright of the labouring classes as much as of the rich, and Chalmers looked forward to the day when his parish would be as well provided with 'all the means of respectable scholarship as any parish which our classical and lettered and intellectual Scotland has to boast of'. This ideal of 'learned operatives' remaining content with their station was hardly realistic at a time when education was one of the few escape routes from poverty, nor was the hope that the Glasgow middle classes would make use of common schools.

Other defenders of the parochial tradition admitted that it encouraged social mobility, but argued that the form which this took actually increased the stability of society. This argument was put in 1836 by the *Aberdeen University Magazine*, founded by the ultra-conservative professors of King's College to oppose the university reform bill of that year. Noting that in the towns 'things seem rapidly advancing to a state of preparation for a war of caste', the *Magazine* applied itself particularly to defending the Aberdeen bursary system, which critics accused of encouraging inordinate ambition among the poor. 'The facilities complained of, for imparting so generally an University education,' argued the *Magazine*, 'constitute that very characteristic of the system which gives to it a powerful influence, to counteract the hostility between the upper and lower orders of society ... and to bind all classes together by the kindliest ties.' Imagine the case of the 'son of the cottager' who rises through the system to

some one of the professional or other walks of life, in which he becomes associated with the higher ranks. There he fixes himself by new ties which he forms; while his connexions by birth, though continuing in the same humble station, are not overlooked or forgotten by him. They are benefited by his rise in various respects; and are thus led to look up to superiority of rank and fortune, not with envious discontent, but with grateful complacence; while the feelings of the whole inhabitants of the district, are influenced by the perception that no impassable barrier exists between them and those they account great and fortunate; and that their own children, or their children's children, may also rise to those elevated ranks of society thus seen to be attainable by all, and in the preservation and prosperity of which, all are thus found to possess a common interest.[14]

This view was persistent enough to surface forty years later in school inspectors' reports. In 1878, for example, the Revd John Macleod argued that the maintenance of the parochial tradition was of national importance. The peaceable nature of the Scottish people 'results from the absence of those sharp lines of demarcation which separate the several grades of society in other countries; and this again is largely, if not entirely, the result of the bridge across which so many youths passed yearly from the common schools to the universities'. If talent can rise to its natural level, men blame themselves rather than society for their difficulties.

The communist of Paris or the republican of London becomes the clergyman, the doctor, the lawyer, or the schoolmaster of Scotland ... Nor is he merely peaceful himself, he is the cause of peacefulness in others. His schoolfellows, who have, perhaps, not been so successful as himself, see that his promotion was the result of his merit, and that their own lot was not due to the despotism of their fellow citizens. His very intercourse with them after the toils of the field are over for the day, is a sweetener of life, and makes them feel the bond of union that runs through all sections of the community. It brings home to them that all have their destined part to play, and that disorder is absurd as well as wicked.[15]

In England, the clergy often lent their authority to crude ideas of education as a form of social control. In Scotland, the belief in popular education took root before fears of the new factory proletariat arose, and men like Chalmers were able to put forward a much subtler idea of social harmony based on common schooling or on a controlled upward mobility. It was important that in Scotland the traditional social authorities supported the wide diffusion of education and endorsed an ethic of individual achievement, even if this Tory-clerical ideal also evoked a hierarchical, paternalist society innocent of

---

[14] *Aberdeen University Magazine,* i (1836), pp. 24-5.
[15] *CCES Rep., 1878-9* (PP 1878-9, xxv), pp. 166-7; cf. similar views of John Kerr in *CCE Rep., 1871-2* (PP 1872, xxii), pp. 93, 99-100.

modern ideas of class, bound together (to use the constantly recurring metaphor) by relationships of a personal, organic kind. It was an ideal which naturally appealed to the clergy, who had often themselves escaped from the 'toils of the field' and who liked to think that their influence rested on an intellectual merit independent of rank. Its applicability to the anonymous, class-segregated life of the cities was, of course, more than doubtful, and kindly feelings between the classes were not a marked feature of early capitalism.

The way was thus prepared for the nineteenth-century ideal of meritocracy. Through the principle of 'removable inequalities', liberal social theory legitimated a competitive, individualist society: if the social hierarchy was open to merit, and genuine talent could always reach the top, then middle-class social domination was felt to rest on ability rather than privilege.[16] It was for the individual to demonstrate his worthiness to succeed through sacrifice and hard work, and this fitted in with the Scottish ideal, which had always emphasized qualities of character and the moral virtue of the struggle with poverty.

It was inevitable that the influence of the clergy should wane, as other professions grew in importance and as social and intellectual life became secularized. The Disruption dealt a fatal blow to the ideal of the parochial community grouped around the church, and—now that there was no longer one Church representing the majority of the nation—accelerated the transfer of public institutions like the schools to secular authorities, a process completed by the Education Act of 1872. In pre-industrial Scotland the landed class had been happy enough to leave education within the clerical sphere, and for some time the clergy were still regarded as the experts on social questions. But the growing middle class had a direct interest of its own in the schools and universities and began to demand both that they should come under closer public (i.e. middle-class) control, and that their teaching should cease to be attuned simply to the training of the clergy. The vanguard of the middle class was formed by the lawyers of Edinburgh, who

[16] Cf. W. L. Burn, *The age of equipoise* (1964), p. 104; G. Best, *Mid-Victorian Britain 1851-1875* (1971), pp. 233 ff.

controlled the Scottish end of the national legislative machine, and who (in conjunction with the intelligentsia of the capital) assumed a conscious role of 'civic leadership'.[17] Later they faded out of the picture, but during the first half of the century the pressures brought to bear on both secondary schools and universities reflected a specifically professional ideal, which emphasized classical education both because of its cultural identification with the old landed élite whom the professional class sought to supplant, and because of the prestige of English models.

Secondary education had already begun to expand in the eighteenth century in response to the quickening of intellectual and commercial life. Most burgh schools were traditionally devoted to the classics, but town councils had begun to found 'English schools', 'commercial schools' and so on to teach modern subjects (the word 'school' being used to mean what was taught by one master), and in some towns, beginning with Perth in 1760, there were more ambitious 'Academies' which sought to offer a complete modern education at a high level, and even to compete with the universities, which were condemned for their irrelevance to commercial needs.[18] Perth Academy was founded by the town council, but elsewhere new schools were often of a 'proprietary' kind, built by a subscription among the local gentry and businessmen, and managed by a board of governors or directors.[19] In the early nineteenth century, there was a movement everywhere for the amalgamation of burgh schools and academies, and in most towns of any size new buildings were erected to house the amalgamated school; many of the resulting schools were called Academies, but the term ceased to denote any particular form of education. Rebuildings and school amalgamations of this kind took place, for example, at Montrose (1820), Dunbar (1824), Dundee

[17] N. T. Phillipson, 'Lawyers, landowners, and the civic leadership of post-union Scotland', *Juridical Review*, n.s. xxi (1976), pp. 97-9, 119-20.

[18] D. J. Withrington, 'Education and society in the eighteenth century' in N. T. Phillipson & R. Mitchison (eds.), *Scotland in the age of improvement* (Edinburgh, 1970), pp. 177-81.

[19] 'Proprietary' schools were those managed by such a board on a non-profit-making basis, and were distinguished from 'private' schools run by an individual as a commercial venture.

(1834), Brechin (1838), Kirkcaldy (1843), Stirling (1855), Arbroath (1861) and Paisley (1864), while simple rebuilding of the burgh schools took place at Ayr (1810), Irvine (1814), Lanark (1840), Falkirk (1845), Greenock (1851), and Aberdeen (1863). This clearly reflects a major expansion of demand, although no statistics are available nationally until the 1860s. But it also resulted from a feeling that a town should have only one major secondary school, and that it should be a public institution under the supervision of the town council, for—according to Sinclair in 1826—a school 'by its connexion with such bodies, is, in some measure, interwoven with the frame of the body politic, and a foundation is thus laid for its future durable prosperity'.[20]

When schools were rebuilt, it was usually in a Renaissance or Greek Revival style, and they were often an important element in the civic landscape, as at Dundee and Edinburgh. This classicism was not just a reference to the type of culture dispensed behind the porticoes, but the expression of a civic consciousness which was stronger in Scotland than in England: English educational architecture was predominantly Gothic, evoking an ecclesiastical past, but in Scotland the 'patronage' of a burgh school gave town councils a certain sense of dignity and intellectual stature. Municipal reform after 1833 intensified this: the new municipal electorate corresponded closely to the class interested in secondary education, and the way was opened to its expansion under middle-class leadership.

Although the town councils were seen as the natural supervisory bodies, the process of amalgamation often resulted in mixed management, in which town councillors sat alongside the representatives of schools which had been absorbed, of endowment trusts, or of subscribers to rebuilding.[21] In the same way, the various departments or 'schools' were often practically independent. Each master collected his own fees, and although the classical master usually had the title of 'rector' he did not exert authority over his colleagues in the style of English headmasters; some schools, like Glasgow High

---

[20] J. Sinclair, *Analysis of the Statistical Account of Scotland* (1826), part 2, p. 103.

[21] For details of rebuilding, management, etc. see *Argyll Comm. 3rd Rep.*, Vol. II; *Colebrooke Comm. 2nd Rep.*; J. Grant, *History of the burgh and parish schools of Scotland. ... Burgh schools* (1876), pp. 115 ff.

School, had no rector at all. At Glasgow, after reorganization by the town council in 1834, there were six independent departments, while at Perth a building called the 'Seminaries', erected and controlled by the town council, also housed six separate operations, including the successors of the traditional grammar school and the Academy. In these conditions no single curriculum was possible, and in nearly all burgh schools parents chose what subjects they wanted and paid the appropriate fees. Modern and commercial subjects were more popular than the classics, and there was no equivalent of the legal restrictions which confined the English grammar schools to the classics and so caused them to stagnate.

Another difference between the two countries was that Scotland lacked large educational endowments. The wealthiest and most ancient were the 'hospitals' in certain towns. Heriot's Hospital in Edinburgh and Hutchesons' in Glasgow dated from the seventeenth century, but more recent foundations were concentrated in Edinburgh. These were residential institutions for children of various deserving categories, especially orphans, and they made only a limited contribution to secondary education until after 1869, when they were mostly reformed as middle-class day schools.

Philanthropy did, however, contribute to the foundation of new schools in towns previously unprovided for. A common type of benefactor was the merchant who made his wealth in London or abroad, and left it to his native parish as a form of gratitude and a way of encouraging others to follow in his footsteps. In this way schools appeared in quite small towns, like Milne's Institution at Fochabers (1846) or Dollar Institution (1818). Philanthropic impulses continued well into the second half of the century, and gifts or bequests helped to create schools at Crieff (Morrison's Academy, 1860), Lerwick (Anderson Institute, 1860), Thurso (Miller Institution, 1861), Newton Stewart (Ewart Institute, 1863), Fraserburgh (Academy, 1870), and Anstruther (Waid Academy, 1884). Of particular interest were the schools founded at St. Andrews and Cupar in 1831-3 by Andrew Bell, the founder of the 'Madras' monitorial system, who left a large fortune for various educational purposes in Scotland. The two Madras colleges replaced the burgh schools, and the town councils handed over their powers to the Bell trustees. At Cupar, the foundation comprised three schools with different scales of fees.

The three schools are not intended to fit into each other, and to be, as it were, departments of one whole, in which the scholars shall be promoted from one to the other as they advance in years. Each is complete in itself, and the distinction between them is founded very much, as in St. Andrews, on the social position of the scholars. The idea of the founder was to have all classes taught, but in separate blocks or divisions, the scale of fees being adjusted according to the ability to pay; and the branches taught in each school being regulated to some extent by the probable requirements of children in different grades of life.[22]

Madras College at St. Andrews proved the more successful school, and developed a large boarding side; following Bell's principles of segregation, the boarders were taught separately from the local children. At Dollar and Fochabers too, the development of a boarding school proved the best way of using a large endowment, with children from the local parish being educated free. There was a good deal of boarding in nineteenth-century Scotland, but it mostly escapes the historian's notice because it was not organized officially by the schools. Parents sent their sons to stay with relatives or live in lodgings while they attended a burgh school, or the rector and masters might take boarders in their own houses as a lucrative sideline. Parish schoolmasters who established a reputation for their classical teaching could also do this: Udny in Aberdeenshire was a parish school which became famous for its upper-class boarders, though this ended in the 1830s. Sometimes an endowment supported secondary education in small schools of this type, as at Fordyce Academy in Banffshire. These developments were not limited to the North-East, for at Carmichael in rural Lanarkshire Thomas Braidwood attracted boarders to his parish school between 1840 and 1873, when he left to open a private school, Stanley House, in the more fashionable location of Bridge of Allan: the 1872 Act had ruled out this kind of enterprise by ending the independent status of the parish schoolmaster.[23]

---

[22] *Argyll Comm. 3rd Rep.*, Vol. II, p. 89, and cf. pp. 63 ff. on St. Andrews.
[23] *The Third Statistical Account of Scotland. The County of Lanark* (Glasgow, 1960), p. 493.

The ethos of the Scottish secondary school remained that of the day school, with the emphasis on intellectual achievement, and with no claims being made to train the character. There were many private boarding schools, but on the whole they lacked prestige, and the element of public management in the burgh schools precluded the kind of development found in England, where ambitious headmasters turned local grammar schools into boarding schools which became part of the Public School system.[24] The first Scottish school to be directly modelled on the English Public Schools was Trinity College, Glenalmond, founded in 1847 by leading Episcopalians like Gladstone. In its early years it included a seminary for the Episcopal clergy; it was expensive and exclusive, and remained a somewhat exotic import to the Scottish scene. These years also saw the development of other schools, however, like Merchiston Castle and Loretto, both near Edinburgh, which were later to be admitted to the Public School community.

The schools of Edinburgh were numerous and diverse, for the city was an educational centre which drew pupils from all over Britain and the British Empire. This large range of choice allowed the traditional burgh school, the High School, to remain almost exclusively classical, with a common curriculum taken by all pupils. The High School was a great object of civic pride, and official oratory laid special stress on the mixture of classes within it. According to the Solicitor-General John Hope, at the laying of the foundation-stone of the new building in 1825, 'It was there where the proud characteristics of Britons was [*sic*] fully exemplified—its classes were open to boys of all ranks and circumstances. It proved what was the use of a school in a free state,—it was not birth, rank, or fortune, that in this country could reach the highest place—but talent, perseverance, and industry.' Hope was a Tory, but twenty years later the Liberal Lord Provost Adam Black struck the same note:

Here the youth of all classes of society—every sect,—the peer and the peasant,—all join in the same form, each possessing no advantages over his neighbour. The most humble of our citizens have an opportunity of getting their children trained up on a par with the highest ranks of society, having their minds improved, their judgment

---

[24] To avoid confusion, capital letters are used for the English Public Schools.

enlarged and strengthened, and their taste refined, so as to be put on a level with the highest of the land. To the great institutions of England none can have access but the wealthy, and yet there is not one of them I hold which is entitled to be placed over the High School of Edinburgh.[25]

The same claim could be made for other burgh schools: as the school song of Perth Academy was to put it,[26]

> Nor Faction's voice nor Dives' nod,
> Nor class nor caste she owns,
> And Peer and Peasant both have trod
> Her well-worn cobble stones.

In Edinburgh the local landed gentry had indeed used the school alongside the middle class in the eighteenth century, but that practice had now ceased, and the 'humble' must have been deterred by the highest burgh school fees in Scotland. In any case, the professional élite of Edinburgh were now dissatisfied with the High School, and in 1824—'an important day for education in Scotland, in reference to the middle and upper classes'[27]—Edinburgh Academy was opened. It was sponsored by such luminaries as Scott, Jeffrey, and Cockburn, all of whom had themselves attended the High School, but who now felt that it was 'lowered, perhaps necessarily, so as to suit the wants of a class of boys to more than two-thirds of whom classical accomplishment is foreseen to be useless'.[28] At the Academy, higher classical standards were to be the aim, and its masters were drawn from the English universities; it was also 'English' in having a prescribed curriculum and a staff of form teachers under the absolute control of the rector, and it could prepare boys for the English universities, although Edinburgh University, the legal profession, and the armed forces were the main outlets. The Academy was a proprietary day school with higher fees than the High School; it was situated in the New Town, to which most of the professional classes had migrated, and one of its aims was to counteract the tendency of the

---

[25] W. Steven, *The history of the High School of Edinburgh* (Edinburgh, 1849), pp. 218-19, 261-2.

[26] E. Smart, *History of Perth Academy* (Perth, 1932), p. 264. The song, characteristically, dates from 1918.

[27] H. Cockburn, *Memorials of his time* (Chicago, 1974), p. 389.

[28] Ibid., p. 388.

Scottish élite to send their sons away to England. The ideal which the Academy represented was significant for the future, but it found few immediate imitators—Glasgow Academy, on the same model, did not open until 1846. In Edinburgh, the response of the town council was to rebuild the High School on a new site and compete for the same clientele.

In 1835 James Pillans, a former rector of the High School who had become professor of Humanity (Latin) at the university, gave some lectures which stressed the importance of the education of the élite and the suitability for the task of the classical training in which the High School and Academy specialized. The numbers affected might be small, yet in them 'are contained the surest hopes of the nation,—the true aristocracy of every civilized community. It is the fund upon which the country must draw for its legislators, its divines, its public teachers, its physicians, its gentry, its nobility.' The progress of 'education for the many', which Pillans strongly supported, had implications for the 'education of the few'. 'If there is any chance of the frame-work of society being strained or disjointed in consequence of the progress of popular instruction, it is not from the diffusion of knowledge that the danger is to be apprehended, but from the higher ranks being left behind in the race of improvement.' Education must reinforce the natural superiority of birth, station, and character. The classics were essential for this élite, but had their value too for 'the great bulk of the middle class of easy and respectable citizens, who can contrive to combine the habits and details of business with the larger views imparted by solitary reading and social intercourse'; it would be a pity to exclude their sons from 'all chance of that general cultivation of the intellectual powers, and that humanizing influence of ancient literature, which result ... from a well-directed course of classical instruction'.[29]

If this classical ideal was to be pursued, it raised questions for other parts of the educational system. The special feature of the Scottish system was that although its different parts were linked by the teaching of Latin as the essential university subject and by the presence of university-trained schoolmasters in both parish and burgh schools, the articulation was a loose

---

[29] J. Pillans, *Contributions to the cause of education* (1856), pp. 258-9, 302-3.

one. Students could go to the university from either sort of school, or direct from adult life, and the level of classical teaching in a traditional burgh school did not put boys from parish schools at a disadvantage when they had to compete at the university. But if the secondary schools taught to a higher level, and became more classically oriented, the universities would be under pressure to raise their age of entry and drop their more elementary teaching, which would imperil the direct link between parish schools and universities and drive a wedge between students of different backgrounds. The logical outcome was that entry to the universities should only be via true secondary schools, and this was what came about by the end of the nineteenth century after seventy years of controversy centring on the issue of a compulsory examination for university entry. Whether or not this reduced opportunities for individuals depended on the arrangements made for scholarships and for transfer from primary to secondary schools. Such arrangements might help the Carlyles and Bains of later years, and save much energy painfully if heroically spent on self-education. More important, perhaps, they might save wasted potential by giving more systematic help to those of average talent, as well as to the exceptional men who were likely to win through whatever the circumstances. Thus the realities of the democratic tradition might be preserved even if its more picturesque and distinctively national characteristics disappeared.

It is a striking fact that in Scotland educational debates invariably included an appeal to the past and to the national tradition, which was used both to defend the status quo and to make genuine innovations more acceptable. When rival models of educational change were put forward, both sides tended to appeal to the Knoxian ideal, often with some plausibility, and to accuse their opponents of abandoning it and of yielding to English examples. It was a common ploy, both then and among later commentators, to stress Scotland's links with the continent, though the precise nature of the continental example appealed to was often left vague. When the history of Scottish education was written in the twentieth century, the First Book of Discipline came to be seen as a kind of expression of the Scottish *Volksgeist*, an Idea which contained in itself every conceivable democratic development and which unfolded over the centuries in Hegelian fashion. Alexander Morgan, for example, claimed in 1927 that 'most of the progress in Scottish education since Knox's day has consisted in advancing towards his ideals. The great Education Acts of 1872 and 1918 are but modern expressions of some of his ideals, others having still to be fulfilled.'[30] Morgan's view was an essentially optimistic one: whatever had in fact happened was declared to be in line with the tradition, and so fitted into the pattern of progress; if some developments seemed out of line (like the foundation of Edinburgh Academy) they could be declared to be alien imports, and were then felt somehow not to count, so that the outline of the story remained intact.

Others, however, might offer a more pessimistic interpretation: there was a Scottish tradition, but in the nineteenth century it was overlaid and distorted, either by insensitive legislation dictated by English preconceptions, or by an Anglicizing bourgeoisie which cared little for the democratic past. This was the reaction of many contemporaries to such developments as the Revised Code of 1862 and the Education Act of 1872, which were thought with some justice to have ignored specifically Scottish conditions and to have destroyed the parish school without creating an adequate substitute. Protest on these lines died away after the 1880s, but it has sometimes resurfaced in modern historiography. The boldest interpretation in terms of Anglicization, however, has been that put forward by George Davie in his book *The democratic intellect*, which is concerned chiefly with the universities and university culture.

Davie's book was a product of the debates of the 1950s about specialization in university education, and it contrasted the Scottish tradition of a uniform and balanced curriculum, in which philosophy and a 'philosophical' and generalizing approach to literature and science imparted a broad and humane culture, with the narrow English university curriculum of the early nineteenth century and the specialization

[30] A. Morgan, *Rise and progress of Scottish education* (Edinburgh, 1927), p. 53, and cf. pp. v, 190. See also H. M. Knox, *Two hundred and fifty years of Scottish education, 1696-1946* (Edinburgh, 1953), pp. xii-xiii.

which later developed out of this. In the course of the century, the Scottish universities lost sight of their own traditions and adopted the English model, a process related by Davie to a general crisis and decline of Scottish culture. Davie's defence and illustration of the Scottish university tradition is both eloquent and historically sound, and few would deny that something went badly wrong with Scottish intellectual life in the nineteenth century, when the achievements of the Scottish Enlightenment ran into the sand. But Davie goes further than this, arguing that the philosophical and general nature of university education was intimately linked (but in a way which he never clearly explains) with the democratic 'social ethic' of traditional Scotland, and by describing the crisis in the universities he claims to 'give a credible and clear account of the tortuous, dark revolution whereby a nation noted educationally both for social mobility and for fixity of first principle gradually reconciled itself to an alien system in which principles traditionally did not matter and a rigid social immobilism was the accepted thing'.[31] Whatever one thinks about this characterization of Scotland and England, it seems doubtful whether conclusions about the highly complex subject of social mobility can be drawn from a study of the university curriculum alone. Davie's account is both strongly idealist, in telling the story as one of clashing concepts divorced from any social context, and somewhat ahistorical, in presenting a conflict between two timeless university ideals and two parties—patriots and Anglophiles—with aims that are apparently consistent over a long period. Thus the historical account of university reform on which his general interpretation partly depends is oversimplified and has some serious inadequacies.

Anglicization was certainly an important element in the history of modern Scottish education, but British and Scottish dimensions coexisted in the minds of the Scottish educated class, and opinion rarely polarized on the issue. If it is true that the defence of the parochial tradition was strongest amongst the

---

[31] G. E. Davie, *The democratic intellect. Scotland and her universities in the nineteenth century* (2nd edn., Edinburgh, 1964), p. 106. My interpretation of events differs considerably from Davie's. Rather than referring to these differences in the text, I have discussed some of them in Appendix II. See also review of the first edition by D. J. Withrington in *Universities Quarterly*, xvi (1961-2), pp. 94-8.

clergy, that was partly because the clergy (like the school-masters, who to some extent took up the struggle in later years) were a profession with interests peculiarly confined to the Scottish cultural sphere. The middle class as a whole had much less objection to borrowing from English experience—the two countries faced very similar problems, after all, and the borrowing was not all in one direction, for English educational progress owed a good deal to Scottish models. Moreover, many Scots wished to use education to further their collective interest in careers in the British and Imperial communities, and were seduced by the prestige of the English Public Schools and universities. Yet at the same time they generally subscribed to the view that Scotland should maintain its cultural identity within the framework of a political union which was unquestioned, and the distinctive character of Scottish education was prized as part of the national inheritance. Many different positions could be taken on specific issues, and it was as 'patriotic' to wish to bring Scottish schools and universities up to English standards where these were seen as superior as to wish them to develop along lines of their own.[32] The democratic myth was certainly alive, and could have a shaping influence; the danger was that constant evocation of past glories might become a substitute for hard thinking about contemporary problems, and that constant and complacent assertion that Scottish education was democratic might cover its actual evolution on class lines. Too often, the Victorian bourgeoisie took refuge from the realities of industrialism by idealizing the social harmony of the older society, and in the sentimental world of the kailyard the parish school, the village dominie and the lad o'pairts had leading roles.

---

[32] Cf. H. J. Hanham, *Scottish nationalism* (1969), pp. 37-42.

2.

THE UNIVERSITIES AND
UNIVERSITY REFORM, 1825-1858

The universities came under earlier and more frequent scrutiny in the nineteenth century than the other parts of the Scottish educational system. They were investigated by two Royal Commissions, appointed in 1826 and 1876, and their organization and teaching were regulated by Acts of Parliament in 1858 and 1889 and by the 'ordinances' of temporary commissions set up by those Acts. University reformers were not concerned only with the curriculum, or with such matters as the universities' relation to the professions and the schools, but also with the internal constitution of the universities and with bringing them out of the shadow of clericalism and under the sway of public opinion. In D. B. Horn's words, the universities 'were ceasing to be regarded as privileged corporations perpetuating themselves by co-option and ultimately dependent upon the Crown and the Church. They were now coming to be regarded as agencies of the State, charged with responsibilities to Parliament and bound to play their part in what was becoming, slowly and painfully, a national system of education.'[1] In particular, they were expected to adapt themselves to meet the professional and status requirements of the expanding middle class.

The Scottish universities had flourished in the eighteenth century, when universities in most parts of Europe were in a state of decay, and their professors had included most of the thinkers of the Scottish Enlightenment (though not Hume). At the base of this lay the continuing vitality of the universities' original task, training the Scottish clergy. The Presbyterian ministry offered few lucrative livings and no posts above the parish level, and consequently did not attract the upper classes as the Church of England did; the Scottish universities there-

[1] D. B. Horn, 'The Universities (Scotland) Act of 1858', *University of Edinburgh Journal*, xix (1958-60), pp. 171-2.

fore had to draw their students from more modest social strata. At the same time, the four-year arts course which preceded the specialized study of divinity gave a general liberal education which was attractive to the leisured classes. This mixture of general and professional education was greatly strengthened by the development of medical schools at Edinburgh and Glasgow in the eighteenth century; these included chairs in subjects like botany and chemistry which had a wider scientific significance, and Scottish chemistry in particular became distinguished for its practical contributions to industry and agriculture.

The Scottish medical schools attracted students from all over the British Isles and overseas. By the 1820s they offered a four-year course combining theoretical and clinical teaching, with an effective examination and degree system not matched in other aspects of the universities' work. At Edinburgh the medical school was the most important part of the university's activities throughout the nineteenth century, and it was the only place to have a large law school. Training in law was much less regular than in medicine. Most students attended part-time while working in lawyers' offices, and this continued for the whole of the century. Law students, like medical ones, often attended arts classes as well, and the development of professional education strengthened the universities and meant that they were well placed to profit from the nineteenth-century growth of professional consciousness.[2]

It also accentuated the differences between the city universities of Edinburgh and Glasgow and the smaller colleges. While the former were large by contemporary standards, St. Andrews was in a small town with a limited catchment area, and had fewer than 300 students; it was also the only university with separate colleges—United College for arts and St. Mary's for theology. Aberdeen's two colleges counted as independent universities, and drew on different clienteles: Marischal was in the modern city and catered for the townsmen, while King's was in Old Aberdeen, a mile to the north, and drew more on the rural hinterland. Although the colleges were developing a

---

[2] For university and faculty enrolment figures see Appendix I. On the universities generally, and the professions, L. J. Saunders, *Scottish democracy 1815-1840* (Edinburgh, 1950) has much of value.

joint medical school, arts and divinity teaching was their main business, and like St. Andrews they were half seminary, half secondary school, since the students there were younger than in Glasgow or Edinburgh—entry at twelve was said to be normal at Marischal.

The characteristic method of university teaching was the professorial lecture. Each professor enjoyed independence from his colleagues and a monopoly of his subject. He was usually paid a small fixed salary, but the bulk of his income came from the fees paid directly by his students. Its size depended largely on whether his subject was part of the standard curriculum: the most lucrative chairs were those in medicine and the classical languages, but there were also chairs, in subjects like astronomy or 'civil history', which had virtually no students, so that the professors often gave up the attempt to form classes. One aim of reformers was to make better use of these sinecures, but there were other ways in which the professorial system could obstruct reform: since each chair enjoyed its own fee income, it formed a vested interest which made it difficult to remove subjects from the recognized curriculum, to propose new ones which might threaten existing classes, or to divide subjects with which one man could no longer cope. Boundary disputes and professorial jealousies were particularly common in the medical field, because of the constant development of new specialisms, but they were not unknown elsewhere.

Students paid for each class separately, and there were no restrictions on entry; in the cities professors were able to reach beyond the audience of full-time students and attract a diverse clientele. 'The Universities of Scotland', reported the 1826 commission,

have always embraced Students of every variety and description; men advanced in life, who attend some of the classes for amusement, or in order to recal [sic] the studies of early years, or to improve themselves in professional education, originally interrupted; or persons engaged in the actual occupations of business, who expect to derive aid in their pursuits from the new applications of Science to the Arts; or young men not intended for any learned profession, or even going through any regular Course of University Education, but sent for one or more years to College, in order to carry their education farther than that of the schools, before they are engaged in the pursuits of trade or of commerce. And all persons may attend any of the classes, in whatever order or manner may suit their different views and prospects. The system of instruction, by a course of elaborate lectures on the different branches of Science and Philosophy, continued daily for a period of six months, is admirably calculated to answer all the objects which such persons may have in view, as well as to afford much useful instruction to regular Students.[3]

For the 'regular students', each university recommended a fixed curriculum, which was based on the demands of the Church and compulsory for those aiming at the ministry. There were six traditional subjects: Latin (usually called Humanity), Greek, Mathematics, Logic, Moral Philosophy, and Natural Philosophy (i.e. physics). It is often said that there were seven, but this is an error based on the common practice of supposing that Edinburgh was typical[4]—Rhetoric, taught elsewhere as a part of Logic, had developed there into a separate subject, and was beginning to evolve from the study of eloquence and composition towards being a course in English literature. There were other local variations both in the number of courses required and in the order in which they were taken, but the common pattern was as follows: Latin and Greek were taken in the first two years, each subject having a 'junior' and a 'senior' class, and sometimes a third class for more advanced students; Logic was taken in the second year, and formed the introduction to the philosophical subjects; Moral Philosophy followed in the third year and Natural Philosophy in the fourth; the position of Mathematics varied, but it was usually studied for two years starting in the second. The progression Logic—Moral Philosophy—Natural Philosophy was found everywhere except at Aberdeen, where Natural Philosophy was taught first and where Logic, having no separate chairs, was incorporated into Moral Philosophy.[5]

---

[3] *Univ. Comm. Rep.*, p. 9.

[4] And perhaps on a supposed connection with the medieval *trivium* and *quadrivium*. In fact the subjects studied had fluctuated over the years, and the professorial system was itself comparatively new: until the eighteenth century teachers took one group through the whole curriculum ('regenting').

[5] Thus making five basic subjects, but at Marischal Natural History was also standard. At St. Andrews, Latin and Greek were studied through all four years.

Thus the standard curriculum gave approximately equal weight to the three fields of classics, philosophy, and mathematics plus physics, and the emphasis on philosophy was the distinctive feature of the Scottish educational tradition. Here Scotland resembled Germany, where philosophy was a central subject in the universities, or France, where it was taught in the last year of the secondary schools (and consequently to boys of the same age as Scottish university students). Philosophical teaching at this level could take advantage of the excitement and stimulation which general ideas and new perspectives give to the developing intellect of the adolescent. Moral Philosophy generally dealt with broad ethical themes, and since the days of Adam Smith had included some teaching of political economy, while Logic was concerned with intellectual method and metaphysics rather than logic in the technical sense. At the beginning of the century, the dominant school was the 'common sense' philosophy developed by Thomas Reid in reaction to Hume. This had the great advantage of providing a rational basis for religious orthodoxy, and was thus particularly suitable as a preliminary to theological training; in this it resembled the natural theology of Paley which was prescribed reading in the English universities, and the 'eclecticism' of Victor Cousin which formed the official philosophy in French state schools and which drew directly on the Scottish thinkers.

The last great exponent of the common-sense school was Dugald Stewart, who died in 1828, though he had resigned the Edinburgh chair of Moral Philosophy in 1810. Stewart's eloquence had made him an inspiring teacher, and had given him an influence which went far beyond the student audience. In later years it proved difficult to reconcile the common-sense tradition with new intellectual tendencies, but it was represented in a modified form by Sir William Hamilton, professor of Civil History at Edinburgh from 1821 to 1836 and of Logic from 1836 to 1856. Under the influence of such teachers a Scottish intellectual style had developed, characterized by a willingness to make connections between diverse subjects, an interest in general theories, and a tendency to make use of systematic classifications and abstract categories. The great achievements of the Scottish Enlightenment thinkers were works of general intellectual synthesis, which may have owed something to the experience of writing university lectures. At any rate, philosophical subjects were particularly well suited to the lecture system: they could appeal to a mixed audience without specialized qualifications, and did not require either intensive classwork (as with the classics) or elaborate apparatus (as with science). Lectures allowed talented professors to establish a unique hold through the force of their personality, and were often a sort of lay preaching. The success of the lecture format, indeed, owed much to the familiarity of the Scots with sermons. In a society where church-going was a binding social convention, students were both inured to tedium and appreciative of the finer points of oral exposition. University lectures were part of that nineteenth-century culture of the spoken word which also accounted for the popularity of long political speeches, of recitation as a form of entertainment, and of the study of 'elocution' as a means to self-improvement.

The Scottish curriculum was not without its critics. Dr Johnson had said that in Scotland every man has a mouthful of learning but no man has a bellyful, and it was true that no subject was really studied in depth. Classics and mathematics were studied for more than one year, but the starting-point was so low that there was no question of competing with the levels of attainment found in England, based as these were on far more effective school training; besides, the classics in Scotland were seen as preliminary subjects to be dropped once the main work in philosophy began. The weakness of the classics was increasingly seen as a defect at a time when they enjoyed much social prestige and when the revival of Greek was a major intellectual movement, and this was one of the main fields of dispute between reformers and traditionalists. But even in philosophy, each subject was taken for only one session, with no scope for following up specialized interests. Professors could open advanced classes if they wished—in chemistry, for example, where the main class formed part of the medical curriculum, the 1826 commission found the professors at both Edinburgh and Glasgow organizing laboratory work for a handful of advanced students, and later the professors of Natural Philosophy were to follow suit; but such work found no recognition in the curriculum.[6]

[6] *Univ. Comm. Rep.*, pp. 145, 256. (The edition used is one where the reports on individual universities are paginated continuously with the general report.)

A second point of criticism was that lectures were not supplemented by more personal forms of teaching. In the classics
much written work was set, but it was difficult for a single
professor to cope adequately with the very large numbers
involved; professors sometimes paid assistants out of their
class income to deal with this sort of routine teaching, but there
were no officially recognized tutors. In philosophy, new techniques had been developed by George Jardine, professor of
Logic at Glasgow from 1787 to 1827. Jardine supplemented his
lecture hour with an additional daily class devoted to 'examinations' (oral questioning by the professor) and to the correction of written essays on a wide variety of general themes.
Jardine expounded his methods in a manual of university
teaching published in 1818, *Outlines of philosophical education,*
and they were widely copied; they had the advantage of keeping all the teaching in the hands of the professor himself, but
could only be used where time and numbers permitted. At
Glasgow a distinction was made between 'public students' who
participated in these 'exercises', and 'private students' who
attended only the lectures. But at Edinburgh, where the number of casual and part-time attenders was greatest, Jardine's
innovations were not adopted, and even for regular students
the philosophy lectures had the character of a public performance to an anonymous audience.

In the 1850s James Bryce attended the lectures of Jardine's
successor Robert Buchanan, and found them tedious and out-
dated. Even so, he recorded that

the atmosphere of College life was highly stimulating, more so than I
found that of Oxford afterwards. The class work kept us on the 'qui
vive' and nearly the whole class wanted to learn and enjoyed learning. Whenever we had a chance we talked about our work, discussing
the questions that came up, an incessant sharpening of wits upon one
another's whetstones. We spoke very little about theology and not
much about politics, and though we cared about classics the ambition
of most of us would have been to be metaphysicians. That seemed the
highest kind of mental exertion.

He added that 'There was no better way of understanding the
Scotch spirit as it has been ever since the middle of the 16th
century than to be a student of Glasgow College in those

days.'[7] There was a touch of the democratic myth about this, but other accounts confirm that for the interested student the lack of personal contact with his teachers could be countered by the stimulation of mutual discussion and private reading, and by the essay and debating societies which were an established feature of university life. What was lacking, however, was the external stimulus of graduation and examination honours, for except at Aberdeen, where the majority of students followed the fixed curriculum and took their degrees, only a handful took the trouble to graduate. The only test of a university education demanded by outside bodies, including the Church, was a certificate of attendance on a professor's class, and indeed this usually sufficed for formal graduation; only at Glasgow does there seem to have been any serious examining.

The universities thus had enough common features to form a recognizable Scottish university model, which had much influence on the foundation both of colleges in North America and of England's first modern university, University College in London (1828). Some of these features, like the parish school link, were peculiar to Scotland itself, but as educational institutions the universities were perhaps closest to their German counterparts, especially in the emphasis on professorial lectures and on students' freedom of choice. Another aspect, which was strongest at Edinburgh, was nearer to French concepts: the idea of an urban university, open to all comers, relying mainly on lectures, and serving as a tribune for the national intelligentsia. Nothing could be further from the residential and inward-looking universities of Oxford and Cambridge, of which Scottish intellectuals were often critical. In the 1830s the *Edinburgh Review* ran a series of articles on Oxford, written by Hamilton, the burden of which was that the colleges and their tutorial system had usurped the educational function of the university itself, and that reform would not be effective until there was a return to the professorial system— a thesis, which was to influence Oxford reformers like Mark Pattison. The contrast between the 'professorial' and 'tutorial' systems became a commonplace, though many Scots, including Hamilton himself, were prepared to borrow the useful features

[7] H. A. L. Fisher, *James Bryce* (1927), i. 24-6.

of the latter.[8] Later the professorial system was also contrasted with the type of 'examining university' represented by the University of London (1836): the divorce between examining and teaching was always deplored by Scottish professors, who saw the universities as essentially teaching institutions. Hamilton's articles, indeed, are striking for their emphasis on this and for their failure to include research among the functions of a university, which he defined at some length. Here English and Scottish universities were at one, for although the former preferred to concentrate on one line of study—classics or mathematics—while the latter gave an all-round education, a liberal education was the aim in both cases.[9] It was only in the 1850s that the German idea of a university which combined teaching and original research began to make its mark.

One obvious contrast was between the 'popular character' of the Scottish universities and the social exclusivism of the English, and between the associated styles of life. Oxford and Cambridge exercised close moral and religious supervision over their pupils, and were schools of manners; Scottish students lived in lodgings or at home, and came into contact with the university only through lectures. Once, indeed, the Scottish universities had had residential accommodation and common tables, but the last traces of this disappeared in the 1820s; it was only at Aberdeen and St. Andrews that some attempts at school-like discipline were made, including the enforcement of church attendance, though since there were no religious tests for students this could never be absolute. In Edinburgh and Glasgow, students were left to make what they would of their university education, and this was seen as a virtue and a test of character. The sacrifices needed to get to a university, and the struggle once there with loneliness and poverty, were held to have shaped the Scottish character, to be part of the Calvinist work-ethic which had carried Scotsmen to success at home and abroad. As Lyon Playfair was to put it, 'The English Universities ... teach men how to spend £1,000 a year with dignity and

[8] See articles of 1831, 1834, 1835 in W. Hamilton, *Discussions on philosophy and literature, education and university reform* (1852), pp. 386-534, and cf. pp. 651-740.
[9] Cf. C. J. Wright, 'Academics and their aims: English and Scottish approaches to university education in the nineteenth century', *History of Education*, viii (1979), pp. 91-7.

intelligence while the Scotch Universities teach them how to make £1,000 a year with dignity and intelligence.'[10]

The Scottish universities were considered to be national and public institutions. The Act of Union provided that they should continue 'for ever', and they were partly financed by parliamentary grants—£5,000-6,000 in the 1830s. The state maintained some of the universities' buildings, and occasionally helped with rebuilding schemes. The state had also founded most of the new chairs required for the expansion of the medical schools, so that by the 1820s appointment to about half of all the chairs was made by the Crown. Otherwise this power generally lay with the existing professors, except at Edinburgh, where because of the circumstances of the university's foundation in the sixteenth century the 'patronage' of the chairs lay with the town council. The town council was also responsible for financial administration, and from about 1815 the 'patrons' were increasingly disposed to interfere in the day-to-day management of the university, giving rise to a series of acrimonious disputes with the professors (the Senate), which lasted until the 1850s and involved several complex legal actions, all of which the Senate lost. In the course of these disputes, the Edinburgh professors were forced to articulate the doctrine of academic freedom, claiming that educational matters should be controlled by them as a matter of right, 'arising from the essential and indefeasible character of a University'.[11] Elsewhere, the professors were free to act as they chose; or rather, they were free to continue in traditional ways, for innovations were obstructed by numerous archaic survivals and organizational deficiencies. Any real development of the universities depended on legislative intervention to remove these, and also on new financial resources, whether from the state or elsewhere, since the dependence of the universities on fixed grants and fee income made them vulnerable to economic crises and fluctuations in student numbers, and gave them no reserve for capital expenditure or the foundation of new chairs.

---

[10] *3 Hansard* cccxxxvii, HC 20 June 1889, col. 381.

[11] A. Grant, *The story of the University of Edinburgh during its first three hundred years* (1884), ii. 20.

From the point of view of reformers, the universities appeared as self-perpetuating professorial oligarchies, dominated by the Moderate party in the Church and by the Tory party machine. The new forces of Evangelicalism and Whiggish liberalism gained an early victory in the 'Leslie affair' of 1805, when attempts to block the appointment of the liberal John Leslie to the chair of Mathematics at Edinburgh were defeated.[12] But more general action eventually came about through one of the universities' medieval inheritances, the office of rector. The rector was a dignitary chosen from outside whose duties included the remedying of abuses; in principle, he was elected by the students, but the system worked fully only at Glasgow and Marischal College. At King's College, the rector was chosen by the professors; at St. Andrews, the older students had the vote, but their choice was limited to four senior professors; and at Edinburgh the town council claimed that the Lord Provost was rector *ex officio*. Liberal stirrings among the middle class spread to the student body, and Glasgow took the lead in using the rectorship as a political outlet. The Whig leader Francis Jeffrey was elected in 1820, after which a political figure became the usual choice after a contest on party lines. At St. Andrews the students tried to defy the system in 1825 by electing Scott, but this was ruled invalid. The most significant election proved to be that of Joseph Hume, the Radical MP for Aberdeen, at Marischal College in 1824. Hume seized the excuse of student grievances about graduation to convene a 'rectorial court' in 1825, the first at Marischal since 1738. The professors were forced to attend this court to be harangued by Hume in the presence of the cheering students, and to listen to evidence of their own failings. Hume declared his intention to 'administer justice in an open and manly manner' and to act as 'a sort of umpire between the governors and the governed', and concluded that the best means of reform would be more public proceedings and the presence of a resident rector. In all this, Hume seems to have been supported by Liberal opinion in Aberdeen and by many of the local professional men in their capacity as graduates of the college.[13]

[12] J. B. Morrell, 'The Leslie affair: careers, kirk and politics in Edinburgh in 1805', *Scottish Historical Review*, liv (1975), pp. 63-82.

[13] *A full and correct report of the proceedings of the Rectorial Court, held in Marischal College and University, Aberdeen, 14th November 1825* (Aberdeen, 1825), *passim*.

This scene coincided with a similar one at Edinburgh, where the conflict between university and town council had reached a climax. The council decided to hold a ceremonial 'visitation', and summoned the professors before it; the disputed policies, which centred on the place of midwifery in the medical curriculum, were forced through at this *lit de justice*. These events of 1825 marked the real beginning of university reform: called on to intervene both by Hume and by the Edinburgh Senate, the Home Secretary, Robert Peel, decided on the Royal Commission which was appointed in 1826.[14] The Crown in Scotland had ancient powers to 'visit' the universities, and there was no attempt by the universities to dispute the commission's powers, as happened later at Oxford and Cambridge.

This commission was a large body, representative of the politically influential classes. Of its twenty-two members, nine were noblemen and ten lawyers, including the leading judges and the government's law officers; the Church had three representatives, headed by the Moderate leader George Cook, but there were no university professors. With the exception of Lords Aberdeen and Rosebery, who acted successively as chairman, the presence of the noblemen was largely decorative, and the effective work of the commission was done by the lawyers and clergymen.[15] After collecting a mass of evidence and hearing witnesses, the commission drew up 'provisional resolutions' embodying its proposals for each university, and after the universities had commented on these the final report was submitted in 1830 and published in 1831. The original plan was for the commission to make 'a Code of proper Rules, Statutes and Ordinances' which would be given immediate executive force, but it was soon realized that many changes would require legislation; in submitting its Code, the commission suggested that any Act of Parliament should be as general as possible, and that a new Board of Visitors should be set up to enforce the details of reform.[16]

The general tone of the report was unsympathetic to the universities in their existing state, reflecting the impatience of

[14] J. B. Morrell, 'Science and Scottish university reform: Edinburgh in 1826', *British Journal for the History of Science*, vi (1972/3), pp. 40-1.

[15] See minutes of their meetings in *Univ. Comm. Ev. Edinburgh*.

[16] *Univ. Comm. Rep.*, pp. 13-14, 24.

practical men with the muddle, financial incompetence, petty squabbling, and general disorganization which they discovered, and which their report laid bare in much detail. Yet these things were not so much the fault of the professors as the result of archaic constitutions which hampered attempts to adapt to modern needs. At Edinburgh, the situation was dominated by relations with the town council, and at Aberdeen by the need to merge the colleges into a single university—a question on which local opinion was fiercely divided. At St. Andrews, the existence of two colleges with a corporate identity separate from that of the university itself compounded the problems of smallness and poverty. One means of relieving that poverty had turned into an abuse: possessing a chair of medicine but no medical school, the university sold medical degrees to practitioners who lacked formal qualifications; this practice was reformed, but not ended, in 1826. At Glasgow, progress was hampered by a dispute within the professoriate: a distinction was drawn between the university proper and the 'Faculty' or 'College'; since 1807 the state had created five chairs in medical subjects, but the existing professors refused to admit them to the 'Faculty', which administered the university's patronage and property. The resulting controversies took on a bitter personal tone, and the commission found itself (as at St. Andrews) having to investigate detailed allegations of financial mismanagement.

The commission's solution to these problems was to give each university a permanent 'rectorial Court' to supervise the professoriate, settle disputes, administer the university's property and revenue, and frame general educational policy. The aim was to 'secure the fair influence of public opinion upon the deliberations of University Bodies'. The commission's proposals, both constitutional and educational, were remarkable for their great detail and for their uniformity, imposing a common pattern of which only the details varied according to local conditions; thus both town-council administration at Edinburgh and the separate universities at Aberdeen would have been swept away. The Courts were to be headed by a rector, elected by the professors, graduates and (except at Edinburgh) students. The commission seems to have envisaged that he would be an eminent outsider, but an active chairman rather than an ornamental absentee. The university Principals would be *ex officio* members of the Courts, which would be completed by a number of 'Assessors' (a term borrowed from the traditional rectorial courts), chosen by various individuals or bodies—usually the rector himself, the Chancellor and the Senate; at Edinburgh the town council would also have an Assessor. These proposals were eventually to be adopted, with little variation, in the Universities Act of 1858.[17]

Under the commission's scheme the powers of the Senates would have been very limited, and it was seen as the prime duty of the Courts to provide for 'the gradual introduction of such improvements in the system of instruction as the progress of Philosophy, or the more enlarged views of the age, may require'. The commission had concluded from its investigations that 'the general opinions of the most competent Judges respecting the System of Education best adapted to the actual state of Society in Scotland, may be much opposed to those entertained by the Professors in the Universities. Eminent Teachers are not always the best qualified to determine the course of instruction most suitable to the general interests of society, or to the preparation for particular professions.'[18] In forming its own opinions on these matters, the commission could draw on a coherent strategy expounded by Thomas Chalmers, who was now professor of Moral Philosophy at St. Andrews; Chalmers expanded his evidence to the commission in a book published in 1827.[19] Chalmers argued that 'The radical error of our system lies in the too early admittance of our youth to universities', and wanted a general raising of the age-level, to be brought about by a strict entrance examination in Latin and Greek. Access to the universities had been made easy in the past because of the shortage of qualified men for the Church, but today the very reverse applied; Chalmers estimated that there were 700 divinity students, but only thirty vacancies to fill every year, and the professions of medicine and law too were 'greatly overstocked'.[20] By restricting numbers, there-

[17] Ibid., pp. 11, 16-17, 19, 21, 24.
[18] Ibid., p. 11.
[19] Reprinted in T. Chalmers, *Church and college establishments* (Edinburgh, 1848), pp. 71-105.
[20] Ibid., pp. 74-5.

fore, nothing would be lost, and the intellectual level of the professions would be raised. The entrance examination would allow a clear distinction to be made between the tasks of the schoolmaster and the professor. The drill of the junior classes would be banished from the universities, and the classical professors could concentrate on their proper task of guiding their disciples 'along the higher walks of literature and refined criticism'. Every subject would benefit, in fact, from the raising of the average age, and the system would be crowned by 'the stimulus of a great public examination at the end of each session, in every way as sifting and severe as those which are held in the English universities, at the dispensation of honours, and affording the same tests of high proficiency in the various sciences as are required at our sister institutions in mathematics and the ancient languages.' Chalmers vigorously defended the broad nature of the Scottish course, and preferred a professorial system reinforced by the methods of Jardine to the 'mere pedagogy of the English colleges'.[21] The key to all improvement, however, was the higher entrance standard: 'I should like the variety, the expansion, and the excursive style of our Scottish Professors to be kept up, but that grafted, as it were, on a basis of solid English Scholarship.'[22]

All this implied a revolution in school education. Chalmers thought that it would be enough to have a 'grammar school' in each university town, or (which he preferred) a preparatory school or 'Gymnasium' attached to the university itself. In the long run, the entrance examination would stimulate the improvement of provincial schools as well. Other witnesses who favoured Chalmers's ideas—like Leslie, Jeffrey, and the Oxonian rector of Edinburgh Academy, John Williams—laid more emphasis on the need for a national network of secondary schools; Leslie in particular admired the state systems of the Continent, and proposed a Board of Education to 'foster the germs of genius, and select the boys of the most promising talents, whose education should either wholly or in part be defrayed by the public'.[23]

---

[21] Ibid., pp. 88, 93, 95.
[22] Chalmers's evidence in *Univ. Comm. Ev. St. Andrews*, p. 64.
[23] *Univ. Comm. Ev. Edinburgh*, pp. 125-6, 159, 397, 591.

Chalmers's programme was reflected in the commission's proposals, but it added elements of its own which showed a greater admiration for English ideas. First, it assumed, without feeling the need for argument, that the classics were the mark of an educated man. 'We are intimately persuaded that no other studies are better fitted, either to improve the taste and exercise the faculties of youth, or to create a love of freedom and a spirit of generous and manly independence.' It was a matter for regret 'that an intimate acquaintance with the Classics, particularly the Greek authors, is not more general than it now is among the best educated classes of society in Scotland'.[24] Second, the commission thought that   .

The main defect in the system of the Scotch Universities is the want of adequate motives and encouragement for continued and vigorous application. ... A young man of the greatest talents and the most vigorous application may pass through the complete course of a Scotch University without the means of gaining distinction, or the opportunities of exertion, which can either determine his habits and pursuits in maturer years, or introduce him, with the advantage of proved talents, into the business or the professions of life. [25]

At Oxford and Cambridge, it was thought, the introduction of Honours examinations and the 'emulation' which they encouraged had been the main instrument of intellectual revival, and the commission was anxious to restore the prestige of graduation in Scotland; this was one reason for giving graduates a share in electing the rector. The commission also wanted educational methods to be more intensive and competitive throughout the course, and particularly condemned the casual approach found at Edinburgh; it admired Jardine's methods at Glasgow, and recommended their extension to the philosophy classes everywhere, with the enforcement of attendance, compulsory essays, and more class prizes.[26]

Whether stimulated by the English example or by the prospect of the Royal Commission's strictures, all the universities except King's College were already introducing new and more rigorous degree regulations, though the examinations involved

---

[24] *Univ. Comm. Rep.*, pp. 38, 26.
[25] Ibid., p. 36.
[26] Ibid., pp. 27-8, 34-9.

were still oral rather than written—Marischal in 1825, Glasgow in 1826, St. Andrews and Edinburgh in 1827. The commission found the Edinburgh scheme rather loose, and its examination of witnesses showed the attitudes which still prevailed there. One professor, presented with the idea of a final examination with 'a classification, according to merit or proficiency', replied that 'The subject is rather new to me, the proceeding is so utterly unknown in this University', and observed that 'There would be great difficulty about it in so *popular* an University as this is, where many students come to us, picking out individual classes which they choose to attend, and not going through the regular course.' A colleague felt that an examination would be useless, as everyone would be allowed to pass: 'there will be a feeling that it is harsh to cut off a young man's prospects, and say he shall not go on because he is not able to answer very strict examinations'.[27]

In presenting its own proposals, the commission emphasized that it had no wish to impose an alien system, or to make Scottish universities more exclusive. Its scheme for the curriculum and graduation would apply only to those who sought a formal qualification, leaving others free to attend classes as they wished.[28] For regular students, however, there would be an entrance examination in Latin and Greek which would 'enable the first Greek class in the University to commence nearly at the point where at present it concludes'. The degree structure was modelled on that adopted at Glasgow in 1826, which (as had always been the case at Glasgow) included a BA as well as an MA. In the commission's scheme, there would be a four-year course leading to the BA, in which the subjects were arranged as follows:

First year	Latin 1	Greek 1	
Second year	Latin 2	Greek 2	Mathematics 1
Third year	Mathematics 2	Logic (including Rhetoric)	
Fourth year	Natural Philosophy	Moral Philosophy	

Examinations, including some written element and conducted by examiners from outside the universities, would lead to the

---

[27] *Univ. Comm. Ev. Edinburgh,* pp. 163, 168 (Brunton), 174 (Meiklejohn).
[28] *Univ. Comm. Rep.,* pp. 8-12, 25.

award of the standard BA, but there would also be two grades of Honours which could be gained by offering additional work, especially in the classics, at the same examination. Once armed with the BA, students could spend an additional year studying for the MA, which involved attendance on classes of Natural History, Chemistry and Political Economy[29] and specialized work in some branch of literature, philosophy or science selected by the student.[30]

Although the commission denied it, it was obvious that this scheme shifted the balance from philosophy to classics, and all the universities condemned the postponement of Logic to the third year and the cramming of Moral and Natural Philosophy into a single year. On these points, indeed, the Church representatives on the commission, Cook and Thomas Taylor, entered a formal dissent, appealing to the long and successful experience of the existing system and claiming that philosophy was more effective than the classics for 'the cultivation of the intellectual and reasoning powers'.[31] The majority, for their part, claimed that the existing course was 'ill contrived for its primary purpose, namely, to awaken and invigorate the intellectual powers, and to train the mind to the acquisition of knowledge'. The multiplicity of subjects studied worked against the cultivation of memory and attentiveness, and the student 'becomes accustomed to a desultory and abortive exertion, and is in danger of turning out a sciolist and smatterer in every thing'. Now there would instead be two solid years of classics followed by two solid years of philosophy. The educational ideal expressed here was one which emphasized mental training rather than exposure to general ideas.[32]

The commission did not confine its attention to the arts curriculum, but also produced elaborate plans for reform in the teaching of law, medicine and divinity, and adopted the general

[29] A somewhat random selection dictated by the availability of chairs; the commission wanted to separate Political Economy from Moral Philosophy and create chairs at Edinburgh and Glasgow.

[30] *Univ. Comm. Rep.*, pp. 39-44. But at Glasgow the BA was simply a shortened MA, omitting Mathematics and Natural Philosophy: *Univ. Comm. Ev. Glasgow*, pp. 530-1.

[31] *Univ. Comm. Rep.*, p. 91. Cook had succeeded Chalmers as professor of Moral Philosophy at St. Andrews.

[32] Ibid., p. 26.

principle that professional training should follow a full liberal education. In the case of divinity, it proposed a full-time course of four years' study leading to a new degree of BD, and sought to bring the faculties into touch with modern scholarship by adding chairs of Biblical Criticism. These ideas were more revolutionary than might appear, for although the existing divinity course also lasted for four years in theory, in practice there was a system of 'irregular' or 'occasional' attendance (condemned as 'preposterous and indefensible' by the commission)[33] under which after one full-time session students needed to appear at the university only once a year for certain formal exercises. This enabled them to combine study with a job, often as a schoolmaster, and when their studies were complete it was the local presbytery, not the university authorities, which decided whether they were licensed to preach. If the commission's proposals had been enforced, they would certainly have excluded many poorer candidates for the ministry—but the commission shared Chalmers's view that this could safely be done since the profession was overstocked.

In the case of law, the commission suggested (at Edinburgh only) a three-year course which would not lead to a degree, but in which law would be studied as 'a liberal and enlightened science' rather than as a course in mere practice.[34] It was assumed that an arts degree would precede this, but it is interesting to find Jeffrey—a spokesman for the Edinburgh bar and in general a supporter of higher standards of liberal education, as befitted a founder of Edinburgh Academy—raising Whiggish objections to this principle. It might harm 'the freedom of industry and ambition', especially by excluding 'persons self-taught, late-taught, home-taught, who, in their youth, had neither the means of getting a degree, nor the learning to entitle them to it. It is a public evil to narrow the practical competitions of talent and industry, by requiring antecedent distinctions; and I should be shy, therefore, of introducing any measure that would have that effect.'[35] The question of preliminary qualifications was also the controversial one in the case of medicine. The commission felt strongly that doctors should

---

[33] Ibid., p. 339, and see pp. 45 ff. for the proposals for divinity.
[34] Ibid., p. 54.
[35] *Univ. Comm. Ev. Edinburgh*, p. 393.

have a full arts education, while the medical professors were determined to resist a proposal which they thought would be a disaster for recruitment—a similar proposal by the arts professors at Edinburgh had already been fought off in 1824. During that dispute it was claimed that 'In England, no professional man, especially with a Scotch degree, is held in much esteem, if he happens to be deficient in classical literature. The want of a previous enlarged education has always been objected to the graduates from Scotland, and not without reason.'[36] What lay behind this was the equation between the classics, professional status, and the manners of a gentleman, and the commission were thinking in the same way when they said that doctors 'should be possessed of such a degree of literary acquirement as may secure the respect of those with whom they are to associate in the exercise of their profession'.[37] On this issue the commission had to compromise, proposing only that medical students should have passed an examination in Latin, Greek, Mathematics, and Natural Philosophy.

The commission's preference for the classics was no doubt an example of Anglicization, but its roots lay in the professional aspirations of the Edinburgh lawyers who formed the commission's majority. Events at Glasgow showed that this preference was not limited to Edinburgh, and also that it might alienate the non-professional part of the middle class. At Glasgow there was a traditional examination (the 'Blackstone examination') between one year and another, and as part of the general tightening-up of regulations this was being strictly applied by Daniel Sandford, the professor of Greek. The effect was that no one could enter the Logic class, except as a 'private student', without Greek. It had been common at Glasgow for 'the sons of the more opulent merchants and traders' to spend several sessions at the university before entering the family firm. They were interested in the three philosophy classes, but not in the classics, and it was feared the new rigour 'will go far to exclude the mercantile classes from College altogether'.[38] Strong feelings

---

[36] Ibid., Appendix, pp. 142-4.
[37] *Univ. Comm. Rep.*, p. 56.
[38] *Univ. Comm. Ev. Glasgow*, p. 184; cf. p. 120, and *Univ. Comm. Rep.*, pp. 242-3.

were aroused in the city and the university, but Sandford was unrepentant:

I think the elementary knowledge of both Greek and Latin is a very essential requisite in the education of every person who is to hold the station of a gentleman in society, whatever his profession be; and if the persons that wish to send their sons without this knowledge to the Logic class, to acquire the principles of composition and of taste, must have it so, let them send them to another institution. Why degrade the character of our University into a mere institution for the accommodation of that class of individuals?

And he was supported by Principal Macfarlan: 'I conceive that, to introduce into our Philosophy classes, as public students, young gentlemen who are nearly unacquainted with the learned languages, would lower the character of the University as a seminary for liberal education.'[39]

When the universities had a chance to comment on the commission's proposals, their reaction was generally hostile, though they concentrated their fire on the entrance examination rather than the details of the graduation scheme. Glasgow feared that it 'would banish from the College that large and most valuable body of students now furnished by the middle ranks of society, and the remoter districts of the country'. Edinburgh pointed out that it required a major reform of the schools, which lay outside the commission's scope. An entrance examination would be 'a blow struck at the peculiar pride and glory of Scotland', and 'inconsistent with the hitherto unchallenged rights of his Majesty's subjects'. The Edinburgh Senate stressed the openness of university classes and the special interests of adult and part-time students, and even claimed that Edinburgh was 'nothing more than a public and free school for instruction in the sciences and literature', and 'rather a great metropolitan school than a University'.[40] The strongest opposition came from King's College, where the commission's policy on bursaries formed an additional irritant. The two Aberdeen colleges were especially well provided with bursaries—134 at King's, 106 at Marischal, which meant that

[39] *Univ. Comm. Ev. Glasgow,* pp. 191-2, 188.
[40] *Univ. Comm. Ev. Edinburgh,* Appendix, pp. 252, 255, 274. Cf. comments of other universities in *Ev. Glasgow,* p. 561, *Ev. St. Andrews,* pp. 415-16.

about a third of the students were bursars—but many of them were very small, and the commission argued that these encouraged too many young men who lacked the resources and ability to profit from a university education, and who dragged down educational standards without gaining any personal success; it would have liked to amalgamate them to provide scholarships for advanced study, or perhaps tutorships.[41] In its comments on the 'provisional resolutions' King's College provided an eloquent exposition and eulogy of the parochial tradition and its advantages for the community, and denounced the entrance examination as part of a 'system of exclusion' which would deprive the common people of their rights.[42]

The 1826 commission was true to its age in giving little thought to the advancement of science or learning as a university function. Its aim was, above all, to make the universities more systematic and efficient educational institutions, turning out doctors, lawyers and ministers with a love of the classics and the manners of gentlemen. It did not wish to exclude the talented poor, but would have used the entrance examination to confine entry to the well-qualified, and it was unsympathetic to the idea of the university as an open arena where talent could take its chance. To this vision of a streamlined university system two distinct ideals were opposed. One was the 'Aberdeen' view that the relationship with the parish schools was a vital national tradition to be maintained at all costs; the weakness of this case, as the commission did not fail to point out, was that it implied the indefinite continuation of low entry standards, and obstructed any general plan of intellectual improvement.[43] The second ideal, equally democratic in its way, was the 'Edinburgh' view of the university as a 'public and free school', a multi-functional institution offering a diversity of intellectual wares. Both ideals could be accommodated by the existing university system, but both were threatened by a strict entrance examination. In proposing this, Chalmers and the Royal Commission laid down the agenda for future debate,

---

[41] *Univ. Comm. Rep.*, pp. 75-6, 337-8.
[42] *Univ. Comm. Ev. Aberdeen*, pp. 321-3. Marischal College, however, approved of an entrance examination, and had introduced its own in 1827.
[43] *Univ. Comm. Rep.*, pp. 9, 75-6.

and anticipated the developments—the evolution of secondary education, the steady raising of the age of entry—which were to take place before such an examination was actually introduced.

The report of the 1826 commission appeared during the Reform Bill crisis, and was neglected partly for that reason. But the Reform Act created conditions which should have been propitious to university reform, giving the parliamentary vote (and the municipal vote after the burgh reform of 1833) to precisely that part of the middle class most interested in educational questions. The MPs for the university towns, invariably Liberals, became the focus of a machinery of lobbying, petitions, and delegations to London which over the next decades all parties learned to use. The Scottish press, too, was expanding, and university matters were frequently discussed in the Edinburgh and Glasgow newspapers and in the more weighty periodicals. Unfortunately, however, Scottish politics, even before the Disruption, were divided along religious lines, and religious dissension over both school and university reform often led to progress being blocked; Scottish legislation had a low priority in Parliament at the best of times, and was most likely to succeed when Scottish MPs of all parties succeeded in sinking their differences and presenting a common front.

The immediate effect of municipal reform was to revive the question of the 'patronage' of chairs. The 1826 commission had said nothing about this, and while removing the town council's powers of government at Edinburgh would have left them to continue appointing to chairs. The situation at Edinburgh was now referred to the Royal Commission on Municipal Corporations appointed in 1833. The most influential witness was Sir William Hamilton, who simultaneously published an article in the *Edinburgh Review* on the 'patronage and superintendence of universities'. Of the three modes of patronage—by municipal corporations, by the Crown, and by the professors themselves— Hamilton considered the first the least unsatisfactory, and the third the worst: 'To be left to divide the cake in the shade, has been the aim of all professorial patronage.' This was also the view of Henry Cockburn, who inclined towards appointment by a minister of public instruction.[44] Hamilton's plan, how-

<hr>

[44] Hamilton, op. cit., p. 377. See *Municipal Corporations Commission. Local Reports,* Part I (PP 1835, xxix), pp. 387 (Hamilton), 391-3 (Cockburn); cf. pp. 372 (Pillans), 373 (Napier), and H. Cockburn, *Journal of Henry Cockburn* (Edinburgh, 1874), i. 106-8.

ever, was to remove appointments from the influence of political jobbery and ill-informed opinion by giving each university a small 'board of curators' of eminent and impartial outsiders, who would make recommendations to be endorsed by the Crown—this was the system, he claimed, followed in Germany. At Edinburgh, for example, representatives of the various legal and other professional bodies might compose such a board. Most of the witnesses before the commission were Edinburgh professors, and they betrayed a good deal of snobbish prejudice against a town council made up of shopkeepers and tradesmen, though more impartial observers thought that their patronage had always been exercised responsibly.

In its report the Royal Commission recommended that the town council's powers of both management and patronage should be transferred to five curators, two appointed by the Crown, two by the town council, and one by the university.[45] The publication of this report in 1835 naturally led to calls for the universities' commission report to be brought out of the government's pigeon-holes, and in the same year the MPs for Glasgow and Aberdeen brought forward their own bills for local reform. The author of the Aberdeen bill was Alexander Bannerman, who had been one of the assessors of Hume's rectorial court in 1825; his bill was the most radical of all the proposals made in this period. There was to be a single University of Aberdeen, with a rectorial Court on the lines recommended by the 1826 commission. But there would also be a body called Convocation, consisting of the members of the Court along with the whole teaching staff, including tutors or 'monitors' financed by surplus bursary funds, and with a right of attendance by students and graduates. Most novel of all, chairs were to be filled by open competition conducted by specially appointed examiners, competitions which were to be 'witnessed' by Convocation, though for this purpose students would not attend; this idea was probably suggested by the unique case of the divinity chair at King's College, where candidates were elected after a 'comparative trial' in public before representatives of the college and the local clergy. The Glasgow bill, introduced by James Oswald, was originally

[45] *Municipal Corporations Commission. General Report* (PP 1835, xxix), p. 72.

confined to the provision of a rectorial Court, but a clause on open competition for chairs was added to it in committee.[46]

These bills coincided with a new outbreak of warfare at Glasgow between the Faculty and non-Faculty professors, and Oswald was working in conjunction with the latter.[47] At Aberdeen, Bannerman's bill was supported by the town council, but violently opposed by King's College, which saw it as a scheme for the aggrandisement of Marischal, and particularly resented the fact that Bannerman had succeeded in securing for Marischal College alone Aberdeen's share of a Treasury grant of £30,000 for reconstructing university buildings.[48] Feelings between the two colleges were so strong that a few years later the medical school which they had been developing jointly broke up. Quarrels of this kind made it difficult for national politicians to take up the cause of Scottish university reform, and while at Glasgow and Aberdeen municipal and business interests seem to have given it general support, at Edinburgh the MPs were forced to defend the rights of the town council, and consequently to oppose any general reform.

Melbourne's government responded to these initiatives by introducing its own bill in June 1836 to carry out the 1826 commissioners' recommendations. Following their suggestion, the bill did not prescribe detailed reforms, but set up a board of 'Royal Visitors' for each university (counting Aberdeen as one), and gave them far-reaching executive powers; there was also a clause on patronage, under which all powers of appointment exercised by professors would eventually have passed to the Crown.[49] This bill was welcomed by reformers like Cockburn,[50] and commended to the House of Lords by peers who had been on the 1826 commission. But it was soon dis-

---

[46] Bills for Aberdeen (June), Glasgow (July) and Glasgow as amended by committee (August) in PP 1835, iv.

[47] J. B. Morrell, 'Thomas Thomson: professor of chemistry and university reformer', *British Journal for the History of Science,* iv (1968/9), pp. 245-65.

[48] *A statement of the proceedings of the University and King's College of Aberdeen, respecting the royal grant to the Scottish universities* ... (Aberdeen, 1835), *passim.* This grant was made in 1826 when the Royal Commission was appointed, but not spent until the 1830s—Marischal and St. Andrews got about half each.

[49] Original and amended versions of the bill in House of Lords Sessional Papers, 1836, ii.

[50] Cockburn, *Journal,* i. 121.

covered that 'this measure had created a great sensation in Scotland, not unaccompanied by considerable alarm'.[51] Opposition came naturally from bodies opposed to any change, like Edinburgh town council and the Glasgow Faculty, but it centred on the Church, which feared that the Visitors, who were not named in the bill, would be radicals out to undermine the religious character of the universities. Protests poured in from presbyteries and other public bodies, and in the commission of the General Assembly Cook pointed out that, though he supported the recommendations of the commission to which he had belonged, there was no guarantee that the Visitors would keep within them.[52] Amendments were made to meet these criticisms: the rights of the Church, especially to consultation on the divinity curriculum, were specifically reserved; it was made clear that the Visitors would be bound by the Royal Commission's report; and the clause on patronage was dropped. But the opposition remained so vocal that the government withdrew the bill, which never reached the Commons. The reforming MPs were pacified by being put on new Royal Commissions to inquire into Glasgow and Aberdeen; these picked over ground that was now familiar, but their reports in 1838-9 had no consequences, except to reiterate that the rectorial Court was the best instrument of reform.[53]

The most passionate attacks on the 1836 bill came from King's College, some of the professors at which founded the *Aberdeen University Magazine* for the purposes of this crisis. As we have seen, this journal developed further the defence of the parochial tradition which the 1826 commission had already provoked. From a political point of view it was ultra-Tory, seeing the bill as the work of revolutionists and democrats, and the Visitors as inquisitorial despots who would overthrow every sound tradition. The *Magazine* also returned to the question of classics versus philosophy, denouncing the Royal Commission as an affair of English-educated aristocrats and Edinburgh lawyers; the clergymen were the only sound men on it, and

---

[51] *3 Hansard* xxxiv, HL 14 June 1836, and 28 June 1836, col. 989 (Lord Aberdeen).
[52] *Speeches delivered in the Commission of the General Assembly met ... to consider "The Universities' Bill for Scotland"* (Edinburgh, 1836), p. 20. Cf. *Scotsman*, 9 July 1836.
[53] There was also a commission on St. Andrews, appointed in 1840 as a result of internal disputes.

Cook and Taylor's note of dissent in defence of philosophy was 'the finest passage of the whole Report'.[54]

These controversies died down, but the Disruption brought the universities back into the political forum in 1843. Their divinity faculties now became those of the Established Church, and the Free Church set up its own colleges for training ministers. Theology professors who joined the Free Church resigned, headed by Chalmers. But lay professors were also affected, as they were supposed on their appointment to subscribe to the Confession of Faith before the local presbytery, so declaring their allegiance to the Church of Scotland. Before 1843 this had not caused any problems. At Edinburgh the test had fallen into disuse, and both Edinburgh and Glasgow had several Episcopalian professors, including one Anglican clergyman (Kelland, at Edinburgh). Subscription seems to have been regarded as a formality which raised no issues of conscience. But after 1843 the Established Church was determined to insist on the letter of its rights, and it began by attempting to unseat the Principal of United College, St. Andrews, the scientist Sir David Brewster. This failed, and incumbent professors were left in peace, but the Church was able to enforce the test on new professors, and if this continued the universities would become sectarian rather than national institutions. The question of 'university tests' was therefore an important one, and it involved the wider issue of the secularization of Scottish society, the impulse to which was implicit in the reform movement as a whole; the abolition of tests had already been included by Bannerman in his Aberdeen bill of 1835. After 1843 Liberal MPs made persistent attempts at abolition, but the unflinching opposition of the Church of Scotland was enough to intimidate successive governments.[55] The issue was eventually forced by Edinburgh town council, which had an anti-Establishment majority. In 1847 it attempted to appoint Charles McDouall, a Free Churchman, to the chair of Hebrew, but was forced by legal action to back down. In 1850 it appointed Patrick

[54] *Aberdeen University Magazine*, i (1836), *passim*, but especially pp. 103-15, 123 ff., 128, 191-212. Correspondence of Hercules Scott in AU Library MS 3073 throws further light on the virulence of the campaign against the bill.

[55] There were bills in 1843, 1844, 1845, 1851, 1852, and 1853, and the issue spilled over into rectorial elections at Glasgow.

Macdougall, professor of Moral Philosophy at the Free Church's New College, to the same chair in the university; this time the appointment stood, but Macdougall had to wait three years before he could be legally inducted. The Universities (Scotland) Act of 1853 retained the test for theology professors and university Principals, but for others it substituted a declaration (itself abolished in 1889) that they would teach nothing opposed to the doctrines of the Church of Scotland. This modest Act was the first legislative measure to result from nearly thirty years of agitation and discussion about university reform.

When university legislation eventually came about in 1858, it was because there were effective pressures from a movement of opinion which had support within the universities as well as outside, in which the leading figures were John Stuart Blackie and James Lorimer. In the course of a professorial career which extended from 1839 to 1882, Blackie became one of the best-known men in Scotland, partly owing to his combative part in controversies, partly because he deliberately cultivated the role of a 'character'. Blackie's tartan trousers and plaid, his wide-brimmed hat and flowing locks, were a startling change from the clerical austerity of orthodox professors. A popular lecturer, poet and romantic nationalist, Blackie worked to give Scots a better appreciation of their own history and literature, and in later years was a radical supporter of the Highland peasantry and the Gaelic language. But he first came before the public as a classical scholar and university reformer.

The son of an Aberdeen banker, Blackie attended Marischal College from the age of twelve, and then completed the divinity course there. But instead of becoming a minister, he went to Germany to study at Göttingen and Berlin, and this was the formative experience of his life: it opened his eyes to the progress of classical scholarship, and the German universities, those strongholds of bourgeois culture and national consciousness, were the model which inspired his ideas of university reform. A stay in Germany was common for academics of this generation, especially for scientists, who found there organized teaching and research laboratories of a kind unknown at home, and for theologians interested in the new Biblical scholarship.

Blackie set his sights on a Scottish university chair, but had to wait some time for a chance to come up. In 1839, at the age of thirty, he was appointed to the new chair of Humanity at Marischal College, an appointment which he owed to the MP Bannerman, who was a friend and political colleague of his father.[56] Blackie went on to demonstrate his Liberalism by challenging the religious test: he signed the Confession of Faith, but announced publicly that, as an undogmatic Christian, he did so purely as a formality. The Senate of the College at first refused to instal him, but was forced to do so by the courts. Not surprisingly, Blackie's writings often had a marked anticlerical tone, and he contributed a pamphlet to the tests controversy in 1843. In 1846 he launched a more general attack on 'our system of clerical and aristocratic arrangements for scholastic purposes', alleging that 'The academical institutions of Scotland, while in respect of breadth and compass, and popular sympathy, they are far superior to those of England, do, in point of scientific and literary elevation, by the admission of all who know any thing about these matters, stand at the lowest grade known in Europe.'[57]

The starting-point of all Blackie's writings was the need to eliminate the 'puerility' of the junior classes in Latin and Greek and to free the professors to do the proper work of a university instead of acting as schoolmasters. His educational programme called for a strict entrance examination complemented by a network of secondary schools or 'gymnasia', which would allow the arts course to be shortened to three years. The average age of entry should be raised to about eighteen, giving the student a sounder general preparation and making possible an element of choice in the curriculum: he could devote himself to 'such general historical, philosophical, philological, literary, and scientific culture, as might best consort either with his individual genius, or his professional views, or both'.[58] Blackie called for the creation of chairs in

---

[56] A. M. Stoddart, *John Stuart Blackie. A biography* (3rd edn., Edinburgh, 1895), i. 174-6. The King's College Tories identified 'Bannerman, Blackie, Hume' as the Radical enemy: AU Library MS 3073, D. Mearns to H. Scott, 18 June 1836.

[57] J. S. Blackie, *Education in Scotland. An appeal to the Scottish people* (Edinburgh, 1846), pp. 4, 10.

[58] *North British Review*, xxiii (1855), p. 81. The attribution of anonymous articles follows *The Wellesley Index to Victorian Periodicals 1824-1900* (3 vols., Toronto, 1966-79).

new subjects, and for 'assistant professors' to take some of the routine work off the full professors' shoulders. He admitted that his entrance demands would reduce student numbers, but thought the universities would benefit from this. He attacked the 'large irruption of unripe boys and crude clowns' into the existing junior classes, and favoured secondary schools over the parochial tradition. In 1857, in a lecture comparing Oxford and Edinburgh, he declared that 'It is a most impertinent and short-sighted idea, which some people in Scotland seem to entertain, that Universities ought to be regulated mainly for the sons of the poorest classes. ... The middle classes certainly and the rich have as great a claim on the Universities as the poor.'[59]

Much of this was a revival of Chalmers's ideas in 1827, to which indeed Blackie referred, and he received a congratulatory letter from Chalmers.[60] But for Blackie the educational changes were only a means to an end, the 'advancement of learning in Scotland'. He claimed that 'No person in Germany ever thinks of looking to a Scottish University for any work of profound learning or original research.'[61] By 'learning' Blackie meant above all historical and philological scholarship, and he found that in these fields 'every display of academic learning ... is absent from the registered culture of the Scotch mind.'[62] His aim was to shame the Scots into improving their universities so that professors had the time and resources to do original work, which should not mean sterile displays of erudition: 'we demand a scholarship with a large human soul, and a pregnant social significance, which shall not seek with a studious feebleness to avoid, but rather with a generous vigour to find contact with all the great intellectual and moral movements of the age'. Such a scholarship, he added, could only flourish 'where there is no exclusive influence of self-electing scholastic corporations, and no jealous control of ecclesiastical persons sympathizing with learning only in so far as it subserves the purposes of the Church.'[63] Blackie's own penchant, in fact, was for treating

---

[59] J. S. Blackie, *On the advancement of learning in Scotland* (Edinburgh, 1855), p. 28; *Scotsman*, 5 Nov. 1857.
[60] NLS MS 2622, Blackie papers, Chalmers to Blackie, 22 Apr. 1846.
[61] Blackie, *On the advancement of learning*, p. 13.
[62] *North British Review*, xxiii (1855), p. 77.
[63] *On the advancement of learning*, p. 10.

general themes in his lectures rather than original research.

In 1848 Blackie published a series of articles in the *Scotsman*, later published as *University reform*, which attacked the existing teaching of the classics, and stung both the Edinburgh professors into long replies. The conservative Dunbar, professor of Greek, pointed to the revolutionary anarchy on the continent as an example of what happened if German professors were given their head.[64] But Blackie had the last laugh, for he was appointed as Dunbar's successor in 1852. There was a party on the town council sympathetic to his ideas, which had already given the rectorship of the High School to a German scholar, Leonhard Schmitz, who was to be active in the cause of university reform. In his new post, Blackie was allowed to try out some of his ideas: an entrance examination was introduced for the Greek class, and the Senate agreed to pay for a tutor to take over some of the routine teaching.

Blackie's move to Edinburgh brought him into contact with James Lorimer. Lorimer was an advocate who had spent three years studying in Germany, and who was impressed like Blackie with that country's intellectual and cultural standards. Lorimer's ambition was to be a legal scholar rather than a practitioner; he was later appointed to the reformed chair of Public Law at Edinburgh, and established a reputation as an international jurist. He began to publish his views on university reform in 1850, and in 1854 published *The universities of Scotland past, present, and possible*, which served as manifesto for a campaigning body founded by Lorimer in 1853, the Association for the Extension of the Scottish Universities. Lorimer's fundamental argument was that Scotland lacked a 'learned class' (or 'clerisy'—he sometimes used Coleridge's term), a set of men with enough leisure to make independent contributions to literature and learning. The Scottish bar, it was true, had a fine record in this respect, but the universities were failing in what should be their proper function. A university 'must be at once a magazine and a laboratory of thought. The notion, which has too much prevailed in Scotland, of its being a mere

---

[64] G. Dunbar, *A defence of the junior Humanity and Greek classes in the University of Edinburgh* (Edinburgh, 1848), p. 10. Cf. J. Pillans, *A word for the universities of Scotland* (Edinburgh, 1848).

teaching institution, a sort of Higher-School, by no means ...
exhausts its true idea. ... it must be an institution where learning is fostered and advanced as well as communicated.'[65]

'Fifty new chairs in all,' declared Lorimer in 1854, 'with
half-a-dozen tutors to each university, would place the Scottish
universities in a tolerably efficient state, as educational institutions, and supply no mean stimulus to the cultivation of learning.'[66] In order to provide posts for scholars, Lorimer envisaged two new grades of staff—'junior professors' and tutors—
so creating a true academic career structure, an idea which was
not to come into its own until the 1890s.[67] His Association
suggested eighteen new subjects in which chairs might be
created, but it is significant that these were mostly in such
fields as politics and economics, history and languages, only
three being in science.[68] Lorimer's view was that the sciences
could 'take care of themselves' because they were paying
subjects: it was the state's duty, and its glory, to support those
higher subjects which the 'multitude' or *hoi polloi* could not be
expected to understand, and to invest the universities 'with a
sacred character. As the birthplace and culmination of the
clerisy, they claim to be surrounded with a glory and a sanctity
no less distinct and impressive than that we are accustomed to
attach to institutions more exclusively devotional.'[69]

Lorimer had an equally lofty conception of the social function of university education, which existed

mainly for the benefit of the higher classes, of those who compose, in
the literal sense of the word, the aristocracy of the community. ... Its
peculiar province consists in *educating the professions*—in preserving
their liberal and scientific character—in preventing them from being
degraded into systems of lifeless formulas, ... or mechanical trades,
by maintaining their union with that higher philosophy which is the
light and life of them all.

Lorimer saw the distinction between a profession and a trade
in the relation of the former to general ideas, and concluded

[65] *North British Review*, xii (Feb. 1850), pp. 293-4.
[66] J. Lorimer, *The universities of Scotland past, present, and possible* (Edinburgh, 1854),
p. 44.
[67] *North British Review*, xiii (Aug. 1850), pp. 311-15.
[68] *The universities of Scotland*, p. 62.
[69] *North British Review*, xiii. 307-8, 317.

that 'it is in communicating this, the properly speaking professional, as opposed to the mercantile habit of mind, that the
university finds her highest and most essential vocation'.[70] The
arts faculty existed to give a professional training to scholars
and schoolmasters, but also had a special function for the
'small but highly influential' leisured class. 'It aims at enabling
them to maintain a leading position in society, less by the
material momentum of mere wealth, than by intelligence and
moral dignity, at qualifying them for making the best and most
extensive use of all those opportunities and means of usefulness which wealth, rank, and the willing respect of a loyal people
enable them to command.'[71] This fitted in with Lorimer's
political views. Himself the son of a nobleman's factor, he was,
according to his obituarist, 'a vigorous defender of country
mansion life, and of the country gentleman system', and he
spent his later years restoring Kellie Castle in Fife.[72] One of his
interests was electoral reform, and in his book *Political progress
not necessarily democratic* (1857) he argued for giving a double
vote to the educated; he also supported the creation of a Scottish
university franchise, partly as an incentive to graduation.[73]

Lorimer's special aim in 1854 was to win over middle-class
opinion and put forward a concrete programme of reforms.[74]
Like Blackie, he thought an entrance examination and the
improvement of secondary education essential. 'There is a
notion which we regard as utterly foolish and irrational, but
which nevertheless is very prevalent in Scotland, to the effect
that, for the sake of the poorer class of students, it ought to be
possible to pass at once from the parish schools to the university,
without going through the intermediate training of the burgh
schools at all.' To break this link would be positively desirable.[75] But 'There is no necessity for calling into existence an
Eton or Harrow, a German Gymnasium, or even an Edinburgh
Academy [where he sent his own sons], in every provincial
town.' The burgh schools could be developed satisfactorily if

[70] Ibid., pp. 302-3; *Edinburgh Review,* cvii (1858), pp. 93-4.
[71] *North British Review,* xiii. 306.
[72] Obituary from *Journal of Jurisprudence* in EU Library, MS Gen. 103, Lorimer
papers.
[73] Lorimer, *Political progress,* pp. 246-7, 273-5.
[74] *The universities of Scotland,* pp. 1-6, 30.
[75] *Edinburgh Review,* cvii. 97.

their masters were paid better salaries, which would have the additional advantage of providing posts for men of learning.[76]

Like Blackie too, he foresaw the end of the junior classes and a three-year arts course, which could be made compulsory for entry to the professions. He would retain the existing curriculum unaltered, although this left open the question of what his fifty new professors would do: as critics pointed out, unless their subjects had some place in the curriculum the result would be the 'multiplication of sinecures'.[77] As for teaching methods, Lorimer thought that the professorial system was 'an error in the constitution of the Scottish universities from first to last', and he insisted that tutorships should be grafted onto it. Tutors were part of a package of reforms which Lorimer was prepared to import from England in order to improve the 'moral and social training of students' and give the universities a sense of corporate life, including common tables, the revival of academic dress, and where practicable a residential system. Scottish families, he thought, would wish their sons to exhibit 'the correctness and quiet dignity of the English gentleman' rather than the boisterous coarseness of the German student.[78]

For all this, both Blackie and Lorimer were faithfully reflecting the contemporary neo-humanist ideal of the German universities, in which learning was pursued not 'for its own sake' but because it helped to form the moral character of the student and give him a purpose in life. The professor, himself pursuing original research, trained his disciples in the pursuit of truth, so that the teaching and research functions of the university were intimately allied. This ideal contrasted with the traditional view of the teaching university in Scotland as well as England. It is perhaps relevant to look in this context at another university reformer, whom Davie has contrasted with Lorimer as a proponent of Anglophile ideas, John Campbell Shairp. Shairp was born into a gentry family, attended Edinburgh Academy and Glasgow University, and went from Glasgow to

---

[76] *North British Review*, xxxiii (1860), p. 77.

[77] Pillans, letter of 1854 to Lorimer's Association reprinted in J. Pillans, *Contributions to the cause of education* (1856), p. 590; cf. P. Kelland, *How to improve the Scottish universities* (Edinburgh, 1855), p. 9.

[78] *Edinburgh Review*, cvii. 103. Cf. *The universities of Scotland*, pp. 72 ff., *North British Review*, xiii. 320, 326, 333.

Balliol College on the Snell exhibition, the greatest academic prize in Scotland, originally intended to maintain the supply of Episcopal clergymen. In Shairp's generation, a veritable mafia of Oxonian Scots passed through Balliol, then in the early days of its Victorian fame, and returned to chairs in Scotland. They included Lewis Campbell, professor of Greek at St. Andrews; Edward Caird, professor of Moral Philosophy at Glasgow, and later Master of Balliol; John Nichol, the first professor of English at Glasgow; and William Sellar, professor of Greek at St. Andrews and Humanity at Edinburgh. Shairp himself absorbed English ideals even more thoroughly by teaching for ten years at Rugby, before returning as 'assistant' in Latin at St. Andrews in 1857; later he became professor, and eventually Principal of United College. Shairp was a prime example of the Anglo-Scot, though he cultivated a literary and romantic nationalism in the style of Blackie. Despite his English experience, his pamphlet on *The wants of the Scottish universities and some of the remedies* (Edinburgh, 1856) differed only in emphasis from Lorimer. Like Lorimer, Shairp wanted to restore the Scottish universities to their former eminence and to make them compete effectively with their rivals, and the pamphlet advocated an entrance examination, the use of tutors, and a searching final examination conducted by a single board of examiners for Scotland. This last was also part of Lorimer's plans, though he saw it more as a means of maintaining the philosophical character of Scottish education, and on this point the two men certainly differed.[79]

In 1860, in an article on 'Scottish nationality', Lorimer argued that if Scotland still had a national individuality it was 'not political, or even institutional, but social, and, above all, intellectual'. The Scottish intellectual character was of a generalizing, abstract, rationalistic kind, nearer to continental than to English models, and to keep it alive was essential to the future of Scottish nationality.[80] Shairp, on the other hand, was a critic of the Scottish 'metaphysical' tradition, which he thought encouraged glibness and superficiality. Scottish students could 'write plausibly on almost any subject in a fluent, semi-metaphysical, semi-rhetorical way', but failed 'when

[79] *The universities of Scotland*, p. 68.
[80] *North British Review*, xxxiii. 57, 66, 70 ff.

some accuracy of scholarship, and some definite historical knowledge is required'. Philosophy was 'the most exhausting crop which the soil of the mind can be called on to grow', and could only flourish when that soil had been prepared by a careful study of solid subjects like the classics, and when philosophical study itself was based on the texts of the great philosophers rather than being 'a course of metaphysics let loose on raw and ill-prepared minds'.[81] There was more to this than mere prejudice: Blackie too thought teaching metaphysics to sixteen- and seventeen-year-olds was a gross educational blunder[82], and both men believed that truth must now be discovered by the techniques of scholarship rather than through speculative philosophy. Shairp commended the study of history, and would have agreed with William Sellar that it was 'peculiarly serviceable as a counteraction to the rhetorical and what are called the metaphysical tendencies of Scotch education'.[83] One might draw a parallel with the French scholar Renan's criticism of French university culture for its rhetorical superficiality and cult of literary elegance, which he thought could be corrected by an importation of German historical and philological seriousness.[84]

A recent historian has said of the German ideal of *Bildung* that 'the leisured, vaguely aristocratic ethos of self-development via the pursuit of scholarship had little in common with the practical and hard-headed thinking patterns of the commercial bourgeoisie, let alone those of the artisans and peasants'.[85] Similar thoughts occurred to some of Lorimer's critics, notably Philip Kelland, professor of Mathematics at Edinburgh. Kelland feared that Lorimer's new chairs would destroy 'our moderate and definite curriculum' and 'transform a tolerably compact school, into a wide-spread chaos of disconnected Lectures, and change the practical character of our prelections into a cold exhibition of intellectual superiority'. He appealed to the authority of Hamilton to show that teaching was the

---

[81] Shairp, *Wants of the Scottish universities*, pp. 5-6, 16, 30, 34.
[82] *North British Review*, xxiii. 78.
[83] *Fraser's Magazine*, liv (1856), p. 122.
[84] R. D. Anderson, *Education in France 1848-1870* (Oxford, 1975), p. 226.
[85] C. E. McClelland, *State, society, and university in Germany 1700-1914* (Cambridge, 1980), p. 121.

prime function of a university, and thought that what suited despotic Prussia was not necessarily best for a free country where the universities did not belong to the state. 'We belong to the people—to the ruled as well as to the rulers—we rest mutually on each other.' This relationship with the community was reflected in the 'total absence of all bars, of the very shadow of exclusiveness', and in the 'catholicity' of the universities, that is 'their being available for all grades of society—for all ages—for all intellects—for all attainments'. Thus, above all, an entrance examination 'will never do for Scotland'. Kelland, himself an Englishman, was essentially reproducing the Edinburgh objections to the Royal Commission of 1826.[86]

Lorimer's ideas were influential because he was able to attract powerful supporters, starting with his fellow-lawyers. He belonged to a committee of the Faculty of Advocates on the qualifications of entrants, whose report—probably written by Lorimer himself, and adopted by the Faculty in 1854—laid down that candidates for the bar must be graduates in arts or pass an equivalent examination.[87] Lawyers also dominated the Association for the Improvement and Extension of the Scottish Universities (as it was renamed): of ninety-five General Committee members in 1853, some sixty were judges, sheriffs, advocates, or solicitors, and there were only six 'merchants' and three ministers.[88] But the Association soon built up support among MPs, ministers (especially of the Free Church) and professors. It was weak in Glasgow, where however a similar pressure-group, the Scottish Literary Institute, founded in 1857, formed a rallying-point for reformers like the publisher W. G. Blackie and the MP Walter Buchanan, a champion of the university franchise.[89] Lorimer seems originally to have

---

[86] P. Kelland, *How to improve the Scottish universities*, pp. 4-5, 8; *The Scottish university system suited to the people* (Edinburgh, 1854), pp. 3, 7, 12. For similar views from a more conservative standpoint see article by W. E. Aytoun in *Blackwood's Magazine*, lxxxiii (1858), pp. 74-93; J. McNeill, *Address ... to the Associated Societies of the University of Edinburgh* (Edinburgh, 1857).

[87] Printed as Appendix A in Lorimer's *The universities of Scotland*.

[88] Ibid., pp. 60-1.

[89] *Report of the proceedings of the Scottish Literary Institute at their first anniversary meeting* (Edinburgh, 1857); *Report of the proceedings of the Scottish Literary Institute, at their second anniversary meeting* (Glasgow, 1858).

seen his Association as a fund-raising body, but campaigning for legislation soon became its main activity, and it threw itself into a round of memorials, circulars, reports and deputations which came to a peak in 1857-8.[90]

There were a number of reasons why reform seemed urgent. At Edinburgh in particular, university numbers had fallen heavily since the 1820s, and the dispute with the town council still awaited a solution—the last of the lawsuits was decided in 1854. Moreover, the abolition of religious tests in the English universities removed the appeal of Scotland to English Nonconformists, and threatened hopes for higher scholarship by opening the lucrative endowments of Oxford and Cambridge to Scots. Another development was the introduction of competitive entry in the civil service following the Northcote-Trevelyan report of 1853. Open competition was not generally applied to the home civil service until 1870, but it was used for the East India Company's service from 1855. Careers in India had always attracted Scots, but in the early years of the examination they did not do well. The marking scheme, devised by Macaulay, was intended to be fair as between British universities, but in fact gave more marks to classics than to philosophy, and put Oxford and Cambridge graduates at an advantage. But the examination also put strong emphasis on English literature and history, subjects neglected in Scotland, and the Indian results were used by commentators to urge the need for new chairs in these modern subjects rather than to complain about bias.[91] The issue attracted much attention in the Scottish press, though Lorimer thought its importance exaggerated, since only a few families were affected—'the professions in this country, and not the civil service in India, are the proper objects of our national universities, both Scotch and English'.[92]

One expression of the growth of the professional classes was the demand that graduates should have a say in university

---

[90] *Report by the Acting Committee of the Association for the Improvement and Extension of the Scottish Universities ... 7th November 1857* (Edinburgh, n.d.), *passim*; many circulars etc. of the Association are in a bound collection of pamphlets, annotated by Lorimer, in EU Library. See also the article by D. B. Horn cited above.

[91] J. Muir, *The Indian Civil Service and the Scottish universities* (Edinburgh, 1855), p. 24; W. G. Blackie, *Remarks on the East India Company's Civil Service examination papers* (Glasgow, 1858), pp. 3-4, 16.

[92] *Edinburgh Review*, cvii. 92-3.

government. The Scottish universities, unlike the English ones, were surrounded by a large body of their own graduates, active in local affairs, and likely to be irritated by inefficiency or the misuse of resources. This had been a factor in Hume's agitation in 1825, and one of the men who spoke at his rectorial court became the leading theorist of graduates' rights. This was Alexander Kilgour, a prominent Aberdeen doctor active in Liberal politics, who published pamphlets on the subject in 1850 and 1857. Like Bannerman he called for a 'Convocation', which in his scheme would be a body of teachers and graduates exercising authority through an executive University Council.[93] Kilgour added a good deal of dubious historical argument about the rights of graduates in the medieval universities, but his real point was that the influence of public opinion should replace the oligarchic and secretive system of professorial control. The Aberdeen reformers won a significant victory in 1856, when the professors of King's College, who had previously chosen the rector themselves, opened this election up to graduates.

A graduate movement also existed at Glasgow, where a Society of Graduates was founded in 1849; as the 'Glasgow Association of Scottish Graduates' this body (or its reincarnation) was active in lobbying the government in 1854-5, and it had offshoots in Edinburgh and St Andrews which were organizing meetings in 1858.[94] But it was Lorimer's Association which made the running. Lorimer gained the support of Lord Advocate Moncreiff, and in February 1857 drew up a bill at his request, which assumed that the government would 'endow' the universities with £20,000 a year, most of which would be spent on tutors, provided lavishly at a rate of one to every thirty or forty students; other features of Lorimer's programme incorporated in the bill were a national board of examiners, a compulsory entrance examination for those aiming at graduation, and a reference to halls of residence and common tables. There was also a graduation scheme, with a BA and MA,

---

[93] A. Kilgour, *University reform* (Aberdeen, 1850), and *The Scottish universities, and what to reform in them* (Edinburgh, 1857), pp. 33 ff.; cf. *In Memoriam. Alexander Kilgour, M.D.* (Edinburgh, 1874).

[94] Documents relating to the Glasgow Association in SRO AD 56 54; *Scotsman*, 1 Feb., 19 Feb., 29 Mar. 1858.

modelled closely on the report of 1830.[95] The possible fate
of this bill is uncertain, for 1857 was an election year, and
Moncreiff was replaced in February 1858 by the Conservative
John Inglis. Inglis was a vice-president of Lorimer's Association, but had ideas of his own on university reform, which he
had expounded as the second rector of King's College to be
elected by the graduates. He advised caution in tampering with
Scottish traditions and copying foreign models, and especially
defended the classics; but he acknowledged his obligations to
the graduates by agreeing that their participation would help
'to bring the power of enlightened public opinion to bear
directly on the government of the University, and to secure to
the University a firmer hold on the confidence and affection of
the people'.[96]

Lorimer's campaign reached its climax with a great public
meeting at Edinburgh in December 1857. The platform was
crowded with professors, lawyers, MPs and peers—including
Lord Rosebery, chairman of the 1826 commission. Eight
resolutions were passed, covering the creation of new chairs,
higher professorial salaries, an improved examination system,
tutorial assistants, and a share in government for graduates—
but avoiding, as the Association always had, the wider issues of
university administration and patronage which were so divisive
in Edinburgh. The most interesting resolution, moved by the
Free Church leader Robert Candlish, was on the need to preserve the distinctive character of the Scottish universities,
which meant specifically the professorial system, and more
generally 'their wide and universal adaptation to the whole
body of the Scottish people'. The growing gap between standards in parochial and secondary schools was a matter for
concern, and it was essential that classical teaching should
remain strong in the former and that the university link was
preserved. Moreover, it was important to remember that 'the
Scottish Universities are of a thoroughly practical character,

[95] Versions of the proposed bill are in the collection referred to in note 90 above and
in EU Library MS Gen. 102, Lorimer papers. On the genesis of the 1858 Act see
Horn, loc. cit., and G. W. T. Omond, *The Lord Advocates of Scotland. Second series,
1834-1880* (1914), pp. 199, 213-18.

[96] J. Inglis, *Inaugural discourse delivered to the graduates of King's College, Aberdeen*
(Edinburgh, 1857), p. 11.

that they profess ... that their students shall be trained for practical life, that they shall be trained as workers fully as much as that they shall be trained as scholars'. One senses here a desire to dissociate the speaker from the 'learned class' element in Lorimer's plans, which must have seemed fanciful to many who supported his general aim of regenerating the universities as national institutions.[97]

Both Moncreiff and Inglis moved resolutions at this meeting, and friendly co-operation was the order of the day when Inglis introduced his universities bill in 1858, though this was quite different from the one prepared by Lorimer in 1857. It dealt largely with constitutional matters, and provided for the long-anticipated Courts. Debate was extensive and free—many quite important details were introduced as backbenchers' amendments—and open political conflict was confined to two points: the union of the two Aberdeen universities, opposed to the end by the city's MP,[98] and the unsuccessful struggle of Edinburgh town council to retain its powers. Despite intensive lobbying, and despite the argument that if the influence of public opinion was what was desired the elected town council was the ideal organ for its expression, the council lost its rights of administration and patronage. The bill had not originally dealt with the latter, but it was brought up on amendment, and as a compromise the town council had to agree to transfer chair appointments to a body of seven 'Curators of Patronage', four appointed by themselves and three by the University Court.

When introducing the bill, Inglis stressed its educational aims—to encourage graduation in arts and the 'raising of the standard of excellence in all departments'.[99] But all curricular changes were left to a temporary executive commission, headed by Inglis himself, which was to legislate through Ordinances, a system borrowed from the reform of Oxford and Cambridge. The commission was also given the power to revise endowments, create new chairs, raise salaries, provide for assistantships, etc.

[97] *Scotsman*, 31 Dec. 1857.
[98] The movement for 'fusion' of the colleges had revived in the 1850s and given rise to much controversy. The root of the problem was that each college wanted to retain its own arts faculty.
[99] 3 *Hansard* cxlix, HC 22 Apr. 1858, col. 1546.

For these purposes an extra annual grant of £10,000 was provided—half of what Lorimer had hoped.[100] The constitutional
details were settled in the Act itself, and centred on the Courts.
These followed the pattern suggested by the 1826 commission,
but with some changes in detail: the rector was to be elected
by the students, and by them alone; the Senates handed their
powers of patronage to the Courts, but retained the administration of university property and revenue; and an Assessor
was to be elected by a new body, the General Council. The
General Councils, consisting of all graduates,[101] were Inglis's
concession to the graduate movement, but their powers were
limited—they could meet only twice a year, and their role was
purely consultative. The composition of the Courts gave representation to each university interest—students, professors,
and graduates—but not to 'public opinion' in the true sense,
except at Edinburgh where the Court included, in deference to
history, the Lord Provost and a town council Assessor; but it
could be argued that the General Councils represented the
section of public opinion likely to be best informed on university
matters.

Although the name 'General Council' was new, the idea of
graduate representation went back through Bannerman to
Hume, while the Courts combined the 1826 commission's plan
for an impartial reforming body with Hamilton's plan for the
transfer of patronage. The Act ended one chapter of university
reform by disposing permanently of most of the constitutional
problems identified in the 1820s: the universities could no
longer be seen as symbols of vested interest and corporate
decay, and attention shifted to more obviously educational
questions. Here too there were complex lines of continuity,
from Chalmers, the founders of Edinburgh Academy, and the
1826 commission to Blackie and Lorimer. It remained to be

[100] In 1864 a 'Scottish Universities and Educational Association', which saw itself as
a continuation of Lorimer's movement, was formed in Edinburgh to campaign for
more state aid, and for 'higher class' (secondary) schools. It attracted influential
names, but did not last. See D. Thorburn, *The endowment of the universities of Scotland an
object of national importance* (Edinburgh, 1863); D. Thorburn, *The university endowment
movement: memorandum relative thereto* (Edinburgh, 1866); *Scottish Universities and Educational Association. Draft report for provisional committee* (Edinburgh, 1866).
[101] Or alumni with equivalent attendance; at first only arts graduates qualified,
MDs being excluded.

seen how far Inglis's commission would meet the long-voiced demands for higher academic standards, more encouragement to graduation, and a stricter organization of professional studies.

3.
UNIVERSITY REFORM 1858-1878:
SCIENCE AND CULTURE

The executive commission headed by Inglis was composed of lawyers, peers, and MPs, but the universities themselves had no representatives. Nor did the churches—an indication of how the Disruption had weakened their influence over public affairs. The commission issued ninety Ordinances, and its final report appeared in 1863. The Ordinance on graduation in arts came into operation in 1861, and was to remain substantially unchanged until 1892. Almost as soon as the commission reported, however, its work began to appear old-fashioned, and the working of its system created many practical problems, leading to the appointment of a new Royal Commission in 1876.

As we have seen, the universities adopted stricter examination and degree regulations in the 1820s, and since then there had been further movement in the same direction. Edinburgh, for example, had overhauled its system in 1835, and there seems to have been a general move from oral to written examining. But the subjects studied remained the same, and the only significant innovation was that Edinburgh (1842) and St Andrews (1839) copied Glasgow by introducing a BA which could be gained in three years by omitting some subjects from the usual curriculum.[1] The BA degree was condemned, however, by the Inglis commission, and had to be dropped by all the universities after 1861. The commission considered that all the subjects of the traditional Scottish curriculum were essential to a well-rounded general education, and the only change was to make English Literature a separate compulsory subject, as it already was at Edinburgh, making a total of seven. The commission also allowed a 'natural science' to be added as an eighth subject if universities wished, though for the time being

---

[1] A. Grant, *The story of the University of Edinburgh during its first three hundred years* (1884), ii. 112-14, 118; J. C. Shairp & others, *Life and letters of James David Forbes* (1873), pp. 132-3.

only Aberdeen took advantage of this to continue its practice of including Natural History. The order in which subjects were taken was left to each university, but the commission did lay down that subjects should be grouped for examination under three categories (classics, philosophy, mathematics), so that examinations were taken in three annual stages rather than at the end of the course.[2]

Cautious conservatism was the keynote of the commission's work. The junior classes were to continue, and only a limited concession was made to the partisans of an entrance examination: in future those who passed a special examination could pass directly into the second classes of Latin, Greek, and Mathematics, and so complete a degree in three years. The way thus remained open to boys from the parish schools, but the new 'three-year examination' provided an incentive, in practice not much used, for the development of classical education in the secondary schools. The commission also introduced a compulsory preliminary examination for medical students, and these two examinations took their place among the growing number of such tests—for the civil service, the army, and the professions—which were giving the schools precise goals and stereotyping their work.

A more important innovation was that the MA could now be taken with Honours. Candidates had to complete the full ordinary curriculum, and offer more specialized work in one of four 'departments'—classics, mental philosophy, mathematics (including natural philosophy), and natural sciences (including geology, chemistry, zoology, and botany). Students prepared for Honours examinations by private reading and study, and though this usually (but not necessarily) involved staying on for an extra year there were no special requirements for attendance and no Honours classes. The scheme was thus more modest than that proposed in 1830, with its separate BA and MA degrees, and this reflected the Inglis commission's limited resources. Much of the £10,000 annual grant which it had to allocate went on setting up a full medical school at Aberdeen and on augmenting existing salaries, and only two new arts

[2] *Scott. Univ. Comm. Rep.*, pp. xxvii-xxx, and Ordinances 14, 18. The examination system was modelled on Edinburgh practice.

chairs were created, in English at Glasgow and Logic at Aberdeen; for thirty years, the working of the new curriculum at Aberdeen and St. Andrews was to depend on English being taught by the professors of Logic. The commission also financed assistantships to help with the teaching in some of the large arts classes, as demanded by Blackie. But there was no trace of Lorimer's scheme for the promotion of learning, and the *North British Review* congratulated the commission on its 'wise conservatism' in refusing to countenance 'a notion—at one time wide-spread, and which in some quarters lingers yet—that University Reform consists in establishing professorships in every branch of human knowledge'.[3] It did try to encourage advanced study, however, by using surplus endowment funds to create postgraduate scholarships; the commission shared the view of its predecessors in 1830 that there were too many small bursaries at Aberdeen, and provoked great opposition there by its policy of amalgamation and diversion.[4]

The Inglis commission was concerned with professional as well as general education. In the case of divinity, it found itself unable to make any proposals because of disagreements between the universities over the position of the various denominational colleges. On medicine, its decisions were regulated by the Medical Act of 1858, which had set up a common system of qualifications for the whole United Kingdom. The commission's medical curriculum, as well as introducing the preliminary examination mentioned above, which included Latin, was designed to ensure attendance on at least two arts subjects at university level. Their most significant decision, perhaps, was to recognize the system of 'extra-mural' medical education which had grown up at Edinburgh and Glasgow, by which the universities recognized for graduation purposes attendance on private lecturers outside their own walls. In Glasgow the lecturers formed extra-mural schools, while at Edinburgh they operated individually, but in both cities they had an important role, and at Edinburgh the extra-mural teaching was at times more distinguished than that of the official faculty.

---

[3] *North British Review*, xxxix (1863), p. 491 (H. H. Lancaster).
[4] *Scott. Univ. Comm. Rep.*, pp. xxxvii-xlii.

The Medical Act was a landmark in the development of the professions, but the same desire for formal qualifications was affecting the legal profession. As we have seen, the Faculty of Advocates decided in 1854 to require graduation in arts or the equivalent from entrants, and the Edinburgh solicitors' bodies also introduced an arts requirement, though falling short of full graduation—the Writers to the Signet in 1851, the Solicitors to the Supreme Courts in 1854. Professional training still combined apprenticeship in a practitioner's office with attendance at university lectures, and after the Law Agents Act of 1873 the latter was made compulsory: entrants to the solicitor's profession throughout Scotland had to go to a university for classes in Scots Law and Conveyancing. The law faculties at Glasgow and Aberdeen taught little more than these staple subjects, but at Edinburgh the Inglis commission set up a three-year degree of LL B to which only arts graduates were admitted, and it revived the chair of Public Law, which was given to Lorimer. Lorimer had ambitious plans for making legal education the normal path, as on the continent, for those aiming at politics, diplomacy, and the public service generally—plans which came too late to challenge the 'Northcote-Trevelyan' ideal of the 'amateur' administrator trained in classics or history.[5] By 1870 Lorimer had to admit that the LL B had failed. As an 'academic' degree which went beyond professional requirements, it attracted only a handful of students. Lorimer therefore recommended a shorter degree to encourage graduation, so that 'the Legal Profession, as a whole, can be bound to the National Universities, and united within itself, as a learned profession'.[6] In 1874 Edinburgh created a two-year BL degree, requiring some arts subjects but not the full curriculum, and Glasgow followed suit in 1878; but the BL did not prove much more successful than the LL B.

The main work of the Inglis commission was thus to reform the traditional arts degree and provide for the needs of the

[5] J. Lorimer, *On the sphere and functions of an academical Faculty of Law* (1864), pp. 21-2. Cf. the very similar views of his counterpart at Glasgow: W. G. Miller, *The Faculty of Law in the University of Glasgow* (Glasgow, 1889), p. 7.

[6] EU Library, MS Gen. 102, Lorimer papers, documents relating to committee on graduation in law, 1870. Cf. Lorimer's evidence in *R. Comm. Univ. Ev.*, Part II (1878), pp. 361 ff.

'learned' professions. Its report showed little consciousness of industrial or commercial needs, nor perhaps was this to be expected of a body drawn from the established political and legal élite. Lorimer and his Association had practically ignored science, and had recognized contemporary social change only in the negative desire to distance the professions from the 'mercantile' spirit. But in the 1860s the demands of science became more insistent. Schools of natural science existed at Oxford and Cambridge, and London University had introduced a B.Sc. degree. In 1864 Edinburgh followed this example. The Edinburgh B.Sc.—which completely bypassed the Inglis commission's safeguards for general education—could be taken in three branches of pure science, and in engineering after Edinburgh acquired a chair in that subject in 1868.[7] At this time, however, the professional openings for scientists were still limited, and of 149 students who had taken the B.Sc. in pure science by 1890, sixty-two became professors and teachers and thirty doctors, and only eleven, all chemists, found posts with industrial applications.[8]

The disinclination of those interested in science to go through a compulsory curriculum in which the natural sciences were themselves under-represented meant that the B.Sc. superseded the Inglis commission's scheme for Honours in natural science. In the six years between 1870/1 and 1875/6 only eleven students took that degree, all but one of them at Aberdeen. Table 3.1 gives some other data about graduation.[9] Despite the incentives of General Council membership and the university vote, by no means all those completing the curriculum took the trouble to graduate, for the practical advantages were limited; the Church, for example, remained content with certificates of attendance. Moreover, those completing the full curriculum were themselves a minority, except at Aberdeen, where both graduating and taking Honours were more popular than else-

[7] Glasgow had a chair of Engineering as early as 1840. At Edinburgh the government founded a chair of Technology in 1855, but this lapsed on the death of the professor in 1859.

[8] SRO ED 9 61, letter to university commissioners from A. Crum Brown, 30 Oct. 1891.

[9] Average figures for six academic years, based on *R. Comm. Univ. Returns & Documents*, pp. 3, 148-50, 211, 341.

Table 3.1.

Arts graduation in universities, 1870/1 to 1875/6

	Aberdeen	Edinburgh	Glasgow	St. Andrews
Average numbers:				
(1) in Arts faculty	337	739	830	129
(2) completing curriculum annually	62	n.a.	57	21
(3) graduating annually	44	62	37	12
(3) as % of (2)	70%	n.a.	65%	55%
(3) as % of (1)	13%	8%	5%	9%
Total degrees awarded	262	372	222	69
Honours degrees awarded	73	42	54	9
Honours as % of total	28%	11%	24%	13%

where. But at Glasgow the average group completing the curriculum was 57 at a time when most of the arts classes had a strength of 140-60, and contemporaries estimated that only one student in seven aimed at the full curriculum. 'Many students, especially in a large city like Glasgow, avail themselves of *two* or *three* of the Arts classes. They are lads in offices, students of law, teachers, lads going into business; they come many of them for the sake of a liberal education, and thus prove very good students. They wish, say, to take literature, logic, moral philosophy, chemistry. They cannot afford time for more.'[10] Statistics collected at Glasgow showed that out of 3,122 students who entered the arts faculty in the period 1861-72, 36 per cent stayed for only one session, 17 per cent for two sessions, and only 47 per cent for more than two. Only 372 of the 3,122 graduated, though a further 654 completed the curriculum, or nearly so.[11] At Edinburgh too, it was said that average attendance was two years and that one in five or six graduated.[12]

As the quotation above indicates, many students were only able to give part-time attendance. In 1876 George Ramsay, professor of Humanity at Glasgow, administered a questionnaire to his junior class. This met twice a day, at 8 and 11 a.m. Of the 283 students who replied, 97 came only to the 8 o'clock class, and then went on to their work, mostly as 'clerks in law offices' (56) or teachers (30). A further 44 came to the 11 o'clock class, but also had full-time jobs. Of the remaining 142 students, 74 were free in the winter but had to work in the summer; they included 17 teachers, mostly from the Highlands, who obtained substitutes during the university session. That left only 60 students who had no other cares, a figure which also applied to Ramsay's senior class. He concluded therefore that 'only a small proportion of our students—only some 60 a year—are really free to go through the entire course from beginning to end,—are, in short, what we may call graduatable material, and that the great bulk of our students attend merely special classes for special objects'.[13] This was even more true of classes which were not part of the arts curriculum. At Edin-

---

[10] *R. Comm. Univ. Ev.*, Part I, p. 39 (J. Caird) and Part II, p. 251 (Veitch).
[11] *R. Comm. Univ. Ev.*, Part II, pp. 512-13 (W. Stewart).
[12] Grant, op. cit., ii. 120-1, and cf. *R. Comm. Univ. Returns & Documents*, p. 341.
[13] *R. Comm. Univ. Ev.*, Part I, pp. 965-6.

burgh, for example, the professor of Engineering gave his class at 9 a.m., and many of his students went on to a full day's work as draughtsmen or assistant engineers, while the professor of Political Economy (a chair newly founded in 1871) had forty-eight students who mostly worked in offices or banks, and he held the class at 5 p.m. to accommodate them.[14] The most successful teacher at Edinburgh at this time was the physicist P. G. Tait, whose Natural Philosophy class had 229 students in 1875; only between a quarter and a third of these, he estimated, were taking the full arts course, while a large number were at the university for only one year, taking his class alone or combining it with subjects like Engineering and Geology.[15] In earlier years, indeed, university science classes had attracted artisans, but this seems to have been no longer the case, for technical education could be obtained in day or evening classes at institutions subsidized by the Science and Art Department. At Glasgow there was 'Anderson's University', which went back to 1796, and at Edinburgh the Watt Institution, founded as the Edinburgh School of Arts in 1821.[16]

Whatever the educational virtues of the Inglis commission's arts curriculum, therefore, they were not being extended to all of those who used the universities, and in the 1860s it was increasingly felt that the curriculum itself was partly responsible for the failure of many students to graduate. It was too long, too inflexible, too much tied to the intellectual requirements of the clergy. At a time when the growing commercial and industrial middle class were taking a more serious interest in extended education and university culture, the Scottish universities risked losing the chance to capture a new clientele, and began to look old-fashioned by comparison with those, old and new, south of the border. The idea that the uniform curriculum should give way to one in which students could choose between options suited to their intellectual interests or vocational needs made

[14] *Royal Commission on Scientific Instruction and the Advancement of Science. Vol. I. First, Supplementary, and Second Reports* (PP 1872, xxv), p. 100 (Fleeming Jenkin); *R. Comm. Univ. Ev.*, Part II, pp. 502-3 (W. B. Hodgson).

[15] *R. Comm. Univ. Ev.*, Part I, pp. 157-8.

[16] Anderson's (or the Andersonian) University was renamed Anderson's College in 1877, and became the Glasgow and West of Scotland Technical College in 1887. It also included an extra-mural medical school.

rapid progress in the 1860s, and was often taken up by the General Councils, speaking for the local business and professional community; their importance was increased in 1868, when they became the constituencies for the new Scottish university seats, and when certain restrictions on the qualifications for membership were removed. Active influence in the General Councils was confined to those who attended the half-yearly meetings, where the professoriate itself was also strongly represented, but from time to time the calm of academic decision-making was disturbed.

The clergy, it is true, remained a large profession whose training provided the arts faculties with a substantial core of students. At Aberdeen in the 1850s, 48 per cent of students graduating at King's College aimed at the ministry, and 40 per cent at Marischal—and these figures included the medical as well as arts faculties.[17] The clerical profession was still an expanding one, as Table 3.2 shows.[18] The table also shows how the teaching profession was expanding. This might seem an obvious field of recruitment for the arts faculties, but various difficulties stood in the way of exploiting it, and in the long run this could only be done properly if the universities were opened to women.

Meanwhile, the universities were already serving the commercial middle class, though not without tension between their demands and what the universities were able to offer. Such tension had arisen at Glasgow in the 1820s over the position of the classics, and in the 1860s it recurred over the length of the university course. Merchants in Glasgow liked to send their sons to the university, but they also believed in an early start in the business of life. 'Scottish shrewdness will readily determine', wrote one observer, 'that a youth destined for business is not in the fair way of gaining success in life if, at the age of eighteen, he is still loitering over his books, when he should be acquiring, if ever he is to acquire, the exact and energetic habits of the man of business, amid the activities of the count-

---

[17] *Rep. R. Comm. Univ. Aberdeen* (1858), pp. 120, 143.

[18] The figures are based on the censuses of Scotland, and their use is subject to various cautions. Those for 1841 are particularly unreliable, and in other years it is not always possible to distinguish students, clerks, etc. The figures are for males over 20, except in the case of teachers.

Table 3.2
Numbers in selected professions at census dates

	1841	1851	1861	1871	1881	1891	1901	1911
Protestant ministers	2,909	3,352	3,641	4,204	4,081	4,553	4,876	4,631
Advocates	270	220	232	179	158	296		
Solicitors	2,589	1,832	1,973	1,946	2,284	2,815	3,911	4,156
Physicians, surgeons	2,601	2,087	1,870	1,760	1,874	2,583	2,904	3,094
Civil, mining engineers			366	586	783	1,034	1,302	1,352
Teachers, male:								
All ages	4,560	6,074	6,933	6,368	7,003	7,144	7,534	8,010
Over 20	4,292	5,396	5,150	4,948	5,325	6,115	6,664	7,939
Teachers, female:								
All ages	2,255	4,415	5,523	6,059	10,412	12,965	17,234	18,778
Over 20	2,099	3,896	4,394	4,689	6,998	9,390	13,289	18,494

ing-house or the exchange.'[19] By the 1860s few were entering the university below the age of fifteen, and the Inglis commission had abolished the three-year BA degree. In 1861 the Glasgow General Council suggested a new way of shortening the course: if the six-month vacation were cut down, and a 'summer session' introduced instead, the MA could be completed in three years. This demand found some sympathy in the University Court, and was backed in 1863 by petitions from various 'Merchants and Inhabitants' and from the town council, which argued that 'it would tend greatly to intellectual elevation, and the advancement of true social enjoyment in the community, were an increasing number of the sons of our citizens to devote their earlier years to the systematic course of study pursued in the University'. The Court added that 'a constantly-increasing number of the sons of the wealthier classes has been sent to proprietary and collegiate schools in England, where tuition is extended over nine months of the year'.[20] The Glasgow bourgeoisie were becoming impatient with the rural rhythms of Scottish education. Although a summer session was already customary in medicine, the Glasgow Senate strongly opposed its extension to arts subjects, urging that three-quarters of the students came from the 'country' and needed to earn money in the summer to support themselves, a view which the Inglis commission endorsed. The professors were naturally reluctant to give up their six months of leisure, which they claimed were essential for recuperation after the labours of the winter, and as a bait to attract eminent men to chairs.[21]

Another line of attack was on the suitability of the curriculum. J. S. Blackie, one of the earliest advocates of choice within the curriculum, lectured in Glasgow in 1861 on the 'advantages of a university education to a mercantile community'. He complained that the curriculum had changed little for 300 years; the mercantile class could hardly be blamed for shunning the

---

[19] A. Anderson, *The Scottish university system* (Edinburgh, 1859), p. 8.

[20] *R. Comm. Univ. Returns & Documents*, pp. 486, 492. For similar problems at Aberdeen see *Ev.*, Part I, p. 439 (Webster).

[21] *R. Comm. Univ. Returns & Documents*, pp. 505-6, and *Scott. Univ. Comm. Rep.* (1863), pp. xxx-xxxi. Some arguments in defence of the long vacation were less plausible—e.g. that at St. Andrews the hot weather which set in after April distracted students from their work: *R. Comm. Univ. Ev.*, Part I, p. 286 (Heddle).

universities when their interests were not consulted, but it was essential for the sake of their liberal culture that 'the influential men in that class should devote their special attention to that enlargement of our school and University system, which is so necessary to harmonise them at once with Nature, with the age in which we live, and with the intellectual needs of the middle classes'.[22] This was followed up by William Gairdner, who was just beginning a distinguished career as a Glasgow medical professor. In a paper submitted to the General Council in 1865, Gairdner pointed out that the Council's 837 members included 473 ministers, 111 lawyers and 91 doctors, but only 39 merchants. The university was failing to exploit its position in a great mercantile city or to exercise the intellectual influence which was its due, and Gairdner attributed this to the fossilization of the arts curriculum, which needed adaptation to 'the broad and varied culture required by the age'. Gairdner proposed a reform scheme which included a revived BA, and followed the issue up in subsequent years.[23] This activity bore fruit in 1869, when the General Council produced a long report on graduation, which attacked the 1858 system as a general failure. It had not increased graduation at Glasgow, and the length of the course was a deterrent to 'those Students who belong to the mercantile section of this great community'. The Council proposed a BA which could be completed in two years, followed by an MA in which students would be allowed to follow various lines of specialization.[24] By this time, as we shall see, similar ideas were being floated at the other universities.

In England the absence of universities in the large towns encouraged the business class to found 'civic' universities representing their own ideals. This opportunity existed at Dundee, where, however, the proximity of the under-used and under-financed university at St. Andrews suggested some collaborative arrangement, especially with a Tay bridge in prospect.

[22] *Glasgow Herald*, 3 Dec. 1861.
[23] W. T. Gairdner, *A plea for an extension and alteration of the curriculum of arts in the University of Glasgow* (Glasgow, 1865), *passim.* For the composition of the GC in the 1870s see *R. Comm. Univ. Ev.*, Part II, p. 154 (Burns).
[24] Glasgow GC Reports, Oct. 1869, and cf. Oct. 1870. The reports and minutes of the General Councils were consulted in the various university libraries, except those for Aberdeen, which were published: *University of Aberdeen. Minutes of the General Council* (3 vols., Aberdeen, 1898-1916).

'There is plenty of money in Dundee if it could be got', mused Principal Tulloch of St. Mary's College.[25] In 1875 professors from St. Andrews began a series of well-attended lectures at Dundee in scientific and literary subjects. St. Andrews was prepared to envisage the transfer of its scientific and medical teaching to Dundee, but conflict arose with the activists in the city, who wanted a college which would include the full range of arts subjects and so compete with St. Andrews. A scheme drawn up in 1874 estimated the initial cost at £150,000, which was not 'too high a price with which to purchase the means of placing alongside of our material prosperity an enlargement of mind and an elevation of character, and of ennobling and purifying the spirit of trade by the influence of culture and scientific knowledge'.[26] This was not idle talk, for the scheme's author, John Boyd Baxter, was related to the Baxter family of linen manufacturers. Sir David Baxter, who died in 1872, had made many educational benefactions (including the Engineering chair at Edinburgh) and it was his sister who in fact gave £150,000 to found University College at Dundee. This was to open in 1883; meanwhile, a committee set up to advance the cause found itself divided between those who wanted a purely scientific college and those who 'were strongly averse to the exclusion of classes falling within the Faculty of Arts, and indeed gave such classes a decided preference, as tending more to advance liberal culture in a trading community like Dundee.'[27] In the event, the new college opened with only one arts chair, in English, the others being in Engineering, Chemistry and Mathematics; the college used the London University examinations, and so escaped the statutory rigidities of the Scottish system.

At both Glasgow and Dundee, there was a feeling that 'liberal culture' was something desirable and that only the arts training of the universities could give it. The term 'culture' was a new one, and was seized on by those who sought to define the elusive liberal character of a university education. Matthew Arnold's *Culture and Anarchy* of 1869, which insisted particularly

[25] *Royal Commission on Scientific Instruction and the Advancement of Science. Minutes of Evidence*, Vol. II (PP 1874, xxii), p. 33.

[26] *R. Comm. Univ. Returns & Documents*, p. 475. Cf. *Ev.*, Part I, pp. 92-9 (Tulloch), 132-9 (Shairp), and *Ev.*, Part II, pp. 431-8 (Baxter).

[27] *Returns & Documents*, p. 479.

on the need to liberalize the values of the philistine middle class, did much to popularize the concept, and references show that it was much read in Scotland, as were Arnold's studies of those continental countries where the state did so much more than it did in Britain to provide for the educational needs of the bourgeoisie.[28]

The concept of culture was also used when teachers from the training colleges were contrasted with those who were graduates. As the work of these colleges expanded, their relations with the universities became a controversial issue. The colleges were nominally controlled by the churches, but were closely dependent on government grants and regulations, and most of their male students came from elementary schools through the pupil-teacher system.[29] While university men continued to staff the burgh schools and many parish schools, the college training was directed to routine elementary teaching, and traditionalists felt that it produced an inferior class of teacher. When the Argyll commission investigated school education in the 1860s, it was alleged that college graduates became 'teaching machines rather than intelligent educators of youth', their minds narrowed by the limited horizons and stereotyped methods of the new form of education. 'I very much prefer University men, on the whole,' wrote one inspector, 'because in tone of mind, taste, and feeling, they are altogether a higher class of men. I should wish the teachers to be gentlemen, and their contact with a higher intellectual life tends in that direction.'[30] In 1847 the Educational Institute of Scotland was formed to represent the interests of teachers; concerned to defend and promote their professional status, it deplored the breaking of the old links between the universities and the schools, and campaigned consistently for education to be made a university subject with its own professors and degrees.[31] For many experts the ideal

[28] By contrast, Newman's *The idea of a university*, dating from 1852 and republished in 1873, does not seem to have attracted attention.

[29] The Church of Scotland and Free Church each had colleges in Glasgow and Edinburgh, and each opened one (for women only) in Aberdeen in 1874-5. The subject is fully dealt with in M. Cruickshank, *A history of the training of teachers in Scotland* (1970).

[30] *Argyll Comm. Rep. on Country Districts*, pp. 145, 180 (J. Black).

[31] D. Ross, *Education as a university subject; its history, present position, and prospects* (Glasgow, 1883), *passim*.

was 'a combination of the two systems,—the one to make the man, and the other to make the teacher'.[32] Some teachers did manage to gain university qualifications through personal sacrifice, but one obvious step, since the training colleges were in the university towns, was to allow students to attend university classes during their training. This was recommended in the 1860s by the senior school inspector John Kerr and endorsed by the Argyll commission,[33] but was not introduced until 1873, when the new Scotch Education Department was able to make its own regulations. This 'concurrent' system of attendance expanded in subsequent years, but since the college course lasted for only two years these students were unable to graduate, which provided an additional argument for reviving something like the BA.

Training-college students were a welcome addition to student numbers at Edinburgh and Glasgow, but the universities themselves were not involved in professional training. The situation was complicated, however, when Edinburgh and St. Andrews acquired chairs in Education, founded out of the surplus funds of the Bell endowment. These pleased the EIS, but were not approved of by the SED or by the training colleges, which succeeded in defeating the government's proposal to supplement the professors' salaries.[34] The chairs therefore began in 1876 with no obvious function and with inadequate resources. At Edinburgh the new professor was Simon Laurie, a forceful personality who also acted as secretary of the Church of Scotland Education Committee and as 'visitor' of the Dick bequest, and who was thus the leading Scottish educationist of the day. Laurie argued that the universities should be allowed to develop their own role in teacher training, but since the SED refused to accept this he was reduced to giving lectures which neither conferred a professional advantage nor had a place in any degree curriculum.

Laurie's colleague at St. Andrews, J. M. D. Meiklejohn, thought that 'It would be a pity not to put a certain University

---

[32] *Argyll Comm. Rep. on Country Districts*, p. 147 (assistant commissioners' recommendations).

[33] *CCE Rep., 1867-8* (PP 1867-8, xxv), pp. 404-10; *Argyll Comm. 2nd Rep.*, pp. cxlv-cxlviii.

[34] *3 Hansard* ccxxvi, HC 31 July 1875.

stamp upon a teacher if he shows himself worthy of it, and it is by a degree alone that the University can give him such a stamp.' He wanted a short BA degree, at least as a stop-gap 'until teaching was as well paid and took as good a place socially as the Bar, or Medicine, or the Church'.[35] Here of course was what lay behind the EIS's demands: professional status was identified in the public mind with university education. In Laurie's words, 'It is the *culture* of a class which ultimately determines the social estimation in which it is held more than any other one fact. For this culture the teachers of Scotland must look to the Universities.' A few picked college students were now allowed to 'sniff the academic air; but this device can never supply the place of a University curriculum and of University life'.[36] Whatever the 'university stamp' was—it was a favourite phrase in the 1870s, and no doubt included matters of accent and manner which elude the historian's grasp—the fact that only the universities could confer it gave them opportunities of expansion which were frustrated by the 1861 curriculum's inability either to respond to the pressures for a shorter degree or to accommodate subjects which the foundation of new chairs brought within the university pale.

The context of these developments in Scotland was a wider British debate about education and science which was taking place in the sixties and seventies. The reform of Oxford and Cambridge, the foundation of new universities in England, and the Clarendon and Taunton reports on secondary education focused attention on the adaptation of education to middle-class needs, while the progress of industry and the growing awareness of competition from France and Germany led to greater recognition of the importance of research and scientifically-trained manpower. Professional scientists formed an influential lobby, and official concern was reflected in the appointment of the Devonshire commission on scientific instruction in 1870; this included Scotland in its surveys, and strongly recommended increased government aid to the universities, though without effect. The utilitarian claims of science gave a

---

[35] *R. Comm. Univ. Ev.*, Part II, p. 439.
[36] S. S. Laurie, *The training of teachers, and other educational papers* (1882), pp. 14, 95.

new edge to the defence of 'liberal culture', as did the advance of political democracy in 1867 and the progress of elementary education. The intellectual defences of the middle classes needed, some thought, to be strengthened.

In 1867 John Stuart Mill used his inaugural address as rector of St. Andrews to give a classic exposition of the ideal of disinterested university culture. His doctrine that the university was 'not a place of professional education' was a somewhat startling one in Scotland, but he congratulated the Scots on retaining their broad curriculum. 'To comment upon the course of education at the Scottish Universities is to pass in review every essential department of general culture.' Mill thought scientific and literary subjects equally essential to a university education, but he saw science as a form of intellectual training rather than a subject with practical applications.[37] Very different were the views of Robert Lowe, the Liberal politician and former education minister, who in a lecture at Edinburgh, also in 1867, attacked the classics, proclaiming that the knowledge of things was more important than the knowledge of words, the present more important than the past; only with an education abreast of the age would the higher classes maintain their social ascendancy.[38] This utilitarianism, which derived ultimately from Herbert Spencer, was more subtly expressed by the historian James Froude, speaking at St. Andrews as Mill's successor in 1869. The ideal of a uniform general education, he argued, had become obsolete through the advance of knowledge; men had to choose between subjects, and 'the only reasonable guide to choice in such matters is utility'. The first consideration should be the profession aimed at: 'The student should learn at the University what will enable him to earn his living as soon after he leaves it as possible.' 'History, Poetry, Logic, Moral Philosophy, Classical Literature, are excellent as ornament', Froude conceded, but he nevertheless deplored 'the devotion of so much effort and so many precious years to subjects which have no practical bearing upon life'. Lawyers, doctors, and clergymen needed to study subjects directly con-

---

[37] W. Knight (ed.), *Rectorial addresses delivered at the University of St. Andrews* (1894), pp. 20, 24.
[38] R. Lowe, *Primary and classical education* (Edinburgh, 1867), pp. 14-15.

cerned with the life of contemporary society, and this meant chiefly science and modern languages.[39]

The debate between liberal and utilitarian ideals was often simplified to classics versus science. One of the leading spokesmen for scientific and technical education, and one of the first to sound the alarm about foreign industrial competition, was Lyon Playfair. Playfair was related to a well-known Scottish academic dynasty. He attended the university at St. Andrews, where his uncle was Provost of the burgh, before studying medicine at Glasgow and Edinburgh. He was then attracted to chemistry, did research in Germany under Liebig, and returned to make a spectacularly successful career in London. A Fellow of the Royal Society by the age of thirty, he was involved in the 1851 Exhibition as a member of the Prince Consort's circle of advisers, and became the first secretary of the Science and Art Department. He returned to Edinburgh in 1858 as professor of Chemistry, but gave this up in 1868 to become a Scottish University MP—one of only two Liberals ever to hold such a seat. Like some other Scots who made their careers in England, Playfair was not above hinting at early struggles which had not really existed, and was proud of his education at a parish school:

I have just left a Scotch town in which I was at a parochial school, and many a friendly grip of the hand did I get from working men and tradesmen who were schoolfellows with me. Neither of us had lost our respect for the other in our different careers in life, and it was a very hearty thing to feel that your old schoolfellows had an honest word of congratulation, if you happened to be in a more conspicuous position than themselves.[40]

During the debates which led to the Scottish Education Act of 1872, there was no stronger champion of the parochial tradition than Playfair.

Playfair expounded his views on university reform to the St. Andrews Graduates' Association in 1873. He defined the distinguishing feature of universities as 'the power of liberalising the professions', and thought that 'all professions have

---

[39] Knight, op. cit., pp. 98-100.
[40] L. Playfair, *Subjects of social welfare* (1889), p. 300 (address of 1870).

reached a stage when a single curriculum for an arts degree is neither possible nor tolerable for them'. The demand for greater variety was

not one of a few half-educated radical reformers. It is the demand of a changed civilisation, which has resulted from three main causes. These are, the rapid advance of science and its numerous applications to industrial life; the free and constant intercommunication of peoples; and the liberalisation of political institutions.... The youth of our country cannot chain itself to the past, and see the modern stream of thought and action flow swiftly past them. Unless our universities go with the stream, by fitting themselves to the changed requirements of modern society, need they be astonished if society soon get accustomed to look upon them as venerable monuments of a past age?[41]

But with a modernized curriculum, the universities could keep pace with the expansion of the middle class.

By this time, the idea of a broadened curriculum was familiar enough in the universities, in each of which it had given rise to internal discussions. The common pattern was that a reforming minority among the professors found support from the General Council, but were opposed by the Senate; the attitude of the Court depended on the balance of forces within it. Frequently the conservative party were willing to concede a BA or B.Sc. degree as a way of accommodating change while leaving the MA intact. At Edinburgh, for example, the chief reformers were Blackie and David Masson, who became professor of Rhetoric in 1865. Under their guidance the General Council pressed for the addition of a natural science to the MA curriculum, as the 1861 Ordinance allowed. A similar movement at St. Andrews was successful, and Chemistry was added in 1869, though it was removed again in 1877 after student protests. At Edinburgh, the Senate approved the proposal in 1869 by one vote, but the Faculty of Arts was hostile, and the Court saw a compromise solution in the revival of the BA. After further controversy a committee of the General Council headed by Masson produced a report in 1871 which endorsed the principle of options and proposed a new degree structure based on five 'departments'—Chemistry and Natural Sciences, and

[41] Ibid., pp. 373, 375, 377.

Law, History, and Political Economy were to be added to the existing classical, philosophical, and mathematical groups. Students would choose three of the five. This scheme was strongly opposed by the Principal, Sir Alexander Grant, who saw it as a threat to the classics, and who put his faith in the BA. The General Council endorsed the Masson plan in 1871 and 1872, but Grant had the backing of the Court, and the issue petered out in deadlock. There was also much discussion during these years of an entrance examination, on the principle of which all parties tended to agree.[42]

At Glasgow, as we have seen, a General Council scheme of 1869 combined a revived BA with options, and it coincided with agitation for a degree in Engineering led by the professor, MacQuorn Rankine, whose students were at a disadvantage now that Edinburgh had a B.Sc. At first a Senate committee was hostile to change, but after prodding from reforming professors like Gairdner and George Ramsay and from the Court it produced in 1871 a plan which combined B.Sc.s in pure science and engineering with a 'B.Sc. in Law' and a 'B.Sc. in Arts'. The latter was really the BA, but this curious terminology was adopted because the university thought it lacked the legal power to revive the BA, whereas the B.Sc. was specifically mentioned in the Representation of the People Act of 1868.[43] Legal doubts eventually prevailed, and only the scientific B.Sc.s were actually introduced.

The most public conflict was at Aberdeen. Whereas in other universities the rector was usually an eminent political or literary figure whose inaugural speech was his only act, at Aberdeen the students from time to time elected a 'working' rector, who presided regularly over the Court and saw himself as the representative of public opinion, as of course the 1858 Act had intended. One such was the Liberal politician Mountstuart Grant Duff, who was rector from 1866 to 1872. There was

---

[42] EU GC Minutes, supplemented by reports in *Edinburgh Evening Courant,* 17 Apr. 1871, 28 Oct. 1871, 17 Apr. 1872. An entrance examination was discussed regularly in the GC from 1863, and curricular reform from 1866. Blackie's original proposal was that a science should be an alternative to philosophy or rhetoric, not an addition. Sèe also A. Grant, *Degree-Standards and other topics* (Edinburgh, 1869).

[43] GU GC Reports, especially Oct. 1864, Apr. 1866, Oct. 1869, Oct. 1870, Nov. 1871, supplemented by Senate Minutes (GU Archives) for 1869-72.

among some of the professors 'a very strong feeling that the present curriculum is not adapted for all the classes of students who wish to avail themselves of it, and that a certain modification would render it more generally useful'.[44] The most radical reformer was John Struthers, the leading figure in the Aberdeen medical school, but he was supported by men like Alexander Bain (Logic) and Frederick Fuller (Mathematics). Grant Duff allied himself with these reformers, and pushed through the Court a series of measures directed especially against the compulsory position of Greek in the bursary examination and the curriculum. By 1873 the Court was committed to a very thorough scheme of reform, including a lightening of the classical load in favour of science, modern languages as an alternative to Greek, changes in the teaching of Greek itself, and the cutting down of Moral Philosophy. Not surprisingly, the Senate was hostile. 'The majority', said Bain, 'have been in favour of retaining the present curriculum as fixed for the M.A. degree in all future time, and giving the desired alternative exclusively as an inferior degree'; they were 'giving to Greek an importance which is altogether irrational, not to say superstitious'.[45] In the General Council, opinion was divided: for a time the reformers captured control of a committee on the curriculum, but its recommendations were overthrown after clerical backwoodsmen had been rallied to a critical meeting in April 1873. By 1874 the Senate had worked out a scheme for a three-year degree, which was accepted as a basis for compromise by the Court. This was to be called the 'B.S.', for the same reasons as at Glasgow, but as there legal doubts prevented its introduction and the result was a stalemate.[46]

Feeling in Aberdeen ran so high that the university refused to give evidence to the Devonshire commission, since 'the majority of our Senatus had no desire to open up questions of scientific or other modern education'.[47] The students, however, expressed their own views by electing the scientist Thomas

[44] *R. Comm. Univ. Ev.*, Part I, p. 645 (Fuller).
[45] Ibid., pp. 672-3.
[46] AU GC Minutes, supplemented by Court and Senate Minutes (AU Library). On these disputes see also A. Bain, *Autobiography* (1904), pp. 346-9, and *R. Comm. Univ. Ev.*, Part I, pp. 594-8 (Christie).
[47] *R. Comm. Univ. Ev.*, Part II, p. 37 (Struthers).

Huxley as Grant Duff's successor. In his inaugural address, Huxley argued the case for science as a part of general education, and combated some of the points made by Mill in 1867.[48] Huxley also chaired the Court in person, and worked with Struthers to carry through some changes in the medical curriculum. Thus the rectorship had been used at Aberdeen to make university reform an open political issue, and it was not surprising that the classical professors disapproved of election by 'the miscellaneous body of students, who are little fitted to determine, as they virtually have done, vital questions of educational policy, such as subjects and standards for degrees' —especially since 'but a short time ago there was an idea amongst the students that they would elect a Rector from their own number'.[49]

These events showed that the universities could no longer resist demands for change, but that the existing legal framework caused a deadlock. If the universities had been free to determine their own curricula, there can be little doubt that the three-year BA would have been generally revived, if only as a means of diverting more radical demands. As it was, only legislation or a new Royal Commission could bring about change, and the General Councils were already campaigning for that for other reasons. Reformers on these bodies were discontented with their limited powers, and from 1870 representatives of all four General Councils were holding frequent joint meetings and drawing up reform plans, which centred on strengthening the Courts and enlarging them so that the General Councils had more Assessors. By 1875 it was recognized that the constitutional and curricular issues went together, and in that year a deputation from all the General Councils except Edinburgh went to London and urged the Home Secretary to set up a Royal Commission; among the MPs accompanying the deputation were Lyon Playfair and the Aberdeen MP W. A. Hunter, an ally of the reforming party in that city.[50] The General

---

[48] P. J. Anderson, *Rectorial addresses delivered in the Universities of Aberdeen 1835-1900* (Aberdeen, 1902), pp. 180ff. Cf. C. Bibby, 'T. H. Huxley and the universities of Scotland', *Aberdeen University Review*, xxxvii (1957-8), pp. 140 ff.

[49] *R. Comm. Univ. Ev.*, Part I, pp. 657 (Geddes), 782-3 (Black), 339 (Principal Pirie).

[50] AU GC Minutes, Oct. 1875.

Councils, because of their electoral function and the prominence of their activists in the local community, always carried a good deal of political weight, and they succeeded in making use of it on this occasion.

The Conservative government which appointed the Royal Commission of 1876 was evidently anxious to maintain continuity with 1858, for Inglis became chairman and there were three other members of his previous commission.[51] Also included, however, were Playfair and Huxley, natural enough choices in view of their official connections with the Scottish universities, and Froude, whose Scottish connections were more tenuous. Playfair and Huxley were to dominate the work of this commission, conducting much of the questioning of witnesses (who included practically all the university professors) and putting their stamp on the final report. A number of constitutional and financial questions were referred to the commission, and they recommended changes in university government which were mostly carried out in 1889; most of the General Councils' claims for greater influence were rejected on the grounds that the handful who attended meetings were hardly representative. The curriculum, however, was the central subject of discussion, and there were really two issues: the introduction of greater freedom of choice, which might be linked with the revival of the BA, and the desirability of an entrance examination. Traditionalists tended to oppose both the examination and any departure from the general nature of the Scottish degree, while reformers saw the examination as a device for raising initial standards and making specialization more practicable. But opinions on the two issues could cut across each other, and the commission itself proved to be strongly in favour of specialization, but more ambiguous in its attitude to the entrance examination.

Struthers told the commission that 'The opening up of the Arts education and degree is the great question of the day in our Universities', and he identified three sources of opposition. First, the 'ecclesiastical opposition', which sacrificed general interests to the needs of the divinity students. Second, 'the

---

[51] Cf. comment in *Fraser's Magazine*, n.s. xx (1879), pp. 56-7.

teachers of classics and some of those who have been educated under the old system. These gentlemen seem to believe in classics, with more or less mathematics, and in little else, as education. With them, English literature, modern languages and literature, mental science and natural science, are but worthless intruders.' The third cause of opposition was the fee system, which gave professors a vested interest in maintaining the existing compulsory classes. The answer, as Struthers saw, lay in a common 'fee fund' to pool this income.[52]

The views of professors were certainly influenced by the interests of their disciplines. By no means all scientists were as anxious for reform as Struthers, but it was true that the classicists were generally conservative. This was because Greek seemed the most vulnerable subject if freedom of choice were allowed, and if Greek went down in the universities it would not last long in the schools. Greek was already the chosen target of the Aberdeen reformers, and of Playfair too to judge by his questioning of witnesses, which returned frequently to the point that the universities had the vital social function of giving a general preliminary education to professional men, and could only do this if the general subjects on offer seemed attractive and relevant; compulsory Greek was therefore a barrier to the universities increasing their usefulness.[53] With the exception of Blackie, who was prepared for Greek to become optional provided that it was required in the entrance examination, the classical professors replied that Greek was 'a *sine quâ non* of University education'.[54] At Glasgow the recently appointed professor of Greek, Richard Jebb, refused to allow that 'as a University, we should be justified in permitting any of our graduates to be virtually ignorant of Greek'. At Aberdeen, John Black of Humanity held that to exclude the classics from any type of degree was 'altogether foreign to the idea of a University, at least as at present conceived', and argued that 'Greek is one of the most powerful and valuable instruments of culture, whether from a linguistic, a literary, or a philosophic

---

[52] *R. Comm. Univ. Ev.*, Part II, pp. 15-18.
[53] See his questions in *Ev.*, Part I to Grant (p. 23), Christison (p.68), Ramsay (pp. 553 ff).
[54] Ibid., p. 953 (G. Ramsay); cf. p. 813 (Blackie).

point of view, and I am not sure if I might not add, from a scientific point of view also.'[55] At Aberdeen more than elsewhere, perhaps, there was a feeling that the classics were at the heart of the Scottish intellectual tradition, and that Latin had a peculiar democratic significance because its teaching formed the link between parish schools and universities. But it was the Englishman Ramsay of Glasgow who said that 'It is to the classics that Scotland is indebted for its position as the best educated country of Europe, and it is impossible to overvalue the debt which Scotland owes to the classics in the formation of the national intelligence.'[56]

At St. Andrews Shairp took the occasion to return to his own criticisms of the Scottish intellectual tradition, commending history as 'particularly necessary to give something of the concrete to the Scotch mind, which is so tremendously apt to run off into abstractions, metaphysics, and logic. I think the utter blank of history, and the absence of all that is meant by the historical spirit and the historical method, is the greatest want in Scotch education.' Shairp would retain logic as part of 'a preliminary basis of disciplinary study' for all students, but would define it more strictly: 'At present all our logic classes are full of psychology, if not metaphysics, but I would knock off all that; I think we have terribly overdone it in Scotland,— cramming metaphysics upon raw minds.'[57]

The cause of philosophy was defended with particular vigour by John Veitch, professor of Logic at Glasgow, both before the commission and in an article in *Mind,* which especially emphasized the subject's long and distinguished history in the Scottish universities. His colleague at Edinburgh, A. C. Fraser, argued that the broad curriculum should be preserved,

on the principle that those three sorts of study—literature, reflective philosophy, and mathematics, including physical or experimental science in varying proportions—are essential to, and a sufficient test of, general academic culture.... the three I have mentioned, from their very nature, are essential to liberal academic education of a

---

[55] Ibid., p. 789, and Part II, pp. 419, 424.
[56] *Ev.,* Part I, p. 543.
[57] Ibid., pp. 127-30.

complete kind, and, besides, are historically distinctive of the Scotch Universities; and I do not see sufficient counterbalancing advantage likely to result from a change in that respect.[58]

Conservatives preferred to keep the existing curriculum with minimal changes, perhaps satisfying new demands through a BA, and some moderate reformers also accepted the framework of three 'departments' of study, wishing only to allow options within them, e.g. modern languages instead of Greek.

But a 'departmental' structure could also take a more radical form. Masson put forward the Edinburgh General Council's five-department scheme, and at Glasgow similar ideas were favoured by Principal John Caird and his brother Edward, professor of Moral Philosophy.[59] Their drawback was that if (for example) students chose three departments out of five, classics or philosophy might be avoided altogether. The alternative reforming approach, which perhaps offered better safeguards for general education, was a two-tier degree, with specialization following a foundation of common subjects; this was especially attractive to proponents of the BA, since the first stage might be integrated with the curriculum for a shorter degree. The two-stage system was most clearly expounded by Principal Grant of Edinburgh. Grant was one of the more impatient Anglicizers: a Harrovian and a Balliol man, an admirer of Jowett and an authority on Aristotle. 'The principle to be adopted', he said, 'is that there shall be a certain point in the Arts degree course up to which general and common studies should be pursued by all candidates, after which there should be ramification, each student pursuing special studies till the conclusion of his course.' The common foundation would take two years, would conclude with an examination, and would cover Latin, Greek, Mathematics, some science, and 'perhaps' Logic. After that there would be five 'schools or triposes', though Grant omitted the natural sciences because he preferred the B.Sc. to continue.[60] Ideas of a similar kind were put forward by several of the St. Andrews professors (Shairp, Knight, Lewis Campbell,

---

[58] Ibid., p. 289. Cf. p. 875 (Calderwood) and views of Veitch in *Ev.*, Part II, pp. 242 ff. and *Mind*, ii (1877), pp. 74-8.

[59] *Ev.*, Part I, pp. 37-9 (J. Caird), 893-5 (Masson), and Part II, pp. 203-6 (E. Caird).

[60] *Ev.*, Part I, pp. 21-2.

Tulloch) and by Ramsay of Glasgow. A common foundation which included compulsory Latin and Greek had a natural appeal for classicists, but all these men also included Logic (except Campbell, who would make Logic and History alternatives.)[61] This was an important point, because if the common basis included a philosophical subject it would have to be taught in the universities, and would probably need two years, whereas if it was based on classics and mathematics it would correspond to the work of the junior classes, whose abolition was already on the agenda of radical reformers, and might ultimately be relegated to the schools themselves, leaving the universities free to specialize. Thus the question was intimately linked with the desirability of an entrance examination.

Principal Grant, who was the first witness heard by the commission, declared that

an entrance examination for the Universities of Scotland is an absolute necessity. The Universities have arrived at a certain pitch of excellence, and they never can advance beyond that without an entrance examination. The schools are in a very unsettled and inferior condition, especially the secondary schools, and they can never be improved until an entrance examination is instituted. I think that all persons who know the Universities will agree in this. I hardly expect that your lordship's Commission will hear a single dissentient voice as to the expediency, and indeed the absolute necessity from an educational point of view, of instituting an entrance examination.[62]

This prediction proved wide of the mark, but Grant was supported by Principal Caird, and indeed Edinburgh and Glasgow had already agreed to introduce such an examination jointly in 1875, though they suspended it when the commission was announced. Grant explained the wider implications of the issue:

I cannot see the advantage of confounding the different stages of education, and that is what at present exists in Scotland. The schools and Universities are confounded together; the Universities do the work of the schools, and the secondary schools are doing the work of the primary schools, and the whole thing is a chaos. The nations that

---

[61] Ibid., pp. 88 (Tulloch), 127 (Shairp), 548-52 (Ramsay), 837-40 (Campbell), and Part II, pp. 70-2 (Knight).
[62] *Ev.*, Part I, pp. 10-11.

have succeeded best in science and learning act quite differently, and place a strong line of demarcation between the different stages, marking off the secondary schools from the primary, and the Universities from the secondary schools: so that in Germany no student at all, with the rarest exception, goes to the Universities, who has not so completely done with his general culture that he is at liberty to choose any special subject he likes, and his first University course is always a course of special study.[63]

Grant and Caird argued that the schools could soon be brought up to the necessary standard, and Caird explained that 'In the district which is the chief feeder of Glasgow University, there are, besides the Glasgow High School, Academy, and other schools, good grammar schools in Paisley, Kilmarnock, Irvine, Ayr, Dumbarton, Greenock, Campbeltown, etc., so that nowhere in this district is the needed instruction very far from those who desire to get it.'[64] The secondary schoolmasters who appeared before the commission were among the strongest supporters of an entrance examination; it would give their schools a common standard to aim at, and the abolition of the junior classes would put an end to the 'poaching' by the universities which, they claimed, stunted the development of Scottish secondary schools. The EIS also supported the examination, though it was careful to point out the need for gradualness and the difficulties which would be caused for the parish schools.[65]

There was also the problem of older men, who could catch up in the existing junior classes, but who might find difficulty in taking a school-based examination, and of the many part-time and non-graduating students—was an entrance examination including compulsory Greek to be imposed on them too? Playfair and Huxley when questioning witnesses showed special concern for older or less well-prepared students, though when Playfair raised their problems with Grant, the latter

---

[63] Ibid., p. 19, and cf. A. Grant, *The present state, prospects, and wants of the University of Edinburgh* (Edinburgh, 1871), pp. 29-30. Grant's views on this point were very similar to Blackie's, for which see *Ev.*, Part I, pp. 813-15.

[64] Ibid., pp. 45-6.

[65] Ibid., pp. 685-8 (James Macdonald, Ayr Academy), 727-30 (W. Sewell, for the EIS), 755-6 (Donaldson, Edinburgh High School), and Part II, pp. 356-7 (H. H. Almond, Loretto), 448-52 (D. Paton, Glasgow High School), 455-9 (D. Morrison, Glasgow Academy), 461-5 (T. Harvey, Edinburgh Academy).

replied, 'I don't see how it is to be obviated. If you want to keep a place select you must have a gate to it.'[66] Classicists tended to support the examination because it would raise the standard in their own subjects, even if they suffered financially from the abolition of the junior classes. But the professors of subjects which attracted many part-time students, like Natural Philosophy and Engineering, were usually against,[67] and there were others who held 'a strong opinion that the Universities are public institutions, and that we have no right to exclude any person who thinks he is able to profit by our instructions'.[68] The professor of Mathematics at Glasgow, Hugh Blackburn, submitted an elaborate paper arguing that 'it is part of the fundamental constitution, or theory, of a University, that the instruction there given is open to all; or, to put it otherwise, that such is the understanding between the nation and the Universities, from which it is not open to the Universities to depart without the national consent'.[69] Laurie did 'not think that the University, speaking generally, has any right to exclude anybody from its benches and its classes'. But like others, he thought an examination legitimate for those aiming at degrees provided that anyone else was still admitted freely.[70]

Over-all, a majority of the witnesses did support an entrance examination, but with reservations of various kinds—that it should be introduced gradually, that it should not be required above a certain age, that it should only apply to degree candidates, etc., while at Aberdeen the issue was felt to be irrelevant since the bursary competition already provided a common standard: of about 100 entrants annually, 40 won a bursary, but 250-300 sat for the competition.[71]

'Whenever the interests of science are concerned', wrote one commentator on the commission's report, published in 1878,

---

[66] *Ev.*, Part I, p. 15. Cf. questioning of Geddes by Playfair, pp. 660-1, of Dickson by Huxley, p. 258.

[67] Ibid., pp. 151-2 (P. G. Tait), and Part II, pp. 57-8 (F. Jenkin), 317-18 (William Thomson), 522-5 (James Thomson).

[68] *Ev.* Part I, p. 709 (James Nicol, Natural History, Aberdeen).

[69] Part II, p. 127.

[70] Part I, p. 501. For similar statements see also pp. 367 (Allen Thomson), 560 (Ramsay), 586 (Kelland), and Part II, p. 425 (Jebb).

[71] Part I, pp. 112-13, 602, and *R. Comm. Univ. Rep.*, p. 107.

'the Commissioners ... are revolutionary, but whenever these interests do not come into question they are cautious and mildly conservative.'[72] Their recommendations on the curriculum certainly went beyond what the universities were prepared to accept, and reflected the influence of Huxley and Playfair. The report rehearsed the arguments for allowing more freedom of choice so that 'the advantages of the culture which the University affords would be extended', and proposed to allow 'after a certain foundation of general culture, a tolerably free choice among several distinct lines of study adapted to various bents of mind, and having relation to different professional pursuits'. The general culture was to be tested by a 'First Examination' covering Latin, Greek, Mathematics, English, and science when the state of science teaching in the schools had improved. This examination could be taken either at school, or while at the university, and the existing junior classes were to be retained for those who needed them. Thus the First Examination would not be an 'entrance' examination; but it would be compulsory for those aiming at the MA, and a similar examination, with modern languages replacing Greek, would be required for the B.Sc., which the commission proposed to retain, and for law and medical degrees.

After the First Examination, the MA course would last for three years. The existing fixed curriculum would remain as one alternative, but alongside it there would be five quite separate 'lines of study'—Literature and Philology, Philosophy, Law and History, Mathematical Science, and Natural Science. Within each of these groups there would be certain basic subjects and a limited amount of optional choice. The commission rejected the idea of a revived BA, though they suggested that there might be a 'certificate in Arts' for teachers and others who attended a limited range of classes, a suggestion which was to be acted on. In arts teaching the commission's recommendations for extra resources were limited to a chair of English at Aberdeen, lectureships in modern languages at all the universities, and three chairs of History, a subject specially favoured through the influence of Froude; on science

---

[72] *Fraser's Magazine*, n.s. xx (1879), p. 66.

and medicine there were numerous detailed recommendations in which the hand of Huxley and Playfair was evident.[73]

The scientific journal *Nature* predicted 'great irritation, amounting in many quarters to white heat at least, and determined opposition. The dry husks of speculative "philosophy" ... will die hard. In their place will come the still oppressed truths of modern science.'[74] It was indeed generally felt that the report was far too favourable to science, and too radical in its views on specialization. At Glasgow a General Council committee headed by Veitch complained that the scheme would 'degrade' philosophy, and that the First Examination would not be an adequate test of general culture: there should be at least one year of general study, including Logic, at the university. Similar points were made at Edinburgh, and at both universities the commission was criticized for not giving more incentive to Honours work.[75] For some years Lewis Campbell of St. Andrews had been campaigning on this subject—his proposals included a common examining board for Scotland—and he found support in several quarters. At Edinburgh in particular, two ideas won favour which were to influence later developments: that students should not have to take the ordinary examinations in the subjects which they offered for Honours, and that there should be organized Honours courses to make the Honours degree more solid and promote 'higher and persevering study in special lines'.[76] But the Royal Commission proposed merely that Honours should be awarded on the examination which all students took, which represented no advance on the system used since 1861.

The First Examination was also controversial, and here one may perceive some dissension within the commission. Its details closely resembled what Grant had proposed, and the inclusion of Greek was a conservative feature. Yet the report went out of its way to stress that this was not an entrance

[73] *R. Comm. Univ. Rep.*, pp. 25 ff., 41, 55 ff.

[74] *Nature,* xvii (1877-8), p. 443.

[75] GU GC Reports, Oct. 1878; EU GC Minutes, report of committee under Masson, Apr. 1879, reprinted in Minutes for Jan. 1890.

[76] Report of Apr. 1879. Cf. L. Campbell, *The Scottish Universities. A practical suggestion for the improvement of the honour-system in the Scottish universities* (Dundee, 1867); St. AU GC Minutes, Nov. 1866, Mar. 1867, Nov. 1867, Mar. 1868, Nov. 1868; EU GC Minutes, Oct. 1867, Apr. 1868, Apr. 1869.

examination, that failing it would not lead to exclusion from
the university, that the junior classes should continue for as
long as they were needed, and that to exclude adult or ill-
prepared students would be 'injurious to the public interests'.
One member, however, dissented formally from the proposal
on the grounds that it did not go far enough. This was John
Muir, a retired Indian civil servant who was a disciple of
Lorimer; in 1864 he had helped to found the 'Association for
the Better Endowment of Edinburgh University', and had
shown his enthusiasm for comparative philology by personally
endowing a chair of Sanskrit. Muir now complained that 'the
interests of the poorer students should not be allowed to interfere with another interest of such high importance as the elevation of the general standard of education and enlightenment in
the middle and higher classes of the community'. A strict
entrance examination was desirable both to raise the level of
secondary education—Muir appealed to the example of the
Abitur and Arnold's reports on Germany—and in the long run
to encourage the formation of a 'learned class'.[77]

The Royal Commission's recommendations, which would
have required legislation to enforce them, went beyond the
reforming consensus in the universities. There was wide agreement that more optional choice needed to be introduced, but
also that it should follow a preliminary basis of general culture
which only the universities were properly equipped to give.
The commission's First Examination looked forward to a
standard of efficiency in the secondary schools which did not
exist in the 1870s. But in the 1880s the development of secondary schools was rapid, and by 1892 an entrance examination
was to be accepted, though even then the task of imparting
general culture was not left entirely to the schools; when the
university curriculum was eventually reformed, specialization
was not allowed to go as far as the 1876 commission had proposed. Nor was the imposition of the entrance examination,
and the withering away of the junior classes which followed,
entirely a painless process, for significant numbers of university students still came from the parish schools. For a fuller

[77] *R. Comm. Univ. Rep.*, pp. 43-50, 165-8, 175.

understanding of these matters we must look in more detail at the relationship between the universities and the school system in the 1860s and 1870s (Chapter 4) and at the evolution of secondary education from the 1870s onwards (Chapters 5 and 6); the history of university reform will be taken up again in Chapter 7.

4.
EDUCATION AND SOCIETY IN MID-VICTORIAN SCOTLAND

The aim of this chapter is to explore the relationship between the schools and the universities and the conclusions which may be drawn from information about the social background of students. This information is more abundant for the 1860s and 1870s than for any period before or after, because this was a period of official inquiry and legislation. The landmarks are the report of the Argyll commission on schools and the Education Act of 1872, and it is necessary to go more thoroughly into their history in order to understand both the type of information which becomes available and the controversies of the period. It was felt at the time that the result of the 1872 Act, and of the government's administrative policies, was to weaken the old link between the parish schools and the universities, while the failure to give state aid to secondary schools meant that new ways of helping the talented to rise in society were slow to emerge. By looking at statistical material from this period, when many of the traditional features of Scottish education were still apparent, we shall attempt to estimate how effective the 'parochial tradition' really was on the eve of 1872, what major changes might have taken place since the early part of the century, and what differences were likely to occur when legislation remodelled the institutional framework within which education was given.

As we saw in Chapter 1, the parish schools themselves were unable to reach the whole population, although they were supplemented by sessional or Free Church schools of a similar type. By the 1850s a movement for 'national' education had appeared, which aimed simultaneously at filling the gaps in the system, especially in the towns, and at countering the trend towards separate denominational schools. Bills introduced by Lord Melgund in 1850 and 1851 and by the Liberal Lord Advocate James Moncreiff in 1854, 1855, and 1856 embodied these aims. All foundered on the rock of opposition from the Established Church, which fought to retain exclusive control of the parish schools, but although debate was conducted almost entirely on religious lines to the neglect of strictly educational issues, the bills did contain features tending to preserve the university link. They all provided for a Board of Education in Edinburgh which would be dominated by university representatives, and while new schools founded to meet educational deficiencies would have school committees (elected or nominated), the old parish schools would remain distinct. Moncreiff's bills would also have given rating powers to town councils as the education authorities within burghs, which presumably would have strengthened the position of secondary education.[1] In 1861 the reformers gained a limited victory when religious tests were abolished for burgh and parish schoolmasters, and the power of examining the latter was transferred from the presbyteries to the universities. Each university had powers within a defined district, and although these were limited—the schoolmasters were only examined after their appointment by the heritors—the universities thus acquired a new influence over the school system, which they would use to keep up the level of classical teaching. If a bill proposed by Moncreiff in 1862 had gone through, the universities' influence would have been greatly extended by giving them the 'superintendence' of all new schools in their districts.

By this time, however, a new threat to the parish schools had appeared in the 'Revised Code' for educational grants, first drawn up in 1861 and reissued in 1862. Scotland had participated in the system of government grants to schools which had grown up since 1833, but this was now radically changed following the recommendations of the Newcastle commission, whose inquiries did not extend to Scotland. There were three ways in which the Code ignored Scottish conditions. First, it introduced 'payment by results' after annual examination of the children in six 'standards', which gave the teacher a strong incentive to concentrate on the three Rs and discouraged him from the higher subjects which were customary in Scotland.

---

[1] The bills differed in detail, and in 1856 there was a separate one for the burghs, but secondary education was not specifically provided for.

Second, it assumed that all teachers were of the 'elementary' type: they had to hold a government certificate, but university qualifications gave no advantages, and only laymen could receive grants. And finally grants were intended only to 'promote the education of children belonging to the classes who support themselves by manual labour'. This caused difficulties for the many Scottish schools which catered for a range of social classes, and (unlike the previous grant system) required invidious inquiries into the parentage of pupils, though even before the Revised Code some burgh schools had been refused grants because they had too few pupils from the 'labouring poor'.[2]

The author of the Revised Code was Robert Lowe, the minister chiefly responsible for education between 1859 and 1864. He held rigidly to the principle that state aid should go only to those who could not help themselves, and seems to have made a speciality of offending Scottish opinion: deputations from the Scottish universities were told that 'all State aid to education must be looked upon as so much outdoor relief', and that 'I'd as soon have the State paying a man's butcher's bill for him as paying for the higher education of his children.'[3] Lowe's general defence of the Code, which became the official orthodoxy of the Education Department, was that the old system encouraged the neglect of the average child in favour of coaching a few bright pupils. Outcry against the Code was so strong in Scotland that in 1864 the government appointed the Argyll commission to report on the general state of Scottish education. Meanwhile the full operation of 'payment by results' was suspended, though the machinery of standards and annual examinations was duly introduced; until 1872, however, most of the parish schools, with their privileged access to rate income, seem to have managed without government grants.

The Argyll commission appointed assistant commissioners to survey education on the ground, and they published several valuable reports—on the 'lowland country districts', the classic

---

[2] *CCE Rep., 1858-9* (PP 1859, sess. 1, xxi, part 1), p. 230; cf. evidence of R. Lingen in *Argyll Comm. 1st Rep.*, p. 324.

[3] As reported by G. G. Ramsay in *Fraser's Magazine*, n.s. xiii (1876), p. 591, and *Classical Association of Scotland. Proceedings, 1904-5*, p. 51.

territory of the parish schools, on the Hebrides, on Glasgow, and on 'burgh and middle-class schools'; this last was written by Thomas Harvey, a future rector of Edinburgh Academy, and Alexander Craig Sellar, an advocate who later became a Liberal MP active in educational debates. The commission's main report was published in 1867, and related only to primary education. It endorsed the complaints against the restriction of grants to the labouring classes, but thought that otherwise the Revised Code was sound and should be put into full effect. It found much evidence of educational deficiency, but its recommendations for legislation were cautious, following Moncreiff's bills in providing for a Board of Education with university representatives and in leaving the parish schools as they were; a 'national' system should be allowed to develop gradually, with local school committees at first supervising only new schools.[4] In 1868 the report on burgh and middle-class schools appeared. Harvey and Sellar had found their general state satisfactory, and the commission did not propose major changes. The secondary schools would remain under their existing management, but there would be limited state grants, for building and repairs and for teachers' pensions; special grants were also recommended to encourage the teaching of higher subjects in parish schools where there was no burgh school. The doctrinaire liberalism of Lowe was thus rejected, and the commission invoked the spirit of Knox against it:

It cannot be too often repeated, that the theory of our School system, as originally conceived, was to supply every member of the community with the means of obtaining for his children not only the elements of education, but such instruction as would fit him to pass to the Burgh school, and thence to the University, or directly to the University from the Parish school.... In any changes, therefore, which may be made in the School-system of Scotland, the connexion between the Universities and the schools should be strengthened and not relaxed, and the ancient theory of Scottish National Education should be scrupulously respected and carefully developed.[5]

In 1869 the new Liberal government introduced a Parochial Schools Bill on the lines recommended by the Argyll commis-

---

[4] *Argyll Comm. 2nd Rep.*, pp. clxxiii ff.
[5] *Argyll Comm. 3rd Rep.*, Vol. I, pp. x-xi, and cf. pp. xxvi-xxvii.

sion, though secondary education was not mentioned. This passed the Commons, but was rejected by the Lords. There was then a pause while attention was concentrated on the English Act, and in 1871 a new bill appeared, which failed that year but formed the basis of the Education (Scotland) Act of 1872. In many respects the Act went beyond the Argyll report and beyond what had been introduced in England: education was to be compulsory until the age of thirteen (subject to certain exemptions), and there was to be a school board, elected on a wide franchise, in every parish and burgh. The school boards were to take over both the parish and other public schools and the burgh schools, and church schools might also be transferred to them: nearly all Presbyterian schools were so transferred, and Scotland thus gained a national system while in England voluntary and board schools developed separately and were the focus of much political and religious controversy; in Scotland only Episcopal and Roman Catholic schools, the latter a growing force, remained outside school board control and continued to receive direct grants from the state. Above the school boards was the Scotch Education Department, which was to administer its own Code; this was based in London, however, and until the creation of the Scottish Office in 1885 it lacked real independence of the English department.

The Act also provided for a Board of Education sitting in Edinburgh, but it was to be a temporary body supervising the changeover to the new system, and even this was a reluctant concession to critics. For the 1872 Act lacked those features of the earlier bills which had seemed to safeguard the parochial tradition. The parish schools disappeared as such, and their teachers became employees of the school boards; the power of certifying schoolmasters was taken away from the universities, and was to remain exclusively in the hands of the Department. These points, and the general failure of the Act to provide specifically for the teaching of higher subjects in the schools, were strongly criticized by the universities and by the EIS, which extended the campaign first mounted against the Revised Code. Within Parliament their spokesman was Lyon Playfair, who complained that 'The three Bills of 1869, 1871, and 1872 are successive steps in the Anglicizing and lowering of Scotch elementary education.'[6] The only concession won was clause 67, which obliged the SED to take 'due care ... that the standard of education which now exists in the public schools shall not be lowered, and that, as far as possible, as high a standard shall be maintained in all schools inspected by the said Department'. This clause went back to the 1869 bill, where it had referred specifically to the parochial schools; with the wording changed to 'public schools', it was too vague to mean much.

Playfair had welcomed the fact that the 1871 bill, for the first time, included the burgh schools.

Primary and secondary education are ... so thoroughly ingrained in Scotland that you cannot deal with them separately, nor would Scotchmen give one farthing for a system of national education in which they were separated. The great Napoleon used to say that every soldier carried his Marshal's baton in his knapsack; so every Scotch peasant, when he goes to school, carries in his satchel a minister's gown, or other emblem of a learned profession, and it is his own fault if he lose it.[7]

Unlike their English equivalents, the school boards were not legally confined to giving elementary education. But the powers given them were vitiated by the devotion of Parliament to *laissez-faire* principles. When Lord Advocate Young introduced his bill in 1872, he stressed that 'It was not ... generally in accordance with the views of the House to grant Imperial money or to authorize local taxation in order to provide for the higher class of education, and it could therefore be provided for only otherwise than pecuniarily in the Bill.'[8] The Act created a special category of 'higher class' schools, defined as those mainly giving 'instruction in Latin, Greek, modern languages, mathematics, natural science, and generally in the higher branches of knowledge'. Eleven such schools were scheduled in the Act, and school boards could add to the list; but they were reluctant to do so, for higher class status was more a burden than an advantage. These schools were free of the irksome restrictions of the Code, but were starved of resources because they could neither receive government grants nor be supported

[6] *3 Hansard* ccix, HC 7 Mar. 1872, col. 1590.
[7] *3 Hansard* cciv, HC 13 Feb. 1871, col. 215.
[8] *3 Hansard* ccix, HC 12 Feb. 1872, col. 259.

out of the school board's rate income. They therefore had to depend on fees, and in smaller towns the fee income was not enough to support a purely secondary school. Those burgh schools which did not become higher class schools, therefore, simply became public schools, legally indistinguishable from those which gave nothing but elementary education.[9]

One reason for the neglect of secondary education in the 1872 Act was perhaps the influence of the English Schools Inquiry (Taunton) Commission, whose report on secondary schools held out the hope that a system of middle-class education could be created without state aid by reviving and re-modelling the endowed grammar schools. This led to the Endowed Schools Act of 1869, and Scotland had a similar Act in the same year, though (as we shall see in the next chapter) this was of limited scope. In Scotland, neither the schools nor the universities enjoyed the rich charitable endowments found in England, and the hope of salvation from this source was illusory. If middle-class education was to develop satisfactorily, it needed public support, which its champions were not slow to demand. To compensate for the inadequacy of the 1872 Act in this respect, the government appointed a Royal Commission on endowed schools under Sir Edward Colebrooke. This was a commission of inquiry which did valuable work in collecting facts and suggesting new lines of policy, and it was to be fol-lowed by two commissions under Moncreiff (1878) and Lord Balfour of Burleigh (1882) which had the power to reform the endowments themselves. Through their work new or revived secondary schools appeared which were the equal of the higher class schools.

For public schools administered under the Code, there was some encouragement for higher subjects in the new Code issued by the SED in 1873. This differed only in detail from the English Code, and finally introduced payment by results, but it did allow extra grants for older children who studied 'specific subjects' beyond the three Rs. On this question the Department came into conflict with the temporary Board of

---

[9] The Act avoided the terms 'elementary', 'primary', and 'secondary', although all were freely used at the time. The term 'public' (sometimes 'state-aided') was generally used for schools administered under the Code, whether run by school boards or voluntary bodies; the higher class schools were also technically 'public'.

Education, which included two university Principals (Grant and Tulloch) and which was anxious to preserve the university connection and maintain the classics. The Board originally proposed that the specific subjects should be mathematics, English, Latin, Greek, French, and German. The Department rejected this as out of line with the spirit of the Act: 'It had too much the look of a middle-class scheme', its Secretary later recalled.[10] The Board was no more successful when it argued that at least the 'university subjects' should attract a higher grant than others, or when it pressed for financial aid to the higher class schools. The Board's annual reports included sharp criticism of the working of the Code, to which the Department replied that improving the general level of education was the first priority. 'We cannot think', they said in 1878, 'that, at the present day, with all the social and industrial changes that are in progress among us, it is right to encourage these [university] subjects at the cost of others, which have hitherto been much neglected, and which, by many high authorities, are held to possess an educational value of their own, at least equal to that of what are called "University Subjects".'[11] These high authorities appear to have included Playfair and Huxley, who were responsible for the prominence of science in the list of thirteen subjects. Apart from the six mentioned above, they included mechanics, chemistry, animal physiology, light and heat, magnetism and electricity, physical geography, and botany.[12] Critics complained that such subjects could be crammed from textbooks, and that teachers would prefer this easy way of earning grants to the long and careful work of teaching languages. Nevertheless, each specific subject had a three-year programme, and the system could be used to finance a secondary curriculum of sorts.

By its campaigns on this issue, the Board of Education did much to persuade Scottish educational opinion that the Code and the 1872 Act were having a disastrous effect on standards. It was supported, for example, by the *Educational News,* a

[10] *Moncreiff Comm. Special Rep.* (1881), p. 23.

[11] *Board of Education. 3rd Rep.,* p. xxvii; *CCES Rep., 1877-8* (PP 1878, xxxi), p. xiv, and cf. *1876-7* (PP 1877, xxxii), p. xii.

[12] *CCE Rep., 1872-3* (PP 1873, xxiv), Scottish Code of 1873, Article 21 and Fourth Schedule. Cf. *Moncreiff Comm. Special Rep.,* p. 32 (evidence of Sir A. Grant).

journal founded in 1876 by the EIS, which joined in the unsuccessful demands that the Board should be turned into a
permanent body. The first editor of the *News* was James
Donaldson, rector of Edinburgh High School, who had already
been active in educational politics as president of the EIS in
1868. Donaldson was later to argue that the 1872 Act was
based on the 'application of English ideas to Scotch education',
whereas the 1869 bill, like those previously introduced by
Moncreiff, was faithful to three hundred years of national
tradition, a view with which some modern historians have
sympathized.[13] Certainly, the 1872 Act abolished the parish
schools as a separate category, where Moncreiff would have
kept them; but how much vitality the parochial tradition
retained in the 1860s, and how far the principle behind it could
be adapted to the needs of an industrial society, are complex
questions which will be discussed below. Donaldson himself,
like most Scottish educationists, thought that it was the duty of
the state to support middle-class education, and condemned
the Act for failing to provide an adequate network of secondary
schools. Perhaps the greatest weakness of the 1872 Act was that
it ended a well-understood but obsolescent tradition without
offering a clear replacement, and left secondary education in a
financial and administrative limbo.

The resulting confusion also complicates the work of the
historian. The Argyll commission's report on 'burgh and
middle-class schools' was a comprehensive survey of secondary
schools in towns, but after 1872 comparable statistical information is lacking. Endowed schools and higher class schools,
because they did not receive government grants, did not figure
in the SED's annual reports; other types of school—former
parish schools, burgh schools which did not attain 'higher
class' status—were merged in the general category of 'public'
schools, and 'secondary' pupils within them were not distinguished.[14] The maintenance of higher education now depended

---

[13] J. Donaldson, *Home Rule and Scottish education* (n.p., n.d. [1913]), pp. 4-7,
and *Addresses delivered in the University of St. Andrews from 1886 to 1910* (St. Andrews,
1911), pp. 466-9; J. D. Myers, 'Scottish nationalism and the antecedents of the
1872 Education Act', *Scottish Educational Studies*, iv (1972), pp. 86-8.

[14] Some former burgh schools which had been under 'mixed' management were not
transferred to school boards, but retained independent governing bodies—e.g.
Dundee High School, Inverness Academy.

on the policies of individual school boards, which might or might not be willing to maintain the traditions of an old burgh school or to make a point of appointing schoolmasters with some university training. Some boards did do this, and indeed built up new secondary schools within the administrative framework of the Code—notably in Glasgow, where in the 1880s the term 'higher grade schools' was adopted from England to describe this development. In the 1870s, however, the best index to the presence of secondary education within the public schools, though it is an imperfect one, is the extent to which the specific subjects, especially Latin, were taught. Fortunately the Board of Education collected much fuller information about this than the SED, and the Moncreiff endowments commission of 1878 also investigated the question.

In order to reach conclusions about the social role of the universities, we must first look at the parish schools and the burgh schools separately. What proportion of students came from each type of school? This was a question which interested the Argyll commission, and its assistant commissioners collected valuable data from the universities which covered ages and parental occupations as well as school origins. The commission was concerned partly with the complaints of secondary schoolmasters that the junior classes in the universities were poaching on their territory. They found some truth in this, but thought it a minor evil outweighed by the need to keep the universities widely accessible, and claimed in support of this view that fewer than half the students—35 per cent at Edinburgh, 46 per cent at Glasgow, 47 per cent at St. Andrews, 48 per cent at Aberdeen—came from 'burgh and middle-class schools'.[15] This did not mean, however, that the rest came from parish schools, since the percentages related to a total which included students educated privately or outside Scotland. If the details in the report are broken down to isolate the students educated at schools in Scotland, a rather different picture emerges, with 60 per cent at Edinburgh, 64 per cent at Glasgow, and 77 per

---

[15] *Argyll Comm. 3rd Rep.* Vol. I, pp. 156-7, 163-6.

cent at St. Andrews coming from secondary schools of different kinds (see Table 4.1).[16] But even these figures are not very satisfactory, for they failed to take account of the fact that it was common to attend more than one school, and in particular to go to a secondary school for a year or two to complete an education started at a parish school. In the North-East, for example, it was accepted by this time that a year's stay in one of the Aberdeen grammar schools was almost essential for success in the bursary competition.[17] We do not know how the commission classified such cases.

At Glasgow, the university carried out its own inquiry in 1868 which showed more awareness of the problem, and published figures which claimed that 46 per cent of its students had attended only 'elementary' schools (see Table 4.2).[18] The Glasgow Senate was campaigning at the time against the Revised Code, and trying to show how important it was to maintain higher education in ordinary schools. At Edinburgh, on the other hand, Principal Grant sought to minimize the parish-school contribution to the university in order to strengthen the case for an entrance examination: he began the regular collection of information about school careers from first-year students, and claimed that only 16 per cent came directly from parish schools.[19] Direct examination of the Edinburgh records, however, suggests that in 1870 about 70 per cent of the students came from secondary schools, and 29 per cent from the nonsecondary sector, mostly from parish or similar schools in the provinces.[20]

The conclusion from these figures is that attending a secondary school was the most common preliminary to a university

[16] Table based on figures in ibid., p. 243. The students covered were those in the Latin, Greek, and mathematics classes.

[17] Only about 12 per cent of successful bursary candidates came *direct* from parish schools: *Moncreiff Comm. Special. Rep.*, p. 205; cf. *Argyll Comm. Rep. on Country Districts*, p. 132.

[18] *University of Glasgow. Report of Committee of Senate on elementary schools in their relation to the universities* (Glasgow, 1868), p. 5.

[19] A. Grant, *The present state, prospects, and wants of the University of Edinburgh* (Edinburgh, 1871), pp. 7-8, and *Edinburgh University Annual Record* (Edinburgh, 1873), pp. 18-19. Other figures in *Argyll Comm. Report on Country Districts*, p. 132 (20-9 per cent at Edinburgh from parish and similar schools), and *Moncreiff Comm. Special Rep.*, pp. 75-6, 81, 102-3.

[20] See below, Table 8.5 (One per cent unknown or doubtful.)

Table 4.1

School origins of arts students, 1866/7

	Edinburgh	Glasgow	St. Andrews
Numbers educated at:			
Academies, grammar schools, colleges	67	123	28
Burgh schools	45	51	8
Institutions, hospitals, endowed schools	23	6	4
Private schools	17	10	6
Total secondary	*152*	*190*	*46*
Normal school	15	18	0
Parochial schools	52	56	12
Free Church schools	32	28	0
Other primary	3	7	2

	102	*109*	*14*
Total primary			
Total at schools in Scotland	254	299	60
Private education	25	7	6
Elsewhere in U.K.	10	23	6
Abroad	11	5	0
Doubtful	16	40	2
TOTAL	316	374	74
As percentage of those educated at schools in Scotland:			
Academies etc.	26·4	41·1	46·7
Burgh schools	17·7	17·1	13·3
Institutions etc.	9·1	2·0	6·7
Private schools	6·7	3·3	10·0
Total secondary	59·8	63·5	76·7
Total primary	40·2	36·5	23·3

Table 4.2

School origins of students at Glasgow, 1868

Totals, and as percentage of those educated at schools in Scotland

	Arts	Theology	Medicine	Law	Total
Educated wholly at elementary schools	235 (45·3%)	34 (50·7%)	76 (58·9%)	26 (26·5%)	371 (45·6%)
Educated partly at elementary schools	130 (25%)	19 (28·4%)	37 (28·7%)	20 (20·4%)	206 (25·3%)
Educated wholly at middle-class schools	154 (29·7%)	14 (20·9%)	16 (12·4%)	52 (53·1%)	236 (29%)
Total at schools in Scotland	519	67	129	98	813
Privately or outside Scotland	49	4	32	0	85
TOTALS	568	71	161	98	898

education. At St. Andrews, the Argyll commission attributed the high figure to the university's experiment with a hall of residence, intended to appeal to the higher social classes, and 'filled mainly from the Edinburgh Academy and such schools'.[21] At Glasgow, on the other hand, the Senate stressed that many students came from elementary schools in the city itself, not just from country parish schools. Twenty-two per cent of the students in the arts faculty were practising teachers, who had usually risen from elementary schools through the pupil-teacher system.[22] This is a reminder of another difficulty of interpretation: there were many older men at the universities, and they included especially those of working-class origin; although they were likely to have attended only an elementary school, it was their private study rather than what they learnt at school which prepared them for the university. Thus the link between elementary or parish schools and the universities was not necessarily a direct one, and its maintenance depended as much on the barriers which the universities might put in the way of entry as on the existence of university-oriented teaching in the schools.

The extent of such teaching in the public schools is the next point to be investigated, and there are two sources of information. First, the numbers studying specific subjects, about whom the fullest details are in the Board of Education's report for 1877. And secondly, a questionnaire sent by the Endowed Institutions Commission of 1878 to the head teacher of every public school, asking about his university qualifications, the number of pupils studying beyond the Code standards, the numbers preparing for university entrance, and the social position of these pupils' parents. These sources reveal the existence of important regional and local differences.

In 1877 there were 2,425 public elementary schools in Scotland, with 363,542 pupils on the roll, of whom only 20,294 (5.6 per cent) were thirteen or over. Only 1,457 schools taught any specific subjects at all, and 41,551 scholars were studying one or more of them. But the most popular were modest

---

[21] *Argyll Comm. 3rd Rep.*, Vol. I, p. 157.
[22] *Report of Committee*, p. 6.

additions to the three Rs such as English and geography, and the numbers studying genuinely 'secondary' subjects were lower:[23]

	Boys	Girls	Total
Latin	8,764	1,666	10,430
Greek	592	31	623
Mathematics	3,990	336	4,326
French	3,027	3,600	6,627

The total of 8,764 boys studying Latin seems quite high, but the detailed figures show that most of these cannot have been aiming at the university. Specific subjects were taught at three stages, and only the third stage of Latin came anywhere near the level required for university entry; schoolmasters who took university preparation seriously went beyond the official schedules altogether and read Virgil, Livy or Sallust with their chosen pupils. Yet very few of those studying 'university subjects' ever reached the third stage, as the 1877 figures show:

	Latin	Greek	Mathematics
Boys studying at 1st stage	6,569	446	3,268
2nd stage	1,720	92	619
3rd stage	570	55	150

The utility of teaching mathematics even for one year can be appreciated, but it is less easy to see why Latin was taught to so many who would make no further use of it. One answer, no doubt, was that this was an easy way for a schoolmaster to earn an extra grant, but the traditional prestige of the subject must also have been a factor. It is difficult otherwise to see why school boards in the large cities taught the rudiments of Latin to a significant number of boys in their elementary schools. As Table 4.3 shows, few of these were to take it further (none at all to the third stage), and in most cases the authorities did not even present their Latin pupils for the specific subject examination.[24]

---

[23] *Board of Education. 5th Rep.*, pp. 150, 502. The figures are for those 'studying' the subjects, as distinct from the smaller numbers presented for examination. These figures, and those in Tables 4. 3-4, appear to relate to board schools only.

[24] Ibid. pp. 224, 267, 376, 404, 421.

Table 4.3

Study of Latin as a specific subject in certain towns, 1877 (boys)

	Nos. studying at stages 1	2	3	Presented for examination at stage 1
Glasgow	445	15	0	31
Govan	87	8	0	36
Edinburgh	49	0	0	11
Dundee	113	4	0	4
Aberdeen	64	2	0	20
Paisley	211	69	0	52

The teaching of Latin at a higher level was a rural rather than an urban phenomenon in the public schools: of the 570 boys who reached the third stage, 406 were in the parishes and 164 in the burghs.[25] This figure is coincidentally almost identical with the number of scholars preparing for the university (574) who were listed by the headmasters questioned by the Endowed Institutions Commission.[26] This might be a very small fraction of all pupils in elementary schools, but they were enough to make a significant impact on the university statistics at a time when the total university enrolment was about 5,000.

These students were, however, unequally distributed through the country, as Table 4.4 shows.[27] The most striking feature of this is the exceptional position in the North-East, which—as appears from Column 1—had a far higher proportion of university-trained schoolmasters than the rest of Scotland, and where the advanced teaching of the classics was far more widely distributed in the rural areas. Columns 2 and 3 show the number of boys who were either studying Latin at an advanced

[25] Ibid., pp. 150-1. 'Burghs' here means those with 'burgh school boards'. Since public schools in burghs included quite important former burgh schools (e.g. Dunfermline, Kirkcaldy, Kilmarnock, Dumbarton), it looks as if these did not use the specific subject grants, but relied on fees to support secondary education.

[26] *Moncreiff Comm. Special Rep.*, p. 201. The total of 574, and the county figures used below, were decided by the commission's officials on the basis of often imprecise answers by the headmasters.

[27] Table based on *Moncreiff Comm. Special Rep.*, pp. 200-1 (columns 1 and 3) and *Board of Education. 5th Rep.*, Appendix X (columns 2, 4-6). The distinction between urban and rural school-board districts is made empirically, since no simple criterion (e.g. population) was satisfactory. The modern names of the counties have been used throughout.

Table 4.4

Regional variations in provision for classical teaching in public schools

	University trained masters (%)	Boys at advanced stage 1877	1879	No. of school board districts	Advanced classical teaching Town	Country
	1	2	3	4	5	6
North East						
Aberdeen	70	89	98	92	5	42
Banff	77	55	73	24	5	9
Kincardine	62	17	12	19	2	3
Moray	82	44	27	22	3	5
Nairn	13	0	5	5	0	0
Highlands & North						
Argyll	26	36	52	46	3	12
Bute	43	3	1	6	1	1
Caithness	23	12	6	12	1	4
Inverness	28	19	16	35	1	10
Orkney	34	23	5	19	1	3
Ross & Cromarty	35	10	23	35	1	8
Shetland	24	0	2	12	0	0
Sutherland	41	6	6	13	1	3

East Central						
Angus	32	18	8	60	2	3
Clackmannan	22	2	0	5	1	0
Fife	25	10	5	69	4	6
Kinross	50	1	0	5	1	0
Perth	32	52	39	82	5	16
Stirling	33	5	21	28	1	0
West						
Ayr	35	14	51	51	6	1
Dumbarton	34	13	19	14	3	1
Lanark	45	25	34	50	8	1
Renfrew	37	5	14	23	4	0
Lothians & Borders						
Berwick	42	2	8	32	1	3
East Lothian	56	3	3	26	3	0
Midlothian	51	5	1	34	3	2
Peebles	35	2	6	14	0	2
Roxburgh	47	2	7	33	1	2
Selkirk	33	2	4	9	1	2
West Lothian	40	0	1	14	1	1
South West						
Dumfries	39	30	14	45	4	6
Kirkcudbright	30	32	6	30	3	3
Wigtown	32	33	7	18	2	4

Table 4.4 (*Contd.*)

SCOTLAND	40%	570	574	982	78	153

Columns 1 Percentage of headmasters of public schools with university degree or attendance, 1879

2 Boys studying Latin as specific subject at third stage, 1877

3 Boys stated to be preparing for university by headmasters, 1879

4 Number of school board districts in county, 1877

5 and 6 Number of these, urban and rural respectively, where either Latin at third stage or Greek at any stage studied as specific subject, 1877

stage in 1877 or said to be preparing for the university in 1879. Not all these pupils, however, were 'rural', for many former burgh schools were now ranked as public schools, and one would expect to find classical pupils in towns which did not have higher class or endowed schools. Columns 4 to 6 attempt to measure the extent of purely rural classical teaching: Column 4 shows the total number of school-board districts, and Columns 5 and 6, for towns and rural parishes respectively, show those where boys (even one boy) were studying the classics at a more than basic level—either Latin at the third stage, or Greek at any stage. There were only 153 rural parishes where this was the case, and of these 100 were in the North-East and the Highlands. In Aberdeen and Banff over half of the parishes had advanced classical pupils, but in most Lowland counties this was true of only a handful, and in some of none at all. The general picture is that in the Lowlands secondary education had already become 'centralized' in the towns (to use a term from later years), and that country schoolmasters were seldom called on to teach the classics.

In the North-East, however, the traditions of Aberdeen University and the operation of the Dick bequest supported the diffusion of secondary teaching. Schoolmasters encouraged a nucleus of pupils to stay on and study the higher subjects, and every year or so sent one or two on to university. According to Laurie's report on the Dick counties, between 1878 and 1888 365 boys from the schools aided by the bequest went on to university, 209 directly and 156 after a brief stay at a secondary school; this was an average of 36.5 a year, from 122 schools, and Laurie thought it an outstanding record.[28] It worked best in Aberdeenshire and Banffshire, where it was favoured both by geography—there were secondary schools only at Aberdeen, Peterhead and Banff—and by social conditions, for these counties corresponded to the 'central wedge' of the North-East identified by Ian Carter, where small farmers and crofters were particularly numerous.[29] There was a more concentrated

---

[28] S. S. Laurie, *Report to the Trustees of the Dick Bequest on the rural public (formerly parochial) schools of Aberdeen, Banff, and Moray* (Edinburgh, 1890), p. 51.

[29] I. Carter, *Farmlife in Northeast Scotland 1840-1914. The poor man's country* (Edinburgh, 1979), pp. 11, 30-1.

pattern, however, in Moray and Kincardine. Moray had secondary schools at Elgin, Forres, and Fochabers, and in Kincardine (which was not covered by the Dick bequest) Table 4.4 shows only three rural parishes, the 'urban' ones being Stonehaven and Banchory.

The replies to the Endowed Institutions Commission's question about the social origins of the pupils who were aiming at the university confirm Laurie's description of them as 'the sons of small farmers, tradesmen, or ministers'.[30] Although the replies are often vague and difficult to classify, they also show the presence of boys from the 'working classes', which in some cases at least included farm servants and rural labourers. Table 4.5 summarizes these data for Aberdeenshire, and one for Banff would give a similar picture.[31] The majority of those who went to the university from a parish school were not poor boys but the sons of the rural middle class—of the minister, of the schoolmaster himself, of farmers, often described as prosperous although of course this category could cover different levels of wealth. Farmers and ministers used the parish schools because they were at their doorstep, but they would probably have sought out secondary education in any case, and it was these parents who sent their sons to finish off their education at Aberdeen.[32] Only rarely did the schoolmaster have the chance to advance the son of a labourer or ploughman. As for the artisans and tradesmen, these were mostly in the schools in small towns, which were developing in a secondary direction. At Keith, for example, which was famed for its classical teaching, the headmaster claimed twenty-eight pupils aiming at the university, belonging to the 'middle class' of 'farmers, professional men, merchants and tradesmen'. At Huntly there were seven, whose parents included two farmers and the bank agent, master slater, master cabinet-maker, veterinary surgeon and journeyman blacksmith listed in Table 4.5. At Banchory there

[30] S. S. Laurie, *Report on education in the parochial schools of the counties of Aberdeen, Banff and Moray* (Edinburgh, 1865), p. 124.

[31] Based on replies in SRO ED 2 10/1-3, Aberdeenshire. The total is higher than that for the county in Table 4.4 because it includes pupils who had recently left and other marginal cases.

[32] Of 24 'country boys' in the rector's class at Aberdeen Grammar School in 1866, 5 were sons of ministers, 11 of farmers, only 3 of labourers: *Argyll Comm. 3rd Rep.*, Vol. II, pp. 281-2.

Table 4.5

Parental occupations of boys aiming at university, Aberdeenshire, 1879

Professional	25
(15 ministers, 9 teachers, 1 doctor)	
Middle class generally	20
('middle class', 'good social position', 'comfortable but not wealthy')	
Miscellaneous middle class	4
(1 veterinary surgeon, 1 excise officer, 1 bank agent, 1 merchant)	
Farmers and crofters	36
(27 farmers, 1 farm overseer, 4 'small farmers', 4 crofters)	
Artisans, small business, miscellaneous	15
(3 shoemakers, 1 carpenter, 1 mason, 1 master slater, 1 master cabinet-maker, 1 blacksmith, 1 journeyman-blacksmith, 1 master miller, 1 meal miller, 1 fishcurer, 1 general merchant, 1 sergeant-major, 1 colporteur)	
Working class generally	16
('working classes', 'labouring classes', etc.)	
Labourers	3
(1 labourer, 1 rural labourer, 1 farm-servant)	
Poor, paupers	4
TOTAL	123

were six 'sons of local tradesmen'; 'This would be a splendid centre for a secondary school if funds could be raised', observed the headmaster.[33] In schools like this, the specific subjects would be used to cater for other needs than university preparation. According to Laurie, 'It is only the picked or more ambitious boys who seek an outlet for their activities in some form of professional or quasi-professional training. The higher education, meanwhile, is shared in by a very much larger number

[33] SRO ED 2 10/7, Banffshire, Keith; ED 2 10/1-3, Aberdeenshire, Huntly; ED 2 10/17, Kincardineshire, Banchory Ternan.

who settle down in their native parishes, or, if they leave them, follow the ordinary work of life as artisans, tradesmen, and clerks.'[34]

Outside the North-East, it was only in the Highlands that the rural schools were really important for university preparation. Secondary schools existed only on the eastern fringes, and little was being done to develop them elsewhere. In 1879, for example, the Nicolson Institute at Stornoway, later a well-known secondary school, was unable to teach any university subject as its sole master had to struggle with ninety-nine pupils, assisted only by one pupil-teacher.[35] In centres like Inveraray, Oban, Portree or Dingwall there were modest clusters of more advanced pupils, but classical pupils were also found in quite remote parishes, and they were as often the sons of crofters or 'working-class' parents as of ministers or the teachers themselves. One striking example was the large parish of Gairloch in Wester Ross, where three separate schools had pupils aiming at the university: two sons of crofters at Opinan, three from the 'upper working classes' at Achtercairn, and one from a 'poor' family at Bualnaluib.[36] In such areas there was little rivalry from commerce or the trades, and university entry was the best road out for anyone with intellectual promise. Higher education was thus well developed in Argyll, Ross and Cromarty, and Inverness-shire, though not in impoverished Sutherland. In the North, Caithness and Orkney had secondary schools and followed a more Lowland pattern, but education at all levels seems to have been neglected in Shetland, though there was a proprietary school at Lerwick, Anderson's Institute, which escaped the official statistics.

Apart from the North-East and the Highlands, classical teaching in rural schools was of little significance. One partial exception, which tends to prove the rule, was Perthshire, a large and partly Highland county, which had only one public secondary school, Perth Academy. Although pupils commuted to Perth by train from a radius of 15-20 miles,[37] there was a

---

[34] Laurie, *Report to the Trustees* (1890), p. 43.

[35] SRO ED 2 10/26, Ross & Cromarty, Stornoway.

[36] SRO ED 2 10/26, Ross & Cromarty, Gairloch. A similar case was Glassary, Argyll: SRO ED 2 10/4-5.

[37] *Argyll Comm. 3rd Rep.*, Vol. II, pp. 236-7.

need for secondary education which could be met by the public schools in the towns of northern Perthshire and in some of the rural parishes. Elsewhere in the Lowlands, advanced teaching was often expanding in growing industrial towns. At Larbert in Stirlingshire, for example, there were nine boys preparing for the university, and at Strathaven in Lanarkshire there were seven; 'District is so situated that Public School must do work of a High Class School', noted the schoolmaster.[38] In 1868/9 a school inspector in the West had reported that about a fifth of his schools gave a more or less secondary education 'comprising languages (Latin and French), a little geometry and algebra, in some instances a little Greek, a portion of English history, some notions of English literature and of physical science.'[39] But where commerce and industry flourished, interest might turn away from the classics and the universities, and in the Lowlands French was beginning to overtake Latin as a popular prestige subject, though even in 1877 there were only five counties where the numbers taking French were larger.

Where a rural school in southern Scotland was still giving classical education, it was likely to conform to the pattern described by the Argyll commission's experts: 'in those of the old-fashioned parish schools which we visited, we found, not unfrequently, a class of three or four boys in Latin, two of them, perhaps, the minister's sons, and one the teacher's'.[40] But working-class boys were rare. 'A labourer's son going to the University, from the country, is nearly unknown', declared one Kirkcudbrightshire headmaster.[41] It was also practically unknown, to judge from the teachers' information about the status of parents, for sons of the industrial working class to do so. The mining population, for example, was spread very widely through the Lowlands in semi-rural villages, and the parochial system of higher education might seem to suit these conditions very well. Yet not a single miner's son was among those aiming at the university in 1879. The nearest to it was at

---

[38] SRO ED 2 10/28, Stirlingshire, Larbert; ED 2 10/18-19, Lanarkshire, Avondale.
[39] *CCE Rep., 1868-9* (PP 1868-9, xx), p. 340.
[40] *Argyll Comm. Rep. on Country Districts*, p. 133.
[41] SRO ED 2 10/17, Kirkcudbrightshire, Bargrennan.

Braidwood, Lanarkshire, where a colliery engineman's son would have liked to attend university, but could not do so unless a scholarship could be found.[42] On the other hand, at Crookedholm, near Kilmarnock, the schoolmaster reported that 'A great number of young men do not begin studying for the University till some time after they have left School. As a proof of this, I have prepared 9 students for Glasgow University, within the last three years, from the age of 17 to 24—the majority of whom were either miners or the sons of miners. Three were preparing for Medical Profession, three for being Ministers, and three were for the Legal Profession. I assisted them in their preliminary studies in the evenings.'[43] It is difficult to know how typical this was, but it was certainly true that many students of working-class origin started their university careers at an advanced age. The school perhaps played its part by arousing an initial intellectual interest, but its role in sending boys direct to the universities, so marked in the rural areas of the North-East, proved incapable of adaptation to industrial conditions. Factory workers were almost as rare among the parents mentioned in 1879 as miners, and even in the North-East itself the fishermen were notorious for their resistance to education of any kind. Both miners and fishermen, it was complained, put their children to work at the earliest possible date. Neither the accessibility of schools nor the presence of well-qualified schoolmasters could counteract the imperatives of poverty.[44]

One region with few classical pupils in its public schools was the Lothians and Borders. This was partly due to the dominance of Edinburgh, whose numerous schools attracted the middle class over a wide area and enfeebled the burgh schools in towns like Linlithgow and Haddington. In the Borders, however, there were only two secondary schools, at Peebles and Selkirk. The explanation perhaps lies in the social structure of the region, which was one of capitalist farming and large landlords. In the case of East Lothian, Dr Cook of Haddington, convener of the Church of Scotland education

[42] SRO ED 2 10/18-19, Lanarkshire, Carluke.
[43] SRO ED 2 10/6, Ayrshire, Kilmarnock.
[44] *Argyll Comm. Rep. on Country Districts*, pp. 7-13.

scheme, explained to the Argyll commission that whereas in the North-East there was a class of small farmers with an interest in the professions, here the rich farmers might use the parish schools for a while, 'but when they come to the classics they are sent to Edinburgh', while 'respectable hinds, and people in the lower classes ... think more of giving their boys an education fitting them to be shopkeepers, and that sort of thing, and therefore they don't care so much for classical education.'[45] His conclusion, shared by the experienced school inspector John Kerr, was that the classics had not declined in the south because they had never been very strong there in the first place, and Borders schoolmasters tended to say the same thing when replying to the 1879 questionnaire.[46]

That questionnaire asked schoolmasters whether the demand for university subjects was declining: 610 said yes, 259 no; many used the question as a cue for venting their grievances against the Revised Code and the 1872 Act. Schoolmasters at this time, especially those who were old parochial teachers, had many complaints about their status and conditions of work under the school boards, and it was natural that they should express these by talking of declining standards. But they were also aware of the social trends which were affecting their schools. The middle classes, who had once used the parish schools for their local convenience, could now afford to send their children to the towns as boarders, or make use of the railways to send them to a neighbouring town every day. At the same time, economic expansion meant that only in relatively remote areas did teaching and the Church still seem the most attractive careers, and the prestige of the classics was declining. Many schoolmasters complained that they were simply unable to interest parents in the higher subjects. At Glamis in Angus, the schoolmaster was a graduate, and about a fifth of his pupils were of the class—farmers and master tradesmen—who elsewhere might aim at the university: but 'there is little or no ambition in that direction here. The opinion being that it does not *pay*.' He had sent only one boy to the university in the last

---

[45] *Argyll Comm. 1st Rep.*, p. 49.
[46] For Kerr see *Moncreiff Comm. Special Rep.*, p. 64.

twenty years, and 'he was a poor man's son whom I took in hand myself, & educated free'.[47] This evidence suggests that when contemporaries attributed the decline of the parish school to the disappearance of university-educated schoolmasters they were wide of the mark: the demand for classical education disappeared first, and the impression left by reading the 1879 questionnaires is of a teaching force which was over-qualified, or wrongly qualified, for the task which it had to perform.

Nevertheless, contemporaries certainly felt that the parochial tradition was declining, and that the opportunities which it had once offered were being closed off, and it is necessary to consider how far this was so. Was the situation in the North-East a model of what had once existed everywhere in Scotland, or did it reflect unique local conditions? Were the regional disparities which have been displayed above symptoms of a tradition in collapse, or do they give a fair picture of how the ideal had always worked in practice? One difficulty in answering these questions is the lack of reliable statistics for earlier years. Another is that the period when the tradition was supposed to have flourished tends to recede through a golden haze. As early as 1827, Henry Cockburn was complaining that 'our ancient system of popular instruction is in an alarming condition, and that, if we really wish to make our parish schools continue to accomplish the purposes for which they were originally designed, we must cease to slumber over them with the half patriarchal half poetical dream, which is apt to come over us when we think of those rural seminaries—and must do something effectual to revive them'.[48]

The hypothesis put forward here is that classical teaching in parish schools was rather more widespread in the 1820s than in the 1870s, and had retreated to its Highland and northern redoubts as urban secondary schools were founded or improved; but the decline was a gradual one, and a matter of degree only, and there had been no sudden collapse of a national system of parochial education. The evidence may be discussed in the form of responses to four questions.

First, was the proportion of students from parish schools in the universities higher in the earlier period? Witnesses before the

---

[47] SRO ED 2 10/13-14, Forfarshire, Glamis.
[48] *Edinburgh Review*, xlvi (1827), p. 111.

1826 commission gave estimates of 50-60 per cent, but these were not backed up by direct inquiry.[49] On the other hand, Nicholas Hans's study of eighteenth-century education showed that of a sample of 650 men educated at Scottish universities, 275 received their prior education at home or from private tutors, 163 in Scottish 'grammar schools', 96 in Scottish parish schools, and 116 elsewhere, mainly outside Scotland. This was a sample of men who achieved distinction rather than a representative one, but it suggests that the normal road to the universities was through secondary education in the eighteenth century as in the nineteenth, the main change being that the upper and middle classes switched from private tuition to formal schooling.[50]

Second, were schoolmasters better qualified to give university preparation in the 1820s? Probably yes. In 1879 40 per cent of the headmasters had attended a university—but only 10 per cent were actually graduates, two-thirds of them in the Dick counties. The 1826 commission established through an inquiry conducted by the presbyteries of the Church that 585 of the 841 parishes possessed university-trained schoolmasters, half of whom had been through the full four years; even then, the superiority of Aberdeenshire, Banff, and Moray was marked, with university men in 91 per cent of the parishes.[51] At that time, of course, there were no training colleges, and since then a new breed of teachers had appeared, while graduates could find new opportunities in commerce, in churches, and in the expanding secondary sector. Changes in the training of the ministry also had their effect: by the 1860s part-time or 'irregular' study for divinity was practically at an end.[52]

The fact that a schoolmaster could teach Latin was itself of limited significance, and such sources as the *New Statistical Account* in the 1840s, or reports of the Church's Education

---

[49] *Univ. Comm. Ev. Glasgow*, p. 75 (Sandford) and *Ev. Aberdeen*, p. 76 (Melvin).

[50] N. Hans, *New trends in education in the eighteenth century* (1951), p. 18. This studies the education of men mentioned in the *Dictionary of National Biography*. There is also information on social background (pp. 26-7): most of those educated at parish schools were ministers' or farmers' sons, and there were very few sons of workers.

[51] *Univ. Comm. Ev. Edinburgh*, Appendix, p. 235. County figures can be worked out from those given for presbyteries.

[52] S. Mechie, 'Education for the ministry in Scotland since the Reformation. II', *Records of the Scottish Church History Society*, xiv (1960-2), p. 172.

Committee in the same period, suggest much the same picture as the Argyll commission's report on the 'country districts' or the Moncreiff questionnaire—that in southern Scotland the demand for higher subjects was limited and occasional. Besides, one should not underestimate the abilities of the college-trained teachers. The colleges taught Latin and Greek, and in 1879, out of 2,046 male teachers 1,989 claimed that they could teach Latin as a specific subject, and 1,397 Greek. Apart from Latin at an elementary level, most of them would rarely have to call on this ability.[53]

Thirdly, did the numbers studying the classics decline or increase? The presbyterial returns of 1827, though very defective, claimed to show that 8,553 boys were studying Latin and 2,042 Greek. These figures covered schools of all kinds, and the four large cities alone accounted for 2,630 of the Latin pupils (31 per cent) and 984 of the Greek (48 per cent). In 1877 8,764 boys were studying Latin as a specific subject and 592 Greek— but these figures excluded most genuine secondary schools, and suggest that the teaching of Latin at least had expanded rather than declined over fifty years. Indeed, it was continuing to do so, for the numbers taking Latin rose steadily until the specific subject system itself disappeared: in 1877/8 the number actually presented for examination was 3,958, and by 1899/1900 this had risen to 11,262.[54] If much of this Latin teaching was at a low level, the same may well have been true in 1827.

Finally, did the proportion of scholars studying Latin rise or fall? This was a calculation often attempted by contemporaries. The Argyll commission, using a sample of rural schools, found Latin scholars to be 3 per cent in the schools as a whole, 5.25 per cent in parochial schools, and concluded that 'if classics are falling off in country schools, it is only to a very small extent'.[55] These figures appear to have included girls, and comparable percentages for 1877 show no decline: 3.7 per cent (all public

[53] *Moncreiff Comm. Special Rep.*, pp. 200-1. Cf. statement by M. Paterson in *Argyll Comm. Appendix to 1st Rep.*, p. 125.

[54] *CCES Rep., 1899-1900* (PP 1900, xxiv), p. 13 (both sexes). Another source of information is the educational census of 1851, which found 11,125 boys studying the 'ancient languages' in schools of all kinds: *Census of Great Britain 1851. Religious Worship and Education. Scotland*, pp. 40-1, 43-4.

[55] *Argyll Comm. Rep. on Country Districts*, p. 165. Cf. discussion by G. Ramsay in *Fraser's Magazine*, n.s. xiii (1876), pp. 409-10.

schools) and 5.1 per cent (schools teaching specific subjects), or 5.7 per cent and 7.8 per cent for boys alone.[56] Unfortunately there were no reliable figures for earlier years; in the 1860s Laurie produced an estimate of 6 per cent for an unspecified date in the past, but he attributed the decline of Latin to natural social factors, and refused to endorse the thesis of a general fall in standards.[57] Laurie was also able to give precise details of the Dick bequest schools, where the percentage studying Latin had risen from 4.6 per cent in 1833 to 6 per cent in 1865; by 1889 it was to be 8 per cent.[58] This is significant, because it shows that the special situation in the North-East was in part a creation of the nineteenth century, and direct comparison of the 1827 and 1877 figures seems to confirm this: the number of boys studying Latin rose in Aberdeenshire (excluding Aberdeen) from 453 in 1827 to 1,007 in 1877, in Banff from 136 to 448, and in Moray from 187 to 275.

Laurie once said of the North-East that 'The problem of "a career open to talent and accessible to the poorest" ... was solved as it never had been solved in the history of education in any country. The schools were constantly referred to as models of the old Scottish parochial schools which have done so much for Scotland.'[59] They might be models in the sense of providing an ideal type, or as the basis of a democratic reinterpretation of the tradition for modern conditions, but it seems clear that the parochial system found working in the North-East in the 1860s and 1870s was the product of peculiar local conditions, and not a surviving remnant of what had once been universal; historical evidence drawn from this region cannot safely be used for generalizations about Scotland. While in this area, and in the Highlands because of the problems of remoteness, the rural schools did continue to provide important opportunities for university access, in the rest of Scotland the continuing 'centralization' of secondary education was not likely to cause more than marginal reductions of educational opportunity.

[56] *Board of Education. 5th Rep.*, pp. xxi, 150.
[57] Laurie, *Report on education* (1865), pp. 307-8, and his evidence in *Argyll Comm. 1st Rep.*, p. 33. But in later years he blamed the Code for causing a decline: *Moncreiff Comm. Special Rep.*, Evidence, pp. 2-7.
[58] Laurie, *Report to the Trustees* (1890), pp. 40, 48. The figure of 6 per cent for 1865 is from this source—elsewhere Laurie said 6.5 or 6.88.
[59] *Ibid.*, p. 13.

Information about the burgh schools is relatively abundant, for as well as Harvey and Sellar's report on 'burgh and middle-class schools' for the Argyll commission, Scotland was visited by an English school inspector, D. R. Fearon, who reported on secondary schools to the Schools Inquiry Commission for England. Fearon visited only sixteen schools, and since they were the leading ones he perhaps formed an unduly favourable impression of the state of affairs, but his report is especially valuable for his interest in the relation of education and society. Harvey and Sellar were more comprehensive; they defined 'public' schools widely to include endowed and proprietary schools—even Glenalmond. Only strictly private schools were excluded, although Harvey and Sellar did look at a sample of eleven, only three of which were named. They also seem to have passed over some endowed schools, for the Colebrooke commission in the 1870s described fifteen which did not figure in the earlier report.

Harvey and Sellar eliminated a number of burgh schools because they gave only elementary instruction, and settled on a list of fifty-nine schools about which data were collected.[60] Twenty-eight were managed by town councils alone, seventeen by mixed bodies, and fourteen independently. There were 14,879 pupils in the schools, giving an average size of 252. But many schools were quite small, and twenty-one were run by a single teacher—the total number of teachers in all the schools was only 216.[61] Table 4.6 shows how the pupils were distributed by age and sex.[62]

Two points may be made about the age distribution. First, the schools took children of all ages, and there were rather more under twelve than over: these were 'secondary' schools because of the level reached by their studies and because they charged fees which made them socially select, not because they formed a second stage in an educational plan. And second,

---

[60] Including Glasgow High School, for which however statistics are imperfect: Harvey and Sellar did not visit it because there was a separate report on Glasgow.

[61] i.e. salaried masters; there may also have been 'visiting' masters charging their own fees.

[62] *Argyll Comm. 3rd Rep.*, Vol. I, pp. lxxvi-lxxviii, 248-64. Both this and Fearon's report were published in 1868, but the inquiries were carried out in 1866/7, and 1866 has been used as the reference date.

Table 4.6

Pupils in secondary schools, 1866

	Boys	Girls
Age under 8	1,317	686
8 to 11	3,488	1,600
12 to 15	3,380	1,379
16 and over	552	199
Total pupils in actual attendance	8,737	3,864
Total pupils on school rolls	9,756	4,323
add Glasgow High School	800	
Total (boys)	10,556	
Total (boys and girls)	14,879	

there were very few pupils over fifteen—in most schools practically none, for the figures are swollen by a few untypical schools, notably Edinburgh Academy.

The presence of girls in public secondary schools was a notable feature of Scottish practice, though it had limitations. In the large towns, there was an abundance of private schools, and no girls were admitted to Edinburgh High School or Academy, Glasgow High School or Academy, or Aberdeen Grammar School. It was generally thought that the girls in burgh schools came from a lower social class than the boys, since the upper middle class disliked mixed education, and some schools responded to this feeling by segregating the sexes. Harvey and Sellar commended the system at Inverness Academy, where the girls were taught the same subjects as the boys by the same teachers, but in a separate building; Fearon, and the full Argyll commission, thought this excessively cautious.[63] But the trend was towards segregation: the Ewart Institute at Newton Stewart, founded in 1863 by the Liverpool merchant William Ewart to give 'a superior education to the children of the middle classes', had a separate 'Ladies' Department' under a 'lady superintendent'. The new Fraserburgh Academy followed suit in 1870, and in the 1870s Sir David Baxter left money to found a separate girls' school at Cupar.[64]

[63] Ibid., pp. xiv, 84-6; *Schools Inquiry Comm.*, Vol. VI, pp. 57-8.
[64] *Colebrooke Comm. 2nd Rep.*, pp. 469, 541-3, and cf. *Colebrooke Comm. Appendix to 3rd Rep.*, Vol. I, pp. 424-5.

The Schools Inquiry Commission worked out a scheme for three 'grades' of secondary education distinguished by their leaving age and clientele, and by these standards nearly all the Scottish schools were of the second grade. Observers agreed that the upper class had long since ceased to use the burgh schools, and by the 1860s the attraction of the English Public Schools for the richer professional and business class was well established. Harvey and Sellar thus concluded that the burgh schools were 'middle-class' in a very precise sense: 'they are almost exclusively supplied from the middle ranks, including in that general description, tradesmen and shopkeepers at the one end, and professional men and the less wealthy landed proprietors at the other, but having few or no representatives of the lowest or highest classes on their benches'. Fortunately the middle class 'is so large, and contains so many grades, that the schools can still boast to represent the great body of the community, and to be really national institutions'. Fearon concluded, on much the same lines, that 'Scotch burgh schools, while they are essentially and emphatically schools of the middle class, are yet so managed that the poorer class is not shut out from them, but shares to some extent the benefit of their influence.'[65]

These generalizations were confirmed both by the brief descriptions of each school's social recruitment and by Fearon's more detailed investigations. At Ayr Academy, for example, Harvey and Sellar found that the pupils 'belong to the usual classes attending a burgh school or academy where the fees exclude the lower classes, while the mixed education of boys and girls, and the greater facilities now-a-days of sending children to a distance, have their effect in keeping the very highest from the school. Bank agents, lawyers, ministers, merchants, shopkeepers, we found all represented in the same class, but no children of labourers, as in our parish schools'. This was a typical mixture, slightly superior to that at Forres, where 'the scholars are for the most part the sons and daughters of bankers, farmers, shopkeepers, tradesmen, and labourers of the more comfortable class'. The degree to which the clientele

---

[65] *Argyll Comm. 3rd Rep.*, Vol. I, pp. 26-7, and cf. 83-4; *Schools Inquiry Comm.*, Vol. VI, p. 23.

extended downward into the working class depended on the level of fees and local circumstances—many of the small one-man schools hardly differed from parish schools. Thus while at Kirkcudbright, 'The boys and girls attending the school belong exclusively to the upper and middle classes', at Lanark an unusually large number of bursaries brought in working-class boys; 'Among the other scholars are found the usual classes attending a burgh or grammar school—sons of shopkeepers, with a few children of professional people.' At Airdrie, where Glasgow was close enough to drain away those with higher ambitions, 'The pupils represent the ordinary classes of a mining town and neighbourhood,—shopkeepers, foremen, superior labourers, and a sprinkling of professional men.' And at Port Glasgow, the small burgh school was predominantly lower middle class, because the better-off used the superior facilities of Greenock; Port Glasgow 'serves as a school for those who do not wish their children to mix with the ordinary classes in a cheap school, and who are yet either unable or unwilling to send them to Greenock'.[66]

It was from the more select schools—typical of those which achieved higher class status in 1872—that Fearon collected the information about social backgrounds which is presented in Tables 4.7 and 4.8 (for Hamilton there are additional data from Harvey and Sellar); the social classifications used are those of Fearon himself, and some of the figures are evidently approximate.[67]

These tables confirm that the schools were used chiefly by the professional and commercial classes, and that the only significant group from lower down the social scale were the small shopkeepers (and perhaps clerks). Labourers and even artisans were practically unrepresented, except at Aberdeen and Inverness High School, where there was the special pheno-menon of country boys preparing for the university: Inverness High School was not a burgh school, but a Free Church institu-tion to which boys went on scholarships from all over the

---

[66] *Argyll Comm. 3rd Rep.*, Vol. II, pp. 6, 113, 137, 164, 173, 178, 266.

[67] Ibid., p. 259 for Hamilton, and *Schools Inquiry Comm.*, Vol. VI, pp. 73 (Aberdeen), 93 (Ayr), 111 (Edinburgh), 126 (Glasgow), 138 (Hamilton), 151 (Inverness Academy), 159 (Dumfries), 166 (Perth), 206 (Inverness High School). Except at Edinburgh, the figures appear to cover all ages and where applicable both sexes.

Table 4.7

Parental occupations of pupils in eight secondary schools, 1866

	Aberdeen Grammar School	Ayr Academy	Dumfries Academy
Landed proprietors	9 (2·9%)	8 (2·1%)	6 (2%)
Professional men	69 (22·4)	64 (16·4)	30 (10)
1st-class merchants, wholesale traders, etc.	52 (16·9)	30 (7·6)	30 (10)
Large farmers, superior employees, managers, etc.	42 (13·6)	71 (18·2)	60 (20)
2nd-class merchants, superior retail traders	38 (12·3)	112 (28·7)	150 (50)
Inferior retail traders, small farmers, clerks	47 (15·3)	80 (20·5)	15 (5)
Artisans, labourers, mechanics	51 (16·6)	25 (6·4)	9 (3)
TOTAL Nos.	308	390	300

Edinburgh High School	Glasgow High School	Inverness Academy	Inverness High School	Perth Academy
4 (7·1%)	20 (2·5%)	0	0	10 (3·1%)
17 (30·4)	50 (6·3)	41 (17·3%)	26 (7·3%)	100 (31·3)
7 (12·5)	200 (25)	16 (6·8)	0	30 (9·4)
—†	150 (18·8)	64 (27)	—†	—†
20 (35·7)	340 (42·5)	56 (23·6)	100 (28·1)	100 (31·3)
8 (14·3)	40 (5)	52 (21·9)	150 (42·1)	80 (25)
0	0	8 (3·3)	80 (22·5)	0
56*	800	237	356	320

* Figures for one class only
† Category not used: possibly merged with others

Table 4.8

Parental occupations of pupils in Hamilton Academy, 1866

(A) Fearon's Report

	Boys	Girls	Total	as %
Landed proprietors	4	3	7	2.8
Merchants, professional men	17	9	26	10.3
Tradesmen, farmers, shop-keepers	93	88	181	71.8
Clerks	13	8	21	8.3
Labourers	9	8	17	6.8
TOTAL	136	116	252	

(B) Harvey and Sellar's Report

	Total	as %
Landed proprietors	4	1.4
Professional classes	14	4.9
Coalmasters	8	2.8
Shopkeepers	85	29.7
Master tradesmen	77	26.9
Agents, clerks, travellers	32	11.2
Farmers	32	11.2
Working men, artisans	22	7.7
Others, without occupations	12	4.2
TOTAL	286	

Highlands. Otherwise both peer and peasant were conspicuous by their absence, and Fearon thought that most of the 'landed proprietors' were bourgeois with small landed investments rather than country gentlemen.[68]

In medium-sized and smaller towns, the burgh school served the whole of the local middle-class community. But in Glasgow and Edinburgh the High Schools faced strong competition from the Academies and from a profusion of private schools, some idea of which can be gained from the Argyll commission's special report on Glasgow. In the Blythswood district alone (the fashionable residential quarter) there were twenty-two 'private adventure' schools; some were girls' schools 'exclusively for the upper and middle classes', but others were mixed.

[68] Ibid., p. 22.

Among the secondary schools in Glasgow were one connected with the Andersonian University, which specialized in modern subjects, and Scotland's leading Catholic school, the Jesuits' St. Aloysius College, which 'will bear comparison with the High School or the Academy. The boys either complete their education at it, and pass from it at once into active life, or, if they wish to carry their education further, they go, it may be, to Stoneyhurst [*sic*], or some other Catholic institution.'[69] For the Catholic bourgeoisie of more limited means, the Marists had recently established St. Mungo's Academy.

Many of the boys' private schools in Scotland were mainly for boarders. Harvey and Sellar described a number of these, but unfortunately concealed their names. The annual cost varied between £55 and £125; they were used by those with a special need for boarding like officers, residents abroad, widows, and country gentlemen, but also by those who 'estimate highly the advantages to be gained at a Boarding school in the way of cultivation and polish, and who believe that better physical development and training, more self-reliance and manliness of character, can be got in them than from an exclusively home education'. These schools laid much stress on games and character training, but were not competing intellectually with the best burgh schools.[70] Boarding schools never became fully domesticated in Scotland, and those who wanted cultivation and polish preferred it without a Scottish accent. England offered a far greater variety of boarding education, and a level of teaching which gave direct access for those who wanted it to the English universities.

In Scotland an education of good quality was available in public day schools which were a part of the local community. This was of great potential significance for educational opportunity, but in practice the fees might form an insuperable barrier for the poor. It is not easy to estimate their level, because the custom was to pay for each subject separately, and because they rose steeply according to the year of study. Crude averages can be obtained by dividing a school's fee income by the number of pupils; Harvey and Sellar arrived at

[69] *Argyll Comm. Rep. on Glasgow*, pp. 9, 41, 82.
[70] *Argyll Comm. 3rd Rep.*, Vol. I, pp. 176-9.

an average annual fee of £3.10 by this method. Fearon attempted, more realistically, to work out typical fees for students taking a full secondary curriculum, and thought the fees higher than in comparable schools in England, which were often supported by endowments. Table 4.9 shows the average fees, and Fearon's calculations where they are available, for schools which became higher class schools after 1872. Also shown are the averages in 1877, and the range of fees in those schools which had by then adopted a consolidated fee scheme; the figures tend to substantiate the view that the restrictions of higher class status forced schools to raise their fees.[71]

Some of the smaller schools were undoubtedly cheap: in 1866 twenty out of fifty-five burgh schools had an average fee under £1 p.a., and fourteen in the range £1-2. These were comparable with the parish schools, where the usual fee for an education including the classics seems at this time to have been around 5s. 0d. a quarter, and such fees were within the reach of artisans and shopkeepers. On the other hand, the middle-class parent had to contemplate a payment of £10 or more for the higher classical forms, to which might have to be added the expense of lodgings, estimated by Fearon at £25-40 in provincial towns.[72] It is not surprising that farmers and ministers used the local school when they could, and when the time came to send a boy away from home it made sense to send him straight to the university, where the fees were hardly more than in a burgh school (usually three guineas a class, or about £10 for a full curriculum), but where the teaching was given by professors and where every year was a step on the road to a useful qualification; from the student's point of view, the status and freedom from discipline also made university life more attractive than staying on at school. Moreover, far more bursaries were offered for the universities than for secondary schools, few of which had any at all.[73] Thus the

---

[71] Ibid., pp. 75, 256-7; *Schools Inquiry Comm.*, Vol. VI, p. 176; figures for 1877 in *Board of Education. 5th Rep.*, Appendix VIII. By contrast, in public schools after 1872, the maximum fee was 9d. per week (under £2 p.a.).

[72] *Schools Inquiry Comm.*, Vol. VI, p. 175.

[73] See details in *Argyll Comm. 3rd Rep.*, Vol. I, pp. 62-6, 248-9. There were only 186 bursaries in burgh schools, concentrated in 9 schools.

Table 4.9

Annual fees in selected secondary schools

	1866 Average	1866 Range for full secondary curriculum	1877 Average	1877 Range where consolidated fee charged
	£	£	£	£
Aberdeen Grammar School	4·19	4·90-9·10	4·96	-
Arbroath High School	2·24	-	4·00	-
Ayr Academy	3·64	5·10-13·80	5·74	1·50-11·00
Dumfries Academy	2·82	7·00-10·00	2·99	-
Dunfermline Grammar School	2·08	-	0·82	4·00
Edinburgh High School	10·15	8·20-19·90	11·60	11·00-15·00
Elgin Academy	1·69	-	3·86	-
Glasgow High School	5·59	12·63-18·73	9·21	-
Hamilton Academy	1·26	1·73-4·15	5·36	5·00-9·00
Inverness Academy	5·81	2·50-10·50	-	-
Irvine Academy	2·88	-	3·85	2·50-7·00
Leith High School	4·29	-	4·56	2·00-10·00
Montrose Academy	3·44	-	3·57	-
Paisley Grammar School	2·29	-	6·51	1·60-10·70
Perth Academy	4·36	15·00-18·00	5·92	-
Stirling High School	1·95	5·00-8·00	3·41	-

burgh schools, while able through relatively low fees at the bottom of the scale to perform a useful service to their own town, found it difficult to compete at the higher classical level, and did not draw very widely on the surrounding countryside.

Fearon thought that Scottish parents willingly paid high fees because the schools gave them what they wanted—this responsiveness to local opinion he saw as the main lesson to be learnt from the Scottish example: the

popularity of the schools with the poorer as well as the richer classes in Scotland depends on the fact of their being *day schools*; on the fact of their having (generally) no forced curriculum, but allowing each parent to choose his own subjects of instruction; on the care with which a due share of honour and attention is given to science and modern subjects, as well as to the classics; and on the impartial energy and active sense of responsibility to all parents, which is created in the masters by the want of endowments and their dependence on fees.[74]

Nearly all the burgh schools allowed parents a free choice of subjects, though they often had a recommended curriculum, sometimes divided into classical and modern 'sides', which parents were encouraged to choose, and for which a consolidated fee might be payable. This free choice reveals what the preferences of parents really were: in the 58 schools for which Harvey and Sellar collected this information, which had 14,079 scholars on the roll, the only practically universal subject was 'English', a term which covered the teaching of history and geography as well as grammar, composition and literature. The full figures are in Table 4.10.[75]

The most striking feature of this table is the almost complete neglect of science, despite the strong mathematical tradition in Scotland. It is remarkable, and in the long run no doubt a source of national weakness, that in one of the most industrialized countries in the world the middle classes generally lacked any training in the natural sciences: the Natural Phil-

---

[74] *Schools Inquiry Comm.*, Vol. VI, pp. 22-3.
[75] *Argyll Comm. 3rd Rep.*, Vol. I, pp. 254-5, 259. Excludes Glasgow High School. Unfortunately sex and age-group are not distinguished. Cf. comments in J. Grant, *History of the burgh and parish schools of Scotland. ... Burgh Schools* (1876), pp. 352-3, 402-3.

Table 4.10

Subjects studied in secondary schools, 1866

	No. of pupils	No. of schools in which taught
English	12,976	58
Writing	10,535	57
Arithmetic	10,367	57
Latin	3,529	58
French	2,682	53
Drawing	1,748	36
Mathematics	1,609	52
Music	1,227	10
Book-keeping	806	34
Greek	801	44
German	554	29
Physics	487	8
Chemistry	146	3
Natural History	124	2

osophy classes in the universities gave them their only foothold in general education, and even medical students were not expected to have studied science at school. In 1866 the only schools which taught the sciences at all seriously seem to have been Edinburgh High School (which had just overhauled its syllabus in an attempt to put up numbers), Dundee High School, Perth Academy, Dollar Institution (which had a specialized line in preparing for the Indian engineering service), and Edinburgh Institution, a private school noted for its scientific teaching.[76]

The table does little to support the notion that nineteenth-century secondary schools were obsessed by the classics. Probably most boys took Latin at some stage, but only at a few schools like Edinburgh High and Aberdeen Grammar was the curriculum centred on it as a compulsory subject. From the university point of view, the neglect of the classics was seen as a weakness, and the Board of Education complained in 1876 that even the higher class schools 'are not as yet distinctively secondary schools; they are not places of preparation for the Universities, but are rather engaged in

[76] *Argyll Comm. 3rd Rep.*, Vol. II, pp. 109, 207-10.

imparting to the greater part of their pupils what is considered to be a plain, useful education to prepare them for commercial or other practical life'.[77] From the schools' own point of view, adaptation to the needs of commerce was the secret of success. The subject called 'writing' taught the skills needed in offices, and French and German—still completely neglected by the universities—were taught for their commercial usefulness. Book-keeping was a popular subject, and attracted more students than Greek. 'This feature in Scottish education is worth remarking,' observed Harvey and Sellar, 'as indicating the extent to which the utilitarian idea of education is carried out.'[78] Whatever views the teachers may have cherished about the cultural value of the classics, it seems that parents took a more hard-headed line: they

look upon education as a means to an immediate end. The great object is to get a lad placed in some situation in which he will gain pecuniary benefit, and keep himself at as early an age as possible. If he can do this by means of classics, as at Aberdeen, they will teach him classics; if by writing, they will teach him writing. If, along with his writing he can pick up a little Latin and a little French, so much the better, but it is not essential. This is the view of education which is adopted by parents of the middle class in Scotland; and those subjects of instruction which conduce to this end are most appreciated by them.[79]

Although the burgh schools were well enough equipped to prepare boys for the university, since the masters were commonly university men, the commercial bias of the schools made this a minority interest. This comes out very clearly from Harvey and Sellar's reports on the careers adopted by pupils in individual schools. Typical comments are, 'Few of these scholars go to any university; only four have gone during the last five years. The majority leave school for writers' and bankers' offices' (Forres). Or, 'Very few go to any university. During the last five years, the rector says that 8 have gone; but the majority enter bankers' and solicitors' offices, or take to mercantile life' (Inverness Academy). Or,

[77] *Board of Education. 3rd Rep.*, p. xxii.
[78] *Argyll Comm. 3rd Rep.*, Vol. I, p. 125.
[79] Ibid., p. 116. Cf. *Schools Inquiry Comm.*, Vol. VI, p. 16.

with a more industrial slant, 'Not more than one or two at most leave school each year for Glasgow or any other college. The boys go mostly to mercantile pursuits, engineers' shops, shipbuilding yards, etc.' (Renfrew, Blythswood Testimonial). A few schools were different—the Madras College at St. Andrews sent about thirteen boys a year to the neighbouring university, helped by linked bursaries—but the successful burgh school was one which sent about three or four.[80] The rector of Ayr Academy explained some of the difficulties to the 1876 universities commission. He estimated that not more than one in ten of his pupils went to the university or reached his highest form. The majority left at 14-15, after only four years of the six-year curriculum, for 'Fifteen is the age at which any business man in Glasgow will tell you he prefers to get a boy into his office.' At Ayr, 'business is the thing. We are very near Glasgow, which swallows up four-fifths of our young men, and could take the whole of them if we would give them.' Glasgow High School had the same problem with early leaving, and some boys preferred to take jobs in offices and combine that with university attendance rather than staying on at school.[81] In prosperous urban areas, the professional careers to which the universities led could look unattractive compared with the openings in business—a factor often adduced by the parochial schoolmasters in 1879 to explain the declining popularity of classics. Among the burgh schools where few or none were said to go to the university were Kilmarnock, Dunfermline, Hamilton, and Forfar, where 'Since the introduction of machine instead of handloom weaving, there has been an increased demand for well-educated boys to keep the books and carry on the office work. The result is, that almost none care to go to the universities. Not one has gone from this school within the last five years.'[82]

From which classes did the boys come who stayed on to study the classics and prepare for the university? Some of

[80] *Argyll Comm. 3rd Rep.*, Vol. II, pp. 6, 70, 83, 121, 295. There is much evidence of the same kind in *Colebrooke Comm. 2nd Rep.*

[81] *R. Comm. Univ. Ev.*, Part I, pp. 683-7 (Ayr), and Part II, pp. 447, 453 (Glasgow).

[82] *Argyll Comm. 3rd Rep.*, Vol. II, p. 32; cf. case of Brechin in *Colebrooke Comm. 2nd Rep.*, p. 368.

them, no doubt, were the sons of professional men aiming to become lawyers or doctors themselves, but there are also indications that the university was seen particularly as an outlet for the less well-off. At Paisley, for example, declining interest in the universities was explained partly by the attractions of business, but partly by 'the fact that the boys in the school belong to the upper middle classes. The class of boys who do go to College from Paisley ... belong mostly to the lower middle ranks', and preferred another school which had lower fees and access to university bursaries.[83] At Kirkcaldy, it was reported that about thirty had gone to the university in the last twenty years. 'Of those thirty, only two belonged to the middle class; these were the sons of a banker and of a Free Church minister. The other twenty-eight belonged to the humbler classes, and were induced to go to the University by the personal influence of the teacher. The other scholars attending the school go very early to offices and factories.'[84] The burgh schools, one may conclude, were drawing heavily on the commercial middle class for their pupils, and were returning most of them to the same economic sector. This was a world where university education had little relevance, where early experience and learning on the job, not paper qualifications, were what employers valued. The universities were oriented to the professions: the professional classes themselves used the larger burgh schools or other schools of superior status, leaving the small burgh schools to provide, in much the same way as the parish schools, for a trickle of recruits to the professions from the more humble social classes.[85]

Harvey and Sellar, as part of their attempt to refute the charge that the universities were entrenching on the secondary schools, collected data which showed that the two sorts of institution drew on different segments of the community. They published details of the fathers' occupations of two samples of students—

[83] *Argyll Comm. 3rd Rep.*, Vol. II, p. 168. The other school was Neilson's Institution.
[84] Ibid., p. 94.
[85] Note the distinction drawn by the Argyll commission when classifying the school origins of students between 'academies, grammar schools and colleges' and ordinary 'burgh schools' (above, Table 4.1).

one of 882 students in certain arts classes in all four universities (covering about a quarter of total student numbers), and one of 1,212 students who had passed through the Greek class at Edinburgh in the six academic years between 1860 and 1866. The results of this inquiry are shown in Table 4.11.[86] The socio-occupational categories used are based on those in the original report, which as was usual in the nineteenth century were related to types of occupation rather than income level. Thus 'farmers' might be large or small, rich or poor, while the category of 'merchants' was ambiguous because it applied at the time both to the commercial élite of the towns and to country shopkeepers.

These figures show without doubt that the universities were serving a wide range of the community. About a third of the students came from the professional classes, and the sons of ministers alone formed 13 per cent of the general sample and 18 per cent of the Edinburgh one. If the 'commercial and industrial' group are added, and some of the farmers, perhaps half of the total came from the solidly prosperous bourgeoisie, with some not unexpected variations between the universities: farmers were better represented at Aberdeen and businessmen at Glasgow, while the social tone was higher all round at St. Andrews. At the other end of the scale, nearly a quarter of the students may be classified as working class, though few of them came from the really poor. In the general sample, for example, there were thirteen miners, thirteen labourers, three shepherds, two crofters, and two farm servants. There were twelve sons of gardeners and four of coachmen, perhaps benefiting from the benevolence of rich employers. But the overwhelming mass of working-class students were the sons of artisans and skilled workers, with a bias towards the more traditional trades. The largest categories were carpenters and joiners (21), boot and

---

[86] *Argyll Comm. 3rd Rep.*, Vol. I, pp. 153-6, 235-42. The general inquiry covered the Latin, Greek, and Mathematics classes, except at Aberdeen, where it was confined to the Junior Latin and Greek classes. The original data include both the actual occupations and a classification into social categories which is the basis of my own: but some individuals have been reclassified, and an arbitrary correction made of one inconsistency. For comparable figures for later years, and for a note on the classification of occupations, see Tables 8. 7-8 below.

Table 4.11

Parental occupations of Arts students in universities

	Edinburgh 1860-6	General, 1866				
		Ab.	Edin.	Glas.	St. A.	TOTAL
Professional group:						
Proprietors, gentlemen	29	-	7	4	3	14
Ministers	213	14	46	50	7	117
Doctors	36	8	8	11	3	30
Lawyers	72	3	20	15	6	44
Teachers	75	7	15	17	10	49
Officers, officials	39	2	11	9	3	25
Other professional	10	-	4	6	-	10
Total professional	474 (39·1%)	34 (28·8%)	111 (35·1%)	112 (29·9%)	32 (43·2%)	289 (32·8%)
Commercial and industrial group:						
Bankers, etc.	21	-	8	7	-	15
Manufacturers, etc.	35	3	5	15	4	27
Large traders	-	-	-	2	1	3
'Merchants'	79	8	34	49	3	94
Managers, agents	14	-	1	2	1	4
Total commercial and industrial	149 (12·3%)	11 (9·3%)	48 (15·2%)	75 (20·1%)	9 (12·2%)	143 (16·2%)

Agricultural group:						
Farmers	175	29	40	50	8	127
Crofters, small farmers	2	2	–	–	–	2
Factors, etc.	17	3	2	–	–	5
Total agricultural	194 (16·0%)	34 (28·8%)	42 (13·3%)	50 (13·4%)	8 (10·8%)	134 (15·2%)
Intermediate group:						
Small business	25	4	5	4	–	13
Shopkeepers	67	3	12	13	1	29
Clerks, minor officials	16	1	7	6	–	14
Total intermediate	108 (8·9%)	8 (6·8%)	24 (7·6%)	23 (6·1%)	1 (1·4%)	56 (6·3%)
Working-class group:						
Artisans, skilled workers	201	12	58	65	9	144
Policemen, etc.	4	1	–	2	–	3
Labourers, farm servants	47	4	10	7	1	22
Miners	–	–	4	9	–	13
Domestic servants, gardeners	35	3	7	7	1	18
Total working-class	287 (23·7%)	20 (17·0%)	79 (25·0%)	90 (24·1%)	11 (14·9%)	200 (22·7%)
Not given, uncertain	11	11	12	24	13	60
TOTAL	1,212	118	316	374	74	882

shoemakers (18) and masons (14), though modern industry was represented by eleven 'practical engineers' and ten 'weavers and warpers'. Printers and such building tradesmen as painters, plasterers, and plumbers were represented by only a handful of students. Thus most working-class students were drawn from the very top stratum of their class, while neither the rural poor, nor the majority of factory workers, nor the unskilled workers of the towns, had more than a token representation.

In percentage terms working-class representation in the universities was significant, but the working class was of course far larger than the middle class. The 117 sons of ministers were drawn from an occupational group of 4,205, while the 46,190 miners in Scotland provided 13 students, which meant that a minister's son was about a hundred times as likely to go to the university as a miner's. These disparities are illustrated by Table 4.12 which shows, for occupations which can be distinguished with sufficient precision, 'opportunity

Table 4.12

Relative representation in universities of selected occupations

Ministers	30.9
Lawyers	22.7
Doctors	18.9
Teachers	8.6
Farmers	2.9
Gardeners	1.2
Clerks	1.1
Shoemakers	0.82
Coachmen	0.80
Carpenters and joiners	0.76
Masons	0.69
Blacksmiths	0.51
Printers	0.51
Seamen	0.44
Shepherds	0.40
Miners	0.31
Labourers	0.12
Farm servants	0.06
Fishermen	0.04

ratios' indicating the relative chances of access to university education. These disparities existed not only between middle class and working class, but within the working class itself, for the sons of artisans had five or six times the chances of the sons of labourers.[87] Artisans had perhaps inherited the traditional respect for learning of their predecessors, and only they were really capable of the long-term planning and saving necessary to contemplate pushing a clever boy on to the universities or the professions. Even so, this must have been the exception rather than the rule, and recent work by R. Q. Gray on the 'working-class aristocracy' of Edinburgh does not suggest that educational advance figured largely among their values.[88] This was true *a fortiori* of the poor, and Sellar was surely deluding himself when he wrote that the universities 'are, in the widest sense of the word, national, and the old theory of Scottish education is carried out by means of them. Their doors are open to the wealthiest of the community and the poorest, even to the beggars. Go into any Scottish family in the country, a shepherd's, or a gardener's, or a village shoemaker's, and the chances are that some member of the family has had a university education.'[89]

Harvey and Sellar's data do not tell us about the school origins of the different social groups, but they do link occupation and age in the case of the Edinburgh sample, and some inferences can be drawn from this information. The age distribution for selected occupational groups, and for the two samples as a whole, is shown in Table 4.13.[90] This table does not show the age of *entry*, since it covers students in their first and second years, but it suggests that, although the presence of older men was very significant, the usual age of

---

[87] Occupational figures (males, all ages) from *Eighth Decennial Census of the Population of Scotland taken 3d April 1871*, Vol. II (PP1873, lxxiii), Table XIV. The figures in this table, which are indicative only of *relative* chances of access, are obtained by dividing the percentage of a group in the 1866 students sample by its percentage in the employed population. Labourers and farm servants could be grouped differently, but the result would be similar.

[88] R. Q. Gray, *The labour aristocracy in Victorian Edinburgh* (Oxford, 1976).

[89] *Fraser's Magazine*, lxxviii (1868), p. 342.

[90] Same source as for Table 4.11, but here the original social classifications are retained, so there are some disparities in the sub-totals.

Table 4.13

Ages of students in certain Arts classes (% by columns)

| Age | Edinburgh 1860-66: Selected groups | | | | | | | | Edinburgh 1860-6 | General 1866 |
	Ministers	Teachers	Other Professional	Commercial	Farmers	Shopkeepers	Artisans	Labourers	TOTAL	TOTAL
13	1·0	3·0	-	0·7	-	-	-	-	0·4	-
14	6·0	3·0	2·3	2·8	0·6	-	1·5	-	2·1	1·1
15	18·1	10·8	14·7	11·2	5·1	6·0	3·9	-	8·7	6·0
16	27·1	26·2	28·8	14·7	13·1	11·9	4·9	6·9	16·8	14·9
17	24·1	16·9	28·2	16·1	12·6	11·9	5·3	3·4	15·8	16·3
18	13·6	9·2	12·4	17·5	9·7	10·4	8·7	20·7	12·3	13·2
19	7·5	6·2	6·8	11·2	12·6	13·4	12·6	13·8	10·4	9·9
20	1·5	7·7	3·4	6·3	10·3	10·4	14·1	6·9	7·7	7·5
21	0·5	1·5	1·7	4·2	8·6	4·5	12·1	6·9	5·9	7·6
22	0·5	1·5	0·6	5·6	4·6	4·5	11·7	3·4	4·6	7·0
23	-	3·0	1·7	3·5	6·9	10·4	9·2	6·9	4·8	4·2
24	-	3·0	0·6	1·4	4·0	7·5	5·8	-	3·2	4·4
25 and over	-	7·7	2·8	4·9	12·0	9·0	10·2	30·9	7·3	7·9
No. of cases	199	65	177	143	175	67	206	29	1,212	882

entry was around sixteen. The third column, which refers to professional parents with the exception of ministers and school-teachers, shows the 'normal' pattern likely to be followed by boys coming from secondary schools, with comparatively few younger or older students. The ministers and teachers, however, were likely to send their sons rather earlier, and they accounted for over half of the thirteen and fourteen-year-olds in the sample. It was these parents who found it most convenient to use the parish schools: they were both the most rural and the least well-off part of the professional class, and were in a position to coach their sons personally for university entry while keeping them at home. They were also well placed for obtaining university bursaries; the absence of older students among the sons of ministers is particularly marked, and suggests that among sons of the manse little talent was left unexploited.

Among the commercial middle class, farmers, and shop-keepers, the pattern of entry was more diffuse, with a significant amount of adult attendance. But this feature was particularly striking among the sons of artisans—the median age of those in the sample was twenty, and evidently few went direct from school. Experience of employment between school and university must have been common for some students in most social groups, but for those of working-class origin it was the norm. Sometimes, perhaps, they studied privately and attended evening classes while working in an office or at a trade, but often the work must have been teaching, for (as we have already seen in the case of Glasgow) the pupil-teacher system and the training colleges were an important avenue of social mobility. The training colleges drew mainly on the upper working and lower middle classes—Table 4.14 gives some figures for the Free Church college at Edinburgh in the 1860s[91]— and the presence of these colleges in Edinburgh and Glasgow perhaps explains the high concentration there of students from both the artisan and the shopkeeping groups.

The evidence on ages suggests, therefore, that the importance of the parish schools for the democratic character of the universities should not be exaggerated. They sent on a handful

[91] *Argyll Comm. Appendix to 1st Rep.*, p. 126.

Table 4.14

Parental occupations of students at Edinburgh Free Church Normal School, 1866

	Men %	Women %
Labourers, artisans, etc.	56	20
Small farmers	16	16
'In places of trust, clerks, etc.'	18	24
'Shopkeepers—generally of a higher class in case of females'	10	40

of rural labourers and artisans, but they were doing little for the industrial working class, and their main importance was for the rural middle class. Most men of working-class origin came to the university as adults, and for them it was the accessibility of the universities, the absence of an entrance examination, and the availability of the remedial teaching of the junior classes, which mattered more than the direct link between parish schools and universities. Hence the importance of this issue in the debates on university reform, and hence too the desire of the universities to establish a link with the training colleges, which were potentially a significant new source of recruits. An entrance examination was eventually to be established, and the secondary schools were to become the normal gateway to the universities. Whether this actually diminished opportunity for the working class depended on the form which changes took, for it could be argued that the presence of so many older students on the university benches only illustrated the inefficiency and capriciousness of the Scottish arrangements for discovering and promoting talent. Why should teachers have to struggle to improve their qualifications in adult life, instead of being able to take a degree before entering their profession? Why should men with the talent to escape the working class have to teach themselves Latin in order to reach the university, instead of being given scholarships to go to secondary schools at the proper age? These questions were beginning to be asked by reformers.

What conclusions can be drawn from the data presented in this chapter about educational opportunity and social mobility? They do not tell us directly, of course, about social mobility, but only about access to secondary education and universities. Nevertheless it is clear that the universities were promoting social mobility, for Table 4.11 suggests that only about half of the students' fathers were likely to have had a university education themselves, and successful completion of a university course opened the way to careers in the ministry, teaching, or medicine—though law presented higher social and financial barriers. Scotland had more university places than other countries—one per thousand population, according to the Argyll commission, compared with 1:2,600 in Germany and 1:5,800 in England[92]—and if this led to the production of more qualified men than Scotland could absorb, Scots were notorious for their willingness to seek posts in England or abroad.

The universities were specifically linked with training for the professions. Today we are accustomed to think of educational qualifications as the passport to middle-class careers in general, but in the nineteenth century that was not so. The dominance of formal degrees and diplomas advanced only gradually, and it had hardly affected the world of industry and commerce. Inter-generational social mobility through education was only one possible type of mobility, and this study can tell us little about the mobility which occurred through men improving their positions in the course of a career, or about the field of opportunity provided by business. It was with that field that the burgh schools were especially linked, since they sent most of their pupils into bankers', merchants' and lawyers' offices. Posts of this kind seem to have been surprisingly numerous even in small towns, but since this milieu has been little studied by historians we cannot say whether these boys would be clerks all their lives or work their way up to the top. What we do know is that industrial and commercial employers insisted on entry at an early age; Glasgow manufacturers and merchants might

---

[92] *Argyll Comm. 3rd Rep.*, Vol. I, p. ix. But one should remember that in England law and medicine were taught largely outside the universities, and that the Scottish universities were performing some 'secondary' functions. The commission also gave comparative figures for secondary school places, but these should not be relied on—the calculation has various deficiencies.

send their own sons to the university, but they did not think of recruiting their personnel there.

It may be useful to distinguish two cycles of social promotion and social reproduction through education—one with an academic, rural, professional bias, the other more urban and commercial. Universities and parish schools belonged to the former, traditional burgh schools to the latter. The established middle class took it for granted that their sons must be given a secondary education, but the path after that depended on vocational considerations. Apart from commerce, important careers like the army, engineering, and most branches of the public service were entered directly after secondary education; the universities were used only when a 'learned' profession was the aim, for to attend them merely for the sake of 'liberal culture' was a luxury which few could afford.

Below this social level, choice was of course much more limited. The rural 'lad of parts', picked out by his schoolmaster or minister for intellectual ability, would naturally be steered towards the academic cycle, to end up as a minister or schoolmaster himself, while his urban equivalent was perhaps more likely to seek an outlet for special ability in the business world, or (in later years) to make use of evening classes and technical colleges. The urban masses lacked the intermittent leisure of agricultural life, which had traditionally given young men a chance to take up an interrupted education; but if their inclinations lay in an academic direction they might make use of the pupil-teacher and training college system, which in the 1860s was still cut off from university influence. The importance of elementary teaching as a channel of social mobility should not be underestimated, although the occupation was one with only modest pay and status.[93]

While the significance of the parish schools for educational opportunity may have been overestimated, their mere existence had the important effect of delaying the introduction of an entrance examination and keeping alive the junior classes, which in turn made it easy for men to enter the universities in adult

---

[93] One beneficiary of the pupil-teacher system (in a rural context) was Ramsay MacDonald: see his reminiscences in W. Barclay, *The schools and schoolmasters of Banffshire* (Banff, 1925), pp. 306-8. This book is an extended panegyric of the parochial tradition.

life. Some Latin was needed for this, but the classics did not become, as they did in many countries, a mark of bourgeois status and a socio-educational barrier which fenced off the secondary schools and the universities to which they alone led. Moreover, the survival of the parish schools meant the survival of the democratic myth, and of the widely accepted view that the state was 'bound to make it possible for all who are under its government to obtain such an education as will enable them to reach that position in life for which their character and talents may fit them'.[94] According to Playfair, 'It is less the number of those who learn higher subjects, though that is large; less the number of those who struggle upwards from the small rooms of the parish school to the wider halls of the University, that produces the character of Scotchmen; but it is more the fact that the possibility of advancement is within the reach of every peasant and artizan in the kingdom.'[95] The road had to exist, but it did not have to be made too easy, for ambition, hard work, and moral resolution were needed as well as talent.

This Scottish tradition of competitive individualism corresponds to what Ralph Turner has called 'contest mobility'. Turner distinguishes between 'contest' and 'sponsored' modes of social ascent through education: in the former, relatively large numbers are admitted to higher educational institutions, and the eventual selection of the élite is left to the operations of competition; in the latter, the élite controls its own recruitment more tightly, imposing early selection tailored to the number of posts available, and using schools and universities as a means of inducting the chosen few into its own values.[96] In Turner's original essay, America and England were the models in mind, but, as Andrew McPherson has pointed out, Scotland showed many features of the contest model,[97] notably the wide accessibility of the universities, the kind of competitive ethos which reached its peak in the Aberdeen bursary competition, and the

[94] *Argyll Comm. 1st Rep.*, p. 69 (Revd Dr Stevenson).
[95] *3 Hansard* ccix, HC 7 Mar. 1872, col. 1586.
[96] R. H. Turner, 'Modes of social ascent through education: sponsored and contest mobility', in A. H. Halsey & others, *Education, economy, and society* (New York, paperback edn., 1965), pp. 121-39.
[97] A. McPherson, 'Selections and survivals: a sociology of the ancient Scottish universities', in R. Brown (ed.), *Knowledge, education, and cultural change* (1973), pp. 165 ff.

emphasis of the secondary schools on intellectual and utilitarian education rather than the classical ideal or character formation. In a sense, the debate about a university entrance examination was a conflict between contest and sponsored ideals, and the same could be said of the debate, to be discussed in later chapters, between those who sought to promote opportunity by admitting an élite of 'merit' to the secondary schools, and those who wanted to revivify the parochial tradition by making secondary education an open-ended continuation of what all received in the public schools.

Soon after Fearon, two French educational officials, Jacques Demogeot and Henry Montucci, toured the Scottish schools and included a full account of them in their report on Britain. The parish schools naturally struck their attention: 'the peasant finds within his reach, in the middle of the countryside, a form of instruction which with us is the privilege of the towns'. But they did not approve of this. 'One can go too far, even in the right direction. There may be cruelty in awakening desires which it is not possible to satisfy. ... A few great names who escaped from the plough or the workshop are cited with enthusiasm; but as for those who, led astray by these rare examples, have suffered the fate of Icarus, no-one counts their number, for their name is legion.' 'Impartiality compels us to admit', they continued in a reference to the Revised Code controversy, 'that our way of seeing the matter finds hardly any partisans in Scotland. We have on our side only the Committee of the Privy Council.'[98] This view, and their fear of the professions becoming 'overcrowded', showed that Demogeot and Montucci preferred their social mobility sponsored.

They also remarked that in Scotland 'one soon perceives a singular neglect of the intermediate terrain between the university and the parish school'.[99] Any advantage which Scotland derived from the parochial tradition was outweighed by the situation in the larger towns. Attempts to transfer the parish-school tradition to an urban setting had been very limited, and most working-class children were educated in purely elementary schools, while middle-class needs were largely met by

[98] *De l'enseignement secondaire en Angleterre et en Ecosse* (Paris, 1868), pp. 407-8, 420.
[99] Ibid., p. 439.

private or proprietary schools which charged high fees. In countries like France and Germany, there were powerful state secondary schools, keeping their pupils until eighteen or nineteen and preparing them for the stringent *baccalauréat* or *Abitur*. These schools, because of their public status, were relatively cheap, and recent research shows that they were being used by the artisan and lower middle classes: in France in the 1860s, and in Prussia in the last quarter of the nineteenth century, the proportion of working-class children was higher than in the Scottish schools examined by Fearon.[100] The Scottish burgh schools perhaps had the potential to develop on continental lines. Unlike similar day schools in England, they had the advantages of antiquity, legal establishment, and public status, and they were not overshadowed by a more prestigious set of boarding schools. But in the 1860s they were poorly organized, understaffed, and underfinanced, and had few pupils over the age of fifteen. The revelations of the Argyll report therefore helped to awaken a movement for the reform of secondary education which grew rapidly after 1872.

The education of the upper middle classes in such schools as the Edinburgh Academy left little to be desired, but in a large city educational needs were many, and the commission pointed out that neither private nor public schools provided adequately the sort of semi-secondary education needed by the artisan and shopkeeping classes.[101] But perhaps the greatest need was to rescue the medium-sized burgh schools, few of which, complained Sellar, 'succeed in giving much more than a clerk's education, and very few indeed can lay even the foundation for a high order of cultivation'.[102] More secondary schools needed to be brought into the academic cycle and connected up with university culture, and this aim converged with the efforts of university reformers to attract to that culture a wider range of the middle class by bringing the curriculum into closer touch with the practical spirit of the nineteenth century.

[100] F. Ringer, *Education and society in modern Europe* (1979), p. 71 (for Germany); P. Harrigan, *Mobility, elites, and education in French society of the Second Empire* (Waterloo, 1980). p. 14. Cf. R. Anderson, 'Secondary education in mid nineteenth-century France: some social aspects', *Past & Present*, no. 53 (1971), pp. 121-46.

[101] *Argyll Comm. 3rd Rep.*, Vol. I, pp. xxii-xxiii, 172.

[102] *Fraser's Magazine*, lxxviii (1868), p. 349.

5.
THE SECONDARY EDUCATION MOVEMENT AND THE REFORM OF ENDOWMENTS

Nineteenth-century Scotland was a society dominated by the values and interests of the middle classes, and it was they who made the fundamental decisions about educational policy which shaped both the schools which they used themselves and those destined for the classes below. In the earlier part of the century, the Edinburgh legal profession had tended to dominate such national decision-making as existed, but the Inglis commission of 1858 and the Argyll commission were the last bodies to be composed, in the old-fashioned manner, of lawyers and noblemen. From the 1860s a new breed of MPs emerged who regarded themselves as educational experts, and who had close links with the kind of professional and mercantile élites which were also represented in the University General Councils. The need for legislation to reform endowments gave politicians a special importance, and the same names recur on the various commissions and committees of the century's last decades. These politicians included both Liberals like Lord Elgin, Sir Edward Colebrooke, A. C. Sellar, Charles S. Parker, and John Ramsay, and Conservatives like James A. Campbell and Lord Balfour of Burleigh.[1] Also influential in this period were various university figures like Grant, Laurie, and George Ramsay of Glasgow. University professors were still expected to be authorities on general educational questions, but the headmasters of secondary schools were also men of authority, and the successive rectors of Edinburgh High School, James Donaldson and John Marshall, took the lead in speaking for their colleagues. Several of these men—Donaldson (who became Principal of St. Andrews), Laurie, George Ramsay—

[1] Parker had been a reforming don at Oxford before entering Parliament. Both Ramsay (who sat on practically every commission of the period) and J. A. Campbell (brother of Campbell-Bannerman) had Glasgow merchant backgrounds. Colebrooke was a Lanarkshire landowner.

remained active in educational affairs into the twentieth century, although after 1885 the development of the SED under its powerful head Henry Craik tended to push both professors and politicians into the background.

In the 1870s men of this kind rallied around the cause of secondary education, and it makes sense to speak of a 'secondary education movement', which aimed at rescuing Scotland's secondary schools from neglect, accentuating their distinct character, forming them into a national system, and making them accessible to the talented poor through the selective principle of 'merit' as the basis of scholarship systems. The report of the Colebrooke commission in 1875 was a victory for these ideas, but it led only to modest legislation in 1878. In the absence of state financing for secondary education, which came in 1892, attention was concentrated on the reform of endowments, and it was not until 1882 that this task was comprehensively undertaken by a commission headed by Balfour of Burleigh.

According to the Colebrooke commission, 'Secondary Schools, in the proper sense of that term—*i.e.* schools which begin the instruction of their pupils where the Elementary Schools end, and prepare them for the higher class of Civil Service appointments and for the Universities—can scarcely be said to have any place in the educational economy of Scotland.'[2] Not all champions of secondary education defined it as restrictively as this, but all started from the belief that secondary schools ought to be clearly distinguished from others in a properly 'graded' system, and that they had a special connection with the universities. The question was closely linked with the demand for a university entrance examination, of which the secondary schoolmasters were strong supporters. As one of them put it,

Secondary or High Schools, whatever purpose besides they may serve in an Educational system, should be regarded chiefly as preparatory schools for the University; and as the object of University training is to render our knowledge strictly reasoned or scientific by showing us the principles on which it is organized, so Secondary education should

---

[2] *Colebrooke Comm. 3rd Rep.*, p. 97.

lead up to it by grouping the subjects of instruction in proper sub-ordination around some central subject, the study of which should form in itself a good mental discipline, as well as supply abundant material for the ever-growing mind of the active student.[3]

That central subject, of course, was Latin, and from the university side George Ramsay claimed, on the basis of his investigations into the school backgrounds of his students, that

a student who has been systematically trained from the commencement with a view to a higher education, has the advantage over other students throughout the whole of his university course. ... Those who consider that it is the main function of the university to reach a high standard of excellence, and that to the country at large the quality of the work done by Honour students is of more importance than the work done by Pass students, must regard the students who have received a high previous training as forming the very life-blood of the university.

The idea here was of certain academic values which the secondary school and the university shared, but to which the elementary schools and the spirit of the Code were alien. The fault of the latter lay not just in the inadequacy of 'specific subject' classics, but 'still more in a want of general knowledge, of disciplined habits of thought and work, and of that sound basis of literary culture without which the mind cannot assimilate the teaching of the university, nor receive its natural and full development'.[4]

If secondary and primary education were different in their very nature, it followed—to quote Marshall of Edinburgh—that secondary education was not 'something added on mechanically at the end of a previous education called Elementary: the two are from the first organically different ... just as a workman's two or three-roomed dwelling is not at all to be likened to a slice out of a rich man's house, but has an organic unity and completeness of its own'.[5] Secondary schools needed their own preparatory or primary departments to make a start on imparting the secondary spirit, and children in the elementary schools who showed special promise should be transferred at

---

[3] J. B. Charles (Dundee High School) in *EN*, iii. 101 (23 Feb. 1878).
[4] *Blackwood's Magazine*, cxli (1887), pp. 835-6, cxlii (1887), p. 69.
[5] J. Marshall, *Secondary education and school boards* (Edinburgh, 1886), p. 17.

the earliest possible age. Secondary headmasters were not averse to admitting talented boys from all classes; but it was a matter of simple social reality, accepted by all orthodox educationists, that the schools' principal function was to meet the diverse and legitimate needs of the middle class. 'A higher class school is not intended, generally speaking, for the poor', said Grant; 'it is intended for the middle classes in general, and for those exceptionally gifted members of the poorer classes, whose intellectual abilities entitle them to be relieved from a career of manual labour.'[6] Marshall was equally realistic.

The wealthier classes of course it is obvious pay for the secondary education of their children whether they are specially clever or not. I do not say there is a larger proportion of clever boys amongst the wealthier classes than amongst the working classes, but they pay for secondary education because they know that through money or influence they can provide a professional career for their boys, although not specially clever, by purchasing a share in a business or otherwise.[7]

For those without these advantages, it was no kindness to raise false hopes, and Marshall wanted to see a new type of school which would give a practical form of education rather than competing with schools like his own.

The skilled artisan class congregates most in towns; and the presumption is a reasonable one, that there is in the urban children, therefore, a certain latent inheritance of special technical capacity, which it would be only wise for us to try to develop. It would surely be a very improvident use of public money to sift out steadily by our educational machinery every able child from the artisan class, and give him a bookish or literary training instead. ... The majority of the children of poor parents ... if thus trained wholesale in University subjects, must inevitably go to increase the glut of moderately capable educated men, who overcrowd the lower range of all the professions, isolated from the class to which by birth they belong, and yet adding no great strength to the class of which they have become the hangers-on.

Only 'the specially capable few' should be admitted to classical education. This way of thinking, with its convenient equation

---

[6] *Transactions of the National Association for the Promotion of Social Science*, 1877, pp. 399-400.

[7] Evidence in *Balfour Comm. 1st Rep.*, p. 756.

of class situation and intellectual faculties, was to grow in influence.[8]

The principles of 'grading' and open competition on the 'principle of merit' were already being applied in the reform of English endowments, but the secondary school movement in Scotland cannot be seen simply as a piece of Anglicization. For one thing, it could be claimed with some plausibility that a graded system, with scholarships for transfer from one level to another, was precisely what Knox had envisaged in 1560; this patriotic argument was used by Blackie, Sellar, and Tulloch.[9] For another, there were few English models for the kind of middle-class day schools which were envisaged. The German *Gymnasien* had always been Blackie's model, and it was to Germany that William Geddes of Aberdeen looked when he called in 1869 for secondary education to be 'boldly taken in hand, and constituted upon a scale worthy of the age, and worthy of the land that led the van of Europe in the diffusion of popular education'. 'Our affinities scholastically are with the land of Luther, and to that as the ideal we make our appeal. The legislature of Scotland accepted from an early period the duty, or, rather, the privilege, of guiding and fostering the educational training of the country, and I hold that the united legislature is bound to do so still.'[10] The 1872 Act was condemned, not simply for its neglect of the secondary schools, but because Scottish opinion was united in rejecting the *laissez-faire* dogmas which were conventional orthodoxy in England. Ramsay, for example, attacked 'the sacred principle, so dear to a certain type of Liberals in this country, so entirely foreign to the practice of those countries which we should most desire to imitate— that no national money should be expended on secondary education'. He argued that the state owed a duty to the community as a whole, including the middle class; and that in modern conditions 'one of the main factors, if not *the* main factor, in the continued prosperity of a nation ... is the disciplined

---

[8] J. Marshall, *Some moot points in secondary education in Scotland* (Edinburgh, 1884), pp. 16-17.

[9] *R. Comm. Univ. Ev.*, Part I, p. 814 (Blackie); A. C. Sellar, *The higher education of Scotland* (Edinburgh, 1875), pp. 6-7; Tulloch in *Blackwood's Magazine*, cxix (1876), p. 285.

[10] W. D. Geddes, *Classical education in the north of Scotland* (Edinburgh, 1869), pp. 53, 68.

intelligence of the great bulk of the community'; it was the state's duty to search out talent wherever it was to be found, and 'by a carefully organised system of graded education, placed within the reach of all such as are able to profit by it, do everything that is possible to swell the bulk and improve the quality of the national intelligence'.[11]

Particularly interesting in this respect were the ideas of James Donaldson. He had proposed a state system of secondary education to the Argyll commission, and attacked its report for 'aristocratic' neglect of the question. 'The aristocracy of Scotland, and those who hang on the skirts of the aristocracy, have done next to nothing for the secondary education of Scotland.' If they had their sons educated in Scotland at all, it was at boarding schools like Glenalmond or the new Fettes College, 'an institution ... opposed in the strongest manner to what is best in Scottish and European education'. They would do better to attend his own High School, where they would benefit from rubbing together with all classes: 'it is by this intercourse with boys in all positions, and subsequently with men, that the real being of men is fashioned'. Donaldson was not alone in hoping to tempt back the upper classes, but he was unusual in seeing Edinburgh High School as a 'national' school which should meet all secondary needs in the city, and he was to oppose the opening of rival schools on this principle. His argument was that public schools subsidized from rates and taxes would allow lower fees, making the rich pay their due to society while putting secondary education within reach of the middle class in a broad sense.[12] This idea was bolstered by historical evidence in a massive history of the burgh schools published by James Grant in 1876, which formed a timely contribution to the secondary movement. In the past, Grant claimed, 'the town councils most earnestly endeavoured to make their schools not limited, select, or exclusive, but really national, adapting them to the best of their ability to the varied circumstances of the different grades into which the inhabitants were socially divided'. But in recent years fees had been forced

---

[11] *Fraser's Magazine*, n.s. xiii (1876), pp. 590, 596.

[12] *Scotsman*, 14 Dec. 1868 (address to a meeting organized by the EIS); cf. his evidence in *Argyll Comm. 3rd Rep.*, Vol. I, pp. 196-8.

up, and they had become 'upper middle-class schools—select schools, in which the poor and rich do not mix now as they did in the past'.[13]

Since there was no chance that Parliament would approve the public funding of secondary education, attention naturally turned to the unlocking of endowment funds, which were first thoroughly investigated by the Colebrooke commission. This commission had no executive powers, but it used its report—largely the work of S. S. Laurie, its secretary—to lay down principles of reform. Since the 1872 Act many endowments had become obsolete, especially in the cities, where free charity schools could not compete with the work of the school boards. The question was how funds originally left to help the poor could best be used in the new conditions. Orthodox Liberal opinion was strongly against free education as such and against helping children on grounds of poverty alone. In the words of A. C. Sellar, a member of the commission, 'The kindest friends of the poor are those who help them to help themselves—not those who with one hand pamper and with the other pauperise them. The man who goes about the country clamouring for free schools and indiscriminate gratuitous education to be provided out of such endowments as these, is no true friend to those to whom he proposes to give his education as a dole.'[14] The commission's report endorsed this view, and also adopted the principle that endowment funds should not be used where there was other legal provision, to 'relieve' the school rate or to help pauper children whose fees were paid under the 1872 Act by the poor-law authorities. Instead, all schools should charge a proper level of fees, and endowments should be used to help 'the more promising pupils' either to stay on for a year or two at the elementary school, or, if they had the talent, to benefit from 'a system of open bursaries or scholarships from the Public Elementary to the Secondary Schools, and from the latter to the Universities'.[15] Endowments in Scotland were rarely large enough to allow the foundation of new schools, nor was this as

[13] J. Grant, *History of the burgh and parish schools of Scotland. ... Burgh schools* (1876), pp. 465, 493.
[14] Sellar, op. cit., p. 19.
[15] *Colebrooke Comm. 3rd Rep.*, pp. 82, 86, 111.

necessary as it was in England, but the commission thought
that they could support an adequate system of competitive
scholarships, and that this was now the correct way of discharg-
ing the community's obligations to the poor. The commission's
survey extended to university bursaries, and showed that open
bursars, like those at Aberdeen, did far better than those who
got their bursaries by presentation or on charitable grounds.
The universities were urged to sweep away local and other
restrictions, and to persuade private patrons to make use of a
common examination administered by the university—Edinburgh and Glasgow were indeed already moving along these
lines.[16] Thus reformed, the university bursary system would be
adequate, but it needed extending downwards, and the commission proposed secondary bursaries of about £25 which would
allow students to lodge in towns with higher-class schools. The
concept was that popularized by Huxley at this time of a 'ladder
from the gutter to the university', and in its emphasis on merit
and competition was in line with orthodox liberal individualism.

Critics on the popular wing of Liberalism, however, saw this
as a very narrow idea of educational opportunity, and argued
that a scholarship system was liable to be taken over by the
middle class—the reform of endowments in England had
already provoked the charge that the rich were stealing the
rights of the poor. According to the Radical MP Duncan
McLaren in the Commons debate on the Colebrooke report,
open competition 'sounds well, and it would also be very well if
the open competition was among persons in equal circumstances. It is then the best possible means of selection; but if
you have to draw into competition raw young lads who have
never been at good schools with those who have had superior
advantages, then I answer that it is not at all a good mode of
selection.' The historian James Grant, discussing the same
problem, called for 'some principle of selection exercised in
favour of poorer persons of merit'.[17] The report had anticipated this criticism by proposing that bursaries at the lower
level should be confined to children in public schools, so that
'preferences to poverty would receive fair and sufficient effect',

---

[16] Ibid., pp. 167 ff., and cf. *2nd Rep.*, pp. 227-47, 613 ff.
[17] *3 Hansard* ccxxv, HC 9 July 1875, col. 1286; Grant, op. cit., p. 500.

but in the case of university bursaries they rejected any plan for the 'discriminating promotion of poverty', arguing that by the end of secondary education initial inequalities would have levelled out.[18]

As for the general organization of secondary education, the commission made clear its support for the secondary school movement, and sympathized with the desire for a university entrance examination. It admitted, with lukewarm approval, that the parochial schools still had a contribution to make in the rural districts. 'But if we look for any real improvement in the standard of Scottish Secondary instruction, we must not rest content with such agencies as these. What we require in Scotland is a supply, adequate to the wants of the country, of thoroughly-equipped Secondary Schools ... giving a really high class of Secondary instruction at reasonable fees, organized on the best principle, and managed and taught by an efficient staff of well-paid teachers.'[19] The report naturally gave a new impetus to the secondary campaign, marked by a wave of articles in the periodical press[20] and by the foundation of an Association for Promoting Secondary Education in Scotland. Colebrooke was its president, Laurie its secretary, and its executive committee was weighed down with political and university luminaries: Moncreiff, Inglis, Lorimer, Playfair, Balfour of Burleigh, Principal Grant, J. A. Campbell, George Ramsay, Donaldson, Sellar, Grant Duff, etc. Its aim was to carry out 'the scheme proposed by John Knox for the establishment of Secondary Schools or "Colleges" between the Parish Schools and the Universities'. It believed in using endowments to help the 'clever poor', and drew up a list of ninety-one towns which should have secondary schools, divided into three grades.[21] The Association's propaganda campaign bore fruit in

---

[18] *Colebrooke Comm. 3rd Rep.*, p. 191.

[19] Ibid., pp. 99, 105.

[20] Apart from those already cited, see Lorimer in *Edinburgh Review*, cxliii (1876). Pamphlets of the period include J. Lorimer, *How to provide for the higher instruction in Scotland* (Edinburgh, 1873); J. Hutchison, *Our secondary education and some of its recent critics* (Glasgow, 1875); J. Macdonald, *Our secondary schools and how to improve them* (Glasgow, 1876); J. Black, *On some defects in our present school system* (Edinburgh 1876).

[21] *Transactions of the National Association for the Promotion of Social Science*, 1877, pp. 403, 404-6. Cf. *Memorandum of the objects of the Association for the Promotion of Secondary Education in Scotland* (Edinburgh, 1876); S. S. Laurie, *The training of teachers, and other educational papers* (1882), pp. 187-99.

two Acts of Parliament in 1878, after which it disbanded. The first created an endowments commission under Moncreiff, which could authorize reform schemes proposed by the endowed bodies themselves, but had no powers of initiative, while the second allowed school boards to use rate income to maintain the buildings of higher class schools. But the rates could still not be used for salaries or for lowering fees, and there was no question of grants from central government. These were therefore modest victories.

The Association showed more interest than the Colebrooke report in higher education in rural schools, recommending that boys should not be transferred to urban high schools before fifteen, and that country schoolmasters should have a university training.[22] This reflected the views of Laurie, the real force behind the Association—like the Board of Education, he both campaigned for stronger secondary schools and accused the SED of allowing the parochial tradition to be undermined. There was perhaps no contradiction between the two positions, but if the secondary education movement had achieved its aim of a 'graded' system there would obviously have been more concentration of higher education in the towns, and the 1872 Act's failure in this respect had the slightly paradoxical effect of prolonging the old tradition. For the same reason, the SED figured in these years as the defender of that tradition, in attempting to show that all was well under the specific subjects regime and that it was maintaining standards as required by clause 67 of the Act. When the Board of Education was allowed to lapse in 1878, critics were appeased by requiring the Moncreiff commission to make a special report on higher education in public schools. This report appeared in 1881, and endorsed the parish school tradition, concluding that 'it is not only possible to combine thorough elementary teaching with instruction in the higher branches, but ... any separation of these subjects is detrimental to the tone of the school, and dispiriting to the master'. New secondary schools might be needed in 'certain populous centres', but this would not help the great majority of rural children, and the aim should be, as

---

[22] Cf. Memorial of the Association in *EN*, ii. 197-8 (21 Apr. 1877); the *EN* supported the movement at this time.

in the past, to have a graduate in every parish and to provide financial encouragement for the higher subjects.[23] Meanwhile the SED was moving cautiously towards the idea of 'central' schools: from 1880 annual circulars were sent to school boards encouraging them to designate one school to concentrate on higher subjects, and talking of 'a scheme of graded schools'.[24] But these circulars were really concerned with the rural problem, and as yet the SED had no general policy for the development of secondary education.

The Moncreiff report marked a swing of opinion away from the Colebrooke doctrines (the two commissions had only one member in common),[25] and provided ammunition for those who believed that secondary education should not be confined to middle-class schools admitting a privileged élite of 'gifted' children, but should be built on elementary education in an organic and open-ended way. In the 1880s this conflict between secondary and primary ideals of education, sponsored and contest ideals of opportunity, became open and explicit, as we shall see in Chapter 6. First, however, we shall examine developments in the four large cities, where the wealthier endowments were concentrated, and where new needs like those for the education of artisans or of girls were most pressing. The cities were the laboratories for educational experiment, and conditions favoured the secondary theorists. Yet the ideal of common education too had its defenders, and they were active in the foundation of new 'higher grade' schools in Glasgow and in a complex dispute over the reform of George Heriot's Hospital in Edinburgh.

'Truly more splendid mausoleums for the memory of individual citizens could hardly have been devised', wrote Principal Grant of the Edinburgh 'hospitals'. 'Conspicuous from a hundred points of view, they draw a half-circle of varied and stately architecture about the city of Edinburgh, adding dignity

---

[23] *Moncreiff Comm. Special Rep.*, p. vii.

[24] Circulars of 15 Apr. 1880, 1 Mar. 1881, 28 Apr. 1882. For the evolution of this policy see *CCES Report, 1881-2* (PP 1882, xxv), pp. 47-50. The idea of 'district' schools went back to Harvey and Sellar: *Argyll Comm. 3rd Rep.*, Vol. I, pp. 145-7.

[25] John Ramsay. The politicians on Colebrooke were mainly Liberal, while Moncreiff was more equally balanced. It also included Donaldson.

and embellishment to the scene.'[26] These residential establishments were not unique to Edinburgh, but it had more than
anywhere else: the Colebrooke commission estimated the income of all Scottish endowments at £174,532, of which hospitals accounted for £79,245; and of that Edinburgh and its
neighbourhood had £59,770.[27] The inquiries of the 1860s
showed that seven of the city's nine hospitals gave a 'liberal' or
middle-class education, but the Argyll commission excluded
them from its account of burgh schools, perhaps because the
children generally left at fourteen and few went to the university.[28] It was not difficult for reformers to argue that very large
sums were being spent for comparatively little educational
gain.

The oldest of the hospitals was George Heriot's, founded in
the seventeenth century on the model of Christ's Hospital in
London.[29] In the 1860s its impressive buildings contained 180
boys, living a somewhat cloistered life, and educated free by a
well-qualified staff. When they left, they were traditionally
apprenticed to a trade, and provided with an 'outfit' of clothes
and with an annual allowance during their apprenticeship. A
few more promising boys stayed on for a year or two as 'hope-
ful scholars', and could then go to Edinburgh University on
Heriot's bursaries. This was the model on which the other
hospitals were founded, and the impulse was by no means dead
in the nineteenth century. As with Oxford and Cambridge
colleges today, rich men preferred to perpetuate their name by
association with a proved model of success rather than by bold
innovation; but in Edinburgh the supply of funds was beginning
to outrun that of deserving objects of charity.

After Heriot's, the most important hospitals were those run
by the Merchant Company, a body representing the corporate
traditions of the mercantile community. The Company had
founded the Merchant Maiden Hospital in 1695 for the daughters of its own members, and since then benefactors had entrusted it with their legacies: George Watson's (1741) and

[26] A. Grant (ed.), *Recess studies* (Edinburgh, 1870), pp. 119-20.
[27] *3rd Rep.*, pp. 13-18; cf. pp. 226-7, and *Appendix to 3rd Rep.*, Vol. II, pp. 337 ff.
[28] *Schools Inquiry Comm.*, Vol. VI, p. 178.
[29] The basic source for all the hospitals is *Colebrooke Comm. 1st Rep.*, pp. 517 ff., and
Appendix to 3rd Rep., Vol. I.

Daniel Stewart's (1855) were for boys, while Gillespie's Hospital was a foundation for old people which also included an elementary day school. In all these cases the founders had had charitable ends in view, and the beneficiaries were either orphans or children whose parents had come down in the world. But in 1870 the residential hospitals were turned into large fee-paying day schools for the middle class; a small core of foundationers survived, but no longer lived in. Heriot's was to follow the same path in 1885, after years of controversy, and amid charges that the poor were being despoiled of their rights. In order to make sense of these controversies, it is necessary to look at the situation before the reforms.

In the case of George Watson's and the Merchant Maiden, the position was fairly straightforward: they were intended to benefit members of the merchant class, and drew on middle-class families suffering from genteel impoverishment; the boys mostly went into shops and merchants' or lawyers' offices, and the girls became teachers and governesses. At Heriot's, whatever the founder's intentions may have been, the school drew mainly on the artisan and lower middle classes, with a preference to orphans. An inquiry in 1868 established that although 111 of 178 boys had both parents alive, nearly all the parents were 'tradesmen or operatives', mostly with incomes under £60 p.a.,[30] and a list of those who went on to apprenticeship or further education between 1864 and 1878 showed that although 24 went to the university, and 62 as 'clerks to merchants etc.', 53 were apprenticed as joiners and cabinetmakers, 27 as printers, and many others to other manual trades.[31] Heriot's offered real opportunities of social mobility· through the quality of its teaching and the existence of university bursaries, and those opportunities were prized by the city's working and lower middle classes. Daniel Stewart's too was a charity aimed at the poor: preference was given to orphans, who in fact formed the majority, and in the 1860s they were

[30] F. W. Bedford, *History of George Heriot's Hospital* (Edinburgh, 1872), p. 194; cf. *Colebrooke Comm. 1st Rep.*, p. 520. For George Watson's and the Merchant Maiden see S. S. Laurie, *Reports on the hospitals under the administration of the Merchant Company, Edinburgh* (Edinburgh, 1868), pp. 42, 87.

[31] SRO ED 2 11/12, list among papers of *c.*1879. The SRO contains the records of the Moncreiff and Balfour commissions (ED 2 and ED 13 respectively).

'almost wholly drawn from the upper labouring or quite the lowest middle class, and it is therefore to be presumed that the mass are destined for the occupation of skilled artizans, shop assistants, and clerks'.[32] Latin was taught, but not Greek, and Stewart's had no university link.

The Merchant Company conducted its business in the public eye, and Heriot's even more so, for the Heriot's governors consisted of the town council and city ministers of Edinburgh. The town council thus retained a stake in education even after handing the High School over to the school board (endowments had the same effect in Glasgow and Aberdeen), and the affairs of Heriot's became entangled with the city's notoriously quarrelsome municipal politics. But other trusts were much less amenable to public opinion, and the vagueness of the benefactors' intentions often gave the trustees the power to indulge their private views. Thus the governors of Donaldson's Hospital, opened in 1850, decided to specialize in the education of the deaf, though that was not prescribed in the bequest. In the case of John Watson's Institution, the benefactor, who died in 1759, had envisaged a foundling hospital, but by the time the institution opened in 1828, after an amending Act of Parliament, the trustees had decided to confine themselves to orphans from middle-class and especially professional families all over Scotland. Despite this social background, the children left as in other hospitals at the age of fourteen, and few if any of the boys went on to a university. The John Watson's trustees were drawn from the Edinburgh legal profession (the 'Keepers and Commissioners of the Signet'), which had a good deal of educational influence through its control of charitable bequests, large and small.[33]

The most remarkable case of this kind, however, was that of Fettes. Sir William Fettes died in 1836, leaving his fortune 'for the maintenance, education, and outfit of young people, whose parents have either died without leaving sufficient funds for that purpose, or who, from innocent misfortune during their own lives, are unable to give suitable education to their children'. Fettes probably envisaged a hospital on the lines of

---

[32] Laurie, *Reports on the hospitals,* pp. 19, 35.
[33] The Writers to the Signet also controlled the Dick Bequest.

George Watson's, but the trustees, headed by John Inglis, thought with some justification that Edinburgh was over-provided with hospitals, and decided instead to found a Public School on the English model, using Fettes's money to support fifty foundationers drawn from the classes who would normally use such a school. The construction of a grandiose building began in 1863, and the trustees appointed a headmaster from Rugby and a staff of Oxford and Cambridge graduates; Fettes College opened in 1870, giving a full liberal education and charging its boarders £85 p.a.[34] As Inglis pointed out, fee-paying schools had been grafted onto charitable foundations in cases like Rugby and Harrow—but that had been the result of a long historical evolution, and had not been unopposed. In this case, since Fettes had never come into existence as a hospital, critics of the change were disarmed.

By this time both Heriot's and the Merchant Company were contemplating reform, for although the Argyll commission had made only the vaguest reference to the use of hospital funds it was not difficult to see that the hospitals would eventually have reform thrust on them if they did not take the initiative themselves. The hospital system had in any case often been criticized in Edinburgh for its 'monastic' nature. Educational experts, including those who had actually taught in the hospitals, agreed that their inmates lacked energy, vigour, and self-reliance, and showed 'dulness in perception and understanding, and a peculiar intellectual inertness and heaviness' which made the educational results disappointing. This was especially attributed to the absence of contact with other boys and with the outside world.[35] As opponents of change pointed out, these criticisms seemed unconvincing at a time when the prestige of the English boarding system was so high, but it does seem that Scottish middle-class opinion was less enthusiastic about boarding than English, and boarding in the hospitals seemed illogical when the conditions of admission meant that most of the pupils came from Edinburgh families.

---

[34] *Colebrooke Comm. 1st Rep.*, pp. 637-49; *2nd Rep.*, p. 175 (evidence of Inglis); *Appendix to 3rd Rep.*, Vol. I, pp. 48-56.
[35] *1st Rep.*, pp. 50 ff., 103-4, 122 ff., 307 ff.

Another motive for reform was that the endowments enjoyed growing wealth for which they were seeking new uses. Heriot's trust were superiors of most of the land on which Edinburgh New Town was built, and as the city expanded rents and feuduties poured in. The income of Heriot's rose from £4,389 in 1800 to £18,546 in 1871, while at the end of the 1860s the Merchant Company trusts had an income of over £20,000.[36] In the case of Heriot's, a new application had been found in providing free elementary schools: these 'outdoor schools' were authorized by an Act of Parliament in 1836, and by 1868 there were thirteen of them, with over 3,000 pupils. The Heriot's free schools were efficient and popular, but the creation of the ·school board made their position anomalous, and ̀they were prime examples of that 'indiscriminate' free education of which experts disapproved so strongly. The free schools, even more than the hospital itself (with which they had no direct connection), were to be at the centre of political controversy.

In 1868 the Heriot's governors made a modest change in the hospital by turning 60 of the 180 foundationers into day-boys, and in the same year the Merchant Company commissioned a report on its hospitals from Laurie, who endorsed all the criticisms of 'monasticism'. Laurie's report revealed that George Watson's was in a state of crisis and decay: the classical teaching was very poor, the headmaster was suffering from 'nervous exhaustion' and had lost control of discipline, and the strap was too freely used. The solution proposed was to wind up the educational side of the hospital altogether, keeping it as a boarding establishment with a more liberal regime, and sending the boys to classes at the High School. For the Merchant Maiden, Laurie's plan was equally radical, but in the opposite direction: boarding should be abolished, and the buildings used for 'a great Ladies Day School, open to all at a moderate fee', with the foundationers continuing to enjoy free education, but boarded out with friends or families.[37] The Merchant Company lost no time in adopting Laurie's plan for George Watson's, and in October 1868 its older boys entered the High School.

[36] Bedford, op. cit., pp. 228-9; A. Heron, *The rise and progress of the Company of Merchants of the City of Edinburgh 1681-1902* (Edinburgh, 1903), p. 283.
[37] Laurie, *Reports on the hospitals,* pp. 56, 59-60, 117 ff., 127-30. He found Daniel Stewart's in a satisfactory state.

They were not altogether welcome, for High School masters and parents protested against the loss of social tone, and some boys were withdrawn. The hospital boys bore the stigma of charity, and at the High School's opening ceremony the Lord Provost had to urge that they should be received as equals, for though touched by misfortune they were still the 'sons of gentlemen'. Donaldson followed this up with reference to his theory of 'national' education, and looked forward to the day when 'there will be one great public classical school in Edinburgh', with up to 1,000 pupils and 50-60 teachers, like the secondary schools of Paris or Berlin.[38]

He was destined to disappointment, for the Merchant Company had actually decided to turn all its hospitals into day schools, and was only awaiting legislation to allow this, legislation which was soon obtained through its influential political contacts. This was the Endowed Institutions (Scotland) Act of 1869, a far more limited measure than the English Act of the same year. It allowed endowed bodies to apply to the Home Secretary for approval of their reform schemes, but did not prescribe any limitations on the nature of the reforms or set up a commission to supervise the process. The bill was attacked for its permissive nature by Playfair, whose own prescription for the endowed schools was that

While not neglecting the education of the middle classes who could pay for it, they should send their roots down into the primary schools, so as to draw out of them, by an open competition, the *élite* of the poorer classes, and advance them by an education suitable to their future occupations; and they ought to throw out their branches into the Universities, so as to knit together the lower and higher education of the country. Instead of being stereotyped in one common mould, they should glory in [their] distinctive character by establishing special schools fully appointed and equipped—such as trade schools, schools of commerce, schools of science, all properly graded and co-ordinated, so that pupils might pass from one to the other.[39]

Instead of the Merchant Company being allowed to act in isolation, the Edinburgh endowments should be replanned as a

---

[38] *Scotsman*, 20 Oct. 1868; cf. 30 July 1869, and Donaldson's evidence in *Colebrooke Comm. 1st Rep.*, p. 185.

[39] *3 Hansard* cxcvii, HC 17 June 1869, cols. 153, 155-6.

whole to allow for these forms of specialization—an attractive idea which was also taken up by Grant and by the Colebrooke commission; in these schemes, Heriot's was usually marked out as a technical school because of its links with the artisan class.[40]

But the Act was passed, and the Merchant Company obtained the orders authorizing its schemes without opposition. In 1870 the educational provision of Edinburgh was transformed, as five large, fee-paying day schools replaced the old hospitals, partly occupying their old buildings. They were George Watson's and Daniel Stewart's for boys, the Edinburgh Educational Institution for Young Ladies (the former Merchant Maiden), and George Watson's school for girls, a completely new foundation; all these were middle-class schools, taking pupils from around the age of eight and giving a full liberal education. James Gillespie's, a large mixed school located in the hospital formerly used for old people, stood apart from the others in being aimed at the upper working class, and was essentially an elementary school. All these schools enjoyed immediate success: George Watson's boys' school and the Young Ladies' Institution took over 1,000 pupils, and by 1872 the schools together had more than 4,000 pupils, compared with 394 in the unreformed hospitals, and where 26 teachers had worked before there were now 213.[41]

As at Fettes, the endowment income continued to pay for foundationers in the new schools, but these now lived either at home or in boarding houses separate from the schools. Their numbers were reduced, and, in the words of the Master of the Merchant Company, 'the special identity of foundationers is now lost, and a spirit of merit runs through all.'[42] A proportion of the foundation places was opened to competitive examination within the Merchant Company schools so that a talented

[40] Grant, *Recess studies*, pp. 134 ff. On ideas for Heriot's see evidence in *Colebrooke Comm. 1st Rep.*, pp. 125 ff. (J. Currie), 279 ff. (Playfair), 334 ff. (F. Jenkin); also *Scotsman*, 21 Mar. 1868, and G. Robertson, *The science education movement* (Edinburgh, 1868), pp. 11-12.

[41] *Colebrooke Comm. 1st Rep.*, pp. 36-7 (figures), 524; *Appendix to 3rd Rep.*, Vol. I, pp. 19 ff. George Watson's girls' school (later Ladies' College) did not open until 1871.

[42] T. J. Boyd, *Educational hospital reform: the scheme of the Edinburgh Merchant Company* (Edinburgh, 1871), p. 14.

child from Gillespie's might go on to one of the secondary schools, but there were no bursaries open to outsiders, no roots sent down into the elementary schools in the way Playfair had demanded. In the original plan, moreover, the Merchant Company claimed to be creating a graded system, and designated Daniel Stewart's as a 'lower' secondary school with a technical bias, but this was rapidly abandoned. By 1872 Daniel Stewart's was charging the same fees as George Watson's, and had a virtually indistinguishable curriculum, both schools offering a choice between classical and commercial sides; and the Stewart's foundation places, given before the reform on grounds of poverty, were now filled exclusively by internal competition.[43] In the case of Daniel Stewart's, therefore, a recent foundation where the intention of the benefactor to help the poor was in no doubt, there was a very clear diversion of resources towards the middle class. The same cannot be said of the other parts of the Merchant Company scheme, since these endowments had always been intended for the middle class. But while providing lavishly for middle-class needs—funds were also used for university bursaries for their own pupils, and to create the Political Economy chair at Edinburgh University—the schemes did less than the ideologists of 'merit' normally recommended to extend a hand to the working class; if they had come under later legislation, rather than the lax 1869 Act, much more provision of open bursaries would certainly have been enforced.[44]

The chief contemporary complaint was that the Merchant Company's resources permitted low fees which undercut other schools, whose interests were seriously damaged by the sudden creation of several thousand new places. Even well-established schools like the Academy suffered, and Donaldson of the High School might well feel aggrieved: his welcoming of the Watson's boys in 1868 had frightened off richer parents, but now those boys were withdrawn, and numbers in the High School fell from 378 to 284 between 1868 and 1872. Donaldson complained of this before the Colebrooke commission, arguing that all

[43] Evidence of Boyd in *Colebrooke Comm. 1st Rep.*, p. 44.

[44] The original scheme included an 'industrial school' for the destitute, but this was not proceeded with. Gillespie's School later became a higher grade school, and was handed over to Edinburgh School Board in 1908.

education ought to be under public control to prevent the arbitrary action of bodies like the Merchant Company, but admitting from experience that the ideal of a single national school conflicted with the social prejudices of parents—and 'there is no place where to a greater extent caste prevails than in Edinburgh'.[45] He had indeed told the Argyll commission a few years before that it was not the quality of education but social status and respectability about which parents cared, matters 'very much determined by the fees charged; and as people pay different prices for box, pit, and gallery to see the same play, so they are willing to pay very different prices for the same education'.[46]

Another headmaster, Ferguson of the Edinburgh Institution, complained that the Merchant Company's system 'does much more to cheapen the highest secondary education to those who need no cheapening, than to render it accessible to people in humble life. It is much more a boon to ladies and gentlemen than to working men. £10 a year for a girl, and £6 for a boy, are sums that cannot be paid by working people.'[47] These figures referred to the highest fees charged by the Merchant Company, but £10 was a third of the fees usually charged by private girls' schools, £6 half of the High School fees. Ferguson's school survived because it had enough prestige to attract parents even at higher fees, but many small private schools closed down, and it is likely that girls' schools were especially hard hit, as the Merchant Company offered entirely new standards of scale and quality in girls' education.

The complaints of the private school teachers,[48] together perhaps with a feeling that the Merchant Company had got away with too much, helped to give the government second thoughts about the 1869 Act. A scheme put forward by Heriot's was refused, on the legal ground that it was 'so subversive of the purposes of the foundation' as to fall outside the powers given by the Act, and after this the Act became a dead letter. The real objection to the Heriot's scheme was that it offended

---

[45] *1st Rep.*, p. 185.
[46] *Argyll Comm. 3rd Rep.*, Vol. I, p. 194.
[47] *1st Rep.*, p. 179.
[48] Expressed in 'Sit Jus', *On the scholastic position and results of the Merchant Company's schools* (Edinburgh, 1870).

orthodox doctrines on the reform of endowments, and this was the beginning of a long political struggle. On three occasions—in 1870, 1879 and 1883—Heriot's put forward a reform scheme, and each time it was rejected. The details varied, and it was not always easy to see what the practical implications of the schemes were, but certain factors were constant. First, the 'outdoor' schools were to be maintained, and even extended to meet new needs; one party among the Heriot's governors was willing to charge moderate fees, but this proved so unpopular that after 1870 the schemes stressed the continuation of free education. Second, the hospital's role was to be expanded, with day boys being admitted, but with some foundationers still living in, and with the emphasis on providing for the working class rather than on merit and open competition. Third, the work of the foundation was to be expanded in various directions—evening classes, girls' schools, 'industrial schools' for the destitute—which were angled towards working-class needs much as the Merchant Company schemes were to middle-class ones.[49]

The Heriot's governors were, in effect, the town council, which felt that the institution should move with the democratic times. The great champion of Heriot's was the veteran Radical politician Duncan McLaren, who had done much to create the outdoor schools in 1836, and who was MP for the city between 1865 and 1881. With the failure of the Heriot's application in 1870, and of further pressures and negotiations in 1871, the feeling grew that both the free schools and the hospital were under attack, and the Heriot's party especially blamed the machinations of Principal Grant, who was seen as the leader of a faction devoted to universities and to middle-class education; he was not forgiven for having indiscreetly hinted that the hospital would make an excellent hall of residence for the university.[50] The next threat came from the Colebrooke commission, which was so full of representatives of the secondary education party that McLaren refused to give evidence to it.[51]

---

[49] The 1870 and 1879 schemes are printed in *Moncreiff Comm. 1st Rep.*, pp. lii–lxvi. For the thinking behind them see *Colebrooke Comm. 1st Rep.*, pp. 209 ff. (Gray), 232 ff. (Bailie Tawse, the aptly named chief spokesman for Heriot's), 259 ff. (D. Lewis).

[50] Speech of Grant in *Scotsman*, 3rd Nov. 1869. For the controversy generally see D. McLaren, *Heriot's Hospital Trust and its proper administration* (Edinburgh, 1872).

[51] *Appendix to 3rd Rep.*, Vol. II, p. 354.

But other representatives were questioned closely and unsympathetically by the commission, including members of the Edinburgh Trades Council, which argued that George Heriot's original aim had been 'to raise up a respectable, thinking, able class of artizans or citizens', that the correct use of the endowment was to benefit the working class, and that it was large enough to provide comprehensively and gratuitously for their needs.[52] It was the kind of skilled worker represented by the Trades Council, rather than the really poor, who got most benefit both from the outdoor schools and from the hospital.

The Colebrooke commission established to its own satisfaction that Heriot had intended to benefit the middle rather than the working classes, and endorsed the Merchant Company model of hospital reform. Its recommendations for Heriot's were that more of the endowment should be spent on university scholarships, that fees should be charged in the outdoor schools, that the hospital should become a purely secondary school 'so organized as to be specially adapted to the wants of the industrial and commercial classes' (the example of the German *Realschulen* was cited), and finally that competition places on the foundation should be thrown open to the whole country.[53] The last proposal was especially offensive to the Heriot's party, who always claimed that the endowment was the exclusive property of Edinburgh. Fortunately for them, the Colebrooke commission had no executive powers, but the publication of its report in 1875 led to the formation of a Heriot Trust Defence Committee which was to be active in later events. Sympathy for it was not confined to Radical circles, for local feeling in many quarters resented interference with an ancient institution whose usefulness and efficiency were widely accepted.

The Heriot's case proved the most controversial of the thirty-two schemes considered by the Moncreiff commission. Although the Act of 1878 setting it up was modelled on the English Act of 1869, the commission did not have compulsory powers. But

---

[52] I. MacDougall (ed.), *The minutes of Edinburgh Trades Council, 1859-1873* (Edinburgh, 1968), p. 356; cf. evidence of its spokesmen in *Colebrooke Comm. 2nd Rep.*, pp. 98 ff.

[53] *3rd Rep.*, pp. 39, 48-55, 69-70.

many governing bodies already had plans for which they were anxious to obtain legal sanction, and in introducing the Act ministers had stressed that bodies like Heriot's were being given a 'last chance', and that there would be more stringent legislation if they failed to come up with acceptable schemes.[54] The Heriot's scheme of 1879 was in fact more radical than that of 1870, showing a determination both to maintain the free outdoor schools and to link them with the hospital itself. McLaren's aim was to 'make Heriot's Hospital a great civic school for the clever boys and girls selected from the elementary schools, to be educated along with the boys placed on the Hospital foundation'.[55] In recent years some day-boys drawn from the free schools had indeed been admitted. The outdoor schools themselves, however, now had a new opponent in the school board, which found that they obstructed its own efforts to provide a rationally-planned school system, and which opposed the creation of a kind of Heriot's empire of working-class education outside the statutory framework. That empire would have extended further than before, for one new proposal was that Heriot's should take over the Watt Institution, which provided most of Edinburgh's technical instruction. This was the only part of the scheme which the Moncreiff commission thought acceptable, for otherwise it offended against orthodoxy by refusing to abandon the hospital system, by failing to divert funds to university bursaries, and above all by glorying in the principle of free education, defended in McLaren's evidence as in line with both Scottish tradition and the practice of other advanced countries.[56] The commission was especially shocked by the evidence of the Defence Committee spokesmen, who boasted of the way in which councillors who had supported fees in 1870 had been turned out at the municipal elections. This manifestation of democracy was not to the commission's taste, and led them to say that 'the kind of control and pressure which is here indicated is one to which the Governors of such an institution ought not to be exposed, and

[54] *3 Hansard* ccxxxix, HL 29 Mar., 5 Apr., 11 Apr. 1878; ccxlii, HC 29 July 1878.
[55] J. B. Mackie, *The life and work of Duncan McLaren* (1888), ii. 192 (citing McLaren's words).
[56] *Moncreiff Comm. 1st Rep.*, pp. 29-30 (Tawse), 122-3, 132 (McLaren), 132 ff., 153 ff. (School Board spokesmen).

is incompatible with due administration'. The Heriot's plans were turned down, and in a special memorandum to the Home Secretary the commission recommended that no reforms should be accepted until the governing body had been changed.[57]

This new question of the composition of governing bodies proved an embarrassing one for the Liberal government of 1880, which was prepared to legislate for the compulsory reform of endowments but found this obstructed by the Radical (and pro-Home Rule) wing of Scottish Liberalism, whose MPs saw themselves as the defenders of 'popular representation' and of the rights of the poor against 'spoliation'. After McLaren's retirement, the most vociferous of these was Charles Cameron of Glasgow, where 'spoliation' was also an issue, but the defence of the Heriot free schools was always at the heart of the campaign. The obstructiveness of the 'Heriot ring' caused much resentment among other Liberals, but it was effective enough to defeat attempts at legislation in 1880 and 1881. By 1882, the government was prepared to make enough concessions to get a bill through, but even so the debates were long and angry; the minister in charge was A. J. Mundella, a strong supporter of the principles of endowment reform accepted in England, and his handling of the bill inspired little confidence among the Scots. As it finally emerged, the Educational Endowments (Scotland) Act of 1882 contained some important safeguard clauses which were absent from the Act in force in England: governing bodies were to include a minimum representation from town councils or school boards, and where this 'popular' element had been in the majority before (as with Heriot's) the minimum was two-thirds; funds intended by benefactors to provide free education or limited specifically to the poor were protected; and a clause which was stronger than the English equivalent obliged the commission which the Act created to make equal provision for girls. In one respect, the commission was to have a freer hand than in England, for their powers covered all school endowments down to 1872; in England there was a fifty-year limit, but Scottish lawyers seemed to have much less reverence than English ones for the

[57] Ibid., pp. xlii ff., lxxxi, 138 ff. (evidence of G. Stephen & J. Thom). Cf. *2nd Rep.*, pp. cxi-cxv, and documents printed in a parliamentary return in PP 1880, lv.

wishes of 'pious founders', as indeed their operations in the Fettes and John Watson's cases had shown.[58]

The executive commission created by the Act was headed by Lord Balfour of Burleigh. It was to sit until the end of 1889, and to review 379 schemes, covering 821 separate endowments with an annual value of about £200,000—the great majority being very small and of purely local interest. Balfour himself and two other members had been on the Colebrooke commission, though one of these was the Liberal John Ramsay, who was to show himself the member most sympathetic to the claims of the poor. Among the other members were the Lord Provosts of Glasgow and Edinburgh, but this was hardly re-assuring to the Heriot's party, for the latter, Thomas Boyd, had been the chief architect of the Merchant Company reforms, and carried weight as a critic of the hospital system.

The commission tried to standardize the form of endowment schemes, and laid down its general principles in its first report in 1884. Since endowments were rarely large enough to allow the creation of a new school, much of the emphasis was on bursaries, but the safeguard clauses in the Act tied the commission's hands and prevented it from applying the principle of merit in pure form. Substantial sums were still to be devoted to paying school fees, or clothing and maintenance allowances, to families in real need. Small 'school bursaries' of £5-10 would be given to encourage children to stay on at the primary schools for a year or two longer, and these too would be subject to a means test. Larger bursaries of £15 upwards would allow older children to go to a secondary or technical school for two or three years, but these, like the university bursaries which were part of some larger schemes, were generally open to all comers. Wherever possible, the commission tried to group smaller endowments to allow bursaries to be distributed more rationally, and to divert funds to the direct support of higher departments in public schools or of higher class schools; at Stirling, for example, a large number of endowments were consolidated and used to strengthen the High School. Technical education,

---

[58] 3 *Hansard* ccliv, HL 9 July, 16 July, 22 July, 26 July 1880; cclxviii, HC 1 May 1882; cclxxii, HC 15 July, 22 July 1882; cclxxiii, HC 2 Aug. 1882, HL 8 Aug., 10 Aug. 1882, HC 15 Aug. 1882. The clause on governing bodies was the most contentious.

evening classes, and secondary schools for girls were other matters to which the commission gave special attention.[59]

The Moncreiff and Balfour commissions had most scope for their activity in the large cities, but their policies could raise issues of principle in smaller towns as well. At Beith, for example, a large sum had been left by Mrs Spier, who died in 1870, to found a traditional hospital for twenty-four local boys, drawn strictly from the labouring class—the sons of shop-keepers and tradesmen were specifically barred. The trustees encountered various difficulties in applying the bequest, and successfully applied to the Moncreiff commission to use it instead for a secondary school, with the twenty-four founda-tioners attending as day pupils. Spier's School, which eventu-ally opened in 1888 after further modifications by the Balfour commission, met a local need and made effective use of a slightly eccentric endowment, but the clear wishes of a very recent benefactor were overridden, and the case raised the same question as some of the Edinburgh reforms: if the usefulness of the foundation was to be extended, were the rights of the poor really respected by maintaining a small number of foundation places in what became a middle-class institution? Why not instead seek a modern use for the endowment which was more directly related to working-class need?[60]

Somewhat similar problems arose where an endowment pro-vided both a secondary school and free elementary education for the locality, as at Dollar and St. Andrews. The creation of school boards with rating powers made this situation anoma-lous. At St. Andrews, for example, the 'foundation department' of Madras College had nearly 300 children who were educated either free or for very low fees—for the trustees, fortified by the belief that 'when any working man leans upon anything but his own exertions and God's providence, it is a bad thing for him', tried to limit the distribution of 'gratis tickets'.[61] But there was a quite separate department for fee-paying primary pupils, and

[59] *Balfour Comm. 1st Rep.*, pp. xviii-xx, and *7th Rep., passim.* Cf. similar statement of principles in *Moncreiff Comm. 2nd Rep.*, pp. vii-xi.

[60] *Colebrooke Comm. 2nd Rep.*, pp. 303-13, and *Appendix to 3rd Rep.*, Vol. II, pp. 264-9; *Moncreiff Comm. 1st Rep.*, pp. xi-xx, 1-21; *Balfour Comm. 1st Rep.*, pp. 838-58.

[61] *Colebrooke Comm. 2nd Rep.*, p. 14 (Revd A. K. H. Boyd).

only the occasional foundationer went on to the secondary school. At the time of the Colebrooke commission, the masters were complaining that the presence of the poor children harmed the success of the secondary school, but the trustees were not considering any change. By the time of Moncreiff, however, they had prepared a radical scheme: they would give the school board £1,000 to build a school to which the foundation children would be transferred, and the endowment would be used to pay fees for deserving cases and provide some bursaries to the college. This was strongly opposed by the school board, which saw it as a blatant attempt to get rid of the poorest pupils while keeping those able to pay fees, and a public meeting called by the town council condemned a scheme which would 'create a most invidious distinction between the children of the industrial and upper classes'; an equally potent objection was that it would sharply increase the school rate.[62] The Moncreiff commission heeded these objections and rejected the scheme, but an only slightly revised version was approved under the 1882 Act. Both this scheme and a very similar one for Dollar were fought right up to the parliamentary stage of the objections procedure, and were taken as examples of spoliation of the poor. 'It is, in my opinion, a great pity that the children of the middle class were ever admitted to this school at all', said one MP of Dollar. 'They were admitted at first as a privilege, and now, like cuckoos, they are driving the poorer children out of the nest.'[63] The principle applied by the reformers was that endowments should not 'relieve the rates', and that the 1872 Act had made the founder's original intentions redundant. But in both these cases, the effect of transferring elementary education to the school board was that henceforth the prestige of the foundation and of its buildings was monopolized by the secondary school.

The 1872 Act did not lead to any greater co-ordination between elementary and higher class schools, even though both were now brought under the same authorities. The school boards

---

[62] Ibid., pp. 1-33; *Moncreiff Comm. 2nd Rep.*, pp. cccxviii, 301-28; *Balfour Comm. 4th Rep.*, pp. 1-43.
[63] *3 Hansard* cccxi, HC 21 Feb. 1887, col. 272.

lacked the funds to set up scholarships, and the city high schools remained detached from the local community. At Edinburgh High School, for example, 61 out of 106 new entrants in 1883 came from outside Edinburgh (often from England or abroad), and of the 45 from the city only four had attended board schools, the majority coming from private preparatory schools.[64] In Glasgow, too, although the High School was reorganized and rehoused by the school board, its fees remained high. What seemed needed were schools accessible to the lower reaches of the middle class, and in Glasgow the solution found was the 'higher grade' school—the term was used from around 1885—which built secondary work on elementary foundations; since the bulk of the school's teaching could be financed through the usual government grants, moderate fees could be charged in the secondary department. The endowments commissions were also concerned to fill the gap in the cities between elementary schools and traditional secondary education, but they thought rather in terms of schools with a technical or commercial bias to suit the classes for whom they were designed.

This was the principle behind the reform of Heriot's which was finally imposed by the Balfour commission in 1885. The Heriot's governors were still proposing to admit day-boys to the hospital and to new schools linked with it, chosen on grounds of poverty and educated entirely free; they would be able to choose 'not only a liberal English, but also an advanced classical, commercial, and scientific education'.[65] The commissioners rejected this, and their plan was a defeat all along the line for Heriot's. The outdoor schools were transferred to the school board, the hospital was turned into a fee-paying day school and the foundationers boarded out, surplus funds were diverted to other institutions instead of being used to expand the Heriot's influence, and the governing body was reduced to twenty-one, with the 'popular' element limited to the two-thirds minimum required by the 1882 Act (eleven from the town council, three from the school board). Most of the endowment was devoted to a complicated array of scholarships and bursaries, only some of which were attached to the new George

---

[64] *Balfour Comm. 1st Rep.*, pp. 759-60 (Marshall).
[65] Quoted from 1879 draft scheme, in *Moncreiff Comm. 1st Rep.*, p. liv.

Heriot's School: the elementary board schools, the High School, and the University also benefited. Provision for 120 foundationers continued, with a qualification based on father-lessness, but most of the bursaries were open to competition. Also part of the scheme was the takeover of the Watt Institution, which now became Heriot-Watt College.

The High School had feared a repetition of the Merchant Company episode, with low fees creating unfair competition; Marshall and his masters proposed dissolving Heriot's altogether and transferring the building to themselves.[66] The commission's solution was to make Heriot's a technical school which would not compete with its classical rivals. Latin was retained, on the grounds that it was 'too much a subject of general education to be entirely excluded', but the teaching of Greek was specifically forbidden; any foundationers who showed special promise for the classics were to be transferred to the High School. Equipped with laboratories and workshops, and with fees which started at £1. 10s., Heriot's school was to be both emphatically modern and directed to the needs of the artisan class.[67]

These proposals provoked a storm of opposition in Edinburgh, and there were heated exchanges at the public hearings held in 1884. Among the bodies making formal objections were the local organizations of both political parties, the Free Church Presbytery, and the Trades Council. The school board and the Liberal *Scotsman* supported the commission, but the Conservative *Courant* bemoaned the final victory over Heriot's of 'the secondary educationists, who for ten years have been trying in vain to gobble it up'.[68] In their own objections the Heriot's governors underlined the differences of principle which lay behind the dispute. Their aim had been to look first to the class of the community which George Heriot had intended to benefit (i.e. in their interpretation, the working class), and not to

---

[66] SRO ED 13 85, printed Memorial by rector and masters of High School.

[67] Ibid., letter from Balfour commission to SED, 7 Mar. 1885. For the scheme itself see PP 1884-5, lxi.

[68] SRO ED 13 85, press-cutting of 17 July 1884, and other objections in this file. See *Balfour Comm. 1st Rep.*, pp. 570-603, 799-809 for views of the Heriot's governors, and *2nd Rep.*, pp. 644-713 for other objections, especially sharp exchanges between the commissioners and working-class spokesmen. Cf. *3 Hansard* ccxcix, HC 23 July 1885.

restrict the type of education which it might be allowed to receive. Under the commission's scheme, 'too much attention is given to the educational merits, and too little to the necessitous circumstances of the parties preferred to the benefits. Every benefit, even for the most elementary education, is to be given by competitive examination. ... the Foundationers, unless they at a prematurely early age show a marked predilection for classical learning, will not be able to follow out a learned profession.' The exclusion of Greek was especially objectionable because it broke the university link, and destroyed what was in practice the only form of access which the poor in Edinburgh had to the classics.[69] The commission, for their part, rejected the Heriot's plan for linking the hospital with the outdoor schools: 'the Commissioners do not see how it would be easy, if indeed practicable at all, to bring a system of merit into operation so long as these free schools are maintained'. Boys would tend to be transferred automatically, and 'inevitably be allowed to remain in the school without any further regard to merit'.[70] No such objection, of course, was ever made to the automatic transfer of fee-paying pupils, but the orthodoxy of the day was incapable of seeing poorer pupils except as a 'gifted' minority admitted as a privilege, and the Heriot's conception of a school which could be both secondary and based on meeting the varying educational needs of a non-privileged clientele seemed merely an example of muddled thinking.

Heriot's school was to be for boys only. The Balfour commission planned to create a girls' school by amalgamating Donaldson's and John Watson's (a plan which went back to Colebrooke), but this was resisted by the governors of those hospitals, and did not go through. The commission's work in Edinburgh thus had an unbalanced result, and the only large girls' schools remained the two run by the Merchant Company, for the school board, unlike those in Glasgow and Aberdeen, took no action to found a High School for girls.

The Balfour commission reviewed existing arrangements for endowments as well as those in need of major change. They made only minor alterations in the Merchant Company

---

[69] SRO ED 13 85, printed objections by Heriot's trust, 1885.
[70] Ibid., letter to SED replying to Heriot's objections, 7 Mar. 1885.

schemes, but Fettes proved more controversial, largely because of a strong political agitation mounted by Duncan McLaren, which alleged misuse of funds left for the welfare of Edinburgh. According to McLaren, the history of Fettes demonstrated both the selfishness of the professional classes, as opposed to the 'mercantile' classes to which he belonged, and the evils of 'close' bodies like the Fettes trustees compared to popular representation. There was particular criticism of the 'open' scholarships at the college, which, as the headmaster himself admitted, were not accessible to the poor because they did not cover the full cost, and were filled from preparatory schools in Scotland and England.[71] McLaren wanted to break up Fettes entirely and turn it into something like Heriot's, but even if the commission had been sympathetic this would hardly have been practicable when the school had been successfully established for fifteen years in a building suitable for no other purpose. Nevertheless the commission felt obliged to reject a scheme involving minimal change submitted by the Fettes trustees, and imposed one which provided for twelve scholarships open only to children in state-aided schools and subject to a means test. The five existing trustees were replaced by a body representing various educational and professional interests in Edinburgh, but the 'popular' element was limited to one representative of the town council—the school board being unrepresented.[72] Otherwise no changes were made. Yet the campaign against Fettes had been a powerful one. It was supported by the town council, and in the parliamentary debate which was the last attempt at opposition three of the city's four MPs spoke against the scheme. Two members of the Balfour commission were themselves against it, including the Liberal MP John Ramsay, who showed his sympathy with the critics of 'spoliation' in a number of controversial cases. But, as with the outcome of the Heriot's affair, popular opposition, however strenuously expressed and over however many years, could not ultimately prevail over the educational orthodoxies established at national level.

[71] D. McLaren, *Fettes College Trustees and the rights of the citizens of Edinburgh* (Edinburgh, 1883), *passim*. See evidence in *Balfour Comm. 1st Rep.*, pp. 678 ff., 701 (headmaster), 859 ff., 868 ff., 887 ff., and *3rd Rep.*, pp. 189-222.

[72] See documents relating to the dispute in *3rd Rep.*, pp. 737-62, and *3 Hansard* ccciv, HC 29 Mar. 1886.

In Glasgow, the reform of endowments had not awaited the work of the commissions. They mostly took the form of free schools giving elementary education to the poor, a provision which was considered obsolete after 1872. The only large endowment was Hutchesons' Hospital, a seventeenth-century charity which spent about two-thirds of its income on pensions to old people and one third on maintaining a free school for boys. This was a day school rather than a hospital in the Edinburgh sense. The beneficiaries were supposed to be, in the first place, the sons of 'decayed burgesses, who have carried on business on their own account in Glasgow with credit and reputation'. In practice, they seem to have come from the artisan and small tradesman class. This had caused controversy, and it was partly in order to clarify the position that the trust had sought an order under the 1869 Act, and in 1872 finally obtained their own Act which gave them extensive powers. There was no shortage of resources, for Hutchesons' was profiting from urban development on its land in the Gorbals. When the Colebrooke commission investigated Glasgow, no changes had been made, and the school was found by their inspector to be fundamentally an elementary one, though described as 'a Primary School of the highest class, with a strong and sound germ of a Secondary School in it'.[73] In 1875, a scheme was approved to bring that germ into growth, and in 1876 the Hutchesons' Grammar Schools, for boys and girls, were opened. These charged fees markedly lower than the High School's, included free education for foundationers along with bursaries of various kinds, and were intended, according to the prospectus, to revive the old kind of grammar school 'where the children of country gentlemen, professional men, tradesmen, and artizans were educated side by side, and were prepared either for the University or commercial life'. Although one aim was to 'connect the School with the University', special attention was given to 'the requirements of those who do not propose for themselves a University career, but intend rather to devote themselves to mercantile, scientific, or technical pursuits, such as mechanics, engineering, &c., or to

---

[73] *Colebrooke Comm. Appendix to 3rd Rep.*, Vol. I, pp. 149-71, 297-300, and evidence in *1st Rep.*, pp. 492-509.

prepare for appointments either in the Civil Service, or other Government employments, open to competition'. The schools immediately attracted 1,002 boys and 728 girls, compared with 286 boys in the last year of the old system, though this early success was not maintained.[74]

Another school which achieved reform through a private Act of Parliament was Allan Glen's Institution, founded in 1853 as an ordinary free charity school for the 'sons of tradesmen or persons in the industrial classes'. In its new guise after 1878, it became 'a secondary school, in which the utmost is made of science as a general instrument of education'.[75] It gave a general scientific education up to the age of fourteen, then two years of specialized training directed to the chemical and engineering industries. With the help of Science and Art Department grants, it was able to impress the Samuelson commission on technical education as 'the only day school in which science teaching was on an altogether satisfactory footing in Scotland; and we consider that it is one of the very best examples of a secondary technical school ... that we have met with in the course of our investigations'.[76]

One of the men behind the reform of Allan Glen's was George Ramsay, who had a powerful influence on the general reform of endowments in Glasgow as representative of the University. The various educational trusts in the city had formed a joint committee in 1879, and this favoured the creation of a limited number of 'graded' secondary schools, with the funds formerly devoted to free schools being diverted to bursaries.[77] The Glasgow hearings of the Balfour commission in 1883 revealed that strong feelings had been aroused about 'the upper classes plundering the poor',[78] and that the school board saw itself as the champion of the plundered. It argued

[74] W. H. Hill, *History of the Hospital and School founded in Glasgow ... by George and Thomas Hutcheson of Lambhill* (Glasgow, 1881), pp. 216-17, 225-9, 230, 233, 289-91.

[75] *Balfour Comm. 1st Rep.*, pp. 177-8 (G. Ramsay).

[76] *Royal Commission on Technical Instruction. Second Report*, Vol. I (PP 1884, xxix), pp. 488-9.

[77] *Report of committee on educational endowments in Glasgow, 1880* (n.p., n.d.); Memorial of Glasgow School Board printed as parliamentary return in PP 1880, lv.

[78] *Balfour Comm. 1st Rep.*, p. 366 (Revd R. Thomson). Cf. objections from the Incorporation of Dyers and Bonnetmakers (271-7), Barony Parochial Board (310-14), Govan Combination Parochial Board (314-20).

that funds left for free education should continue to be used to help the poor parents directly, since poverty had certainly not disappeared since the charities were founded, and, moreover, that the school board 'as the popularly elected managers of national education in this district' should have general control of all educational developments.[79] In Glasgow the school board played something of the part of the Heriot's trust in Edinburgh, while the Glasgow town council, which was the largest constituent of the Hutchesons' trust, was on the side of Ramsay. The Revd Frederick Robertson, a close ally of Ramsay, observed that the school board electorate 'is composed of a large number of persons who pay no rates—hundreds and hundreds of paupers who pay no rates,—but have all votes, and actually exercise their votes. I do not think the School Board represents the mind—certainly not the general mind—of the community so well as the Town Council does'.[80]

The Balfour commission's schemes for Glasgow were a defeat for the school board, and laid heavy emphasis on bursaries. Most of the city's endowments were merged into two general trusts, whose governing bodies overlapped with each other and with that of Hutchesons': Robertson became secretary of all three. Together they offered a bursary system at various levels which was very similar to that based on the Heriot's funds in Edinburgh. The Hutchesons' schools themselves were left much as before, as was Allan Glen's, which as a technical school played the same role as Heriot's in the commission's educational grand design. The only important change at Hutchesons' was that scholarships which had formerly been open were restricted so as to favour the poor, a move strongly criticized by George Ramsay, in an article which praised the principle of 'absolutely free and open competition' and, for good measure, attacked the 'ignorant and

[79] Ibid., pp. 214-52 for school board's views, and 256-66 for Ramsay's. For the school board's case see pamphlets by its clerk and chairman respectively: W. Kennedy, *The school boards of Scotland: their relation to higher education* (Glasgow, 1883); J. N. Cuthbertson, *Secondary education from the school board point of view* (Glasgow, 1887).

[80] *Balfour Comm. 1st Rep.*, p. 81. The school board franchise (householders with a rental above £4, including women) was wider than the municipal one. In Glasgow there were 130,743 school board electors, 79,774 for the town council: SRO ED 13 460, Memorial of Glasgow School Board, 21 Mar. 1883.

vindictive outcry' over Fettes and the whole set of misguided opinions which had fettered the commission's powers in the 1882 Act.[81]

The Balfour commission heard contradictory and confusing evidence about which classes were using Hutchesons' and whether the fees were pitched at the right level. For whatever reason, numbers were to fall drastically in the 1890s, and on two occasions the governors tried to get rid of the school by offering it to the school board. One reason for this was that its situation in the slums of the Gorbals deterred middle-class patronage, but another was no doubt competition from higher grade schools. Ever since starting its operations, Glasgow School Board had attempted to maintain Scottish traditions by appointing graduate schoolmasters and encouraging the teaching of specific subjects, including Latin. This had meagre results, and such teaching was soon concentrated in schools where local social conditions were favourable. By 1883 there were seven of these, with 626 pupils above Standard VI; by far the most successful, with 250 pupils, was Garnethill. Under an able headmaster, Garnethill soon acquired a reputation for university successes, and in 1894 it was converted into a High School for Girls.[82] The other higher grade schools grew more slowly. The higher grade policy was also pursued by Govan School Board, whose area covered the western suburbs of Glasgow, both north and south of the Clyde. Govan had no burgh school under its wing, and had to provide for the needs of 'a large section of the middle class, composed chiefly of warehousemen, foremen, clerks, shopkeepers, and persons of limited income occupying houses of from three to five and six rooms and kitchen'. Like the Glasgow board, Govan claimed to be following the parish school tradition, and in the 1880s opened five higher grade schools, of which the most successful and controversial was Hillhead (1885).[83] Hillhead was situated in an area already over-provided with secondary schools: Glasgow Academy had moved there from the city centre, and

---

[81] *Macmillan's Magazine*, lii (1885), pp. 35-48.

[82] *Balfour Comm. 1st Rep.*, p. 239. Cf. *Parker Comm. 3rd Rep.*, pp. 55-60, 164-5; J. M. Roxburgh, *The School Board of Glasgow 1873-1919* (1971), pp. 49-50, 98 ff., 132-42, 151, 167.

[83] *Parker Comm. 3rd Rep.*, pp. 166-8.

Kelvinside Academy had been founded in 1878. Hillhead's fees were higher than those of Garnethill (about £6 rather than £4), but much lower than those of the proprietary Academies (Glasgow £19, Kelvinside £24), which complained bitterly about this unfair competition. Hillhead—which soon became known as Hillhead High School—attracted a middle-class clientele, and the Academies wanted the SED to enforce the 'ninepenny rule' under which public schools were supposed to charge a maximum fee of 9d. per week; this, it was thought, would ensure that the school appealed only to the lower middle class, as seems to have been the case with the other Govan higher grade schools.[84]

While attacked from one direction as illegitimate extensions into the secondary field, the higher grade schools came under simultaneous fire from Radical MPs as 'genteel academies' financed from the rates paid by working people. 'The working-class children were excluded from the school', it was complained, 'and what was now desired was to have two or three separate schools under the same school board for elementary instruction, in order to correspond with various social grades.'[85] These were the words of James Caldwell, who had been a leading critic of 'spoliation', of the Balfour commission, and of the 'intellectualists' like Robertson 'who simply look at intellectual results, as brought out by competitive examinations, as the end and aim of all education'. But he was no more sympathetic to the school board, whose grading policy meant that middle-class parents could enjoy subsidized education while being 'relieved of the discomfort of the presence of the poorer classes'.[86] These charges were not without foundation, for the higher grade schools had higher fees throughout the age range, which were payable quarterly in advance. Their aim was to meet the special needs of an 'intermediate' social class, not to take clever children from other elementary schools, though the

[84] Ibid., p. 63. There were complex legal disputes about the '9d. rule' and the power of the SED to suspend it.

[85] *3 Hansard* cccxxv, HC 30 Apr. 1888, col. 1010 (Caldwell), and cf. col. 1008 (Cameron). See also *4 Hansard* i, HC 25 Feb. 1892, col. 1267 (Trevelyan); iii, HC 2 May 1892, col. 1807 (Cameron).

[86] J. Caldwell, *Educational endowments of the city of Glasgow. ... How the poor are being robbed of charity funds bequeathed solely to them* (Glasgow, n.d. [1884]), pp. 26-7, 49.

fact that they were based on the Code curriculum made the transfer of such children easy if bursaries became available.

In Glasgow higher grade schools did more than endowed ones to meet new needs, but in Edinburgh the school board seems to have lacked energy faced with the plethora of existing schools, and did not even make much use of the specific subject grants.[87] Both Aberdeen and Dundee, however, saw higher grade developments. In Aberdeen the school board developed three higher grade schools in the 1880s, and later pioneered the idea of a 'central' higher grade school taking children from all over the city. The board was accused of neglecting the Grammar School, refusing to spend any rate income on it even after the 1878 Act allowed this. The rector of the school complained that the board was 'virtually dominated by the Trades' Council, which consists of the radical working men in the city', and the chairman admitted the existence of this ratepayer pressure.[88]

The main innovation in Aberdeen was Robert Gordon's College, created by the Moncreiff commission out of an old-established hospital of the Edinburgh type. According to the original scheme, Gordon's was to be 'mainly devoted to the higher branches of a commercial education', and the classics, while not specifically excluded, were not among the 'chief subjects' prescribed. In practice the school came to specialize in scientific and technical education rather than commercial, but it also developed its classical teaching and began to send boys to the university. The school board complained about this competition with the Grammar School and (as in the Hillhead case) wanted the fees lowered, from £5 p.a. to £3, to make clear that Gordon's was for a lower social class. This was done, though the Trades Council complained that even the lower fees put the school out of the reach of working men: their view was that the school should be mainly for bursars from the element-

---

[87] *Elgin Comm. Minutes of Ev.*, pp. 4-5, 67-8. Cf. *Parker Comm. 3rd Rep.*, p. 89.

[88] Ibid., pp. 94, 121; *Elgin Comm. Minutes of Ev.*, pp. 22, 71-2. The Trades Council did have representatives on the school board after 1882, but they were a minority: K. D. Buckley, *Trade unionism in Aberdeen, 1878 to 1900* (Edinburgh, 1955), pp. 120-8.

ary schools, but in 1885 there were 120 foundationers, 60 free scholars, and 620 pupils paying fees.[89]

In Dundee, developments had followed a rather different path. Dundee High School had been under mixed management before 1872, and had not been transferred to the school board. After disputes about the provision of free places, the board threatened legal action to get control of the school, at which point a local philanthropist, William Harris, stepped in with an offer of £30,000: he would give the school board £10,000 to establish a school of a lower type, and £20,000 to the High School 'on condition of its being managed by governors such as he trusted more than a popularly elected School Board to keep up and raise the standard of liberal education.' This was accepted, and the school board opened Harris Academy in 1885.[90] In the 1890s this was charging £2 p.a., and providing for 'the children of foremen, mill managers, shop-keepers, and a few of the clergy'.[91] By then it had been joined by Morgan Academy, converted by the Balfour commission from Morgan's Hospital. The latter, opened as late as 1868, was a traditional hospital with 100 boys, two-thirds of them orphans, and all 'children of artisans, or of men who have held a similar, or even lower, position, such as cabmen or porters'.[92] The commission dissolved the foundation entirely, handing funds and buildings over to the school board. Dundee thus acquired two higher grade schools, which soon became of full secondary standard, alongside the High School, and the city illustrates both the power of private money to shape future social relationships (for Dundee High School remains an independent school today) and the summary treatment which the reformers could give to institutions, even recently founded ones, which did not conform with their views. The history of Morgan's Hospital may be contrasted with the kid-glove handling of Fettes.

[89] *Colebrooke Comm. 1st Rep.*, pp. 424-47, 702-10; *Moncreiff Comm. 2nd Rep.*, pp. cxliv-clxxxiii, 112-39, 154-71, and *3rd Rep.*, pp. 30-43; *Balfour Comm. 3rd Rep.*, pp. 505-25, 545-7; *Parker Comm. 3rd Rep.*, pp. v, x.

[90] Ibid., pp. iv-v, 156 ff. Harris's sister gave a further £16,000 for the girls' department of the High School.

[91] *Elgin Comm. Minutes of Ev.*, p. 119.

[92] *Colebrooke Comm. Appendix to 3rd Rep.*, Vol. I, pp. 78-81; *Balfour Comm. 4th Rep.*, pp. 351-7, and *5th Rep.*, pp. 18-48. The dissolution of the hospital was opposed by the town council, who were its originators, but supported by the school board and Trades Council.

In all the cities, a hierarchy of schools thus emerged in the 1880s. The attempt to make it a hierarchy of functions was on the whole unsuccessful: all three of the schools marked out for a special role—Heriot's, Allan Glen's, and Robert Gordon's— soon developed strong classical sides, and the prohibition of Greek at Heriot's was later removed. In the same way, the higher grade schools, influenced by the parish school model, aimed from the start at the universities and the professions. The real hierarchy was one of social differentiation, and the complexities of urban society were reflected in the fees charged, which varied from £20 or more in the Academies to £2 or less in the higher grade schools. In the more exclusive schools, high fees reassured parents that there would be no social mixture, and such schools did not necessarily suffer from financial competition; as we have seen, they often attempted to force a rival school's fees down rather than up. The real secret of success was to combine moderate fees with social cachet and a reputation for high academic quality: the Merchant Company schools and Hillhead managed to pull off this trick, but Hutchesons' failed to find the right formula. The great service which these schools performed was to put secondary education of a guaranteed quality within reach of the lower ranges of the middle class, giving them access both to the universities and to the numerous professions and careers which set examinations for entry. The working class was less well served by the developments of the 1880s, for even a fee of £2 was a real barrier, and transfer from elementary to secondary schools depended on the chancy workings of the various bursary schemes.

The work of the Moncreiff and Balfour commissions, the emergence of the higher grade schools, and the creation of the Leaving Certificate as part of the newly dynamic policy of the SED after 1885 mark out the 1880s as the formative period of the modern Scottish secondary school. The Balfour commission was especially important because its schemes for endowed schools followed a common organizational model which was imitated by school boards when they reorganized their higher class schools: this provided for a headmaster with absolute authority on English lines, aided by a staff of assistants, and for a planned and balanced curriculum with a common scale of fees. 'Endowed' and 'higher class' schools came to be thought of together as forming the first rank of secondary schools, contrasted with those—whether the new higher grade schools in the cities or the old common schools elsewhere—where secondary education was not the sole purpose of the school. The Balfour commission was also significant because it showed that even the most comprehensive reform of endowments could only be, in its chairman's words, 'a very essential and proper preliminary to securing a complete system of secondary education'. The commission's final report pointed out that a bursary system based on local funds was bound to be capricious, and that 'a complete and satisfactory system of higher education for Scotland as a whole' could not be established 'until some order is introduced into the system of Higher Education which these endowments are designed to foster, because thus only can the path upwards from the elementary school be opened to every child that is worthy to pursue it, to whatever class it may belong, or in whatever part of the kingdom it may live'.[93] By the end of the decade, the time was ripe for the extension of state aid.

---

[93] Balfour of Burleigh, *Secondary education in Scotland* (Glasgow, 1887), pp. 6, 19-22; *Balfour Comm. 7th Rep.*, p. xxi.

6

SECONDARY EDUCATION
FROM THE 1880s TO 1914

In the 1870s there seemed to be no contradiction in campaigning simultaneously for better secondary schools and for maintaining the 'higher' subjects in rural schools, but in the 1880s the development of higher grade schools began to threaten the prosperity—insecure at the best of times—of established secondary schools, and there was a growing rift between the secondary and primary teachers, who competed for political influence.[1] The EIS and its organ the *Educational News* developed a critique of the secondary education movement which attracted enough sympathy among MPs to defeat the SED's attempt to channel the first state grant to secondary education in 1892 mainly to the higher class schools. This rivalry continued into the 1900s, but the SED—whose authority and expertise in this field developed rapidly— then introduced a series of changes which were accepted as a compromise: secondary education continued to be given in a large number of schools, and received the same financial aid whatever the type of school, but it was sharply distinguished from the mere prolongation of elementary education, and the claims of democracy were held to have been met once efficient arrangements had been made for transferring promising pupils at an early age.

Neither side in these disputes thought of primary and secondary schools as successive stages in an educational plan: this idea was foreign to nineteenth-century thinking, and with few exceptions all schools in Scotland aimed at educating their pupils from initial entry until they were ready to leave. The argument was about whether there needed to be two different types of school. The secondary education party, as we have seen, thought that secondary schooling had a character of its

---

[1] Similar conflicts in England seem to have come a decade later: O. Banks, *Parity and prestige in English secondary education* (1955), pp. 15-19.

own which should apply from the start, and one trend which followed from this in the 1880s was the opening of elementary or 'preparatory' departments where these did not already exist; such departments, freed from the constraints of the Code by charging high fees, were now regarded as essential for a successful school.[2] Most higher class and endowed schools were organized like this, and were essentially middle-class in their clientele. The anti-'secondary' party were not necessarily against class differentiation in education, as the example of the Glasgow higher grade schools showed, but they argued that secondary education should grow naturally out of an elementary schooling which could be the same for everybody in its content and methods. In the traditional parish school, both types had been given by the same teacher. This was passing into history, but the tradition was reinterpreted to mean in the cities that transfer into secondary schools should encounter as few barriers as possible, and in the countryside that secondary education should be encouraged to develop wherever the means and the demand existed. For a long time, indeed, it was argued that it should be offered by at least one school in every parish. 'There must be one school within reach of every pupil of twelve years, where a secondary education can be had', wrote the *Educational News* in 1880; 'and any attempt to dispense with the public school for that purpose, by the substitution of a purely secondary school, commanding a district of ten or twelve miles' radius, would be positively mischievous.'[3]

For a time, however, the initiative was held by the Balfour commission, which was dedicated to the creation of full secondary schools. The *Educational News* joined in the cries against robbing the poor. 'The spoliation of the lower by the upper classes is as prevalent at the present day as in the wildest period of Scottish history', it complained in 1883, with special reference to Fettes and the Glasgow endowments.[4] The *News* criticized the 'bursary mania', and accused the commission of

---

[2] See evidence in *Parker Comm. 3rd Rep.*, p. 60 (J. Kerr), *Balfour Comm. 4th Rep.*, p. 18 (Madras College, St. Andrews). Such departments competed with private rather than board schools.

[3] *EN*, v. 432 (24 July 1880).

[4] Ibid., viii. 711 (27 Oct. 1883). Cf. pp. 35 (13 Jan.), 88 (3 Feb.), 247 (14 Apr.), 586 (8 Sept.).

having *'bursary on the brain'*. The principle of merit was specious, it argued, when the rich started with so many advantages, and although the 1882 Act contained various safeguards for the poor, 'all the fine-spun words, designed to limit upper-class cupidity, are of as little avail as a spider's web in a hurricane'.[5] The *News* recommended instead that the funds released by endowment reform should be used to make secondary education generally cheaper. The value of the higher class schools was acknowledged; indeed, they should be supported out of the rates, but in return they must become genuinely public schools, with places reserved for elementary pupils and with the curriculum harmonized to make transfer easy.[6] Edinburgh High School, for example, was criticized for maintaining high fees in a vain attempt to compete with more exclusive schools, which left it half empty. 'But if the classes are hopelessly lost, the masses are ready to fill the deserted classrooms to overflowing', and the school should be opened up to become 'the school of the people'.[7] These remarks were especially directed against the school's rector, John Marshall, who was the leading 'secondary' spokesman in the 1880s. In 1885 he founded the Association of Teachers in the Secondary Schools of Scotland,[8] which campaigned both for more state aid to secondary schools and for their management by separate authorities which would appreciate the nature of secondary culture and foster the university link; many heads of higher class schools were restive under school board control, and envied the endowed schools their independent governing bodies.

The EIS, conversely, insisted on a single authority for all types of school, and combated 'the growing pretensions of the secondary teachers'.[9] Professional rivalries here came into play, for as the *Educational News* pointed out 'an elementary school, pure and simple, does not command much social con-

[5] Ibid., xi. 75 (23 Jan. 1886), xiii. 421 (16 June 1888). Cf. v. 445 (31 July 1880), vii. 402 (24 June 1882).
[6] Ibid., iv. 199 (12 Apr. 1879), vi. 191-2 (19 Mar. 1881), xi. 761-2 (23 Oct. 1886), xii. 853 (3 Dec. 1887).
[7] Ibid., xiii. 751 (27 Oct. 1888). Cf. viii. 503-4 (4 Aug. 1883).
[8] Ibid., xi. 7 (2 Jan. 1886), xvi. 706-9 (17 Oct. 1891). An earlier Association of Higher Class Schoolmasters existed from 1874 to 1878. A London-based organization, the Teachers' Guild, also had a branch in Glasgow favoured by secondary teachers.
[9] Ibid., xiv. 70 (26 Jan. 1889).

sideration; and none are more ready to regard elementary teachers with scornful eyes than their secondary brethren. ... To the public teachers of Scotland, it is really a matter of life and death, pecuniarily and socially, to uphold by every means in their power, the traditional idea of combined primary and secondary education in every suitable school.'[10] In its early years the *News* tended to join in the complaints about the Code and the 1872 Act, but as time passed it came to see the Code as a sound basis for higher studies, and the specific subject system as an instrument which could be developed further. In 1882 it thought that these subjects could be brought up to university entrance level, leading to the 'establishment of a recognised connection between the poor man's secondary school and the University'. In 1890, following a scheme which the EIS had submitted to the SED, it proposed five stages of specific subjects, with an ascending scale of grants, which would cover the full range of secondary schooling.[11] 'Secondary Education', the *News* maintained, 'is not a thing apart, a new Educational departure. It is but the natural development of the Elementary training, the fuller growth of the primary plant.' Thus, 'The secondary school of the future will be the higher department of the ordinary public school; and it is futile to attempt any other arrangement.'[12] The *News* naturally approved of the higher grade schools, and welcomed Glasgow School Board as an ally in the fight against its *bêtes noires* Marshall and Ramsay.[13]

The talk of 'culture' in which the secondary party so freely indulged caused particular irritation. 'Secondary schools, University entrance examinations, compulsory Latin and Greek, and other ideas born in times long ago ... are yet the guiding notions in the educational world', the *News* complained in 1883, and it was a persistent critic of the classical dominance in the universities. Any subject could impart 'culture' if it was properly taught: 'the highest ideal of culture is not that which makes it the direct object of a special curriculum, but that which makes it the outcome of a curriculum adapted to the

---

[10] Ibid., xv. 334 (17 May 1890).

[11] Ibid., vii. 763 (25 Nov. 1882), xv. 169-70 (8 Mar. 1890).

[12] Ibid., xv. 135 (22 Feb. 1890), 833 (6 Dec. 1890).

[13] Ibid., xii. 834 (26 Nov. 1887), comment on speech by chairman of Glasgow School Board. For other hostile comments on Ramsay see pp. 230-1 (26 Mar.), 539 (30 July), 581-2 (20 Aug.).

necessities of life. The business of life has the first claim on the educational institutions of the country; and their success must be measured by the extent to which they prepare for the business of life. Culture is a necessary product of any form of thorough intellectual training.'[14] Elementary education, far from being a sterile routine as the secondary teachers implied, provided a solid foundation for whatever vocational option the student later chose.

Thus two distinct ideals of secondary education were in the field: one which saw it as organizationally and socially distinct, and based on a classical culture whose rigour marked off the élite and regulated the admission of a privileged handful to their ranks, and one which would make it 'available for all who desire to take advantage of it',[15] modern in its outlook, and flexible in its social function. The question was which way the SED would incline, now that it was at last taking an interest in the secondary schools. In 1885 the Department was reorganized under the new Secretary for Scotland, and Henry Craik became its permanent head. Craik was to dominate the making of educational policy until 1904, and exploited the SED's powers to give it an influence over secondary education which the 1872 Act had hardly envisaged. Craik was a typical 'London Scot': the son of a Glasgow minister, he was educated at Glasgow High School and University, and went to Balliol as a Snell exhibitioner; the whole of his subsequent career was on the Education Department's London staff. After his retirement Craik became a Conservative MP for the Glasgow and Aberdeen university seat, and he held strongly unionist views.

In a small department, Craik's authority was absolute, and the Scottish Secretaries, who had many other responsibilities, followed his advice; the only one who knew much about education was Balfour of Burleigh, who in any case had a strong sympathy with Craik's ideas. Craik's aim, as far as it may be judged from his policies, was to encourage distinct secondary schools, to rescue the higher class schools from the financial neglect which they had suffered since 1872, and to achieve much higher and more uniform academic standards. At the

---

[14] Ibid., viii. 233 (7 Apr. 1883), xv. 301 (3 May 1890).
[15] Ibid., xii. 853 (3 Dec. 1887).

same time, Craik wanted to encourage science and modern languages to take their place alongside the classics, and seems to have been genuinely anxious to bring down fees so that secondary education was more accessible, and to ensure that bursaries and transfer arrangements for poor pupils worked effectively.

His first move was to begin the inspection of secondary schools, which had been allowed by the 1878 Act, but which did not take place until 1886; the first report revealed that 'the signs of failure ... are numerous'. Weaknesses arose from the shortage of resources, the apathy of parents and their readiness to take their children away prematurely (this became a standard complaint in Craik's annual reports), and antiquated curricula. 'In many schools the subjects studied appear almost exactly to follow the choice of fifty years ago or more; and this naturally produces in the minds of parents a doubt as to the utility of the education offered, in its application to the practical necessities of life.'[16] In the next year, however, the inspection found 'evidence of renewed activity, of a curriculum developing so as to meet modern requirements and of a more defined aim and improved organization'.[17] In future the 'defined aim' was to be provided by Craik's second weapon, the Leaving Certificate, introduced in 1888. This examination met a practical need by largely replacing the numerous government and professional examinations which had complicated the schoolmaster's task, and when the universities eventually laid down entrance requirements the Leaving Certificate served that purpose too. It also gave the SED direct influence over what was taught in the schools, for Craik managed to fend off any participation of the universities in its running, and it could potentially be used to impose a common curriculum. For the moment this power was not used, certificates being awarded in whatever individual subjects candidates chose to offer; at first too the Leaving Certificate was confined to higher class and endowed

[16] *CCES Rep., 1886-7* (PP 1887, xxxii), p. xxix. SED inspection was also extended to endowed schools under the 1882 Act.
[17] *CCES Rep., 1887-8* (PP 1888, xli), pp. xxix-xx (comma inserted for sake of clarity).

schools, following Craik's policy of concentrating secondary education in the schools best equipped for it.[18]

In 1886 Craik himself became one of the members of a departmental committee on various educational questions, chaired by the MP C. S. Parker. Secondary education was dealt with in its third report, published in 1888. The Parker committee's first and general conclusion was that 'for secondary education the country should look mainly to schools specially appropriated to that work'. It also recommended that 'in each country parish a public school should be maintained, as of old in Scotland, capable of preparing its best pupils for University education'. But the mechanisms to allow this were not discussed at length, and the committee was far more concerned with the problems of urban education.[19] Much of the evidence which it heard was about the state of the burgh schools and the competition between different types of school in the cities. The Secondary Schoolteachers' Association gave evidence at length, and there was a separate memorandum from one of their most prominent members, James Macdonald of Kelvinside Academy.[20]

Four issues before the committee were of special interest. First, the finance of secondary education. The committee endorsed the longstanding complaints about the neglect of the higher class schools, and proposed that they should receive parliamentary grants, contingent on a contribution from the rates. Second, there was the question of helping the 'promising children of poor parents': broadly speaking, the Parker committee shared the Balfour commission's belief in bursaries, but concluded that the reform of endowments was unable to provide what was needed. More than half of the bursaries created by the Balfour schemes were allocated to Edinburgh, and another quarter to Glasgow and Lanarkshire, leaving less than

[18] The examination was on three grades—lower, higher, and honours. The universities had run 'local' examinations for school-leavers since the 1860s, but these were never very successful. The subject is well covered by T. B. Dobie, 'The Scottish Leaving Certificate, 1888-1908', in T. R. Bone (ed.), *Studies in the history of Scottish education 1872-1939* (1967).

[19] *Parker Comm. 3rd Rep.*, p. xx. Cf. Parker's views in *Elgin Comm. Minutes of Ev.*, p. 90, and C. S. Parker, *Secondary education in Scotland and the state* (Ayr, 1888).

[20] *Parker Comm. 3rd Rep.*, pp. 92-6, 171-4. The EIS evidence (86-7) was much less incisive.

a fifth for the rest of the country. The committee therefore wanted bursaries financed out of the rates, and suggested that in return for state grants the schools should offer 10 per cent of their places free to pupils from state-aided schools. The idea of lowering fees all round was rejected; they should rather be raised to whatever the market would bear, in order to maximize income.[21] Third, the committee considered the complaints about unfair competition from higher grade and endowed schools, especially those against Hillhead. It refused to recommend the restrictions on higher grade schools which some secondary headmasters wanted, but it did warn that higher grade education based on specific subjects should not be confused with true secondary education, and enjoined both higher grade and endowed schools to charge realistic fees. On all these points, it was the secondary ideal which was favoured.[22]

The fourth issue was a new one: should there be separate administrative authorities for secondary education? The secondary schoolmasters suggested district boards for secondary education, with rating powers, and they found even more attractive a plan in Macdonald's memorandum for four special boards based on the university regions, which would coordinate the secondary schools and strengthen their links with the universities. Macdonald himself, and his colleague at Glasgow Academy, suggested that with such an arrangement they might be prepared to bring their schools into the 'national system'.[23] The Parker committee did not adopt this plan, but looked rather to the county councils which were then about to be set up; some kind of county authority with rating powers was envisaged, and in the meantime there should be special arrangements so that surrounding districts could contribute to the upkeep of burgh schools. The Parker recommendations, which were on balance favourable to the secondary party, provided the context of debate when secondary education returned to the parliamentary agenda in the 1890s.

[21] Ibid., pp. vi-vii, xx.
[22] Ibid., pp. x-xiv, xx-xxi.
[23] Ibid., pp. vii-viii, 70, 78-9, 81-3, 93, 172-3. The two Academies were in financial trouble at this time; but see a similar suggestion by A. McBean of Edinburgh Academy in *EN* xiv. 50 (19 Jan. 1889).

The first state grant to secondary education came about through a complex set of changes in local taxation, which released funds which could be earmarked for educational purposes. In 1889 and 1890 these were used to make education in primary schools free,[24] and a further sum in 1890—the 'residue grant', or 'whisky money'—was allocated to county and burgh councils for technical education; some of this money, though not much, came to secondary schools.[25] In 1891, new funds were used to make education free in England, and since this had already been achieved in Scotland it was agreed that the Scottish share of £60,000 (the 'equivalent grant') should be used to promote secondary education. Legislation had to wait until 1892, but throughout 1891 the rival parties lined up their claims and mobilized their political influence. At first the EIS and the ATSS hoped to produce a joint scheme, but the differences between them soon became clear, and for the next few years relations were very strained. The system of local management was one issue, finance another: the secondary teachers followed the Parker committee in favouring a regime of high fees with bursaries for the poor, while the EIS wanted a general lowering of fees. Broadly speaking, the former wanted the money spent to strengthen individual secondary *schools*, the latter to support secondary *education* in whatever school it was found. A subsidiary issue was the Leaving Certificate, which the EIS and the school boards sought to have opened up to state-aided schools. The school boards as a whole, orchestrated by Glasgow, generally took the anti-secondary line. As 1891 progressed, the pages of the *Educational News* were filled with news of meetings, of deputations to London, of lobbying of MPs. In August the EIS held a special conference on the issue at Oban; the Glasgow School Board produced its own scheme which other boards accepted, and in January 1892 a Conference of School Boards passed a series of resolutions calling for a grant of £75,000, to be used mainly to help school boards improve the existing

---

[24] Up to Standard V; extended to children aged fourteen in 1891 and fifteen in 1893. See H. M. Knox, *Two hundred and fifty years of Scottish education, 1696-1946* (Edinburgh, 1953), pp. 113-14.

[25] It was mostly spent on evening classes and technical institutions. A Technical Schools (Scotland) Act of 1887 allowed school boards to open technical schools, but remained virtually unused.

schools and organize new higher departments in public schools.
The higher class schools should be 'specially and favourably
dealt with', but all schools with effective post-primary education should share in the grant.[26]

Thus the ground was well prepared when the bill which
became the Education and Local Taxation Account (Scotland)
Act was introduced in February 1892; it was followed in April
by a Memorandum from the SED which provides interesting
evidence of the policies favoured by Craik. He began with
some statistical estimates: there were about 270,000 children in
the age-group 13-16, among whom some 32,000 (12 per cent)
were potential secondary pupils 'either from the circumstances
of their parents, or the special capabilities of the children'. The
numbers actually in secondary schools were 20,000 (12,000 in
endowed schools, 5,500 in burgh schools, 2,500 in private
schools); but only 18,000 of these were over 13, so that there
were 14,000 extra pupils who might be attracted. This was to
be done by using the Equivalent Grant to reduce fees in higher
class and endowed schools: a capitation grant of £3 p.a. would
be given on condition that the average fee did not exceed £3
(compared with existing averages of £6 in higher class schools,
£7 in endowed ones), and that a similar sum came from 'local
resources' (rates or endowments). This would cost £42,000,
and a further £15,000 would be spent on helping selected
'higher departments' of rural schools; with £3,000 set aside for
the expenses of inspection and the Leaving Certificate, this
made £60,000.[27]

In opting for a low-fee policy, the Memorandum favoured
the 'primary' party; on the other hand, the capitation grant
was to be limited to full secondary schools and to a limited
number of others designated by the SED, so that the policy of
spreading it around the rural schools was ruled out. The grant
system would also have strengthened the centralizing hand of
the SED, and although there was a vague reference to joint

[26] *EN*, xvi. 117, 123 (14 Feb. 1891), 128-30 (21 Feb. 1891), 171 (7 Mar. 1891),
297-9 (2 May 1891), 324, 326-7 (16 May 1891), 541 (15 Aug. 1891), 569-72 (29 Aug.
1891), 625 (19 Sept. 1891), 649 (26 Sept. 1891); xvii. 27-9 (9 Jan. 1892), 51-2 (16 Jan.
1892), 84 (30 Jan. 1892), 116 (13 Feb. 1892), 356-7 (28 May 1892). Cf. J. A. Campbell, *Secondary education and the state: the present position of the question in Scotland* (Glasgow,
1891), *passim.*

[27] Memorandum printed in *Elgin Comm. Minutes of Ev.*, pp. 141-2.

action by school boards there was no mention of county or district authorities. Opposition to the 'despotic' tendencies of the SED was one reason why the scheme was badly received by the Liberal opposition in Parliament, though Liberal MPs differed in their grounds of criticism. On the one hand, representatives of popular Glasgow constituencies (Sir George Trevelyan, James Caldwell, Charles Cameron) opposed spending the money on education at all, and especially on schools for the middle classes; the grant should be used instead to relieve the hard-pressed ratepayer. On the other hand, those who welcomed the grant tended to maintain that it should be used to build up secondary education in the ordinary schools.[28] Yet another point of view was that of the Aberdeen MP Hunter, who wanted the whole sum spent on a giant bursary scheme, which would ensure (he claimed) that it went only to the poor; but bursaries were a less popular panacea than in the 1880s, and this view was not widely shared.[29]

In 1882 MPs had succeeded in imposing conditions on the reform of endowments because they felt that the rights of the poor were under attack. In 1892 they succeeded in getting Craik's memorandum withdrawn because of the vague but potent feeling that the separate development of secondary education was alien to the Scottish democratic tradition, and because they favoured local control over bureaucratic centralization; Liberal MPs were attracted by the model of the Welsh Intermediate Education Act of 1889, which had created county authorities.[30] In 1892 as in 1882, MPs were relying on their political instincts rather than on any very close examination of the educational realities, but that did not make their opposition less effective. In 1892 the government was anxious to get the bill passed before the dissolution of Parliament, and in May it secured this by a major concession: the means of distributing the Equivalent Grant would be left open, and a departmental committee would report on how it should best be done. The

---

[28] *4 Hansard* i, HC 25 Feb. 1892; iii, HC 31 Mar., 4 Apr., 2 May 1892; iv, HC 3 May, 5 May 1892; v, HC 31 May 1892.

[29] *4 Hansard* iii, HC 2 May 1892; iv, HC 3 May 1892; v, HC 31 May, 13 June 1892. Cf. W. A. Hunter, *The future of higher education in Scotland* (Aberdeen, 1890), pp. 14-18.

[30] A group of Scottish MPs had introduced an abortive bill on similar lines in 1888 (in PP 1888, vi).

committee was to be headed by Lord Elgin, and it included Craik himself, the Conservative J. A. Campbell, the chairman of Glasgow School Board (J. N. Cuthbertson), and A. H. D. Acland, a Liberal educational expert who had special experience of the working of the Welsh Act.

The evidence given to this committee traversed familiar ground. The EIS and the ATSS put forward their rival views. The endowed schools urged their claim for a share in the grant. The virtues of 'central' secondary schools in rural areas, rather than multiplying small 'higher departments', were canvassed. Above all, there was much discussion of the finance of urban schools, for the most criticized proposal in the Memorandum was the £3 limit on fees. Schools which had high fees claimed that their loss of income would not be replaced by the new grants or by increased numbers—on the contrary, any influx of poorer pupils would tend to drive away the existing clientele. According to Marshall, if a hundred free pupils were admitted a hundred others would leave, as 'the idea would have got abroad that the school was getting more and more socially ineligible. It is not an idea of which I necessarily approve.' Craik's questioning of Marshall and others on this point was especially critical, implying that the schools and school boards were influenced by middle-class selfishness.[31] Whether because of these strictures or not, Edinburgh School Board reduced the High School fees substantially in 1893, to the Merchant Company level, and this proved successful in attracting new pupils.[32]

The Elgin committee's report appeared in August, by which time a general election had brought a Liberal government to power, with Trevelyan as Scottish Secretary. The report recommended retaining Craik's principle of capitation grants, but with various modifications to meet the criticisms which had been made—for example, higher class schools which did not want to accept the £3 fee limit could opt instead to take a grant of £6 for every free scholar they accepted. The main new suggestion was for county secondary education committees, whose

[31] *Elgin Comm. Minutes of Ev.*, pp. 42-3. Cf. Craik's questioning of witnesses at pp. 4-5, 70, 94.
[32] *EN*, xviii. 486 (22 July 1893), and Craik's evidence in *Royal Commission on Secondary Education*, Vol. IV (PP 1895, xlvi), p. 193.

role would be to inquire into local conditions and designate schools which should be given grants. The proposals in this report were embodied without change in a Minute of the SED, and although its submission to Parliament was delayed all seemed set to go ahead, and the county committees were brought into being. They comprised equal numbers of county councillors and school board representatives, with a school inspector to offer expert advice; there were separate committees for the four cities, with representatives of endowed bodies as well as town councils, and for Govan and Leith.[33]

In 1893, however, new political pressure by the Scottish MPs forced the SED to accept a quite different idea: that the county committees should become permanent bodies, drawing up their own schemes for allocating a lump sum distributed amongst them on a population basis. When their views were sought, the majority of the committees themselves preferred the original plan, but the minority included influential committees like Edinburgh and Glasgow: distribution on a population basis obviously favoured urban areas where secondary education was already well provided for, and ignored the fact that it was most expensive to organize where the population was sparsest.[34] Nevertheless, the new scheme went ahead, and the principles of the 1892 Memorandum had to be scrapped altogether. Craik had been defeated by the power of localism, and he did not forget or forgive this. His aim had been to use the new grant to put the finances of the higher class schools on a sound footing, but there was no guarantee that the county committees would think this way; whereas the 1892 Memorandum had planned to give these schools £42,000, by 1895 only £15,000 was reaching them.[35] The SED's standard complaint against the committees was that they 'dissipated' the grant in too many small packets. It was true that the county schemes had to follow regulations made by the Department, and receive individual approval, and some restrictions could be imposed in this way: in 1894, the smaller counties were helped by making a fixed grant of £200 to each committee before the balance was shared out, and a revision of the scheme in 1897 obliged them

[33] *Elgin Comm. Rep.*, pp. 2 ff., and order setting up committees in PP 1893-4, xxviii.
[34] Parliamentary return showing replies of committees, in PP 1893-4, lxix.
[35] *CCES Rep., 1894-5* (PP 1895, xxx), p. xxix.

to spend this £200 on higher class schools, and to make other cash grants only to separate secondary departments approved by the SED.[36] But even so, the 'chaotic diversity' of the schemes remained, and at the end of the decade the secondary schoolmasters still felt that the system was 'a travesty of the intentions of Parliament, which intended to stimulate secondary education, and specially secondary education in the burgh schools'; Marshall, at least, consoled himself with the thought that this muddle was the 'British way of doing things'.[37]

The *Educational News*, which had at first attributed the political reversal of 1893 to the machinations of the secondary party, and which remained hostile to the secondary committees in principle because they embodied the separate treatment of secondary schools, nevertheless declared once the county schemes had been published that 'With certain modifications, Scotch education is back again on the lines of the old parish schools; and it seems destined to advance on these lines to a higher perfection than was possible under the circumstances of the past.'[38] This was an exaggeration, but it was true that the system allowed committees which wished to support rural education to do so. Although the Equivalent Grant schemes showed great variety, there were three main ways of using the money: cash grants to individual schools; grants related to pupils' examination performance, either in specific subjects or in the Leaving Certificate; and bursaries for individuals, which would be additional to but uncoordinated with any bursary schemes which might happen to exist after the work of the Balfour commission. Some counties did concentrate their resources on a small number of schools—in Berwickshire, for example, the grant was used to create a completely new higher class school at Duns—but the general effect of the system was to encourage a network of small 'higher' or secondary departments built on primary schools. In Dumfries, a typical rural county, five schools received direct grants in 1899 as well as Dumfries Academy; in Fife, five higher class schools were aided (two public, three endowed), but so were ten secondary

---

[36] Minute of 10 June 1897, in *CCES Rep., 1896-7* (PP 1897, xxix), p. 151; cf. *1897-8* (PP 1898, xxviii), pp. xxxi-xxxii. Some of the changes went back to 1896.

[37] *EN*, xxiii. 839 (W. Maybin), 840 (3 Dec. 1898), and cf. 73-4 (22 Jan.).

[38] Ibid., xviii. 821 (9 Dec. 1893), and cf. 789-90 (25 Nov.)

departments in smaller centres; in Midlothian, despite the proximity of Edinburgh, ten schools were aided, and in Lanarkshire twenty-two 'central' schools in addition to two higher class ones.[39]

In the cities, the pattern varied. At Aberdeen, grants were made only to higher class schools (the Grammar School, the new Girls' High School, and Robert Gordon's), while in Govan the school board's six higher grade schools shared out the largesse. In Glasgow the grants were linked with free places for children from public schools: £3,820 went to the High School, the Girls' High School, the two Hutchesons' schools, and Allan Glen's, and £2,640 was shared among four Roman Catholic and five higher grade schools. In Edinburgh, the affairs of the secondary education committee were controversial. Because of the presence of Merchant Company and Heriot's representatives, the school board members were in a minority. The school board's chairman, Colin Macrae, was a strong champion of higher grade schools, but the committee refused to support them. As in Glasgow, grants were tied to free places, and went to the High School, the four Merchant Company schools, and Heriot's; the Merchant Company schools alone received £1,363 of the committee's budget of £3,116, in return for 127 free places. Only £800 went to board schools, in the form of capitation grants for Leaving Certificate passes. In 1898 it was still the case that 'To the representatives of the Merchant Company the mere mention of anything resembling higher education in a Board school is like a red rag to a bull', and it was not until 1900 that the school board opened two higher grade schools.[40]

Since the Edinburgh scheme provided places only in full secondary schools, there were problems of transfer, and there was special criticism of the examination by which free places were awarded. The age limits were ten to twelve, yet as well as the usual primary subjects the examination included Latin, French, German, or mathematics (two of these at first, later reduced to one). This academic bias obviously favoured parents

[39] *CCES Rep., 1899-1900* (PP 1900, xxiv), pp. 45 ff. For interesting details of the politics of secondary education in the Borders see *1894-5*, pp. 323-4.

[40] *EN*, xxiii. 267 (16 Apr. 1898). For Macrae's views see ibid., xix. 33-5 (13 Jan. 1894), xx. 223-4 (6 Apr. 1895).

with a positive interest in secondary education and those who could afford to pay for special tuition.[41] According to the *Educational News*, the scheme illustrated all the vices of bursary systems, and was likely to prove an 'unmitigated curse to the working class population of the city'. It also harmed the public schools themselves by 'the removal of the cream of the pupils', and was naturally unpopular with headmasters who would have preferred to keep their bright children themselves.[42] The *News* also argued that the need to transfer to schools with an alien atmosphere formed a cultural barrier for working-class parents, who would not actively seek secondary education, but might be persuaded to take advantage of it if it was on the spot: 'the working man's son very much prefers to continue his higher studies in the school with which he is familiar rather than in that associated in his mind with a gentility which is distasteful to him. ... There is a great amount of latent talent among the young of the working classes. ... But the ordinary Board school is the only one by which the initial step in the development can be taken.'[43]

Thus in the 1890s—and before then where the Balfour commission had reformed endowments—the movement of 'scholarship' children from elementary to secondary schools was becoming a familiar phenomenon, and some of the problems which it caused were being discussed. The Elgin committee heard complaints that the poorer children were 'ostracized' in the secondary schools, and that the early teaching of Latin in the latter imposed an artificial handicap. On the other side, the secondary teachers complained of the inadequate preparation of the scholars, and feared the social consequences of admitting too many. These fears were confirmed by the experience of Perth Academy, where a wide extension of free places in 1899 led to protests from the parents of fee-paying pupils, after which the school board imposed a numerical limit.[44]

---

[41] *CCES Rep., 1894-5*, p. 321; *1895-6* (PP 1896, xxix), p. 305; *1896-7*, p. 326.

[42] *EN*, xix. 458 (14 July 1894), xxi. 345-6 (23 May 1896), xxiii. 208-9 (26 Mar. 1898).

[43] Ibid., xxi. 867 (26 Dec. 1896); cf. xxiii. 717 (15 Oct. 1898).

[44] E. Smart, *History of Perth Academy* (Perth, 1932), pp. 190-1. Cf. views of W. Maybin (Ayr Academy) in *EN*, xxiii. 839-40 (3 Dec. 1898), of Marshall in ibid., xxviii. 892 (21 Nov. 1903).

If secondary education was developed in public schools, as the *Educational News* recommended, such transfers might not be necessary: higher class schools could be left to do their own work, while board-school secondary education met the special needs of the working class. Such a conception lay behind the higher grade plans of Edinburgh School Board, whose chairman stressed that the aim was to prepare for practical life.[45] In 1897 very similar ideas were expressed in a speech by Laurie. Laurie believed that university preparation should be concentrated in true secondary schools, but he now drew a distinction between the 'professional' and the 'industrial' forms of secondary education, and agreed that the latter should be given in selected board schools. This was seized on by the *Educational News*. 'There was a time when the pulpit and the teacher's desk were almost the only positions open to working-class boys of "pregnant pairts." The Grammar School was then their natural destination, if they did not go direct to the University.' But now that other careers are open,

The secondary school is no longer a stepping-stone on the way of Board pupils to success in life. ... The industrial curriculum is what the Board pupils desire; and the Board schools must furnish it. The Code provides a good education for all who remain to exhaust it; and a truly liberal secondary education may be built on that foundation without the loss of a day in adapting the pupils to the new circumstances of alien schools. An English education quite equal to that of the ordinary secondary school is the natural outcome of the grammatical and literary drill of the Code.

French and science can be added, to form an education equal to the classics. 'The secondary school will find useful work in preparing clergymen, lawyers, doctors, and schoolmasters for their work. But the great industrial army must be provided for by the Board schools.'[46] This notion of separate spheres of action provided ground for a rapprochement with the secondary teachers, but it was a retreat from the *News*'s earlier assertions that public schools should prepare for the universities just as in the past, perhaps reflecting the way in which the leadership of the EIS had passed from classically trained parochial

[45] Ibid., xix. 34 (13 Jan. 1894), xxii. 714 (16 Oct. 1897).
[46] Ibid., xxii. 741-2 (30 Oct. 1897). Cf. 713-14 (16 Oct. 1897).

schoolmasters to the headmasters of higher grade schools, proud of their achievements and conscious that their schools had a distinctive character.

If there had ever been a chance of concentrating secondary work in a small number of schools, it disappeared with the events of 1892 and the work of the secondary education committees, which ensured that it remained available in many small centres, and that something like the parochial tradition survived where school boards wished it to. One indication of this is the number of schools which sent forward candidates for the Leaving Certificate, the list of which for 1900 forms the basis of Table 6.1.[47] In that year, 83 higher class schools presented 5,307 candidates, but a further 11,464 came from 348 state-aided schools. Apart from private and proprietary schools, the former included 32 higher class schools under school boards (compared with 11 in 1872) and 24 endowed schools, and there were many creations of the 1880s and 1890s in both categories: at Callander, Duns, Hawick, and Kelso, for example, among the board schools, and at Anstruther, Beith, Crieff, and Stonehaven among the endowed ones.

In the case of the ordinary public schools, it is the regional variations which are interesting, and comparison of columns 1 and 2 shows a high degree of continuity between the 1870s and 1900. In Scotland as a whole, about one school in nine offered some sort of secondary education—not necessarily enough for university entry, for the lower grade of the Leaving Certificate hardly went further than the old specific subjects. But the North-East and the Highlands accounted for nearly half (160) of the schools in column 3. In Banff, and to a lesser extent in Aberdeenshire, the county committees had used their grants to

[47] *CCES Rep., 1899-1900*, pp. 394-400. Includes Roman Catholic (etc.) as well as board schools, and excludes 270 schools which presented pupil-teachers only. The high figure in Edinburgh arose because before the creation of higher grade schools many ordinary board schools presented candidates—but the standard achieved was low: see A. G. Hogg, 'The Leaving Certificate and the development of secondary education in Edinburgh' (unpublished M.Ed. thesis, Edinburgh, 1970), pp. 64-9. In 1897/8 the EIS promoted an inquiry into higher education in public schools, with hearings in various towns, but it was unsystematically planned and produced little of value: *Educational Institute of Scotland. Report of the commission on higher education in secondary and public state-aided schools ... 1897-1898* (Edinburgh, n.d.).

Table 6.1

Regional variations in provision for secondary education, 1900

	Availability of 'secondary' education in state-aided schools			Total no. of schools	(3) as % of (4)	No. of higher-class schools
	No. of parishes		No. of schools			
	1877	1900	1900	1900		1900
	1	2	3	4	5	6
North East						
Aberdeenshire	47	45	56	252	22·2	0
Banff	14	18	27	82	32·9	0
Kincardine	5	6	7	52	13·5	1
Moray	8	8	11	53	20·8	1
Nairn	0	0	0	15		1
Highlands & North						
Argyll	15	11	12	170	7·1	0
Bute	2	1	1	21	4·8	0
Caithness	5	7	9	64	14·1	0
Inverness	11	11	12	181	6·6	1
Orkney	4	2	2	60	3·3	0
Ross & Cromarty	9	12	14	138	10·1	1
Shetland	0	2	2	62	3·2	0
Sutherland	4	6	7	45	15·6	0

East Central						
Angus	5	4	4	122	3.3	4
Clackmannan	1	3	3	17	7.6	1
Fife	10	15	17	145	11.7	5
Kinross	1	2	2	7	28.6	0
Perth	21	10	10	174	5.7	4
Stirling	1	6	10	87	11.5	2
West						
Ayr	7	17	19	167	11.4	3
Dumbarton	4	7	12	55	21.8	0
Lanark	9	20	26	219	11.9	1
Renfrew	4	8	10	101	9.9	2
Lothians & Borders						
Berwick	4	1	1	49	2.0	1
East Lothian	3	4	4	39	10.3	2
Midlothian	5	6	7	89	7.9	0
Peebles	2	0	0	21		1
Roxburgh	3	1	1	68	1.5	2
Selkirk	3	2	2	22	9.1	2
West Lothian	2	3	5	43	11.6	1
South West						
Dumfries	10	6	6	104	5.8	1
Kirkcudbright	6	3	3	65	4.6	1
Wigtown	6	3	3	52	5.8	3

Table 6.1 (*Contd.*)

Cities	(3)	(4)	(5)	(6)
Aberdeen	4	38	10·5	3
Dundee	3	38	7·9	1
Glasgow	9	93	9·7	5
Govan	7	31	22·6	0
Edinburgh	18	54	33·3	6
Leith	2	16	12·5	0
SCOTLAND	348	3,111	11·2	56

Columns:
(1) School-board districts with higher classical teaching, 1877. (See Table 4.4).
(2) School-board districts where state-aided schools presented to Leaving Certificate, 1900.
(3) No. of actual schools presenting to Leaving Certificate, 1900.
(4) Total no. of state-aided schools, 1900.
(5) (3) as percentage of (4).
(6) Higher class public and endowed schools, 1900.

encourage individual examination passes in any school—in some Banffshire parishes there were four schools presenting for the Certificate. In the Highlands too secondary education was still available in quite remote parishes, and had indeed been strengthened by a system of additional grants for advanced work introduced by Craik in 1886 (the 'Highland minute'). But outside these areas, the schools in column 3 were practically without exception in towns or industrial centres, and with the development of new schools rural secondary teaching had vanished from areas like Perthshire and the South-West where it still lingered in 1877. The biggest change was in the industrialized counties like Lanark, Stirling, Ayr, and Fife, where school boards had built up selected public schools as secondary centres. The parish school tradition, already a regional affair in 1877 (and probably for many years before that), was still more so in 1900, and when in the 1900s the SED adopted a policy of 'centralizing' secondary education in suitable schools it was only in the North-East and Highlands that this meant withdrawing secondary provision from a significant number of schools.

'The Twentieth Century will certainly sweep away all class and caste distinctions, so far as national educational arrangements are concerned', predicted the *Educational News* in 1900.[48] The new century saw a firm attempt by the SED to impose a coherent pattern on Scottish education, but whether this was in the direction of democracy was a matter of dispute. Between 1898 and 1908 there was a complex succession of organizational changes, with a distinct shift of emphasis around 1903: until then the Department was especially concerned to promote scientific and technical education, afterwards more with differentiating between schools in terms of social function, a concern which especially reflected the influence of John Struthers, who took over from Craik as Secretary in 1904.[49]

---

[48] *EN*, xxv. 53 (20 Jan. 1900).
[49] The fullest account is in J. Strong, *A history of secondary education in Scotland* (Oxford, 1909), pp. 257 ff. The SED itself published a 'selection of circular letters' in 1904 which reviewed policy since 1898—in *CCES Rep., 1904-5* (PP 1905, xxix)—but this glossed over the false starts.

The last years of Craik's regime coincided with the tenure of the Scottish Office by Balfour of Burleigh (1895-1903), and the two men worked closely together. In 1898, in a speech which he admitted was the result of a 'constant interchange of ideas' with Craik, the Scottish Secretary reviewed the changes which had given 'new life and vigour' to secondary schools since 1885, and looked forward to further reforms in which 'every school must bear a share in what is a connected work—viz., the construction of an educational highway from the infant class to the ultimate entry upon the business of life. Along which highway all must travel, so far as circumstances and mental capacity enable each one to go.' To ensure this 'we propose to keep steadily in view two grades of schools—the Elementary and the Secondary. Each has its own sphere and its own primary aim.' To confuse the two can only produce mutual injury, waste and inefficiency. In secondary schools, the improvement particularly needed was a 'widened curriculum', for 'the aim of those schools has hitherto been too exclusively professional. The claims of science have not received sufficient attention.'[50]

This new concern with science was partly administrative in origin, since in 1897 the administration of the Science and Art Department's grants in Scotland had been transferred to the SED (the former department was merged into the new Board of Education in England). These grants, given largely for attendance and examination passes, subsidized higher technical institutions, evening classes, and drawing and science instruction in ordinary schools. Most secondary schools shared in the standard grants, and a few had become 'schools of science', which could earn extra money by having a fully-organized science curriculum. But in 1897 there were only thirteen such schools in Scotland, against 143 in England and Wales: apart from Robert Gordon's and Allan Glen's, specially destined by the Balfour commission for this work, these were ordinary provincial secondary schools, and did not include any schools in Edinburgh or the higher grade schools in Glasgow, which

---

[50] Balfour of Burleigh, *Higher education in Scotland* (Edinburgh, 1898), pp. 3, 7, 17-18, 20.

unlike many of their equivalents in English industrial cities do not seem to have felt that their mission was a scientific one.[51]

The years around the turn of the century saw a bout of concern, of a kind perennial in late Victorian Britain, about German competition and the practical deficiencies of technical and commercial education. It was a popular subject for addresses at educational conferences, and a Scottish Association for the Promotion of Technical and Secondary Education was active for a time.[52] Commercial education attracted particular attention, and in 1900 a committee representing the Edinburgh business community produced a report on the subject which called for the teaching of commerce at the universities. At the secondary level, what was demanded was not so much commercial specialization as an education based on modern subjects, especially foreign languages, since the classics had 'the disadvantage of being altogether divorced from everyday life'.[53] The enlightened educational views of this committee, however, were not shared by most of the ordinary businessmen who submitted evidence to it, who preferred to take boys at around fifteen and let them learn on the job. The schools generally had commercial departments—at George Watson's Boys' for example, the classical side had 460 pupils and the commercial 310, the latter learning book-keeping, shorthand, and even typing; but according to the headmaster of Daniel Stewart's 'boys have no difficulty in getting into banks, mercantile offices, and very good commercial houses if they can write a fair hand, spell correctly, and do simple arithmetic. And further, it is in many cases not a boy's attainments so much as the influence which he can bring to bear on the directors or managers of banks, insurance offices, etc., that secures him the appointment.'[54] The value placed on commercial education by traditionalists

[51] *Forty-fifth Report of the Department of Science and Art* (PP 1898, xxix), p. ix, and *CCES Rep., 1899-1900*, p. 151, list of twelve schools of science (earlier known as 'organized science schools').

[52] *EN*, xxiii. 881-2 (24 Dec. 1898), report of its fourth annual meeting. It was presumably an offshoot of the English Association of the same name.

[53] *The Edinburgh Merchant Company. The Edinburgh Chamber of Commerce. The Leith Chamber of Commerce. Report by Joint Sub-Committee on Commercial Education* (Edinburgh, 1900), p. vi. The question was discussed at EIS congresses in 1900 and 1901: *EN*, xxv. 31, 33-7 (13 Jan. 1900), 69-70 (27 Jan. 1900); xxvi. 10-18 (5 Jan. 1901).

[54] *Report by Joint Sub-Committee*, pp. 4-7.

may be judged from some remarks of Marshall, who had set up a commercial side at the High School not because of demand from businessmen, but because 'he had found a certain number of boys ... who did not seem likely to do any good with a classical training, and yet their parents wanted them to go on at the school. He had wanted to find them something that would keep their attention, and to make the commercial education which had been introduced educative.' He added that 'He had never yet had commercial men who applied for a boy asking what the boy had done in book-keeping or any other so-called commercial subject. The usual request was simply for "a nice boy", and a very sensible thing too.'[55] All this meant that the Leaving Certificate, taken around seventeen and based on university subjects, was not a qualification which interested employers.

The changes introduced in 1898-9 had three main aspects: reform of the Code regulating public schools, the creation of an official category of Higher Grade schools, and changes in the grant system to secondary schools proper. The 1899 Code finally abolished the specific subject system, already considerably abridged in 1890, and replaced it with fixed capitation grants to approved 'advanced departments' in public schools. Twelve was fixed as the age of entry to these, and a Merit Certificate examination had to be passed to qualify.[56] In the Advanced Departments, the SED prescribed the teaching of English, history, geography, and other modern subjects, since the maximum leaving age was likely to be fifteen, and 'a very considerable proportion of these pupils will on leaving school follow occupations of an industrial or commercial nature'. But the teaching of languages and science might also be approved, and in practice classical education was allowed to continue where it was established. The *Educational News* welcomed the Advanced Departments as a revival of the parochial tradition, and by 1902 Banffshire had twenty-seven of them, sending pupils direct to the university.[57]

[55] *Classical Association of Scotland. Proceedings 1903-4*, pp. 39-40, 50.
[56] The Merit Certificate was originally introduced in 1892 to encourage specific subject work, and was then taken at a later age.
[57] *CCES Rep., 1898-9* (PP 1899, xxvi), p. xxxv, and Article 21 of Code for 1899; *EN*, xxvi. 766 (19 Oct. 1901); *CCES Rep., 1901-2* (PP 1902, xxxiii), pp. 762-3.

The new Higher Grade schools were a departure from tradition. As previously used unofficially, this term had referred to schools founded by the school boards which aspired to the standard secondary type, but in Craik's new regulations it meant schools specializing in modern subjects. The original plan was for 'Higher Grade (Science) Schools', but it was expanded to allow also for commercial education and for 'special courses' to meet local conditions, which might include a curriculum designed for girls. Higher grade schools were to give at least three years of instruction, and were given higher capitation grants than the Advanced Departments. The circular on Higher Grade (Science) Schools laid down various requirements including the practical teaching of science with properly-equipped laboratories and workshops, and excluded the teaching of Latin. The schools were seen as part of a scientific and technical sector of education which also embraced evening continuation courses and the 'central institutions', the name now given to the various technical colleges, art schools, etc. which had been taken over from the Science and Art Department. The SED also envisaged keeping the former 'schools of science' as a distinctive type of secondary school in large towns, but this idea was not developed. Underlying the Higher Grade policy was the idea of an 'industrial curriculum' as the most suitable for schools with a working-class appeal.[58]

Since the Higher Grade experiment was radically altered in 1903, it was evidently not regarded as a success. By 1902 35 schools were financed under the regulations, including nine of the old higher grade schools in Glasgow and Govan; the majority of the others were in the western industrial counties. The regulations did not stimulate the creation of new schools, except perhaps for those in Edinburgh, but were simply used by existing schools to set up scientific or commercial departments alongside the more traditional course. The science courses (1,040 pupils) proved less popular than the commercial (2,190), and there were only 3,821 pupils altogether, of whom 2,209 were in the first year, 1,006 in the second, and a mere 606 in the third or subsequent years. If this was the new education

---

[58] *CCES Rep., 1898-9*, pp. 87 ff. (Code, Chapter IX and Appendix 5), 201 ff.

demanded by the twentieth century, it seemed slow to take off.[59]

The third matter reorganized in 1898-9 was the financing of secondary schools proper. A new reform of local taxation in 1898 made a grant of some £35,000 available, and Craik was determined to use this for the purpose which had been frustrated in 1892, the support of higher class schools. The 'frittering away' of the Equivalent Grant, and still more of the Residue Grant of 1890, was regarded by the SED as a lesson in the evils of local control, and the county committees were practically excluded from the administration of the new grant, which took the form of direct allocations varying between £300 and £750 to higher class public and endowed schools; counties which lacked such schools therefore received no benefit, and the measure was attacked for that reason. There was also a feeling that the financing of secondary education was becoming absurdly complex, involving numerous grants administered on different terms; but attempts to unify them did not succeed until 1908. In the meantime, the Science and Art grant, which remained separate, was used by the SED to encourage the integration of science into the standard secondary syllabus, and science was included in the Leaving Certificate for the first time in 1899.[60]

The relative failure of the Higher Grade schools was one reason for the new direction given to policy around 1903. Another was the Education (Scotland) Act of 1901, which abolished most of the exemptions which had allowed children to leave early.[61] This meant the retention of a mass of children to the age of fourteen, whose needs were not met by the secondary or quasi-secondary Advanced Departments. The solution adopted—controversial at the time and of fundamental importance for the later evolution of Scottish education—was to distinguish at the age of twelve between extended elementary education and secondary education proper, the former to be available to all primary pupils who were capable of benefiting from it, the latter only, in principle, to those who transferred

---

[59] *CCES Rep., 1902-3* (PP 1903, xxii), pp. 3, 655
[60] *CCES Rep., 1900-1* (PP 1901, xxii), pp. 26-7, 303.
[61] The Education (Scotland) Act of 1883 had raised the theoretical leaving age from thirteen to fourteen, but children could leave earlier if they passed the fifth Standard.

at twelve to properly organized and recognized secondary schools.

Under the new arrangements, most primary pupils stayed at school to attend 'supplementary courses' for two years, after passing the 'qualifying examination' which replaced the Merit Certificate. The curriculum of the Supplementary Courses was to be firmly elementary in nature, with no languages taught, and with 'differentiated lines of work' following vocational requirements—commercial, industrial, rural, and (for girls) household management. Any pupils who were interested in true secondary education should be transferred by the age of twelve to schools where secondary subjects 'form the staple of the curriculum', for

My Lords are of opinion ... that the tendency—not confined to any one class of school—to make one and the same school with one and the same staff serve many different functions is the weak point of educational organisation in Scotland as compared with that of other countries, ... and They are satisfied that increasing division of function as between different types of schools is an essential condition of further educational progress. This division of function [it was hopefully claimed] ... does not necessarily imply a distinction of higher and lower, but simply a difference of aim and purpose with a corresponding difference in the subjects of instruction.

Although it was admitted that exceptions would have to be made in remote areas, this clearly marked the end of the road for the parochial tradition.[62] The practical consequence of the change was that the smaller and weaker Advanced Departments were turned into Supplementary Courses, and had to give up language teaching, while the majority of them became Higher Grade schools or departments: this term now lost its connotation of specialization, and was applied to any secondary school financed through the Code rather than through the separate Secondary School Regulations which applied to endowed and higher class schools.

There were parallels between these changes and those introduced in England by Sir Robert Morant, the controversial head of the Board of Education, following the Education Act of

---

[62] *CCES Rep., 1902-3*, pp. 287-8. The name 'Merit Certificate' was now transferred to an examination at the end of the Supplementary Courses.

1902. But in England the new county authorities were creating many new schools, and Morant faced the special problem of fusing these and the old grammar schools into a single system; he adopted an educational ideal which stressed the classics and the Public School model. On both sides of the border, the aim was a balanced curriculum, but whereas in England science was felt to have been over-stressed in the old higher grade schools, in Scotland the SED was prepared, as we shall see, to deal heavy blows to the classics in order to insist on a proper teaching of science. What the two departments had in common, however, was a belief in the functional differentiation of education and in the need for a sharp distinction between secondary and (to use the English term) 'higher elementary' schools.

If the new higher grade schools were now distinguished from other public schools, the idea lingered that they were somehow different from 'real' secondary schools. In 1904 the SED published a justification of its policies which seemed to look forward to a tripartite system: after a 'common foundation' until the age of twelve, 'Their Lordships think that three types of further instruction may be defined—the Supplementary Course for pupils who leave school at 14, the Higher Grade School for pupils who stay on to 16, and the Higher Class School for those who remain to University age.' Each would have an appropriate curriculum. Despite this talk of a 'common foundation', the Department was not thinking of an 'end-on' organization of schools. Each type of school would cater for all ages, and the plan was illustrated by a diagram showing the 'elementary', 'intermediate', and 'secondary' schools as three separate ladders, leading from the infant department to various occupations and educational outlets, though a profusion of red arrows showed how pupils might leap from one ladder to another. The real barrier was that between the elementary schools and the rest, for seizing the opportunity to transfer would depend on the parents' initiative rather than on any positive selection mechanism, and once the child was in a Supplementary Course the chance had effectively gone; the arrow on the diagram pointed firmly 'To Unskilled Occupations'.[63]

---

[63] *CCES Rep., 1904-5*, pp. 253, 263, diagram opposite p. 264. Cf. speech by Balfour of Burleigh, in *EN*, xxviii. 789-92 (17 Oct. 1903).

In 1904 the government introduced a bill which proposed to replace the school boards by district authorities. The composition of the authorities and the question of rating powers proved so controversial that the bill was dropped, but it seems to have revived tension between the different types of secondary school by making some endowed schools fear for their independence.[64] The Merchant Company, whose schools had been hit financially by the development of higher grade schools in Edinburgh, called a conference of endowed school and university representatives in 1905, at which its Master complained that 'The public still labour under the idea that the Primary school leads to the Secondary in natural succession; and neither Members of Parliament, nor their constituents, realise that under the new conditions of Education the ordinary Board School, in the main, trains, not for the Secondary, but for the Higher Grade School, which does not lead to the University.' 'Under the new Educational plan', he continued, 'the mass of School Board children have no chance of passing to the Secondary School and so to the University. This is only common sense: but there is the small minority, the children of real promise—what in the Book of Discipline are called, "the bairns of pregnant pairts." For them a way must be found to pass at an early age from the Board School into the freer intellectual atmosphere of the Secondary School and so to the University.' But this conference broke up in confusion when it became clear that the Merchant Company's hostility to the public sector was not widely shared; the Hutchesons' representatives, for example, thought that endowed schools had 'served their day', and were anxious to hand over to the school board.[65]

Struthers, who took over from Craik in 1904, soon abandoned the idea of higher grade education as something distinct in its nature. While he reinforced the distinction between

[64] The 1904 bill, unsuccessfully revived in 1905, also provided for four advisory 'provincial councils'; there was a demand at this time, resisted by the SED, for a national advisory council. For contemporary views on these issues see J. Clarke, *Short studies in education in Scotland* (1904); C. M. Douglas & H. Jones, *Scottish education reform* (Glasgow, 1903).

[65] *Secondary education. Report of conference of delegates from governing bodies of endowments for secondary education in Scotland* (Edinburgh, 1905), pp. 9, 13. The scheme for handing over Hutchesons' had reached an advanced stage in 1903-4, but was successfully opposed by Ramsay and others.

elementary and secondary education, and insisted on the 'centralization' of the latter in properly equipped schools, his policy was to assimilate all secondary schools to a common pattern and to treat them in the same way whatever their legal status— endowed, higher class, or higher grade. This policy was enforced through the Department's control of grants and of the Leaving Certificate. The Leaving Certificate had originally been taken in single subjects, but in the 1900s a policy of 'grouping' was progressively introduced, and schools could not enter pupils for the Certificate (or receive grants) unless they followed an approved curriculum. In 1903, a new Intermediate Certificate was introduced to sanction the higher grade curriculum; there were also Commercial and Technical Certificates at a rather higher level, though these proved a failure. In 1908 the Intermediate Certificate was made a compulsory preliminary to the full Leaving Certificate, so that all secondary schools had to adopt the 'intermediate' curriculum, which was designed to meet the needs of those leaving at sixteen as well as those aiming at the universities, and which put a special emphasis on science. Henceforth all secondary courses were divided between the intermediate stage lasting for three years and the post-intermediate which added another two, and the only distinction officially recognized was between full secondary schools which taught for five years, and intermediate schools (usually the smaller rural ones) which gave only the three-year course.[66]

The new unity seems also to have been felt by the teachers. In 1909 the old Association of Teachers in Secondary Schools merged with the Scottish Association of Secondary Teachers, which had originated among Glasgow higher grade teachers in 1898, to form the Secondary Education Association of Scotland; this soon had over a thousand members, whose special point of view was articulated by the *Secondary School Journal*, founded in 1908.[67]

---

[66] SRO ED 44 1/7, Circular 413, 3 Oct. 1908. Cf. *CCES Rep.*, *1907-8* (PP 1908, xxviii), pp. 915-18, 926.

[67] *EN*, n.s. iii. 163-4 (19 Feb. 1909), 1161 (5 Nov.). In 1901, Marshall and others, disaffected with the ATSS, had founded an Association of Scottish Headmasters, but this does not seem to have lasted: ibid., xxvi. 85-6 (2 Feb. 1901).

The training of teachers was also assimilated to the new order, in a series of changes in 1905-7 under which the training colleges were taken over from the churches and more closely connected with the universities. The system of individually apprenticed pupil-teachers had long been in decline, and authorities like Glasgow had centralized their training in Pupil Teachers' Institutes.[68] Now pupil-teachers were renamed 'junior students', and they were to study in ordinary secondary schools, though there were complaints that the new junior student courses were too narrowly angled to the needs of primary teachers. For the new regulations laid down quite separate lines of training for secondary teachers, who would in future have to be Honours graduates, and elementary teachers, who might or might not be graduates, but would normally come up through the training college system. Though attacked at the time for destroying the unity of the profession and the principle of 'free interchange of teachers from the Butt of Lewis to Glasgow High School', the 1906 regulations were to last for more than fifty years.[69]

A final piece of tidying-up concerned bursaries. The Education (Scotland) Act of 1908, although it left the school boards intact, at last consolidated the complex grant system for secondary schools. The county secondary education committees survived, and with the disappearance of the Equivalent Grant as a distinct entity their chief task became to administer a 'district bursary scheme', into which all but the largest endowment trusts had to integrate their own bursaries. The SED had been pursuing a uniform bursary policy since 1906, part of which was that 'The principle of the award of bursaries by general competitive examination is inadmissible.' To avoid the unfair chances which open competition gave to the better-prepared, the committees were to allocate bursaries to individual schools, and if internal competition was necessary school records and teachers' recommendations were to be used as well as examinations. Committees were urged to give priority to the needs of rural pupils, and they could pay for travelling expenses

---

[68] J. M. Roxburgh, *The School Board of Glasgow 1873-1919* (1971), pp. 200 ff.

[69] *EN*, n.s. v. 242 (10 Mar. 1911). Cf. M. Cruickshank, *A history of the training of teachers in Scotland* (1970), pp. 138-9.

and boarding allowances, while for older pupils subsistence payments could be made in order to encourage parents to keep them on at school. The effect, it was claimed, 'will be to substitute for ill-regulated, unwholesome competition a principle of careful selection'.[70] After 1908 these bursary schemes were absorbing £65,000 a year, and although there was no Scottish equivalent of the English 1907 regulations requiring a quarter of the places in state-aided secondary schools to be free, the Scottish arrangements went well beyond the mere payment of fees—which in any case no longer existed in many schools, whereas in England a minimum fee of £3 p.a. was normally prescribed.

Struthers, the son of a Glasgow provision-merchant, was very much a product of the Scottish tradition: he was educated at a parish school, and rose through the pupil–teacher system and the training college to Glasgow University; he then went on to Oxford, but served for twelve years as a school inspector before joining the London office. He later recalled his 'pitiable disillusionment' when he examined at first hand the vaunted parish schools of the North-East.[71] In seeking to differentiate education sharply on functional lines, Struthers was following the expert opinion of the day, as may be seen by a glance at the writings of Alexander Darroch, who succeeded Laurie as professor of Education at Edinburgh in 1903. Whereas Laurie had taken an essentially ethical approach, putting the teacher's moral and religious influence at the heart of education, Darroch spoke the fashionable language of 'national efficiency' and Hegelian neo-idealism. The aim of education was to 'secure the fitness of the individual to perform efficiently some specific function in the economic organisation of society', to discover the innate capacity of individuals and to fit them for the work in which they could best serve the state. Darroch thought in terms of 'equality of opportunity' for a 'specially gifted' élite, and had ideas on the virtues of selective education which were to become common currency in later years: 'schools of various types, sufficient in number, and suited to meet the need for the

[70] *CCES Rep., 1906-7* (PP 1907, xxiii), p. 894. Cf. SRO ED 44 1/7, Circular 420, 24 Apr. 1909.
[71] SRO ED 7 1/33, Struthers to Revd R. Goodwillie, 20 May 1913.

supply of the various services required by the State; a common basis in elementary education; means of higher education open to all who can profit thereby; selection of the best; restriction of those unable to benefit from higher education—these are the principles which must in the future guide the State organisation of the means of education'.[72]

It was perhaps appropriate that Laurie was one of the strongest critics of Struthers. Laurie's views on educational policy were never easy to pin down. On the one hand, as examiner for the Dick bequest he extolled the parochial tradition, and had severely criticized the SED in the 1870s for letting higher subjects run down. On the other, he was a champion of secondary schools and a university entrance examination, and took a narrow view of educational opportunity: he saw this as a social safety-valve ('It makes the clever poor contented, and thus saps the foundations of Socialism'), criticized the concept of the ladder from the gutter to the university, and insisted that only 'the very best brains of the poorer classes' deserved to be encouraged.[73] In the 1890s he accepted that preparation for the universities and the Leaving Certificate should be concentrated in urban secondary schools, 'where the country pupils may mix with others of their own educational and social standing, and enjoy the benefits of generous rivalry'.[74] Yet he welcomed the 1899 Code, and attacked the changes made in 1903 as 'little short of a national calamity'.[75] The key to Laurie's attitudes was that he thought of the classics not as an instrument of social ambition, but as a liberalizing influence which could give 'tone' to the rural school, through the graduate schoolmaster, even when they were only studied by a handful of children. Before 1899 any schoolmaster in Scotland could earn a specific subject grant for teaching Latin, and the Advanced Department regulations had not made much practical difference; but

[72] A. Darroch, *The children* (1907), pp. 11, 84. Cf. his *Education and the new utilitarianism* (1914), pp. 38-40.

[73] S. S. Laurie, *The training of teachers, and other educational papers* (1882), p. 183; *The training of teachers and methods of instruction* (Cambridge, 1901), pp. 194, 196.

[74] S. S. Laurie, *Report to the Trustees of the Dick Bequest* (Edinburgh, 1890), p. 44, and cf. pp. 98, 104-5.

[75] S. S. Laurie, *The Scottish Code of 1899 and other matters* (Edinburgh, 1899), pp. 13-14, 20; *Dick Bequest Trust. General Report to the Governors 1890-1904* (Edinburgh, 1904), p. 32.

the Supplementary Course system forbade this, and Laurie called for an additional Supplementary Course option based on the classics, mathematics and modern languages.[76] These ideas were shared by the veteran classics professor George Ramsay, who became the leading critic of the SED after Laurie's death in 1909. Ramsay had been an even firmer champion of secondary education, but he too found the new spirit of vocationalism and segregation uncongenial. It was all very well to talk of transferring gifted children, said Ramsay, but if they could not sample secondary subjects in the ordinary school, how was their talent for them to be discovered?[77] 'The object of the State in educating the people', argued Laurie, 'is not so much the equipping of future citizens for their work in this or that special industry as the disciplining of the young to the vigorous exercise of their intelligence; and above all, training them up to the moral and religious ideal of the nation to which they belong. ... The primary school, above all, should, in my opinion, be sacred to a liberal education, and technical instruction should be postponed to a later stage.' Laurie believed, after all, that 'The Shorter Catechism has done more to make Scotland efficient in the world's work than mathematics and chemistry can ever do.'[78]

The *Educational News* agreed that the current 'desire to segregate the schools into groups or classes' was suited 'neither to the history of our educational developments nor to the peculiar social stratification of our people', and feared that 'However anxious its promoters are that it should be based solely on educational grounds, ... [segregation by function] will work out more and more on lines corresponding to the social status of the parents.'[79] As might have been expected, the application of the centralizing policy caused particular difficulties in the North-East: 'rural teachers and School Boards alike are seething with indignation', it was reported from Banffshire in 1905. Craik himself, now retired but a candidate for the Aberdeen university seat, confronted a deputation of

[76] *General Report to the Governors*, pp. 35-40.
[77] *Classical Association of Scotland. Proceedings 1903-4*, pp. 23-4. (Intelligence testing was to provide the answer to this question.)
[78] *General Report to the Governors*, pp. 44-5; *Scottish Review*, xix (1892), p. 168.
[79] *EN*, xxix. 625 (3 Sept. 1904), and 22 (2 Jan.).

North-Eastern headmasters, and dealt fairly effectively with their complaints, pointing out that it was impossible for any one man, however well qualified, to teach the range of subjects now required. 'How many graduates can speak French in a way that would render them useful as French teachers?', he asked, to which the teachers replied unconvincingly that 'They could teach a pupil the elements of the language, and he could learn the pronunciation afterwards.' The popularity of French as an alternative to Latin, and the rise of science, were making the old notion of 'university subjects' obsolete.[80]

By 1905 the *Educational News* admitted that the new system was working well in most parts of Scotland, and that 'The trend of public opinion, quite apart from Departmental sugges-tion, has set in towards centralisation, whether we like it or not.'[81] Controversy died down, at least for the time being, and what had once been presented as the defence of a national tradition was reduced to the 'problem of rural education', a problem which was regional in nature and which could be solved if the physical and financial means were found to bring pupils to the 'central' schools. Railways had long carried children to school, and now the bicycle and the beginnings of the rural motor bus added new facilities; another possibility was the provision of boarding-hostels, the first of which, the result of a private benefaction, opened at Dumfries in 1909. Nevertheless, those who saw themselves as 'the upholders of the Scottish ideal' continued to claim that 'the bed-rock of Scottish education is that, as a rule, all the essentials of a sound and liberal education should be available to every boy and girl of ability up to the age of 15, or 14 at least, within *walking* distance of their homes'. Admittedly rural schools could no longer prepare directly for the university, but for them to at least make a start on secondary education would avoid 'sever-ing that fine spiritual bond which has linked the lowest and highest rungs together for over two hundred years'. From this point of view, the official idea that rural Supplementary Courses should have a special 'rural' bias was particularly

---

[80] Ibid., xxx. 59-61 (21 Jan. 1905), 101-2 (11 Feb.), 136-8 (25 Feb.). For a less abrasive meeting between Struthers and Banffshire teachers see xxxi. 840-1 (2 Nov. 1906).
[81] Ibid., xxx. 172 (4 Mar. 1905).

offensive, cutting children off from their birthright of national culture. After all, 'much of the intellectual vigour which has hitherto characterised the work of the Scottish Universities has been due to the fact that the beginnings of higher education have been associated, not with the cramped and artificial conditions of town life, but with the opener, freer, more natural life of the country'. These views—which were those of J. D. Cheyne, schoolmaster of Alves in Morayshire—strongly influenced the policy on rural education adopted by the EIS at its 1905 conference.[82]

This ruralist mystique was later harnessed by Ramsay to the defence of classical education. In the meantime there was a more direct threat. Ramsay was the president and chief founder of the Classical Association of Scotland, whose formation in 1902 (two years earlier than the English equivalent) reflected alarm at the decline of the classics, and especially of Greek, in both schools and universities. Its meetings had an embattled atmosphere, and the utilitarian emphasis in the policies of Craik and Struthers naturally aroused little enthusiasm. The question became critical in 1908, with the new Leaving Certificate regulations which required all schools to adopt the 'intermediate' curriculum. Struthers's policy was that this should be 'a well-balanced course of *general* education suitable for the requirements of pupils who leave school at 15 or 16'. The balance in question was to be 'between the linguistic and the realistic sides of intellectual discipline', and the curriculum had to be the same for all pupils, with no options allowed. There were minimum requirements for various subjects including science and drawing, on which the Department always insisted as custodian of the 'Science and Art' legacy. Two languages could be included, but no more: since these would normally be Latin and French, Greek was effectively excluded from the intermediate curriculum, and could not be started until fifteen or sixteen.[83] (German was affected in the same way, and so presumably were commercial subjects.) The Classical Association circularized headmasters, held special meetings, and sent deputations to Struthers, but without much result. The official

[82] Ibid., xxx. 427-8 (10 June 1905), 445-6 (17 June); cf. 709-11 (23 Sept.).
[83] *CCES Rep., 1907-8*, pp. 920-1.

view remained that it was 'to the post-Intermediate curriculum that we must mainly look for the special development of the linguistic or any other side of school study. That is the soil in which Greek at least will most naturally flourish.' This view of the classics as one form of specialization among many was of course anathema to those who saw them as the basis of a true liberal education. Struthers finally made a concession in 1912, by which individual pupils might drop another subject in the last intermediate year in order to start Greek, and would be exempted from taking the Intermediate Certificate. With this the Classical Association had to be satisfied.[84]

In the course of this agitation, John Harrower, professor of Greek at Aberdeen, had emerged as a vociferous critic of the Department. In 1912 he published a *Map of the Greekless areas of Scotland* based on figures collected by the Association. These figures showed that 689 students of Greek—over half the total— were in Edinburgh, Glasgow, and Aberdeen, and led Harrower to claim that 'to-day there is many a glen and many a village in Scotland where Greek was taught forty years ago and where now the ambition of such learning is a vain dream'.[85] This picture was largely mythical: as we saw in Chapter 4, only 623 pupils were studying Greek as a specific subject in 1877, and even in 1827, when there were 2,042 students of the language in schools of all kinds, 47 per cent of them were in the same three cities. Greek was undoubtedly on the decline in the 1900s, mainly because it was no longer compulsory in the universities, but in truth despite the efforts of Blackie and others in the nineteenth century it had never struck really deep roots in Scotland, and was seriously studied in only a few select schools.

By 1912 Harrower was applying his mythogenic powers to a new campaign which Struthers was forced to take seriously, a revival of the question of rural education. In that year he and Ramsay launched the 'Association for Securing Higher Instruction in Scottish Rural Schools' (at first called the Scottish Education Protest League), which attacked the policy of centralization for reducing the opportunities open to the poor. Higher education, it was alleged, had disappeared from schools

---

[84] *SED Reports, 1908-9. Secondary Education Rep.*, p. 6; *Classical Association of Scotland. Proceedings 1912-13*, pp. 61-2.
[85] Ibid., *Proceedings 1910-11*, p. 11, and *Proceedings 1911-12*, p. 81.

where it had once flourished, and the need to travel to central schools was a barrier which excluded many poorer children. Much stress was laid on the supposed moral dangers of railway travelling, and on the virtues of rural life. 'The brains of the country of Scotland are a most important asset, I believe the best asset intellectually in our whole country. I never would compare the brains of a good honestly prepared country lad with the sort of lad who comes from the lower streets of our big cities. The cry today is "back to the land," and we say, "back to the country schools" ...' So spoke Ramsay, and he cited the case of Yarrow, which was once 'the headquarters for all the glens behind, which were full of farmers and shepherds—the most reflective, thoughtful class in Scotland, who now may be obliged to send their children twenty miles in order to come to Selkirk where they will learn the first deterioration of their manners and do no particular good to their character'.[86] Schools preparing for the universities had once existed 'throughout the length and breadth of Scotland', claimed Ramsay;[87] but it was only in the North-East that the grievances had real force.

The Association's activities caused much discussion, and culminated in a deputation to the Secretary for Scotland in April 1913. On this, the *Educational News* commented that it 'was more imposing and influential than representative. Among the distinguished University Professors, Chairmen of Urban School Boards, City Clergymen, Ex-School Inspectors and others, there was a noticeable absence of representatives of two groups of persons who are in close touch with the matter—members of rural School Boards and teachers of rural schools.'[88] Although the *News* had some sympathy with the movement, the educational world generally treated it with reserve. The EIS created a Rural Education Committee to survey the question, but this refused to endorse the agitation, and recommended a

---

[86] SRO ED 7 1/32, speech of Ramsay at deputation of April 1913. The example of Yarrow was well chosen: it was one of those presenting for the Leaving Certificate in 1900, and one of the two rural schools in Selkirkshire cited in Table 4.4 for 1877. It was thus an untypical rural school, and the number of such schools which had not become at least 'intermediate' ones by this time was quite limited.

[87] *Association for Securing Higher Instruction in Scottish Rural Schools. Statement of the aims of the Association* (Aberdeen, 1913), p. 14.

[88] *EN*, xxxviii. 355 (25 Apr. 1913).

Royal Commission to ascertain the true facts.[89] On the other hand, the themes of the movement's propaganda—past glories destroyed, 'broken links in Scottish education',[90] Plato at the door of every cotter's son,[91] 'the old boast of Scotland, that education of a sterling character was open to all ranks of her people, and that her Universities were truly national institutions'[92]—clearly struck a chord in Scottish public opinion which brought the Association influential support from MPs and the churches.[93]

Struthers's private opinion was that, in so far as the campaign was not based on misunderstanding of official policy and on 'hazy sentiment' which idealized the past, it reflected not the views of teachers but those of the classical party, which was renewing its attack on the intermediate curriculum and especially on science and drawing.[94] Struthers prepared a battery of statistics and arguments to refute the Association's claims, and refused to give way on the central point of his policy: only schools recognized and organized as intermediate schools should present for the Intermediate Certificate, and secondary pupils should be transferred to such schools wherever possible. On the other hand, he stressed that the Department was quite prepared to permit rural schools in suitable circumstances to offer one or even two years of the intermediate curriculum before passing pupils on to the central schools. These were called 'feeder' or 'sub-intermediate' schools, and in the three years up to 1913 fifteen primary schools had been allowed to present pupils directly for the Intermediate Certificate, while 343 (mostly, but not all, in the North-East and the Highlands) acted as feeders. Struthers admitted that it was no longer possible—given the higher standards in the universities as well as

---

[89] Ibid., n.s. vi. 942-4 (4 Oct. 1912), 957 (11 Oct.), 977 (18 Oct.), 1123 (29 Nov.), 1134 (6 Dec.), 1182-4 (20 Dec.); xxxviii. 41-4 (10 Jan. 1913), 450 (16 May).

[90] The title of a book (1913) by the Revd John Smith, chairman of Govan School Board and an active member of the Association.

[91] Harrower in *Classical Association of Scotland. Proceedings 1910-11,* p. 10.

[92] Ramsay in *Statement of the aims,* p. 32.

[93] See, for example, *5 Hansard* lvi, HC 4 Aug. 1913; *Reports on the schemes of the Church of Scotland ... 1913* (Edinburgh, 1913), pp. 48-51; Glasgow GC Reports, Oct. 1913. There was also a separate agitation in 1912 based in Orkney.

[94] SRO ED 7 1/32, memorandum from Struthers to [Scottish Secretary], 8 Apr. 1912; ED 7 1/33, Struthers to G. Macdonald, 29 Nov. 1912, and copy letters Struthers to Revd R. Goodwillie, 20 May 1913, 13 May 1914.

the changes in the school system—for a child to go straight from a primary school to the university, but he argued that practically every primary school which had actually given serious secondary education in the past had now become an intermediate school, and that a system of central schools surrounded by primary schools which were encouraged to feed into them made the real opportunities much greater than before; the recent development of secondary education in Lewis was cited as an example.[95]

Struthers's arguments prevailed, and seem to have been widely accepted by teachers. The initial protests over the Supplementary Courses had died down after a few years, and the assimilation of the different types of secondary school put an end to the division between 'secondary' and 'primary' ideals which had been so sharp in the 1880s and 1890s. An efficient transfer and bursary system was felt to constitute 'Knox's ideal, at last about to be realised',[96] and the problems caused by inequalities of family background were only dimly perceived. The teachers' acceptance of official views is indicated by the report published in 1917 of a 'Scottish Education Reform Committee' representing the EIS, the SEA, and another teachers' association. This fully accepted the distinction between the 'literary or professional type' of education in the intermediate curriculum and the 'practical or industrial' type in the Supplementary Courses, and its plans for post-war reconstruction showed great enthusiasm for vocational training, especially in agriculture for rural pupils, and for girls in 'ideals of conduct directly connected with women's function in life, and with activities which centre in the home'. This committee did think that centralization had reduced rural opportunities, and was critical of the SED's complacency on the question, but there was no trace in its thinking of the kind of nostalgia for the parochial

---

[95] Figures among papers in ED 7 1/32. Struthers rehearsed the arguments at length in his annual reports: *SED Reports, 1910-11. Secondary Education Rep.*, pp. 5-6; *1912-13. Secondary Education Rep.*, pp. 3-5; *1913-14. Rep. of Comm. of Council*, pp. 28-30. Cf. his evidence, slightly less confident, in *Royal Commission on the Civil Service. Appendix to Third Report* (PP 1913, xviii) pp. 168-9.

[96] W. J. Gibson, *Education in Scotland. A sketch of the past and the present* (1912), p. 146. Gibson, headmaster of the Nicolson Institute, Stornoway, supplied Struthers with his data on Lewis, and defended his policies in this book.

tradition on which the pre-war rural education movement, led by classics professors, had relied so much.[97]

The classification of schools as 'secondary' or 'intermediate' led for the first time to the publication of statistics which treated all schools in a uniform manner, and the results of this are summarized in Table 6.2.[98] There were 249 secondary schools in 1912, of which 143 gave the five-year course and 106 the three-year one. The intermediate schools were generally those in small towns rather than subsidiary schools in large ones, and outside the four cities there were only four towns with more than one secondary school (Inverness, Hamilton, Greenock, and Paisley.) Intermediate schools were normally higher grade in origin (i.e. financed under the Code), but so were 87 of the five-year schools, and these were mostly free. The extent to which free secondary education was available should perhaps be emphasized, since this is often thought to be a post-war development. When free education was introduced around 1890, school boards were allowed to retain fees in selected schools, and this was usually done where public schools descended from old burgh schools and in the case of the urban higher grade schools which existed at that time.[99] But schools which developed their secondary status later did not usually become fee-paying, and the result was that in 1912 all secondary education was free in Aberdeenshire and Banff, in several northern counties, in Midlothian, and, with the single exception of Hamilton Academy, in Lanarkshire. For the higher grade schools as a whole, fees now provided a trifling amount of revenue, as Table 6.3 shows.[100]

The table also shows that endowment income had lost much of its significance, and the old endowed schools were now among the most expensive—ironically, since their founders had usually intended them to be free. In counties which had old-established secondary schools the survival of fees, and the need to think of boarding or railway travelling in order to reach

[97] *Reform in Scottish education, being the report of the Scottish Education Reform Committee* (Edinburgh, 1917), pp. 39-40, 66, 86.
[98] Based on *SED Reports, 1914-15. Secondary Education Rep.*, Appendix I. Figures refer to the school year 1912/13.
[99] See list of these schools in a parliamentary return in PP 1890, lvi.
[100] *SED Reports, 1914-15. Secondary Education Rep.*, Appendix I, Table I, pp. 98-9.

Table 6.2

Regional variations in provision for secondary education, 1912

	No. of schools			'Secondary' schools		'Intermediate' schools		No. pupils in post-intermediate courses	Total pupils per thousand population
	Endowed & Higher Class	Higher Grade	Roman Catholic	Fee paying	Free	Fee paying	Free		
North East									
Aberdeenshire	-	18	-	-	7	-	11	135	8·9
Banff	-	10	-	-	6	-	4	100	13·4
Kincardine	1	1	-	1	-	-	1	17	7·2
Moray	1	6	-	1	3	-	3	54	11·7
Nairn	1	-	-	1	-	-	-	4	9·6
Highlands & North									
Argyll	1	7	-	1	2	-	5	33	9·4
Bute	1	-	-	1	-	-	-	12	7·4
Caithness	-	5	-	-	2	-	3	50	13·6
Inverness	1	5	-	1	3	-	2	90	7·7
Orkney	-	3	-	-	2	-	1	19	8·5
Ross & Cromarty	1	7	-	1	3	-	4	106	8·5
Shetland	-	1	-	-	1	-	-	4	4·2
Sutherland	-	6	-	-	1	-	5	28	11·4

East Central									
Angus	4	2	–	5	1	–	–	105	8·4
Clackmannan	1	2	–	2	1	–	–	56	13·3
Fife	5	7	–	5	1	–	6	142	6·2
Kinross	–	–	–	–	–	–	–	–	–
Perth	3	4	–	3	2	–	2	84	8·4
Stirling	2	3	–	2	1	–	2	52	5·2
West									
Ayr	3	13	–	5	1	–	10	172	7·3
Dumbarton	–	6	–	2	3	–	1	36	6·6
Lanark	1	18	2	1	8	–	12	206	6·2
Renfrew	3	10	2	2	4	1	8	93	7·3
Lothians & Borders									
Berwick	1	–	–	1	–	–	–	19	4·4
East Lothian	2	2	–	1	2	–	1	16	6·2
Midlothian	–	6	–	–	2	–	4	15	4·1
Peebles	1	–	–	–	1	–	–	2	5·9
Roxburgh	1	2	–	1	1	–	1	7	4·7
Selkirk	2	–	–	2	–	–	–	13	7·3
West Lothian	1	3	–	1	2	–	1	30	6·2
South West									
Dumfries	1	5	–	1	–	1	4	76	8·4
Kirkcudbright	1	2	–	1	–	–	2	3	4·2
Wigtown	3	2	–	3	–	–	2	25	8·3

Table 6.2 (*Contd.*)

Regional variations in provision for secondary education, 1912

Cities	No. of schools Endowed & Higher Class	Higher Grade	Roman Catholic	'Secondary' schools Fee paying	Free	'Intermediate' schools Fee paying	Free	No. pupils in post-intermediate courses	Total pupils per thousand population
Aberdeen	3	1	1	3	2	-	-	239	11·4
Dundee	1	2	1	4	-	-	-	142	7·5
Glasgow	5	7	4	11	1	1	3	460	6·8
Govan	-	6	1	5	-	-	2	134	8·5
Edinburgh	6	5	1	6	3	1	2	473	13·8
Leith	-	2	1	-	3	-	-	24	8·3
SCOTLAND	57	179	13	74	69	4	102	3,276	7·9
	249			143		106			

Table 6.3

Sources of income of secondary schools, 1912 (%)

	Endowed & higher class	Higher grade
SED grants	30·3	44·1
Rates	17·6	37·7
Fees	25·9	2·5
Endowments	12·8	1·3
Other sources	13·5	14·4
Total income	£302,799	£419,145

the towns where the schools were situated, perhaps made opportunities more restricted, whereas the pupil/population ratio in the last column of Table 6.2 shows that the most favourable conditions were in the counties where the parochial tradition had been strongest and where consequently there were more small schools; a comparison with Table 6.1 also shows how centralization had operated in the North-East and the Highlands to reduce the number of schools offering secondary education.

In 1912 the schools had on their rolls 38,312 pupils (19,611 boys, 18,701 girls), but only 3,276 were in the post-intermediate courses, and as the table shows the numbers in some counties were exiguous.[101] Consequently numbers tapered off rapidly after the age of sixteen, as may be seen from Table 6.4. Premature leaving was a longstanding weakness of Scottish education, and although more pupils took the Leaving Certificate every year Struthers still felt that Scotland was out of line with 'the majority of other civilised countries' in this respect, and looked forward to a six-year rather than a five-year course becoming the norm.[102]

Forty per cent of all secondary pupils were in the four large cities, thirty-one per cent in Edinburgh and Glasgow alone.

[101] Ibid., Appendix I, Tables II, IV. The figures in Table 6.2 for post-intermediate pupils and pupils per thousand population are based on 'average attendance' rather than those 'on the roll'. Other statistics are: teachers—permanent full-time: 2,099; part-time or visiting: 1,359; junior students—boys 565, girls 2,877.

[102] *SED Reports, 1908-9. Secondary Education Rep.*, p. 7. On these figures secondary pupils were 11 per cent of the age-group at age 14, 8 per cent at 15, 4 per cent at 16.

Table 6.4

Pupils in secondary and intermediate schools by age, 1912

Aged under 12	339
12	3,473
13	9,632
14	10,079
15	7,387
16	4,043
17	2,012
18	956
19 and above	391
TOTAL	38,312

Agitation over rural education and nostalgia for the old ways diverted attention from the real problems of inequality in Scottish education, which lay in the cities. Ramsay might see little good in 'the sort of lad who comes from the lower streets of our big cities', but why should he be less deserving than the proverbial ploughboy or crofter's son? In the cities the stratification of schools and the barriers between them were more rigid than elsewhere. The best schools had high fees, and free secondary education was not widely available. There was none, for example, in Dundee; and in Glasgow and Govan, though there was some movement towards the abolition of fees in the 1900s, the schools affected were the weaker ones which did not go above the intermediate stage.[103] Another important barrier was that with few exceptions every secondary school (not only in the cities) had its own primary or junior department, and if the school was fee-paying this applied to the whole age range; in some cases, as in Leith, schools which were themselves free had fee-paying primary departments, which helped to keep the school select, for those who started in the primary department could normally expect to transfer to the senior school.[104] Middle-class parents who used such schools took secondary education for granted as a part of their world, but for a working-

---

[103] For changes in Glasgow, see Roxburgh, op. cit., pp. 142-9, 168-70.

[104] In the case of endowed and higher class schools, the primary departments did not usually claim grants under the Code, so the influence of the SED over their syllabus was limited.

class child to break into this environment required parents to take the initiative in seeking transfer by the age of twelve, in finding a bursary or free place, and of course in forgoing the child's earnings. The 'central' higher grade school without its own primary department was potentially more democratic but these were still rare—one in Aberdeen, one in Edinburgh (Boroughmuir), a few elsewhere.

In his polemics with the rural education movement, Struthers recognized that the question of transfer from elementary schools was crucial, and produced statistics showing that almost exactly half of those entering on the intermediate curriculum came from within the same school, half from elementary schools outside. Three-quarters of all primary schools sent pupils on to secondary education, and such pupils formed 1 in 6.5 of the total, compared with 1 in 22 in England. Thus, he claimed, although the pattern of education had changed, the real extent of opportunity for reaching the top was greater than ever before.[105] One is left feeling that, for all that, Struthers's critics did have a case, and that the parish schools might have picked up and encouraged some talent which centralization deterred. One may also feel that while opportunities in the cities were certainly increasing—for there had been no past golden age there—the educational ladder was most inviting and most efficient in small and medium-sized towns, where the secondary school was likely to be free and the elementary schools less overwhelmed by the task of drilling basic education into the industrial masses.

The pattern of secondary schools established before 1914 proved remarkably persistent in its effects, and if Scottish education was more advanced then than English, this lead was lost as the system was affected by the general immobilism which seems to have overtaken Scottish society in the inter-war years. The Education Act of 1918 replaced the school boards by county authorities, and introduced free education as a general principle. But local authorities were allowed to retain fee-paying schools alongside free ones, and the cleavage within the secondary sector apparent before 1914 remained: an upper tier

---

[105] *SED Reports, 1912-13. Secondary Education Rep.*, p. 5; *1913-14. Rep. of Comm. of Council*, pp. 28-9, and *Secondary Education Rep.*, pp. 3-5. For the comparison with England see SRO ED 7 1/33, memorandum for Scottish Secretary.

of fee-paying schools, which also retained their own primary departments, enjoyed a prestige within the educational world which far outweighed their numbers, and played a vital part in the life of the middle class, especially in Edinburgh and Glasgow. Endowed schools and fee-paying local authority schools survived the move towards 'secondary education for all' in the 1930s, and complicated the task of introducing comprehensive education in the 1960s and 1970s. The local authority schools eventually succumbed, but not the endowed schools. Public opinion came to regard the latter as 'independent' and to reject political 'interference' in their affairs, a development which would have surprised the nineteenth-century reformers. Thus legal distinctions which went back to the 1870s and 1880s, and which had seemed of historical interest merely by 1914, sprang into life in later years. The ironies of history became apparent in 1979 when the local authority which was the successor of Edinburgh town council and school board on the governing body of Heriot's proposed to integrate the school into the public system: this provoked a 'Hands Off Heriot's' campaign whose aims—the retention of fee-paying and resistance to popular control—were the precise opposite of those of the Heriot Trust Defence Committee 100 years before.

Even a perfect machinery of selection and social promotion would not have satisfied all critics. Speaking to a secondary education conference in 1914, Ramsay MacDonald declared that

There is ... no form of national waste more appalling than human qualities which never ripen. When we began to be aware of this a few years ago, we set up what we called an education ladder along which a few selected children were to climb. ... It was only a scheme for helping a few individuals to rise from one class into another; it had nothing to do with the improvement of national education. It was individualism run mad.

As a product of the parish school, MacDonald was at one with traditionalists like Ramsay in holding that 'every child should have enough of what was called secondary education, before he left school, to give him inducements in the form of tastes and of awakened educational interests to continue his education after he had left school'. There was nothing democratic about 'increasing the facilities given to working-class children to pass into the First Division of the Civil Service or into the managerial ranks in commerce through the doors of universities. That was stereotyping society with a vengeance. It was drawing lines across our social unity, dividing it up into a governing and a subordinate class.' Our educational system 'would fail, and ought to fail, if its effect was to form a new series of classes and sub-classes, of servants and masters, of subordinates and superiors, determined by the schools through which they had gone'.[106] MacDonald was able, as so many were not, to link nostalgia for the past, and an instinctive distaste for the kind of vocationalism preached by Struthers and Darroch, with a critique of the powerful tendencies of industrial society which were ensuring that the latter got their way.

[106] *Secondary School Journal,* vii (1914), pp. 44-7.

7.
UNIVERSITY REFORM 1878-1914

Although the Royal Commission report of 1878 had no immediate effect, the problems which had caused the commission's appointment did not go away, and the views of the General Councils continued to have an influence which reached its peak in the 1880s. Many of the Royal Commission's recommendations were embodied in the Universities (Scotland) Act of 1889, which opened the way to a new age of university expansion. Not only were new subjects admitted within the academic pale through the demise of the uniform MA degree, but it became accepted that a modern university needed new buildings, laboratories, and junior staff if it was to meet the demands of the age for practical teaching and the advancement of research. The state, though reluctantly, assumed responsibility for supplying some of these, and by the eve of the First World War its relations with the universities were taking on their characteristic twentieth-century pattern.

One reason why the universities had felt able to brush aside the 1878 report was that in the 1870s they were enjoying a period of exceptional prosperity. Reliable enrolment statistics were first collected in 1861, when there were 3,399 students. Numbers rose only slowly in the 1860s, to 3,785 in 1870, but there followed a period of rapid expansion until 1885, when there were 6,947 students—a figure not reached again until 1906.[1] The success of the medical schools was especially marked in this period, but the arts faculties did not lag far behind. The only dark side to the picture was at St. Andrews, where numbers fell in the 1870s to as low as 130 in 1876, causing a fall in income which was compounded by the agricultural depression, for St. Andrews depended more than the other universities on revenue from rents and teinds. For a time its future seemed threatened, but by the 1880s it was recovering. Numbers in general, however, began to fall after 1885, and there was a steady decline which was not reversed until 1896. The financial

[1] See Appendix I.

problems which this caused made the universities all the more anxious to see the removal of the legislative straitjacket on the curriculum.

The universities could see two obvious ways of extending their appeal: a greater role in the training of teachers, and the admission of women. In the case of the teachers, this was difficult without the co-operation of the SED, which controlled the training regulations and was strongly committed to the training colleges. The 'concurrent' system of attendance had been working since 1873, and the numbers settled down at about 120—half of the men in the colleges.[2] But these students did not stay long enough to take a degree, and the 1876 commission had refused to approve of a short BA, though in 1880 both Edinburgh and Glasgow introduced a 'Literate in Arts' certificate based on two years' work, which was a BA in all but name. Edinburgh also introduced a 'Schoolmaster's Diploma' based on Laurie's education lectures, which was useful for university students hoping to teach in the expanding secondary sector, but it failed to persuade the SED to accept this in place of the special government examination which graduates had to take before they could teach in public schools.

At Aberdeen and St. Andrews there were more ambitious plans. Aberdeen felt frustration and 'a keen sense of services ill requited' since, despite the traditions of the North-East, it could not even take in training-college students: the two colleges in Aberdeen were for women only until 1886.[3] In 1884 Aberdeen proposed to create a college under the university's own supervision, and similar proposals came from St. Andrews. These claims were among the matters referred to the Parker committee which reported in 1888, and it came down against them. That committee, it will be recalled, generally favoured a clear differentiation of secondary and elementary education, and it thought that the college-trained teacher

brings to his business qualities not easily acquired, habits of order, discipline, and organisation, everywhere highly conducive to success, and especially valuable in dealing with the unruly mass of children often found in the large schools of great cities. In some

---

[2] *Comm. on Scottish Univ. Rep.* (1910), p. 43, memorandum by Struthers; M. Cruickshank, *A history of the training of teachers in Scotland* (1970), p. 98.

[3] *Parker Comm. 1st & 2nd Reports*, p. 15 (statement by Aberdeen Senate).

places, especially in country districts (where, however, he is less often found), the University graduate is able to give opportunities, not otherwise procurable, for higher education which may compensate for his want of special training. Yet the want is felt...[4]

Rather than encourage the untrained graduate, the committee proposed various improvements in the system of concurrent attendance, and in 1889 the SED extended financial aid to allow attendance for a third year. The Department, along with the church committees which ran the training colleges, had argued that all those students who were capable of profiting from university attendance were already doing so, and that the universities could not provide either the teaching practice or the moral and religious supervision which the colleges could guarantee. Moreover, the university curriculum excluded subjects which teachers needed, like history and geography, so that progress on this front depended on general university reform.

As secondary education expanded and offered more attractive careers to graduates, elementary teaching was becoming increasingly feminized, and its inclusion within the university sphere naturally raised the question of the admission of women, in which the Scottish universities were beginning to lag behind those in the south. Burgh schools had traditionally taught girls alongside boys (with the important exception of Edinburgh, Glasgow, and Aberdeen), but in some respects this delayed the growth of higher education for women, because there was less urgent demand for women teachers. Public opinion in Scotland did not object to girls being taught by men, and the prestige of the graduate meant that men normally monopolized the headships of elementary schools as well as all secondary posts.[5] It was difficult to break out of this vicious circle, whose strength was shown when the Merchant Company opened its new girls' schools in Edinburgh: these had male heads and male teachers for all the principal subjects, while women taught the younger girls, or, with the title of 'governesses', performed pastoral rather than academic functions. In Glasgow too, Hutchesons'

---

[4] Ibid., p. vi.
[5] L. I. Lumsden, *On the higher education of women in Great Britain and Ireland* (n.p., 1884), pp. 6-7.

grammar school for girls and the new Girls' High School had male headmasters.

It is understandable, therefore, that the first new initiatives were linked with the general education of women from the leisured classes rather than with secondary education proper, and took the form of part-time lectures at university level given by sympathetic professors. Courses of this kind began at Edinburgh in 1867 and Glasgow in 1868, often attracting older or married women. The pioneering organization, the Edinburgh Ladies' Educational Association, became the Edinburgh Association for the University Education of Women in 1879. A similar Association had been formed in Glasgow in 1877, and in 1883 it took institutional form as Queen Margaret College, where regular lectures were given. Through courses of this kind, women could experience the equivalent of a degree curriculum; at Edinburgh the Ladies' Association gave a Diploma based on seven subjects, and the university itself offered a Certificate in Arts for women, which required fewer subjects but had Honours as well as pass grades.[6] This idea was pushed much further in the St. Andrews 'LLA' scheme which started in 1877. Attempts to run lecture courses at St. Andrews failed to survive, as did those at Aberdeen, but the LLA was an 'external' examination which could be taken anywhere after independent study. The standard was of degree level, and the LLA was especially valued by teachers in search of a recognized qualification. By 1896 1,542 diplomas had been awarded, and the university had made a substantial profit on the scheme, which was to continue until after the First World War.[7]

St. Andrews was also the scene of an innovation in girls' secondary education, St. Leonards School, opened in 1877 as a boarding school on English Public School lines. The first headmistress, Louisa Lumsden, had been one of the first students at Girton (in its early days at Hitchin), where she had cherished

[6] Sources for these developments are: C.S. Bremner, *Education of girls and women in Great Britain* (1897), pp. 265 ff.; K. Burton (ed.), *A memoir of Mrs Crudelius* (n.p., 1879) (on Edinburgh); Mrs R. Jardine, *Janet A. Galloway, Ll.D. Some memories & appreciations* (Glasgow, 1914) (on Queen Margaret College). For secondary works see Bibliography, section III.6.

[7] The LLA (so called from 1879) stood for 'Lady Literate in Arts'. See W. Knight, *A history of the L.L.A. Examination and Diploma for Women, and of the University Hall for Women Students at the University of St Andrews* (Dundee, 1896).

the dream of founding 'a really good school for girls, inspired by Dean Stanley's story of the great schoolmaster, Dr. Arnold'.[8] The foundation of St. Leonards was the work of a group of St. Andrews professors, and professors' daughters were prominent among its pupils; Julia Grant, the daughter of the Edinburgh Principal, later became headmistress of the school herself. As a girls' Public School, St. Leonards remained unusual in Scotland, and it appealed to a social stratum where careers were not a high priority for women, but its aim of offering a liberal education on the same academic plane as that given to boys was shared by a cluster of proprietary schools which appeared around this time. Glasgow had Westbourne (1877), the Park School (1880), and Craigholme (1894). In Edinburgh, St. Georges (1888) grew out of part-time classes for secondary education organized by the Ladies' Educational Association, and incorporated a training college for women aiming at secondary teaching. Such women, or those who had attended the various university-level courses, were more likely to find jobs in these new proprietary schools than in the public or endowed sector, and indeed, as Lumsden complained in 1884, 'Scotchwomen who have gone through University training are compelled to look almost entirely to England for a worthy professional career.'[9]

Besides teaching, the career which most attracted women was medicine, and the best-known episode in the history of women's education in Scotland is the attempt of a group of women led by Sophia Jex-Blake to persuade Edinburgh University to give them a medical training. In 1869 the university seemed to agree, and the women were allowed to matriculate. But opposition from the medical professors soon arose, and further progress was blocked. A series of legal actions ended in the women's defeat, as did attempts at legislation by their supporters in Parliament. These transactions were not very creditable to the Edinburgh professors, who tended to shelter behind and even to stir up the prejudices of the male students. In 1886 a solution was found outside the universities when the

---

[8] Quoted in *St Leonards School* (n.d.), p. 150. Cf. L. I. Lumsden, *Yellow leaves. Memories of a long life* (Edinburgh, 1933), pp. 60 ff.

[9] Lumsden, *On the higher education of women*, p. 7.

three Scottish medical corporations agreed to open their qualifications to women. Jex-Blake returned to Edinburgh to open an 'extra-mural' School of Medicine for Women, and at Glasgow medical teaching began under the auspices of Queen Margaret College.[10] Agitation over the admission of women played surprisingly little part in the debate on university reform, either in the 1870s, when it was quite ignored by the Royal Commission, or in the 1880s, when provision for it in the various university bills aroused little comment or opposition; university education for women actually began in the new college at Dundee, which was open to them from the start. Elsewhere many leading university figures sympathized with the cause, but nothing could be done without legislation; and while lecture courses might help girls from the upper middle class in the cities, it was not until the universities themselves (and their bursaries) were open on equal terms that opportunities would be extended to girls in provincial and country schools. To the history of university legislation we must now return.

The university reaction to the 1878 report showed that although the Royal Commission was thought to have leant too heavily in favour of science, there was widespread support for more flexibility in the arts curriculum, and also for a strengthening of the Honours system. The question of an entrance examination was more controversial, but Edinburgh and Glasgow had planned one before 1876, and in 1883 Glasgow established its own, though it was imposed only on entrants under seventeen. Such unilateral action was difficult, for under the 1858 Act any university could object to Ordinances proposed by the others, and it was felt that unless a common scheme was imposed from above there was a danger of delay and deadlock; furthermore, if the curriculum was changed the financial interests of many professors would be harmed, and government aid would be needed to compensate for this, as for other desirable purposes like the founding of new chairs and the rescue of St. Andrews. Within a few years of the 1878 report, therefore, there were calls for an 'executive commission'

[10] Bremner, op. cit., pp. 274-7; M. Todd, *The life of Sophia Jex-Blake* (1918), *passim*.

like that of 1858, and the fact that the 1876 commission had recommended increased state expenditure was held to imply some kind of pledge by Westminster. At the end of 1881 the University Courts of Edinburgh and St. Andrews, prodded by their General Councils, brought pressure to bear on Lord Rosebery, the member of the Liberal government who managed Scottish affairs, and after deputations to London the government promised to introduce a bill.[11]

This did not appear until 1883, and when it did so it contained some disagreeable surprises. The bill created a body of commissioners, and seemed to give them indefinite powers to remodel the university constitutions, thus removing this matter from parliamentary discussion. They were also empowered to abolish tests for the theology chairs—i.e. to end the Established Church's monopoly of the divinity faculties, a proposal guaranteed to stir up sectarian feeling. As for St. Andrews, the commission could not only abolish 'any one or more' faculties there, and affiliate other colleges to it (this with Dundee in mind), but it was also required to prepare a special report within a year on whether the university should not be dissolved altogether. This threat to St. Andrews caused an outcry in Scotland, and its defenders claimed that the worst of the crisis there was already past; in 1886 it acquired as Principal of the United College James Donaldson, the former rector of Edinburgh High School, who was to prove a heavyweight among university politicians during his long tenure of office.[12] In the version of the bill which reappeared in 1884, the reference to dissolution was dropped, though the idea of affiliation remained. Other grievances were also met: the text of the bill specifically included the constitutional recommendations of the 1876 Commission (chiefly relating to the composition of the Courts), and the tests question was evaded by enjoining the commissioners to make a special report on it.[13]

[11] EU GC Minutes, Apr. 1880, Apr. 1881, Oct. 1881; St. AU GC Minutes, Nov. 1881, Mar. 1882.

[12] He became Principal of the University after the 1889 Act established this office. Donaldson's *Addresses delivered in the University of St. Andrews from 1886 to 1910* (St. Andrews, 1911) provide a running commentary on university politics.

[13] In the event no change was made, except that the 1889 Act excluded the theological chairs from a share in any new public funds.

One objectionable feature of the 1883 bill, however, did not disappear: its financial side. The bill provided for an annual grant of £40,000, which 'shall be deemed to be in full discharge of all claims, past, present, and future, of the said Universities'. This 'finality clause', as it came to be known, implied that the state was washing its hands of the Scottish universities, and another clause allowed the Treasury to commute this payment at any time for a lump sum at thirty-three and one-third years' purchase. This aroused alarm among the Scottish MPs, and the Lord Advocate warned the Treasury that

the plan of disestablishing the Universities, apart from the terms on which it is to be done, has not been well received in Scotland. ... This feeling is not confined to the Universities or to University men. ... As national institutions they have been a conspicuous success. The endowments have benefited a poorer class and a much greater number of students than frequent the great universities of England, and the taxpayers of Scotland consider that the money thus spend on education has been well spent.

The Treasury's reply revealed that they did indeed have a theory of disestablishment. Their policy, wrote the junior minister Leonard Courtney,

is to start the Universities with a fair and sufficient endowment from the State in addition to their other resources, whilst relieving them at the same time of the fetters of State interference in the management of their funds. ... in the interest of financial management, and, I would for myself add, in the interest of educational independence the Universities should be remitted to a state of freedom, so that as far as possible they should economize for themselves their resources and mould for themselves their forms of active life.

The Treasury attached particular importance to putting the grant on the Consolidated Fund, for the advantages of the scheme 'would be destroyed if any branch of expenditure were still left to be provided for annually by Parliamentary grants; and our interest in the Bill would practically cease if it did not relieve the taxpayer from these continuous demands'.[14]

---

[14] SRO AD 56 48, Lord Advocate to Courtney, 21 June 1883, and Courtney to Lord Advocate, 2 July 1883; cf. ED 26 8, memoranda of Lord Advocate to Home Secretary, 19 Jan. and 22 Feb. 1884.

Here was a clear conflict between English and Scottish ideas. In Donaldson's words, 'this conception of our Scottish Universities and the proposals based on it run counter to the entire history of these institutions and to the ideas of the Scottish people in regard to them. The Scottish Universities are not private corporations—they are national seats of learning, existing for the nation, and controlled by the Parliament of the nation. And the Universities have no wish to become independent of the State, or to be removed from the control of the State.'[15] The argument that the universities were 'national institutions' used by all classes, which recalled the earlier protests by Donaldson and others against the refusal of Parliament to subsidize secondary education, was echoed in the protests made in 1883 by all the universities, though these concentrated too on the inadequacy of the amount. The government originally claimed that £40,000 would give a clear £10,000 of additional income, but Playfair and other MPs showed that this was not so, and also protested that the payment of professorial pensions, whose growth could not be predicted, was being transferred from the Treasury to the universities.[16] In the 1884 bill, the government raised the annual sum to £43,000, and made a concession on the pension question. But this still seemed inadequate to meet the needs identified by the 1876 commission, let alone those which loomed in the future at a time when, as the Edinburgh Senate observed, 'Education in science becomes constantly more expensive, as well as more valuable, owing to the modern development of practical instruction.'[17]

Besides, the Treasury refused to abandon the finality clause itself. This controversy, and the difficulty of finding parliamentary time for a bill which would be contested, meant that neither the 1883 bill nor its successors in 1884 and 1885 reached a second reading debate. It was given a rest during the 1886 political crisis, and revived the next year. But during this period, the debate had broadened out and new interests had

[15] Donaldson, *Addresses,* pp. 47-8 (1887), and cf. his views in *Scottish Review,* iii (1883), p. 11.
[16] See details in parliamentary return in PP 1883, liii; W. Jack in *Macmillan's Magazine,* xlviii (1883), pp. 53-5.
[17] SRO ED 26 7, Memorandum of Apr. 1883.

come into play, with the General Councils, which knew how to command the attention of MPs, reviving their constitutional claims. An issue which especially absorbed the General Council activists was 'extra-mural' teaching in arts, i.e. the demand that men with suitable academic qualifications should be allowed to give lectures in competition with the professors. This was inspired both by the existing system of extra-mural medical teaching and by the example of the *Privatdozenten* in Germany, and it suggested a model by which the work of the universities could be expanded into new fields. The extra-mural idea had been part of the claims of the graduate movement before 1858, and was raised from time to time in the 1860s in the General Councils. The 1876 commission had considered it, but rejected it on the grounds that it would degrade teaching into cramming for examinations.[18] From 1884, however, the university bills included extra-mural teaching among the subjects to be considered by the new commission, and the Edinburgh General Council passed regular resolutions in its favour. There was also a vociferous extra-mural party at Glasgow, but it was less successful in winning over the General Council, and in both cities Associations were formed which could propagandize more freely than the Councils themselves. The Edinburgh General Council Association claimed in 1885 that 'the monopoly of teaching, which at present prevails in some Faculties in the Universities, should be broken up, and that the same healthy system of free competition that has proved so beneficial for commerce, should be applied and introduced, both within and without the Universities, under the careful guidance and control of the University Court.'[19] The critique of 'professorial monopoly' was given a wider application by W. R. Herkless, one of the leaders of the Glasgow movement. 'Monopoly of administrative and legislative power in the hands of the Senate; monopoly of the right of teaching, such as results in some cases in a single professor having 500 or 600 students; monopoly in favour of a few subjects as qualifying for graduation;—these are obviously fixed

[18] *R. Comm. Univ. Rep.*, pp. 81-4.
[19] SRO ED 26 9, Petition of Edinburgh GC Association, Apr. 1885.

ideas with most of the office-bearers in the universities.'[20] As well as supporting extra-mural teaching, therefore, Herkless— and indeed the General Councils as a whole—favoured a radical opening-up of the curriculum.

As Herkless's remarks indicate, the reformers were hostile to the Senates, championing the rights of the Courts against them. They called for the Courts to be enlarged, with a strong representation of the General Councils, and for the administration of the universities' property and revenue to be transferred to them. The Senates were sometimes attacked as if they were corrupt corporations, the Edinburgh Association, for example, resolving in 1886 that 'as the University is nothing more than the highest Public School in the Kingdom, it is contrary to public policy, principle, and precedent that its property and funds should be held and administered by a Teaching Staff of nearly forty Professors, who are elected for life, hold their meetings in private, and are themselves beneficiaries under the trusts which they administer'.[21] The Courts, on the other hand, were seen as bodies representative of public opinion, and a favourite demand of the General Councils since the 1860s was that they should meet in public and admit reporters. The reader of the *Scotsman* or the *Glasgow Herald,* it was felt, should be able to follow their proceedings just as he did those of the Town Council or the Merchant Company. Occasionally the Courts yielded to this demand, but generally they confined themselves to issuing press releases after their meetings.

The reforming Assocations could hardly be ignored, for they claimed about 900 members at Glasgow and 1,200 at Edinburgh.[22] But the professors could use their own membership of the General Councils to fight back, and at Glasgow a rival organization, the Glasgow University Club, was formed to campaign for reform 'on the principle of Expansion within the organization of the University and under the control of the University Court'.[23] The extra-mural movement at Glasgow

---

[20] W. R. Herkless, *Scottish university reform: the main problem and its solution* (Glasgow, 1884), p. 4. Cf. pamphlet by the leader of the extra-mural party at Edinburgh: A. T. Innes, *Open teaching in the universities of Scotland* (Edinburgh, 1885).

[21] SRO ED 26 14, Memorial of Edinburgh GC Association, Mar. 1886. Cf. similar statements in ibid., Memorial of Glasgow University Council Association, 1886; ED 26 13, Petition of GU Council Association to House of Commons, June 1885.

[22] Documents in SRO ED 26 14.

[23] SRO ED 9 39, printed constitution of GU Club (italics in original omitted).

was closely linked with the foundation of St. Mungo's College, a medical school based on the Royal Infirmary, which seems to have had wider ambitions, since we hear of a 'law faculty' in which Herkless was a professor; another supporter was the publisher W. G. Blackie, who formed a link with the reformers of the 1850s. The University Association began campaigning in 1886 for the 'affiliation' of St. Mungo's to the University, which itself strongly opposed the idea.[24] Thus when the universities bill was reintroduced in 1887 it was opposed by the Edinburgh and Glasgow Associations because it failed to provide either for affiliation (except in the special case of Dundee and St. Andrews) or for increasing the power of the Courts, and it made no progress. But the situation was shortly transformed when R. W. Cochran Patrick, a former MP who was president of the Glasgow Association, became Permanent Under-Secretary at the Scottish Office, and thus in charge of drafting the bill. The 1888 version, which differed little from the Act of 1889, included some radical innovations, and was found by the Association to be 'in all essentials adequate to the ends of a great reform'. As well as meeting their demands on the powers and composition of the Courts, it provided for colleges to be 'affiliated' to any of the universities by agreement, in which case the affiliated colleges would be directly represented on the Court.[25]

The 1888 bill also recognized for the first time a new interest, the Students' Representative Councils. The first SRC had been founded at Edinburgh in 1884, and the movement—which was part of the contemporary growth of corporate and social life among students—soon spread to the other universities. By 1887 the Edinburgh SRC was putting forward a student viewpoint on the universities bill, including such questions as whether the traditional lecture method should be supplemented by tutors, whether appointments to chairs

[24] Various documents relating to this are in SRO AD 56 48. See also *EN,* xiv. 792 (16 Nov. 1889), 824 (30 Nov.); H. Jones & J. H. Muirhead, *The life and philosophy of Edward Caird* (Glasgow, 1921), pp. 102-7. St. Mungo's College continued as a successful medical school.

[25] SRO ED 26 23, Report of Executive of GU Council Association, 19 Apr. 1888. Various documents in ED 26 24 show the close links which Cochran Patrick retained with Herkless, W. G. Blackie, etc. The change of Scottish Secretary in 1887 from A. J. Balfour to Lord Lothian may also have had some significance.

'should be vested in a Board specially selected and qualified to judge the merits of Candidates both as Teachers and as Specialists', and 'Whether other tests than examination (e.g. thesis) might be admitted as qualifying for Graduation?'[26] The 1888 bill (and the 1889 Act) gave the SRCs the formal right to make representations to the University Court, and provided that the rector might consult them before appointing his assessor, though he was not obliged to do so. A joint Memorial of the four SRCs found this inadequate, and pointed out that 'the practical working of University Institutions is a matter of at least as great and direct importance to the Students of the University as to the General Council'. They demanded two directly elected assessors on the enlarged Courts, and the same statutory right to consider Ordinances as the General Councils.[27] These demands were not heeded, but at least the existence of the SRCs was officially recognized, and this was more than was achieved by the non-professorial staff, who were also forming their first organizations at this time—the Assistants' Club at Edinburgh, the Assocation of Assistants to Professors at Glasgow.

The 1888 bill, therefore, was less welcome to the universities than its predecessors. The clauses on affiliation were both obscure and novel, and taken in conjunction with the possible extension of extra-mural teaching they threatened to dissolve the unity of the universities and turn them into examining institutions. The Senates protested strongly both collectively and individually, the Aberdeen professors pointing out that 'The professorial system of instruction has been the prominent feature of the Scottish Universities, and it has been their boast to be able to say that their system corresponds to that of the Universities on the Continent, and to the historic University system, rather than to that of England, and that the Scottish system is the most useful one to the nation.' Affiliation seemed to derive from the English collegiate system, and was 'uncalled for and objectionable'.[28] But the provisions remained in the

[26] SRO ED 26 12, Memorial of Aug. 1887.

[27] SRO ED 26 18, undated Memorial; J. I. Macpherson, *Twenty-one years of corporate life at Edinburgh University* (Edinburgh, n.d.), pp. 30-8. One of the founders of the Edinburgh SRC, R. Fitzroy Bell, became secretary to the 1889 commissioners.

[28] SRO AD 56 48, Memorial by Aberdeen Senatus, 14 Apr. 1888. Cf. Memorial by Edinburgh Senatus, 12 Apr. 1888, and Resolutions of a joint Conference of Senates, 7 Apr. 1888.

bill, for the attack on the 'professorial monopoly' was popular among MPs and in wider educational circles. It had long been a theme of the *Educational News,* and the EIS favoured anything which would allow teachers to complete their qualifications without university attendance. The EIS's committee on university reform, reporting in 1887, in addition to calling for the abolition of 'the existing monopoly of seven classes in arts', recommended more recognition of extra-mural teaching, the affiliation of colleges doing work of university standard, and the extension of university influence through lectures in provincial centres.[29] This last idea—'university extension' as it was practised in England—was taken up by the universities at this time, but little demand was found to exist, and the schemes were dropped after a few years.[30]

The 1888 bill got no further than the House of Lords, but in 1889 MPs at last got their chance to debate university reform. The question of tests and theological chairs came up again, and Radical and Home-Rule MPs were prominent in attacking the bill of a Conservative government. The extra-mural cause was championed especially fervently by Robert Wallace, an Edinburgh MP with a chequered background. He had been a liberal minister whose appointment to the chair of Church History at Edinburgh had caused theological controversy in 1872; in 1876 he had resigned his chair on losing his faith in the dogmas of the Church, and had been editor of the *Scotsman* for a time before becoming an MP. He now sought to amend the bill so as to make university degrees 'accessible to any man who showed he was possessed of the necessary qualifications in point of knowledge, culture, or skill, wherever or however he had acquired them'. He also complained that the bill would restrict opportunities for the poor, though without making the grounds of his criticism very clear.[31] An MP of similar cast was W. A. Hunter, who had strong views on the curriculum, an issue otherwise neglected in these debates. As a member for Aberdeen, Hunter shared the hostility to Greek which was the hallmark

[29] *EN,* xiii. 42 (14 Jan. 1888).

[30] W. H. Marwick, 'The university extension movement in Scotland', *University of Edinburgh Journal,* viii (1936/7), pp. 227-34.

[31] *3 Hansard* cccxxxvii, HC 20 June 1889, col. 374; cf. 27 June, cols. 945-6, 952-4, 1 July, cols. 1213-18.

of reformers in that city, and extended his condemnation to the 'antiquated and totally inadmissible Arts programme' as a whole. He demanded that 'modern subjects, which are of the highest importance to the individual in the struggle for life, shall not be relegated to a back seat, and that students shall have an opportunity of obtaining an education which will equip them properly for the work they have to perform'. In moving an amendment which would require the MA to take full account of science and modern languages, he observed that this ought to be superfluous, 'as it is impossible to conceive that any 15 men of intellectual sanity would meet round a table and approve of the present restricted course of the Arts' curriculum in the Scotch Universities'. He also observed that 'Parliament has been a cruel stepmother to the Scotch Universities. If we had had a Home Rule Parliament, we should not have starved our higher education and stunted its growth.'[32]

One issue on which the Liberal opposition united was the inadequacy of the men proposed as commissioners. According to Wallace, they were 'feeble and reactionary', especially the 'Scoto-Anglican element' of Scotsmen 'caught young, and Rugbyfied and Oxfordized out of all decent shape and recognition'.[33] There was some truth in this, but the real objection to the commission was that it represented the Unionist establishment, comprising a rather dull selection of peers, lawyers and doctors. It did include men already active in educational reform like Lord Elgin, J. A. Campbell and A. C. Sellar, but one such expert, Sir Francis Sandford, was particularly disliked for his record as Secretary of the Education Department, and the only academic on the original list, Sir Henry Roscoe, was a distinguished but English chemist. The government made some concessions on this point, and four names were changed, the newcomers being the Glasgow physicist Sir William Thomson, S. H. Butcher, the Irish-born and English-educated professor of Greek at Edinburgh, and two representatives of the General Council movement, including W. G. Blackie from Glasgow. Hunter still complained that Aberdeen

---

[32] *3 Hansard* cccxxxvii, HC 20 June 1889, cols. 333-4, 1 July, col. 1212. Cf. address by Hunter to Aberdeen branch of EIS, in *EN*, xiv. 144 (23 Feb. 1889). Hunter, an Aberdeen graduate, had become professor of Law at University College, London.
[33] *3 Hansard* cccxxxvii, HC 20 June 1889, col. 375.

was under-represented, and at the very end of the debate the Liberals tried unsuccessfully to secure the addition of the eminent philosopher and educationist Alexander Bain; but his agnosticism made him too controversial, and the critics had to be content with Frederick Fuller, another retired Aberdeen professor, and an ally of Bain in the reform movement there in the 1870s.[34]

Following the precedent of 1858, most of the strictly educational changes were entrusted to the commission, though there were sixteen sub-clauses defining the subjects which they were to deal with. The Act itself settled the main constitutional questions, which met the desires of the General Council reformers. The Courts were enlarged, some changes were made in the basis of representation on them, and they took over the administration of the universities' property and revenues, leaving the Senates responsible for discipline and academic matters. One minor innovation was that municipal representation on the Courts was extended from Edinburgh to all the universities. A major one was the provision for affiliation, and here the Act and the commission ran into trouble. In 1890 the commission carried out the 'affiliation' of University College, Dundee, to St. Andrews on terms which seemed to be agreed at the time and which centred on the creation of a 'conjoint medical school'. But within a few years dissension arose and the legality of the union was challenged in a long series of court actions, ending only in 1900. One problem was the ambiguous nature of 'affiliation', for while Dundee gained representation on the St. Andrews Court and Senate it also retained its own endowment, chairs, and governing council. But the real source of the trouble lay in St. Andrews, where the professor of medicine, James Pettigrew, opposed the transfer of all medical teaching to Dundee. He found an ally in the Marquess of Bute, who was elected rector in 1892 and who carried out his duties in person. Bute was a Roman Catholic, a romantic admirer of the middle ages, and a man who had his own ideas for the development of St. Andrews and immense wealth to back them. Although himself a member of the new universities commission, he threw his energies into frustrating its policy

[34] For this controversy, which had already arisen over the 1888 bill, see ibid., 20 June, 27 June, 28 June 1889; cccxxxviii, HC 17 July, 24 July 1889.

and developing Pettigrew's plan for two years of medical instruction at St. Andrews. The Bute party was able to win over the Court and the General Council, against the professoriate led by Donaldson. Bute was re-elected in 1895, but compromise was on the way by the time his term of office ended in 1898. The union between Dundee and St. Andrews continued, but it was never harmonious, and St. Andrews went ahead in 1901 with founding two new medical chairs, one of them financed by Bute. This extremely complex and acrimonious dispute was perhaps of limited wider significance, though it showed the potential for conflict in the universities' constitutional structure, and probably deterred any other college from experimenting with the affiliation clauses of the Act.[35]

The commission appointed by the 1889 Act, chaired by a judge, Lord Kinnear, remained in being until the end of 1897, and got through a heavy programme of work; it held 251 meetings, which resulted in the passing of 169 Ordinances, many of them on such routine matters as the remodelling of bursaries. The core of the commission's work was formed by the changes which it made in the arts degree, which were closely related to the introduction of a compulsory entrance examination and to the creation of new chairs and the expansion of the non-professorial staff. Changes were also made in the degrees in law and medicine, and a significant innovation was the setting up of separate Faculties of Science, which would supervise the independent development of the B.Sc. degree, which all the universities now possessed, and which covered subjects like engineering and agriculture as well as pure science. Also significant were Ordinances which provided for the machinery of modern postgraduate study—research students, research fellows, and doctoral degrees awarded by thesis, a recognition of the universities' research function which met one of the

---

[35] The union was suspended altogether between 1895 and 1897. For details see *General Rep. of Comm. under 1889 Act*, pp. xliii-lxi; Donaldson, *Addresses*, pp. 159-94, 302-51 (including a strong attack on Bute). The Royal Technical College affiliated to Glasgow University in 1913, but this involved only the recognition of courses for graduation, and constitutional links were avoided.

oldest demands of the reform movement.[36] There were many complaints that Scottish graduates had to go to England for higher training, and that, as Donaldson put it in 1882, 'with the educational revolution of the nineteenth century, a revolution has also taken place in the competition for distinction in science, scholarship, theology, and all the higher intellectual pursuits. The Scotsman has to fight with bow and arrow against men armed with rifles and cannon. He is the hand-loom weaver of the intellectual world.'[37] The case for higher standards was also made by Lord Reay, in a rectorial address at St. Andrews in 1885 which attracted much attention. 'The chief wealth of Scotland', he told the students, 'consists in the natural resources of Scottish brains. The development of brain-power on a wide scale is what a Scottish statesman has to look to. If we had a Scottish Parliament sitting in Edinburgh, I have no doubt that the organisation of the Universities would be the first number on the legislative programme. ... This is not a question of local importance. It concerns the greatness of the Empire. Development of more brain-power in Scotland means increased national efficiency and less danger from democratic ignorance.'[38]

Donaldson, like Blackie thirty years before, complained that 'The Scottish universities are schools', and that the curriculum was still 'fixed nearly on the old Reformation programme.'[39] In approaching the problem of the curriculum, the commission did not lack advice. The Act gave the University Courts the right to submit their own proposals, and the commission's draft Ordinances were commented on at length by the various university bodies. The existing situation, it will be recalled, was that all students had to study the same seven subjects (eight at Aberdeen); at the time of the 1876 commission, university opinion had generally agreed that it was necessary to introduce 'options', but had been divided between two ways of achieving this—a common basis of one or two years' work,

---

[36] Ordinances 61, 62. These are conveniently collected in *The Universities (Scotland) Act, 1889, together with Ordinances of the Commissioners under the said Act* ... (Glasgow, 1915). These doctoral degrees were five-year affairs: the modern Ph.D was introduced after the First World War.

[37] *Contemporary Review*, xli (1882), p. 150.

[38] W. Knight (ed.), *Rectorial addresses delivered at the University of St. Andrews* (1894), pp. 302-3. Reay was active in English educational reform.

[39] Donaldson, *Contemporary Review*, xli (1882), pp. 148-9.

followed by specialization, or a system of 'departments' which would limit student choice in such a way as to preserve the broad educational character of the degree. By the 1890s, the latter solution was the favoured one. The most traditional approach was at Aberdeen, which proposed to keep eight compulsory or semi-compulsory subjects (e.g. modern languages could replace Greek, history or education could replace moral philosophy) while adding two others to be chosen freely —a scheme which would have given students a heavy burden.[40] The other universities produced schemes which, without retaining any one subject as compulsory, gave a privileged position to the traditional classes. The plan which the commission adopted was based very closely indeed on that proposed by Glasgow.[41]

In the first place, students who wished to could still take the subjects prescribed in the previous regulations. But otherwise they could choose seven out of the whole range of arts and science subjects, which were grouped in four departments— language and literature (including the newly introduced modern languages), mental philosophy, science, and history and law. Four of the seven, however, had to be: Latin or Greek; English or a modern language or history; logic or moral philosophy; and mathematics or natural philosophy. The other three subjects could be chosen freely, but the curriculum as a whole had to include either both Latin and Greek, or both logic and moral philosophy, or two out of mathematics, natural philosophy, and chemistry. Thus every student had to take at least one subject from each of the traditional fields of classics, philosophy and science, and two subjects from at least one of these fields.

This was for the Ordinary degree, as it was now called, for the commission also introduced a separate Honours degree. Under the system established after 1858, Honours work was additional to the standard curriculum, but there were no

[40] SRO ED 9 33, Representations of Aberdeen Court, July 1890. Cf. AU GC Minutes, June 1890.

[41] SRO ED 9 61, Draft Ordinances of Glasgow Court, June 1890. See also ED 9 31, ED 9 34, ED 9 44 for other proposals including those of Edinburgh and St. Andrews (which differed in proposing a common preliminary course). The revival of the BA was no longer proposed, presumably because training college students could now attend for three years.

special Honours classes. The commission now moved in the direction of greater specialization, and adopted with some modifications the proposals which came from Edinburgh.[42] Eight Honours groups were provided for, and Honours classes were to be organized. A student would take the Honours as well as the Ordinary classes in two subjects within his group, and three Ordinary classes outside it. Various restrictions were imposed whose effect was that an Honours curriculum, like an Ordinary one, had to include Latin or Greek, a philosophical subject (normally logic or moral philosophy), and a science. Thus although Honours students studied five subjects instead of seven, and aimed at an Honours degree from the start, this was hardly a scheme for early specialization: Honours students shared five courses with their Ordinary companions. The commission had done its best to maintain breadth of study, and one of its requirements—compulsory Greek for philosophy Honours —had to be modified in 1896 because the universities found it too stringent.[43]

The commission's Ordinances were about as cautious and conservative as was compatible with the generally accepted aim of giving students more choice and bringing new subjects fully into the curriculum, and little fundamental criticism was heard. The entrance examination was a more controversial question. The existing situation was that the junior classes in Latin, Greek and mathematics could be bypassed by the 'three-year' examination. Under the 1892 Ordinance, the normal curriculum lasted for three years, and could not be entered without passing a Preliminary Examination which was administered jointly by the four universities; the junior classes were allowed to continue as long as they were needed, but henceforth their function was to prepare for the Preliminary Examination, if it had not already been taken at school, and they no longer counted for graduation. The Preliminary subjects were English, Latin or Greek, mathematics, and a fourth

[42] The Edinburgh proposals for Honours can be traced back to the 1860s. In the 1890s Glasgow had similar but less precise ideas, but Aberdeen and St. Andrews preferred the old system.

[43] Details of degree regulations in Ordinance 11 (1892). The philosophical group of subjects included education and political economy, and candidates in some Honours groups (but not all) could theoretically avoid logic or moral philosophy by taking one of these.

subject which might be a second classical language, a modern language, or 'dynamics'. The standard was similar to that of the Leaving Certificate, which was accepted as an equivalent.[44]

The traditional argument against an entrance examination was that it penalized older students and boys from country schools, but there was also the issue of principle, put by P. G. Tait. An entrance examination as a condition of graduation was acceptable, but one which closed off entry to all university classes 'is a very different matter, and seems to threaten in a direct manner one of the most valuable of a Scotsman's birthrights. The Scottish Universities have hitherto made it their proudest boast that they are the property of the Scottish people, without distinction of rank, age, or sect. Any one who can pay his matriculation fee has at present a right to *demand* enrolment in my class. Is he now to be deprived of this right, or are obstacles to be gratuitously put in the way of his enjoying it?'[45] Tait's Natural Philosophy class was one of those with a large number of students not aiming at a full degree, but such partial attendance was now becoming a thing of the past. Still, Laurie too thought that 'every professor and every subject should be accessible to the general public without reference to graduation'.[46]

The *Educational News* attacked the entrance examination as an example of Anglicization, fearing that it would introduce the social exclusivism of Oxford and Cambridge.[47] A more specific objection put by the EIS was that it would prove an obstacle for training college students, who lacked a background of classical training; the commission responded to this by allowing them to enter with a lower grade of pass, to be made up after arrival at the university.[48] The secondary teachers, on the other hand, were strongly in favour of the examination, as might be expected, as were the General Councils. The Glasgow

[44] Ordinance 11, as modified by Ordinance 44; *General Rep. of Comm. under 1889 Act*, pp. x-xiv. The account given here is simplified.
[45] P. G. Tait, *Address to the graduates. ... Graduation ceremonial, 18th April 1888* (n.p., n.d.), pp. 10-11.
[46] S. S. Laurie, *The training of teachers and methods of instruction* (Cambridge, 1901), p. 194 (written in 1893).
[47] *EN*, xviii. 118-19 (18 Feb. 1893); cf. 188 (18 Mar. 1893), xxii. 273-4 (17 Apr. 1897).
[48] Ibid., xvi. 739-40 (31 Oct. 1891), submission of University Reform Committee of EIS.

General Council, in particular, wanted an early end to the junior classes, which lingered for about ten years, disappearing entirely by 1905.[49] What made the examination acceptable, as it had not been in the 1870s, was the rapid development of secondary schools after the mid-1880s, and once it was established it set a goal which further raised standards in the schools and which worked—along with other factors which have been discussed, including the policies of the SED—to give the parochial tradition its *coup de grâce*.

If the demise of the junior classes lessened the burden of teaching in the universities, the introduction of Honours classes created new demands, and one of the most significant parts of the commission's work was to open the way to an organized expansion of the non-professorial staff. The professors themselves were affected by the creation of the 'fee fund': students still paid for each class individually, but the fee income was pooled and the professors paid fixed (though not uniform) salaries. Thus ended, after many years, the 'painful sight of eminent professors with their own hands raking in the dirty one-pound notes which are the most distinctive product of the Northern kingdom'.[50] The fee fund was an essential accompaniment to the reform of the curriculum (by separating financial from educational interests), but it did not create new resources. The 1889 Act had eventually fixed the universities' grant at £42,000, but after money was set aside for pensions only about £9,000 of this would have been available for new expenditure. In the parliamentary debate of 1889, the government had agreed that some further finance might be made available, and this promise had been embodied in a Treasury Minute. In the event, the Act of 1892 which gave the 'equivalent grant' to secondary education also provided £30,000 for the universities, and this increased the Kinnear commission's freedom of action. In order to provide for the newer subjects which were now incorporated in the curriculum, it was able to create chairs of English at St. Andrews and Aberdeen, History at Edinburgh

---

[49] SRO|ED 9 44, printed Resolutions of ATSS, Mar. 1890; GU GC Reports, Mar. 1892, Mar. 1893, Oct. 1895, Apr. 1900. For dates of disappearance of junior classes see *The Carnegie Trust for the Universities of Scotland. Sixth Annual Report* (1906), p. 57.

[50] *Westminster Review*, cxxxii (1889), p. 412.

and Glasgow, and Political Economy at Glasgow. These were, however, the only new non-medical chairs, for five new chairs had to be created for the 'conjoint' medical school at Dundee; the modern languages received only lectureships, which were not converted into chairs until after the First World War.[51]

The practice of professors appointing assistants was an old one. A parliamentary return in 1888 revealed that most chairs had at least one assistant, but that their status, duties, and re-muneration varied in a chaotic manner. Teaching assistants, who marked essays or conducted tutorial work, were not clearly distinguished from demonstrators in the medical faculty or from technical and laboratory assistants. Since 1858 public funds had provided assistants in the main arts classes at Glasgow and Edinburgh, but otherwise it was common for them to be paid by the professors out of their class fees, and the control of the Courts over these private arrangements was lax.[52] Assist-antships were normally temporary posts, taken by recent graduates and used to support them while they carried out research, established a career (in medicine and law), or waited for a teaching post to turn up. There were also a few lecture-ships, mostly in the medical faculties; the term was usually reserved for the teaching of new subjects not covered by pro-fessorial chairs, for a lecturer gave an independent course and collected his own fees.

There was little here that resembled a career structure. But in 1886 the Glasgow General Council had endorsed a far-reaching plan, drawn up by a committee under Edward Caird, for the creation of new chairs and for a graded staff of Senior Professors, Junior Professors, and Lecturers.[53] The organi-zations formed by the assistants had similar ideas. The Assist-ants' Club at Edinburgh thought it 'highly undesirable that men who have adopted the career of Academic Teachers ... should not have an honourable and definite status in the Uni-versity', and called for 'some system of graded appointments, calculated to induce young men of ability to devote themselves to the prosecution of original research, and to the acquirement

[51] Ordinances 25, 26, 27, 46; *General Rep. of Comm. under 1889 Act*, pp. xxxiv-xxxix. Bequests etc. were also used for some of these chairs.

[52] Parliamentary return in PP 1888, lxxviii. The Edinburgh Assistants' Club criticized this return as inaccurate: see their report in SRO ED 26 21.

[53] GU GC Reports, Apr. 1886.

of a knowledge of how to teach'.[54] But this ideal was challenged by the 'extra-mural' party, who claimed that the need for more teachers would be better met by the appointment of men who enjoyed financial and academic independence, rather than by assistants under professorial control. These reformers had, after all, succeeded in getting a reference to extra-mural teaching written into the Act, and they were indignant when it became clear that the commission had decided against this policy. Like the Royal Commission before them, the commissioners were persuaded that it would undermine the Scottish professorial system and encourage cramming by divorcing teaching from examining; 'the true principle of sound University education [is] that the course of study should govern the examination, instead of the examination determining the course of study'.[55] On this issue, the Edinburgh and Glasgow General Councils took opposition to the 1892 arts Ordinance to the parliamentary stage, but they failed despite the support of MPs like Wallace, Haldane, and Trevelyan.[56] The commission's Ordinance on lecturers and assistants preserved the distinction between the two posts, but regularized the system and put their appointment and payment firmly in the hands of the Courts. There was no real movement towards a graded career, since the assistantships were still temporary posts, and the new grades of staff did not gain any constitutional rights within the universities. The commission thus paved the way for the autocratic professorial department which became characteristic of the Scottish universities in the twentieth century.

The work of the Kinnear commission seemed to promise an era of expansion. Schoolmasters thought that the remodelled curriculum would attract parents who had formerly been put off by the universities' traditionalism,[57] and the admission of women,

---

[54] SRO ED 9 40, printed statement of 27 Jan. 1890; cf. ibid., Memorial of Association of Assistants to Professors in Glasgow.

[55] *General Rep. of Comm. under 1889 Act,* p. xxvii.

[56] EU GC Minutes, May 1890, Oct. 1890, Feb. 1892, Apr. 1892, Oct. 1892; GU GC Reports, Mar. 1892, Apr. 1892, Oct. 1892; *4 Hansard* iv, HC 9 May 1892. Cf. Ordinance 17.

[57] e.g. *Elgin Comm. Minutes of Ev.,* p. 121 (G. Smith).

which took place in 1892,[58] led to further developments in teacher training. With the Dundee union in prospect, St. Andrews had renewed its claim to share in training—Donaldson was a strong critic of the training colleges, and looked forward to an all-graduate profession. The commission recommended allowing this claim, and in 1895 the SED reluctantly introduced a 'Queen's Student' scheme which allowed university attendance without the college link; Aberdeen as well as St. Andrews took advantage of this. The number of teacher trainees in the universities rose to 644 in 1900 and 754 by 1905, when the system was completely reorganized.[59] By that time 80 per cent of the men in training were attending the universities, and the reduction of the Ordinary curriculum to three years (with Education recognized as a graduating subject) meant that both men and women could now graduate. Prospective teachers became, indeed, the largest single element in the arts faculties. In 1890 Ramsay had found that of his 395 Latin students at Glasgow 42 per cent aimed at the Church, 17 per cent at teaching, 15 per cent at law, and 8 per cent at medicine. But by 1909 54 per cent of the women and 35 per cent of the men in the Glasgow arts faculty came from the training colleges, and at Edinburgh the percentage was higher still.[60] At Aberdeen, 15-20 per cent of graduates became teachers between 1860 and the 1890s, but around half by 1914; of 2,912 male graduates at Aberdeen between 1901 and 1925, 1,235 went into medicine, 777 into teaching, and only 247 into the Church, but of the 1,627 women graduates 1,101 became teachers.[61]

This influx of new students helped to compensate for a fall in numbers caused by the entrance examination, which seems to

[58] Ordinance 18. The terms of the Ordinance allowed the Edinburgh medical faculty to continue to refuse women full status. At Glasgow Queen Margaret College was now incorporated into the university, but separate lectures for women continued there for some years in arts as well as medicine.

[59] *General Rep. of Comm. under 1889 Act*, pp. 288 ff; *Comm. on Scottish Univ. Rep.*, pp. 43-4; Donaldson, *Addresses*, pp. 23-6, 129-39; Cruickshank, op. cit., pp. 119-20. The SED also now recognized Laurie's Schoolmaster's Diploma.

[60] SRO ED 9 44, report to GU Court Committee on Ordinances, Apr. 1890; *Comm. on Scottish Univ. Minutes of Ev.*, pp. 42 (Glasgow), 80 (Edinburgh), and cf. 15 (Aberdeen).

[61] G. Mercer & D. J. C. Forsyth, 'Some aspects of recruitment to school teaching among university graduates in Scotland, 1860-1955', *British Journal of Educational Studies*, xxiii (1975), p. 60 (table presumably referring to all faculties); T. Watt, *Roll of the graduates of the University of Aberdeen 1901-1925* (Aberdeen, 1935), p. 943.

have been sharper than expected. Numbers in the arts faculties had reached their peak in the early eighties, after which they declined until 1895, as Table 7.1 shows. Recovery then started, but it was not until 1904-6 that the previous peak figures were reached again, and even then the admission of women concealed the fact that (except at St Andrews) the number of male students of arts and science did not return to the level of the 1880s before the First World War.[62] The fall in arts numbers coincided with a particularly sharp decline in the medical faculties in the 1890s—attributed to the growth of new medical schools in England and the colonies—and with a decline in law teaching caused by changes in professional practice. This in turn affected the arts faculties, where law and medical students often attended classes. The root of the decline perhaps lay in the economic crisis of the 1880s, but it was reinforced by the entrance examination and by changes in the secondary schools: now that these reached a higher standard, and the Leaving Certificate endorsed the acquisition of a 'liberal' education, the old habit of sending boys to the university for a year or two died out.[63]

By the end of the 1890s observers were talking of 'the Scottish university crisis',[64] and arguing that the universities must repair their finances by finding new ways of serving the community. Around 1900, as we have seen, there was much agitation about commercial education, and there were demands for Faculties of Commerce in the universities and new degrees based on courses in subjects like economics and geography. This was recommended both in the Edinburgh businessmen's report of 1900 and by the Glasgow Chamber of Commerce in 1901, when much was made of the need for Britain to retain its supremacy in the international commercial struggle. The response of Principal Story of Glasgow was not encouraging. 'There was a supremacy', he pointed out, 'which, in the long run, was of a higher value, and of a higher meaning, than that

[62] Based on figures in Appendix I.
[63] See EU GC Minutes, special report on crisis, Oct. 1901, and special report on BL degree, Apr. 1902.
[64] The title of an article by W. Wallace in *Fortnightly Review*, n.s. lxviii (1900), pp. 982-93. Cf. article by him in *Quarterly Review*, clxxxviii (1898), pp. 139-59; and *EN*, xxiv. 309-12 (6 May 1899).

Table 7.1

Fluctuations in numbers in arts and science

	Aberdeen	Edinburgh	Glasgow	St. Andrews
Peak year	1884 (462)	1885 (1,147)	1880 (1,406)	1886 (178)
Trough year	1895 (339)	1895 (850)	1895 (868)	1891 (162)
Year when peak regained (men and women)	1904 (466)	1904 (1,149)	1906 (1,510)	1898 (193)
Year of maximum male students 1904-14	1912 (426)	1912 (1,141)	1913 (1,285)	1909 (186)

of mere commercial or trade supremacy. There was no trade or commerce to speak of in Athens ...'.[65] The Glasgow General Council kept up pressure for a Faculty of Commerce, but without success.

The main practical issue was the position of modern languages, which still took second place to the classics in the universities, and especially in the bursary examination: the Kinnear commission, on the grounds that modern languages were easy to learn, had laid down that Latin, Greek, English, and Mathematics should have double the marks of any other subject, and continuing attempts to change this regulation were not satisfied until 1908 (1913 at St. Andrews).[66] Educationists put great faith in modern languages as a commercial tool, and argued that if they were encouraged 'a considerable increase of students would be attracted from the commercial classes, who would appreciate and benefit by it, but who do not at present avail themselves of University studies, and the Universities would acquire a fresh claim upon the sympathy and pecuniary support of the mercantile community'.[67] Businessmen themselves, to judge by the Edinburgh report, were more sceptical. Commercial firms used German clerks for their foreign correspondence, and it was only the more professionalized branches of commerce, like accountancy and banking, which were interested in the universities, and then only in part-time attendance by the young men in their offices: in 1900 the accountants required attendance on the Edinburgh law classes, and in 1909 the bankers followed suit and founded a lectureship in banking at Edinburgh.[68] Otherwise, while the science faculties continued to provide industry with engineers and chemists, commerce did not become a significant outlet for arts students, except to the extent that the sons of the owners and directors were sent there for a liberal education before

---

[65] *EN*, xxv. 31, 33-7 (13 Jan. 1900); xxvi. 152-4 (2 Mar. 1901), 171 (9 Mar. - Story quotation).

[66] This regulation had done much to sustain Greek in the schools, and its abolition coincided with Struthers's 'intermediate' policy.

[67] Memorandum of Scottish Modern Languages Association, 3 Mar. 1900, found in St. AU Library, Donaldson papers, Vol. 33.

[68] *The Edinburgh Merchant Company [etc.] ... Report by Joint Sub-Committee on Commercial Education* (Edinburgh, 1900), pp. 8-9, 13, 19-21, 25, 30.

joining the family business.[69] The main task of the modern language courses was not turning out export salesmen, but training secondary teachers who could replace the Frenchmen and Germans to whom this teaching had traditionally been entrusted.

A new wave of curricular reform began within the universities around 1901, and the desire to attract more students was one motive for it. At Edinburgh the chief reformer was George Chrystal, professor of Mathematics, who argued—much like Playfair thirty years before—that the universities had to adapt their teaching to the whole range of middle-class occupations.[70] It was felt that the 1892 system, under which seven subjects were studied, each for one year only, led to superficial work and inadequate concentration, and the desire for reform converged with moves at Glasgow to adopt a three-term year. The traditional university session lasted from late October to Easter, with a break at the New Year. In medicine there had always been a 'summer session' as well, and in the 1860s a summer session in arts appeared at Edinburgh and Glasgow, in the form of voluntary classes conducted by assistants. The 1889 commission had regularized the summer session, and allowed courses in it to count for graduation; in practice it was used mostly for Honours classes, and students could not be compelled to attend in the summer. The argument now used at Glasgow was that cramming all the work into six months put an undue burden on students, and that a longer year would allow a more reflective approach. Lectures could be spaced out, and more tutorial and practical work introduced—this was all the more necessary, some argued, because of the influx of teacher-training students with an examination mentality, who needed to be forced to work more independently.[71] Changes in the curriculum and in teaching methods therefore seemed to go together, and a joint scheme was worked out by a conference of Faculties of Arts in 1903. Delays then set in, chiefly because a

[69] See the thorough examination of this question in M. Sanderson, *The universities and British industry 1850-1970* (1972), pp. 173-81.

[70] For Chrystal's views see *EN*, n.s. ii. 415-16 (17 Apr. 1908) and *Comm. on Scottish Univ. Minutes of Ev.*, p. 77. Similar views in A. Darroch, *The place and function of the Scottish universities in our educational system* (Edinburgh, 1906); A. Morgan in *The University Review*, ii (1905/6), pp. 445-63.

[71] *Comm. on Scottish Univ. Minutes of Ev.*, p. 42 (Glasgow evidence).

party at Aberdeen, led by Harrower, claimed that many students still needed to take jobs in the summer months, although Harrower's own estimate was that this only applied to one in ten.[72] Reform eventually came about in 1908, when Ordinances in similar terms were put through by three of the universities; the dissenter was St. Andrews, which produced a scheme on slightly different lines in 1910.

The 1908 reforms introduced a three-term year, and reduced the number of lectures prescribed for a course from 100 (five a week under the old system) to seventy-five (three a week), leaving more room for tutorial work. For the Ordinary degree, students would take five subjects instead of seven, but two of them would be studied for a second year at a higher level. The new Ordinary degree thus resembled the Honours degree of 1892, and the latter now became more specialized, with only two instead of three subjects studied outside the Honours group; classics, philosophy, and science could thus no longer be insisted on.[73] In order to avoid future recourse to the cumbersome procedure for changing Ordinances, the details of subject choice and grouping were left to the individual universities. For the Ordinary degree, the four 'departments' of 1892 were retained, but with only five separate subjects it was less easy than before to insist on breadth of choice. Glasgow was the most cautious, prescribing three types of curriculum all of which included a language, mathematics or a science, and logic or moral philosophy. At Edinburgh and Aberdeen, on the other hand, the requirement was simply to choose subjects from three of the four departments, which meant that philosophy, or a language, could be avoided altogether. Perhaps the most significant change, which proved permanent, was that an arts degree could now be taken without including Latin or Greek, though a classical language was retained in the entrance requirement.[74] The neglect of philosophy, however, proved

[72] AU GC Minutes, Oct. 1907.
[73] Court Ordinances XXII (Edinburgh), XXIII (Glasgow), XXIV (Aberdeen), XXIX (St. Andrews). At Glasgow, it was possible to take six subjects, in which case only one was taken at the higher level. At St. Andrews there was first a 'General' examination, followed by a 'Special' examination which was either Ordinary or Honours, but the effect in terms of subjects taken was much the same.
[74] Details from University Calendars. At St. Andrews logic was compulsory in the General examination, and Latin was more difficult to avoid than elsewhere.

temporary, for the extreme freedom allowed by the new regulations soon caused disquiet at Edinburgh, and in 1919 logic or moral philosophy was made compulsory; in 1926 Edinburgh went over to the Glasgow system, requiring a language and a science as well, and Aberdeen had already done the same.[75] The net effect of these changes was to give the two philosophical subjects a privileged status which they had not had before, either under the uniform curriculum when all subjects were 'compulsory', or under the 1892 scheme, when Latin and Greek, mathematics and natural philosophy, had formed pairs of equal status.

By the end of the war some professors had begun to look back with nostalgia to the uniform curriculum of the years before 1892. In 1917 John Burnet, professor of Greek at St. Andrews, compared the German and Scottish methods of forming the national élite, and concluded in favour of a general course with a strong philosophical element before specialization began.[76] In 1918 Harrower launched a strong attack on the 1889 commission. 'Behind the old Arts curriculum, which held its ground from 1860 to 1892, there lay an Educational idea nothing short of this, that the faculties of the student's mind should be exercised over a diversity of subjects so chosen as to secure that on the conclusion of his University course the whole field of human thought and knowledge should lie open to the graduate.' That curriculum had an 'architectonic character', but the result of the commissioners' work was to 'leave chaos where order was before, and one is forced to the conclusion that compromise and opportunism in educational reform may produce results indistinguishable from the havoc wrought by Bolshevism'. Harrower, a conservative who cared above all for the standards of classical teaching, added two points: first, that 'The modern Tutorial system is a mere ghost of that in use under the Old Ordinances, when every class met at least twice a week for purposes of revision in addition to the daily lectures'; and, second, that the end of compulsory subjects had

---

[75] A. L. Turner (ed.), *History of the University of Edinburgh, 1883-1933* (Edinburgh, 1933), pp. 180-96. Given a free choice, a quarter of the students had studied no language, almost half no philosophy, and over 40 per cent no science - p. 189. Logic was actually called 'Philosophy' in Edinburgh in 1919.

[76] J. Burnet, *Higher education and the war* (1917), pp. 218, 223 ff.

destroyed 'the spiritual essence of the vanished Class bond. What his Regiment is to a Soldier, what his College is to an Oxford man, all that was meant by his Class to the Aberdeen student in Arts'.[77] Harrower's points were repeated in a more moderate form by Herbert Grierson, professor of English at Aberdeen until 1915 and thereafter at Edinburgh, in a collection of essays on post-war reform; Grierson too romanticized the old common class and the unique intellectual stimulus which it had given in his student days.[78] After the post-war years, these arguments ceased to attract attention until they were revived by George Davie in 1961. Whatever their force, it was perhaps unfair to load all the blame onto the commissioners of 1889, who had after all maintained compulsory classics and philosophy for all students; the reforms of 1908, though based on the 1889 principles, represented a much more radical step towards specialization.[79]

Table 7.2 illustrates the long-term impact of these changes on graduation. In the 1870s, it will be recalled, only a small proportion of the arts students actually took degrees, especially at Glasgow. By 1890, when the old system was near its end, the proportion had doubled at Glasgow, and also increased at Edinburgh. In the 1900s the numbers graduating steadily increased, and the figures of 20-25 per cent on the eve of the First World War implied that practically all students aimed at a degree. Casual attendance had disappeared, though this was a result of the entrance examination and of changing social habits rather than of the changes in the curriculum itself. The table also shows that those aiming at Honours remained a minority, especially at Glasgow, and only at Edinburgh do the 1908 reforms seem to have led to a sizeable increase. Most students still took the Ordinary degree, and the broad character of this was still quite marked.[80]

[77] J. Harrower, 'Then and now', *Aberdeen University Review*, vi (1918-19), pp. 3, 12, 14-17; cf. reply by J. Lees in ibid., pp. 116-28.

[78] Grierson in J. Clarke (ed.), *Problems of national education, by twelve Scottish educationists* (1919), pp. 318-23.

[79] Grierson acknowledged this in 1919, but forgot it when he repeated his argument in a 1937 Edinburgh rectorial address: H. Grierson, *Essays and addresses* (1940), pp. 195-200.

[80] Based on annual Statistical Reports of the universities: for the 1870s see Table 3.1 above. In 1890/1 the B.Sc. is included. St. Andrews is excluded as the numbers fluctuated, especially in the 1900s, but the percentage of Honours degrees there was usually high.

Table 7.2

Statistics on graduation in Arts

	Arts degrees awarded as % of total number of Arts students			Honours degrees as % of Arts degrees awarded		
	Aberdeen	Edinburgh	Glasgow	Aberdeen	Edinburgh	Glasgow
1870/1 to 1875/6	13	8	5	28	11	24
1890/1	18	14	9	30	17	12
1895/6	17	12	9	35	18	16
1900/1	21	16	15	35	22	14
1905/6	20	18	18	25	29	16
1910/11	25	18	18	26	27	21
1913/14	24	20	22	31	40	21

The new arts curriculum of 1908 required the main subjects to be taught at three levels—Ordinary, 'second' (the universities used different names for these new classes), and Honours, and with the new emphasis on tutorial work this increased the need for staff. The development of new subjects—in all the faculties—had already led to a large expansion, and in 1907 there were 127 professors, 140 lecturers (compared with a handful before 1892), and 172 assistants or demonstrators; this gave a staff/student ratio of 1:16.[81] As Table 7.3 shows, the salary bill consumed over two-thirds of the revenue, and although expanding student numbers increased this there was little to spare for capital expenditure, for which the universities had to turn to the state or to private donors.[82] The state's grants to the universities had increased considerably during the nineteenth century. They were originally in the form of salaries tied to particular chairs, but also included such fixed sums as the £2,232 p.a. in return for which the copyright status of the university libraries had been surrendered in 1837. For many years the total payment came to about £9,400, but

Table 7.3

University expenditure in 1894/5 and 1907/8

	Aberdeen	Edinburgh	Glasgow	St. Andrews
1894/5				
Total expenditure	£31,171	£73,556	£54,441	£15,223
Salaries & pensions	£22,962	£57,213	£41,143	£11,737
(% of total)	(74)	(78)	(76)	(77)
Total expenditure per student	£39·50	£25·03	£28·00	£58·32
1907/8				
Total expenditure	£40,651	£91,162	£76,587	£28,014
Salaries & pensions	£28,405	£67,104	£50,123	£20,239
(% of total)	(70)	(74)	(65)	(72)
Total expenditure per student	£43·62	£27·69	£29·95	£51·12

[81] *Comm. on Scottish Univ. Rep.*, pp. 18-19.
[82] Ibid., pp. 41-2. This illustrates how smallness made St. Andrews less efficient.

the 1858 Act made an additional £10,000 available for new posts. The Act also introduced professorial pensions, which became a substantial charge on the Treasury, and by the time of the 'finality clause' controversy in 1883 existing state expenditure was calculated to be £28,321.[83] From 1892, as we have seen, the old arrangements were replaced by an annual grant of £72,000, and it remained at that figure in the 1900s.

Occasionally the state could be persuaded to support a large building project, but only where private money was raised as well. The chief example of this was the rebuilding of Glasgow University, when it moved from its ancient central site to Gilmorehill in the western suburbs. The government provided £120,000 for the new buildings, which opened in 1870, but the total cost was nearly £400,000, and £159,705 came from a public appeal.[84] The state helped Edinburgh in the same way when it rebuilt its medical school in the 1880s, but there was no question of regular grants for capital projects. The prospects of private benevolence were greater. After 1858 the General Councils brought the universities into closer contact with both graduates and the local community, and in the 1860s Edinburgh pioneered the idea of an 'endowments association' to organize appeals and make the university's wants known. A steady stream of gifts and bequests began to flow, though often in the traditional form of bursaries and prizes, which did not directly benefit the universities' funds; more welcome were scholarships and fellowships for higher study, although all too often they merely carried a promising student off to Oxford or Cambridge. Benefactions of this kind were useful, but larger sums were needed to build a laboratory or endow a chair (which needed £10,000-15,000), and rich industrialists were the most likely source. Michael Sanderson has analysed the contributors to Glasgow's rebuilding appeal, and finds that although most of the funds came from the business community, a few rich men gave disproportionately, and the support lacked a broad base, just as at Dundee employers as a whole failed to back up the initiative of the Baxter family in founding University College. Nevertheless, industrial and commercial money

[83] Figures in parliamentary returns in PP 1865, xliii; PP 1883, liii; PP 1889, lix.
[84] *University of Glasgow New Buildings. Report by the chairman of the University Removal Committee* (Glasgow, 1877), p. 43.

did endow chairs at Glasgow which were obviously relevant to the city's concerns—naval architecture (1883), political economy (1896), geology (1903), and mining (1907).[85] Another chair, in Scottish history and literature, resulted from a public appeal connected with the international exhibition held at Glasgow in 1911; this recalled the Celtic chair at Edinburgh, founded in 1882 after an appeal to Highland patriotism organized tirelessly by J. S. Blackie. Edinburgh also had a chair of Scottish history, founded by bequest in 1901. Such chairs were part of the universities' debt to the national community, but there were cases where appealing to private wealth meant humouring the whims of the donors, as the Bute episode at St. Andrews showed. Moreover, the growth of student 'corporate life' from the 1880s was beginning to divert benevolence away from academic purposes to student unions, playing fields, and halls of residence.

Sometimes the universities had windfalls, as with the Berry bequest at St. Andrews in the 1890s, £100,000 left by an Australian whose connection with St. Andrews was of the vaguest. The greatest example of this, and of the exile syndrome which had led so many successful Scots to found educational endowments, was the gift of Andrew Carnegie, the steel millionaire, who in his retirement diverted part of his fortune to Scotland and to his native Dunfermline. He seems to have taken from the Dunfermline-born MP Thomas Shaw the idea of paying the university fees of all deserving students, and proposed to devote $5m. to this purpose. Wider consultation with the universities and with such figures as Balfour of Burleigh revealed a critical reaction: the universities pointed out that such a scheme would do nothing to meet their direct financial needs, and that the existing bursaries already gave extended help to poor students. Carnegie stuck to his original scheme, but doubled his donation to allow for the promotion of science and scholarship.[86] The Carnegie Trust for the Universities of

---

[85] Sanderson, op. cit., pp. 167-72; P. L. Robertson, 'The finances of the University of Glasgow before 1914', *History of Education Quarterly*, xvi (1976), pp. 468, 471-3.

[86] See Shaw's article in *Nineteenth Century*, xli (1897), pp. 113-23; B. J. Hendrick, *The life of Andrew Carnegie* (Garden City, 1932), ii. 218-20; J. Robb, *The Carnegie Trust for the Universities of Scotland 1901-1926* (Edinburgh, 1927), pp. 7-8.

Scotland, which began work in 1901, disposed of an annual income of £100,000, which was split equally. Under 'Clause A', capital grants were made to the universities, and fellowships and grants supported individual research projects; under 'Clause B', the trust paid the class fees of students who met its qualifying demands. These did not include a means test, for Carnegie himself insisted that the 'manly independence' of young Scots would prevent them from applying if their need was not genuine. Carnegie's critics may have been right in saying that his gift did not transform the conditions of access to the universities,[87] but it was hardly negligible, and must especially have helped girls, to whom bursaries, with their classical bias, were less easily available. By 1904, Carnegie beneficiaries formed half of all Scottish university students, although later the proportion diminished as the funds began to come under pressure. The universities took advantage of the trust's existence to raise the standard class fee from three to four guineas in 1906/7, and the trust was forced to impose tighter requirements on its students and, from 1911, to pay a proportion of the fees rather than the whole.[88]

Under Clause A, the Carnegie Trust made the universities an annual capital grant of £40,000, the first guaranteed income of this kind which they had ever had. Since the trust was spending more than the state, and combining functions later to be exercised by different public bodies (capital grants, support of research, student grants), it became practically a ministry for Scottish universities, and its secretary, William McCormick, formerly professor of English at Dundee, occupied a position of some power. He became a member of the Treasury committee which dispensed university grants in England, and was appropriately enough the first chairman of the University Grants Committee in 1919, taking with him the system of quinquennial planning which the Carnegie Trust had devised. The UGC was to take over the state grants to Scottish universities, a

[87] See especially J. Donaldson, *Memoranda by Principal Sir James Donaldson on the Carnegie Trust and its administration* (St. Andrews, 1913); W. Ramsay in *Contemporary Review*, xciii (1908), pp. 709-25.
[88] Robb, op. cit., pp. 93-4, 98 ff.; *The Carnegie Trust for the Universities of Scotland. Ninth Annual Report* (1909/10), pp. 2-7. The Trust was criticized for using its influence to force changes on the universities, and this was certainly an element in the 1908 reforms.

development already foreshadowed before the war. Carnegie's munificence had underlined the inadequacy of the £72,000 grant at a time when the grants to English universities, which had started only in 1889, were increasing year by year; even though in 1900 Scotland still received twelve times as much per head as England, state support for universities was no longer a Scottish peculiarity.[89] In 1907 the Scottish universities approached the government for an increased grant, and were received sympathetically; but first there was to be an inquiry by a Departmental Committee. The universities gave evidence to this, stressing the new teaching needs created by the forthcoming arts reform and the way in which their very success in attracting private endowments led to additional current expenditure on staff and equipment.[90]

The Committee was chaired by Lord Elgin, a veteran of such inquiries, who was also chairman of the Carnegie Trust. Its report, published in 1910, showed how dependent the universities already were on public money.[91]

Table 7.4

Sources of university income in 1894/5 and 1907/8 (%)

	Aberdeen	Edinburgh	Glasgow	St. Andrews
1894-5				
Fees	33·8	49·7	41·4	17·3
Endowments	19·5	13·8	19·7	33·0
State grants	45·8	35·9	37·9	49·3
Other	0·9	0·6	1·0	0·4
1907-8				
Fees	37·9	53·3	51·4	22·7
Endowments	19·6	14·4	19·5	34·8
State grants	33·8	27·8	27·3	37·4
Other	8·7	4·5	1·8	5·1

[89] Robertson, op. cit., p. 449.

[90] Memorial of the Scottish universities printed in *Comm. on Scottish Univ. Rep.*, pp. 18-19.

[91] Ibid., pp. 41-2. The universities had become more dependent on fees as the state grant had not risen, but the latter had already become a constraint on expansion, in that greater student numbers did not bring in sufficient fee income to cover the extra cost.

The Committee recommended an additional grant of £40,000, and this was accepted by the government.[92] But when it fell to be paid in 1910, the Treasury insisted in return that the universities should introduce an 'inclusive fee', i.e. that students should pay a single fee for their degree course instead of a separate one for each class. The Carnegie Trust had been pressing for this for some years, and the proposal no doubt reflected McCormick's influence at the Treasury; but it was resisted by the universities, who saw it as an interference with their independence. By 1912, however, they were forced into line by the Treasury's refusal to pay the full £40,000 until they complied; the new annual fees were ten guineas for the MA, fifteen for the B.Sc.[93] This controversy, and the work of the Departmental Committee in general, showed that university history had moved into a new and more prosaic era. No longer did university reform attract the public attention which it had between the 1850s and the 1890s, when the issues were passionately debated in pamphlets, reviews, and General Councils. The latter were now polite pressure groups rather than the scourges of professorial monopoly, and academic matters were left to the academics. Negotiation between university Principals and the Treasury replaced public debate, and even before the Elgin Committee the work of the Carnegie Trust had accustomed the universities to drawing up regular plans and deciding their priorities internally before presenting their demands to the funding body.

The inclusive fee was also regarded as a turning-point in the history of university autonomy, at least by Principal Donaldson, whose dealings with Treasury officials convinced him that they were Conservatives out to sabotage the work of the Liberal government. The controversy impelled him to publish a pamphlet for the International Scots Home Rule League which ran through the history of English interference in Scotland's educational development since the days of the Revised Code, and concluded that 'the control of the Scottish Universities, so far as control is advantageous, should be in

[92] Dundee also received a separate grant, now increased, under the 'English' grant system.

[93] *Scottish Universities and the Inclusive Fee* (PP 1912/13, lxvi), *passim*. Resistance was strongest from Edinburgh.

the hands not of a British, but of a Scottish Parliament'.[94] He argued that Scottish opinion regarded state support for the universities as a duty, and that previously Parliament had recognized their historic role by trusting them to spend their grants without the kind of regular supervision on which the Treasury was now insisting. This interpretation passed over the fact that, in 1858 and 1889, Parliament had only made new grants in return for changes in university government which included outside representation, and that the destination of the new grants had been largely fixed by executive commissions on which the universities themselves were not represented. The state in the nineteenth century had indirectly regulated in minute detail matters which might well be regarded as part of any definition of academic freedom—entrance standards, the subjects and hours of teaching, the content of courses and the structure of the curriculum, graduation, etc. McCormick, explaining this to a surprised English professor on the Elgin Committee, thought that the universities and their professors were far more controlled by the state in Scotland than in Germany.[95]

This legislative straitjacket was causing increasing frustration. Although inter-university meetings to iron out differences had become regular practice, the Ordinance procedure still allowed objectors to cause long delays, and in protest against this a conference on university 'autonomy' was organized by the General Councils in 1908. By 'autonomy' most participants meant freedom for each university to act independently of the others, but one of the Edinburgh representatives, A. P. Laurie, Principal of Heriot-Watt College, raised the question of autonomy from the state. The kind of detailed regulation experienced in Scotland, he argued, tended to paralyse the universities' inner life, and to stereotype their teaching so that it fell behind changing demands. Like others at the time, Laurie was alarmed by competition from the new English universities, with their more flexible constitutions, and he cited

[94] J. Donaldson, *Home Rule and Scottish education* (n.p., n.d. [1913]), p. 44. The League was a Liberal organization of which Donaldson became honorary president. Cf. St. AU Library, Donaldson papers, Box 13, typescript of address of 25 Feb. 1914; Box 15, Donaldson to Liberal MPs J. W. Gulland, 23 Jan. 1911, W. Menzies, 2 Jan. 1913.

[95] *Comm. on Scottish Univ. Minutes of Ev.*, p. 53.

the example of the B.Sc., which had not changed since 1892: the regulations included a broad 'first Science examination' which stood in the way of the specialization required by students.[96] Others pointed to the failure to act on commercial education, or to the lack of any training for the new profession of social work.[97] For the reform of 1908, whatever its virtues, held to the old circle of subjects, and such concessions to the social sciences as were made were academic rather than practical in nature—towards economic history, political philosophy, or sociology; sociology was introduced at Aberdeen in conjunction with political science by R. M. MacIver, and acquired a lectureship of its own at St. Andrews in 1913.[98]

Laurie's point of view led him to challenge Donaldson's theory that the universities were state institutions,[99] and in the long run the latter idea—held in all quarters during the 'finality clause' controversy—was to fade from the universities' collective memory. Assimilation under the sway of the UGC led to general acceptance of the view that 'in this country' (i.e. Britain) universities

have always been and they are private institutions, constituted by legal process but largely self-perpetuating, self-governing and under no orders from the State. ... the essential factor is that here the State's active concern with and responsibility for education is of quite recent growth. ... There has never been a national system of University education at all. The Universities have been established and have developed, not without Government interest and aid, but as the result of local initiative and local finance.

These were the words of the Principal of Glasgow, Sir Hector Hetherington, in 1954. Hetherington was so hostile to external 'interference' that he even opposed the rectorship and the election of the Chancellor by the General Council, but he was a fair representative of orthodox academic opinion in the

[96] Report on the conference (which led to no further action) in AU GC Minutes, Apr. 1908. A. P. Laurie was S. S. Laurie's son.
[97] On social work see *Comm. on Scottish Univ. Minutes of Ev.*, p. 80 (favoured by R. Lodge at Edinburgh); Mrs Ogilvie Gordon in *EN*, n.s. v. 76 (27 Jan. 1911).
[98] *As a tale that is told. The autobiography of R. M. MacIver* (Chicago, 1968), p. 73.
[99] See their debate in *The University Review*, ii (1905/6), pp. 1-16; iv (1906/7), pp. 1-7; v (1907), pp. 1-17, and Donaldson, *Addresses*, pp. 500-3, 506-9.

twentieth century.[100] Yet the idea that the Scottish universities were ever 'private' institutions is as historically doubtful as the view, with which it is often associated, that the universities evolved as academic communities in which education was a secondary function to research.

In the nineteenth century Scottish public opinion had little doubt that the universities formed a national system, and the Act of Union was held to guarantee their existence, as the Treasury discovered when it planned 'privatization' in 1883. That opinion was strong enough, working through the Westminster Parliament, to maintain and increase the grants made by the State, but in return it expected a say in how the universities were run. Before 1858 all except Edinburgh had effective autonomy of a negative kind, being hampered by archaic restrictions which they were powerless to remove; while at Edinburgh the vagaries of town council control made the professors there the first to consciously define the sphere of academic freedom. The 1858 Act set the universities on a new path, but only at the cost of detailed regulation by statutory commissions, and of introducing the General Councils, which allowed the local middle class to express their views on university matters and take a hand in university legislation. Home Rule MPs in the 1880s sometimes claimed that if Scotland had its own Parliament the universities would be treated far more generously; this may have been true, but the price would have been more detailed intervention by the MPs and their local supporters. In the event, public distrust of the universities had evaporated by the early twentieth century, and they were again left to govern their own affairs. Under the UGC they enjoyed more genuine autonomy than ever before, and by the time of the Scottish devolution debate of the 1970s this had led to yet another historical myth which finds little support in nineteenth-century experience: that the universities were essentially 'British' institutions which could not survive, or at least maintain their international repute, without the bounty dispensed by the UGC.

[100] H. Hetherington, 'The British university system 1914-1954', *Aberdeen University Review*, xxxvi (1955/6), pp. 1-2; cf. C. Illingworth, *University statesman. Sir Hector Hetherington* (Glasgow, 1971), pp. 47-8. For the very similar views of James Irvine, Principal of St. Andrews, see his *The aim and the end* (Edinburgh, 1956), pp. 150-1, 270.

8.
UNIVERSITIES, OPPORTUNITY, AND ÉLITE RECRUITMENT

After the Act of 1858 each university kept matriculation records in a more or less standard form, and in the first part of this chapter an attempt is made to assess the changes which took place between then and 1914 by examining a sample of entrants at ten-year intervals: at Aberdeen and St. Andrews the whole entry is taken, and at Edinburgh and Glasgow a 50 per cent sample; the sample years are from 1860 to 1910, but 1905 has been added in order to give a fuller picture of the years when women were first admitted. All the universities recorded details of age and birthplace. Fathers' occupations were noted only at Glasgow and (from about 1895) Aberdeen, while Edinburgh was the only university to record its students' school careers. This information, taken together, shows that the average age of entry rose markedly, but despite this, and the changes in secondary education which accompanied it, the social composition of the student body was not transformed; such movement as there was was in the direction of greater 'democracy', with rather more students coming from the working and lower middle classes.[1]

The first table relates to birthplaces, and shows the importance of students from outside Scotland, who will generally be excluded from the later tables. Edinburgh always had the highest proportion of students from overseas, who formed a fifth of the total by 1910. In the early years, overseas students usually came from families with Scottish links, being the sons of settlers in the white Empire or of planters and missionaries in the East. But by the 1900s many Indian students were coming to study arts, medicine, or law; the early development

---

[1] The matriculation registers are in AU Library, St. AU Library, GU Archives, and EU Library (Matriculation Office from 1900). Although they were kept in different forms, I have tried in each case to isolate first entrants. The 50 per cent samples are composed by taking alternate cases. There are no data usable for my purpose for Edinburgh or St. Andrews in 1860, or for Aberdeen medical students before 1900.

in Scotland of university education in engineering had also
attracted students from the United States and Europe, and
there was always a trickle of divinity students from continental
Protestant communities. Edinburgh also had at first the
highest proportion of English students, but this tended to
decline over the years, as did the traditional contingents at
Glasgow of Irish Presbyterians and Welsh Nonconformists.
At St. Andrews, however, the English students increased,
and this was the result of a deliberate recruitment drive, for
in the 1870s its professors began touring English towns to
advertise the virtues of a small and collegiate university.[2]

Table 8.1 also shows the regional origins of the Scottish-born
students, and underlines the essentially local character of all
the universities, including Edinburgh. During the period
Aberdeen became rather less intensely regional, but Glasgow
more so as the population of the industrialized West grew.[3] In
Table 8.2, the figures from each university have been put
together and compared with census figures to give some indication of the regional disparities.[4] This shows that the North-
East, with its parish school tradition, always provided more
university students than the national average, while the industrialized West always provided fewer. The Lothians and Borders
performed well mainly because of Edinburgh, but the East Central region seems to have slipped back. The Highlands made
very marked progress over the period, and by 1910 the rural
areas as a whole were providing more students proportionately
than the industrial ones, which confirms the suggestion that the
mechanisms of opportunity were more suited to rural conditions than to the needs of the urban working class.

It will be recalled that university numbers reached a peak
in the mid-1880s, and that although they recovered after the
subsequent decline this was partly due to the admission of
women. These fluctuations are reflected in Table 8.2, and also

---

[2] W. Knight, *Some nineteenth century Scotsmen* (Edinburgh, 1903), p. 326.
[3] For the counties comprised in these regions see Table 4.4. For earlier data on
regional origins see R. N. Smart, 'Some observations on the provinces of the Scottish
universities, 1560-1850', in G. W. S. Barrow (ed.), *The Scottish tradition* (Edinburgh,
1974), pp. 91-106.
[4] For this table the Edinburgh and Glasgow figures, being based on 50 per cent
samples, were doubled. This also applies to Table 8.4.

Table 8.1

Birthplaces of university students (%)

	1860	1870	1880	1890	1900	1905	1910
Aberdeen							
Scotland	94·8	95·2	92·0	90·8	86·8	88·6	89·4
England & Wales	3·3	3·2	3·3	6·1	6·4	5·7	5·5
Ireland	-	-	-	-	0·5	0·8	-
Outside UK	2·0	0·8	4·7	2·3	5·9	3·7	4·7
Not given	-	0·8	-	0·8	0·5	1·2	0·4
No. of cases	154	124	150	131	219	245	274
Distribution of Scottish-born students:							
North East	84·2	86·4	82·6	78·2	78·4	76·0	79·6
Highlands & North	8·2	6·8	5·8	12·6	12·1	12·9	12·2
East Central	6·2	4·2	8·0	6·7	3·7	4·2	2·9
West	-	1·7	2·9	0·8	3·2	3·7	2·9
Lothians & Borders	1·4	0·9	0·7	1·7	2·6	3·2	1·6
South West	-	-	-	-	-	-	0·8
No. of cases	146	118	138	119	190	217	245
Edinburgh							
Scotland		70·9	64·6	62·4	65·8	65·7	69·0
England & Wales		17·9	18·4	18·3	14·9	12·4	10·3

Ireland	1·7	2·5	4·7	3·4	4·4	0·7
Outside UK	9·3	14·1	14·1	15·7	17·5	20·0
Not given	0·3	0·4	0·5	0·2	-	-
No. of cases	302	517	426	409	411	465

Distribution of Scottish-born students:

North East	7·9	7·5	6·8	7·1	5·2	5·3
Highlands & North	6·5	11·7	10·5	10·4	13·3	10·3
East Central	29·4	29·6	28·2	22·3	17·8	23·4
West	11·2	10·2	13·2	8·9	8·2	10·0
Lothians & Borders	40·2	36·5	36·1	46·8	51·5	47·0
South West	4·7	4·5	5·3	4·5	4·1	4·1
No. of cases	214	334	266	269	270	321

Glasgow

Scotland	84·3	80·8	87·8	85·7	86·7	86·1	81·1
England & Wales	6·9	12·8	6·5	7·5	4·6	6·2	5·4
Ireland	6·4	3·4	1·8	1·9	2·5	0·6	1·5
Outside UK	2·0	3·0	3·9	4·9	6·2	7·1	12·0
Not given	0·5	-	-	-	-	-	-
No. of cases	204	203	337	265	323	338	391

Distribution of Scottish-born students:

North East	1·7	1·8	2·7	3·1	1·1	2·8	1·9
Highlands & North	8·7	14·0	10·1	8·8	7·5	6·2	8·8
East Central	15·7	12·2	8·1	11·0	9·6	8·2	8·8

Table 8.1 (*Contd.*)

	1860	1870	1880	1890	1900	1905	1910
West	62·2	67·7	72·0	70·9	74·6	77·0	73·8
Lothians & Borders	8·1	1·2	2·4	4·0	3·2	3·1	3·2
South West	3·5	3·1	4·7	2·2	3·9	2·8	3·5
No. of cases	172	164	296	227	280	291	317
St. Andrews							
Scotland		86·3	87·5	86·0	71·6	82·7	74·4
England & Wales		2·0	8·9	14·0	21·6	8·0	19·5
Ireland		-	1·8	-	-	1·3	1·2
Outside UK		11·8	1·8	-	4·1	4·0	4·9
Not given		-	-	-	2·7	4·0	-
No. of cases		51	56	57	74	75	82
Distribution of Scottish-born students:							
North East		4·6	4·1	6·1	5·7	4·8	3·3
Highlands & North		6·8	6·1	10·2	7·5	6·5	3·3
East Central		75·0	85·7	69·4	69·8	67·7	68·9
West		-	2·0	10·2	5·7	8·1	13·1
Lothians & Borders		13·6	-	2·0	1·9	9·7	8·2
South West		-	2·0	2·0	9·4	3·2	3·3
No. of cases		44	49	49	53	62	61

Table 8.2

Proportion of Scottish-born university entrants to population, by regions

Students per thousand population

	1870	*1880*	*1890*	*1900*	*1910*
North East	0·36	0·43	0·34	0·43	0·52
Highlands & North	0·22	0·38	0·31	0·34	0·43
East Central	0·31	0·42	0·32	0·27	0·29
West	0·22	0·34	0·24	0·24	0·25
Lothians & Borders	0·35	0·43	0·33	0·39	0·44
South West	0·19	0·38	0·26	0·35	0·36
SCOTLAND	0·27	0·39	0·29	0·30	0·33

illustrated by Table 8.3, which provides a crude measure of university access by simply relating student numbers to the total population.[5] Over the period 1861-1911 the expansion of the universities did keep pace with the growth of the population, even if men alone are counted, but the boom of the 1880s was cut short and its promise never fulfilled.

One cause of lower numbers was of course the entrance examination introduced in 1892, and the impact of this is shown in Table 8.4, which shows the changes in the age of entry; this table covers only Scottish-born arts students (and science students from 1900), since we are concerned here with the age of passage from school to university, and the law and medical faculties were often entered later.[6] The general figures do conceal some differences between the universities: St. Andrews students tended to be younger than others, those at Aberdeen bunched more closely around the 'typical' ages of entry because of the importance of the bursary examination, and Edinburgh had more adult students. The percentage of male entrants over twenty-one at Edinburgh never fell below twenty-three, and those aged twenty-five or more were more than ten per cent in every year except 1910. But there were adult students at all the universities, and the entrance examination does not appear to have discouraged them.

[5] Based on figures in Appendix I.
[6] At Aberdeen the year of birth rather than age at entry was recorded, which introduces a slight upward bias.

Table 8.3

University places per thousand population

	Men only	Men and women
1861	1·11	
1871	1·19	
1881	1·77	
1891	1·64	
1901	1·20	1·40
1911	1·24	1·63

It did, however, practically eliminate younger students, and by the 1900s there were very few below the age of seventeen, which was the minimum age for the Leaving Certificate. The Leaving Certificate, and perhaps even more the Carnegie regulations, did much to impose a more standard pattern of attendance. But Table 8.4 also shows that the rising age of entry was not a consequence of the entrance examination, but something which preceded it and indeed made it acceptable. In 1860 fourteen-year-olds were rare,[7] but university entry at fifteen or sixteen was normal; by 1890, there had already been a shift of about two years upwards, a shift which may be attributed to the contemporary improvements in the secondary schools.

When women were first admitted to the universities, they came at a later age than men, and though the gap narrowed in the 1900s it was still there in 1910. This was perhaps due to the deficiencies of girls' schools, perhaps to the reluctance of parents to send daughters away too young, but probably most of all to the fact that more women than men were students in the training colleges, where the minimum age of entry was eighteen. Fewer women than men came either very young or in adult life.

Only Edinburgh recorded its students' school histories, and the results there may not be typical in view of the peculiarities of the city's schools, where a third or more of all entrants—

---

[7] Were they ever really common? There is much anecdotal evidence for very young students in earlier years, but it may be that, as with the presence of working-class students, what was striking was too readily thought to be typical.

Table 8.4

Ages of Scottish-born arts (and science) students on entry (%)

Age	MEN							WOMEN		
	1860*	1870	1880	1890	1900	1905	1910	1900	1905	1910
13	-	0.9	0.2	-	-	-	-	-	-	-
14	4.2	2.4	1.8	1.0	-	-	-	-	-	-
15	24.7	10.6	10.3	3.6	-	0.2	0.2	-	0.3	-
16	20.0	23.2	16.3	13.5	5.0	7.1	2.4	2.1	2.0	1.1
17	17.9	17.5	16.7	22.5	20.9	19.2	15.8	4.8	8.9	10.4
18	6.5	12.3	13.4	17.2	19.3	24.7	33.0	12.3	32.0	35.3
19	7.0	8.2	9.6	16.2	20.6	20.2	19.1	17.1	32.3	31.3
20	5.7	4.6	8.4	7.3	10.3	8.2	9.3	32.5	14.0	10.6
21	2.1	5.2	4.0	2.1	7.0	5.0	3.9	16.4	4.6	5.3
22	2.1	3.5	3.8	3.7	2.8	2.0	3.3	11.0	1.4	2.3
23	1.6	0.6	2.3	3.4	3.9	1.6	2.7	0.7	2.3	0.6
24	1.8	2.4	3.6	1.8	2.2	2.8	3.5	0.7	1.1	-
25 and over	6.2	8.0	8.7	7.5	7.7	8.9	6.6	1.4	1.1	3.0
Not given	0.3	0.6	0.9	0.3	0.6	0.4	0.3	1.0	-	-
No. of cases	256	407	546	381	332	351	385	176	223	296
Median age	17	17	18	18	19	18	18	20	19	19

* Aberdeen and Glasgow only

including those not born in Scotland—were educated. The main purpose of Table 8.5 is to show how the balance between secondary and 'primary' pupils changed.[8] Defining the different types of school is not easy, and it was a common practice to start at an elementary school before moving on for a short stay at a secondary school better equipped for university preparation. Fortunately the Edinburgh data allow such cases to be distinguished, and in the table those who went from a parish or elementary school to a secondary one for up to two years have been put in the 'primary' category. Even so, 70 per cent of the students came from secondary schools in 1870, and although the numbers from parish schools increased with university expansion in 1880 they declined thereafter, so that the 'secondary' pupils were 85 per cent by 1910.

In the early years, those coming from 'primary' schools were mainly from country parish schools rather than from Edinburgh itself; the figures in line (11) refer to a few Free Church or sessional schools which were not typical of the schools generally available. After 1880 a handful of students from Edinburgh board schools appear, but it is only in 1910, after Edinburgh School Board had developed its two higher grade schools, that a significant number come from the 'elementary' sector—though the higher grade schools might as easily be classified as secondary. For girls the pattern is rather different, because they used the pupil-teacher system. Hence the numbers in line (11) in 1900 and 1905, and the shift into the higher grade schools after the reorganization of the training system, for the higher grade schools were also the 'junior student' centres. One finds for women (though not for men) the phenomenon of movement from a middle-class secondary school into an elementary or higher-grade school for teaching preparation, so by no means all these girls were of modest parentage.   .

---

[8] This table covers the full sample (all faculties, all birthplaces). 'Secondary' (line 19) = lines 7, 8, 10, 13, 16; 'Primary' (line 20) = lines 9, 11, 12, 14, 15, 18. The register usually gives details of all schools attended, and for how long. Lines 8-10 refer to cases where an education was begun elsewhere and completed in Edinburgh; in line 9 (and 14) up to two years' attendance at a secondary school is allowed for. Lines 3 and 18 refer to cases where a training college, but no school, is mentioned. Cases in lines 16 and 17 are allocated between lines 1 and 2 as appropriate.

Table 8.5

University of Edinburgh: school origins of entrants (%)

		MEN						WOMEN		
		1870	1880	1890	1900	1905	1910	1900	1905	1910
Educated:										
Wholly or partly in Edinburgh	(1)	34·4	32·7	30·3	33·8	38·4	42·2	47·6	48·0	53·5
Elsewhere in Scotland	(2)	41·7	37·5	32·4	31·2	26·5	26·2	36·5	37·3	39·5
Scotland: training college only shown	(3)	0·7	1·2	0·7	-	-	0·3	-	1·3	-
Outside Scotland	(4)	20·2	26·3	32·4	26·6	31·9	29·1	9·5	10·7	4·4
Privately	(5)	2·0	1·9	2·3	-	0·6	0·3	1·6	-	-
Not given, uncertain	(6)	1·0	0·4	1·9	8·4	2·7	2·0	4·8	2·7	2·6
No. of cases		302	517	426	346	336	351	63	75	114
Breakdown of students educated in Scotland:										
In Edinburgh:										
Wholly or mainly at secondary school	(7)	33·2	37·7	40·7	45·3	52·3	52·3	47·2	46·2	32·1
Provinces (sec.) + sec. school	(8)	4·7	1·9	0·7	1·3	1·8	1·2	-	1·5	1·9
Provinces (prim.) + sec. school	(9)	0·9	1·9	0·7	1·3	1·4	0·8	-	-	-
Outside Scotland + sec. school	(10)	2·2	0·8	1·5	0·4	2·8	0·4	-	1·5	0·9
Elementary school	(11)	3·9	3·5	4·1	2·2	0·5	-	7·6	6·2	-
Higher grade school	(12)	-	-	-	0·9	0·5	5·4	1·9	-	21·7

Table 8.5 (*Contd.*)

		MEN						WOMEN		
		1870	1880	1890	1900	1905	1910	1900	1905	1910
Elsewhere in Scotland:										
Wholly or mainly at secondary school	(13)	30·2	23·0	32·2	34·2	28·4	31·1	39·6	40·0	38·7
Primary + secondary school	(14)	5·2	3·0	2·2	0·4	0·9	0·8	-	-	-
Primary (parish school, etc.)	(15)	18·1	26·3	16·3	12·9	11·5	6·2	9·4	3·1	2·8
Miscellaneous:										
Roman Catholic school	(16)	-	-	-	0·4	-	-	-	-	0·9
Unclassifiable	(17)	0·9	0·3	0·4	0·4	-	1·2	-	-	0·9
Training college only shown	(18)	0·9	1·6	1·1	-	-	0·4	-	1·5	-
No. of cases		232	369	270	225	218	241	53	65	106
TOTAL PERCENTAGES										
Secondary	(19)	70·3	63·4	75·2	81·8	85·3	85·1	81·1	89·2	74·5
Primary	(20)	28·9	36·3	24·4	17·8	14·7	13·7	18·9	10·8	24·5
Unclassifiable	(21)	0·9	0·3	0·4	0·4	-	1·2	-	-	0·9

One striking fact is the virtual absence of students from Roman Catholic schools: there were only two in this sample of 1,779 students over forty years. This reflects both the marginal position of Catholics in relation to Scottish official culture and the general inaccessibility of the universities to the unskilled working class. No doubt the position was different in Glasgow, and the early development of higher grade schools there must have made the general pattern of relations with the schools different from that of Edinburgh. George Ramsay, who had collected statistics on this question in the 1860s, continued to do so at intervals, and claimed that there was little change throughout the 1870s and 1880s. In 1886/7, for example, he found that 42 per cent of his students came from elementary schools only, 30 per cent from secondary schools only, and 22 per cent from a combination of the two. But by 1904/5 there had been a revolution: 59 per cent had spent three or more years at a secondary school (including some higher grade ones), and 34 per cent had come through the elementary system as pupil-teachers, but otherwise only a handful came from elementary schools.[9]

In Glasgow the board schools may have offered chances of getting to the university, but in Edinburgh these were insignificant until the 1900s. The overwhelming majority of students educated in Edinburgh had been to secondary schools, and Table 8.6 shows which ones they attended.[10] What this shows above all is the remarkable success of the Merchant Company schools, for both boys and girls. Heriot's, the most 'democratic' of the secondary schools, lagged far behind, and the Merchant Company schools were essentially middle-class. Of 1,503 boys at George Watson's in 1892, 564 were the sons of 'merchants', and the professional and commercial bourgeoisie accounted for most of the rest; there were 60 sons of clerks, but no manual workers at all were listed among the parents.[11]

---

[9] *Blackwood's Magazine,* cxli (1887), p. 833 (5 per cent from private schools, etc.); *Classical Association of Scotland. Proceedings 1904-5,* pp. 50-3.

[10] Covers the students in lines 7-10 in Table 8.5.

[11] H. L. Waugh, *George Watson's College. History and record* (Edinburgh, 1970), pp. 207-8. Cf. similar list in J. Thompson, *A history of Daniel Stewart's College 1855-1955* (Edinburgh, 1955), p. 110. Manual workers may lurk in the 'unclassified' categories in these lists, which precede the creation of free places by the secondary education committee.

Table 8.6

University of Edinburgh: attendance at secondary schools in Edinburgh (%)

	1870	1880	1890	1900	1905	1910
Men						
Edinburgh High School	17·9	17·3	10·2	11·9	6·3	13·6
Edinburgh Academy	27·4	14·7	12·7	12·8	14·2	9·8
Edinburgh Institution	14·7	7·1	8·5	4·6	4·7	2·3
Fettes, Loretto, Merchiston	2·1	5·1	5·9	8·3	11·8	12·9
Musselburgh, Leith*	2·1	-	0·9	2·8	1·6	1·5
Unreformed hospitals	4·2	2·6	-	-	-	-
G. Watson's, D. Stewart's	-	30·8	44·1	45·0	48·8	43·2
Heriot's	-	-	5·9	9·2	4·7	12·9
Private schools	31·6	22·4	11·9	5·5	7·9	3·8
No. of cases	95	156	118	109	127	132
Women						
Musselburgh, Leith*				-	3·1	10·8
Merchant Company (2 schools)				68·0	68·8	51·4
St. George's				16·0	21·9	10·8
Private schools				16·0	6·3	27·0
No. of cases				25	32	37

* i.e. the former burgh schools in these towns, which adjoined Edinburgh

The success of the Merchant Company schools was gained partly at the expense of the High School and the Academy (they were both, perhaps, becoming more interested in the English universities), but chiefly at the expense of the private schools: in 1870 these sent nearly a third of the total, but by 1900 their role was insignificant. This reflected a major change in middle-class habits. The 1870 registers show that many boys attended a great variety of schools for short periods, and that the line between private schooling and private tuition was still fluid. W. M. Begbie, for example, ran the well-known Circus Place School (and a girls' school linked with it), but many students put down 'Mr Begbie's private classes' as part of their schooling. There were half a dozen schools with the same prestige as Circus Place, but over the next few decades all were to disappear. The private school, typically run by the proprietor with a small staff in a converted house, could not offer enough for its high fees to compete with the new public and endowed schools with their graduate staffs, laboratories, and playing-fields. Private schools were listed in three parliamentary returns between 1880 and 1897, and their decline took place largely within that period, in the other three cities as well as Edinburgh.[12] A few schools turned themselves successfully into proprietary schools, like the Edinburgh Institution (listed separately in Table 8.6), and a few were sold to school boards, like Bellahouston Academy, which became one of Govan's higher grade schools. But the majority simply closed; at Aberdeen, for example, the Gymnasium, a school once famous for its university successes, closed its doors in 1887.[13] Private schools remained important for girls, because parents valued their domestic atmosphere, but by 1900 the only successful boys' secondary schools outside the public sector were either fully-equipped proprietary schools of the Edinburgh Academy type or boarding schools on the English pattern.

---

[12] These returns are in PP 1880, lv; 1888, lxxviii; 1897, lxxi. They purport to list every school, but various inconsistencies make it unwise to rely on them too closely, especially for pupil numbers. For the earlier history of private education see A. Law, *Education in Edinburgh in the eighteenth century* (1965).

[13] A. Shewan, *Spirat adhuc amor. The record of the Gym (Chanonry House School)*, Old *Aberdeen* (Aberdeen, 1923), pp. 11-12.

Tables 8.7 and 8.8 show the occupations of the fathers of Scottish-born students at Glasgow from 1860 and Aberdeen from 1900, and use the same social categories as Table 4.11 for 1866.[14] They show that the women who entered the universities in the 1900s had rather more middle-class backgrounds than the men,[15] and that, as one might expect, Aberdeen was a more rural university than Glasgow. The rural poor—crofters and farm servants—made a small but significant showing at Aberdeen, but over-all the university seems to have been no more 'democratic' than Glasgow—the high proportion of 'unknown' cases makes direct comparison difficult. The most significant long-term change emerges only from the Glasgow figures: the university growth of the 1880s brought more working-class and 'intermediate' students into the university, and when the expansion ceased their numbers remained at a new plateau; this is seen more clearly by looking at totals than at percentages. Students from the urban working class replaced those from farming backgrounds, of whom there were few by the 1900s, but over the whole period the balance between 'bourgeois' groups (professional, commercial) and those where the

[14] Interpreting and classifying nineteenth-century occupational descriptions is never easy, and no system is perfect. It may be useful to list some of the choices which have been made.

> *Teachers*: includes university professors, but also elementary teachers, not usually distinguishable from other 'schoolmasters'.
> *Officers, officials*: includes only higher civil servants.
> *Other professional*: e.g. architects, civil engineers, journalists.
> *Bankers, etc.*: includes stockbrokers, accountants.
> *Manufacturers, etc.*: includes ironmasters, shipowners, shipbuilders, etc.
> *Large traders*: includes merchants in specified commodities, wholesalers, warehousemen. Some overlap with Shopkeepers.
> *Small business*: e.g. builders, contractors, millers, innkeepers.
> *Shopkeepers*: overlap with working class, e.g. includes tailors, bakers.
> *Clerks, minor officials*: includes commercial travellers, stationmasters, local government officials.
> *Artisans, skilled workers*: interpreted liberally to include most named trades; railwaymen, factory workers, etc. become more important in later years. On the other hand, some (e.g. joiners, building trades) might be considered as small businessmen. Includes 'engineers'.
> *Policemen, etc.*: includes soldiers, janitors.
> *Labourers, farm servants:* includes fishermen.
> *Domestic servants, gardeners*: includes coachmen, gamekeepers.

[15] The 1900 figures are exceptional, because they include a large number of training college students only taking education classes.

fathers were unlikely themselves to be graduates (agricultural, intermediate, working-class) remained about equal.

By the eve of the First World War, the proportion of working-class students was as high at Glasgow as it was later in the twentieth century,[16] and although the gap between skilled and unskilled workers was almost as great as in the 1860s, workers in modern industry were now represented as well as old-fashioned artisans. This is shown by some figures for students receiving Carnegie grants in the 1900s, which cover all the universities. The Carnegie trust used its own social classifications, but Table 8.9 shows that Glasgow had more 'manual' students than the others.[17] Carnegie beneficiaries accounted for about half of all university students (but 70 per cent of the arts faculties), and the better-off parents did not apply. This is shown by Table 8.10: ministers and teachers provided many of the 'professional' claimants, and clerks of the 'official' ones. Within the manual group, those described as 'factory and foundry workers' were numerous, and the evidence of the Glasgow matriculation registers confirms that the university was drawing on the steelworks, shipyards, and engineering industries of Clydeside. Of the 114 'artisans and skilled workers' referred to in Table 8.7 for 1905 and 1910, 53 came from this background—19 'engineers' and 34 others (blacksmiths, patternmakers, steel smelters, platers, etc.), while 36 were from the traditional trades, the largest group (14) being joiners. The remainder included such groups as textile workers and railwaymen.

At this point one may draw some general conclusions about access to the universities and their relations with the schools

---

[16] See I. J. McDonald, 'Untapped reservoirs of talent? Social class and opportunities in Scottish higher education, 1910-1960', *Scottish Educational Studies*, i (1967), p. 53. McDonald also uses the 1910 matriculation registers and (using the Registrar-General's social classifications) gives a rather higher figure than mine for working-class students. See also A. Collier, 'Social origins of a sample of entrants to Glasgow University', *Sociological Review*, xxx (1938), pp. 182-3. For earlier years see W. M. Mathew, 'The origins and occupations of Glasgow students, 1740-1839', *Past & Present*, no. 33 (1966), pp. 78-80. This article has valuable material on geographical origins, careers, etc. as well as social origins: it is based on the pre-1858 matriculation registers, which, however, are difficult to interpret because the occupational descriptions are in Latin.

[17] *Royal Commission on the Civil Service. Second Appendix to Fourth Report* (PP 1914, xvi), pp. 560-1. The 'official' group actually included salaried employees of various kinds.

Table 8.7

University of Glasgow: parental occupations of students

Men	1860	1870	1880	1890	1900	1905	1910
Professional group:							
Proprietors, gentlemen	-	4	7	3	1	3	-
Ministers	13	12	13	12	13	14	16
Doctors	5	4	7	7	5	7	8
Lawyers	17	11	3	4	9	10	12
Teachers	10	7	11	9	11	12	8
Officers, officials	2	-	1	2	2	5	2
Other professional	2	-	6	7	7	10	13
Total professional	49 (28·5%)	38 (23·%)	48 (16·2%)	44 (19·4%)	48 (24·2%)	61 (28·9%)	59 (25·8%)
Commercial and industrial group:							
Bankers, etc.	1	3	3	3	5	7	7
Manufacturers, etc.	10	14	12	10	11	8	7
Large traders	4	4	10	16	15	15	21
'Merchants'	19	12	16	8	7	3	2
Managers, agents	4	4	13	8	11	15	19
Total commercial and industrial	38 (22·1%)	37 (22·6%)	54 (18·2%)	45 (19·8%)	49 (24·7%)	48 (22·8%)	56 (24·5%)

Agricultural group:							
Farmers	19	17	32	14	10	7	3
Crofters, small farmers	-	-	1	2	-	-	3
Factors, etc.	1	1	-	1	-	-	-
Total agricultural	20 (11·6%)	18 (11·0%)	33 (11·1%)	17 (7·5%)	10 (5·1%)	7 (3·3%)	6 (2·6%)
Intermediate group:							
Small business	6	3	13	4	4	6	6
Shopkeepers	18	12	36	17	30	22	25
Clerks, minor officials	5	7	11	12	12	15	14
Total intermediate	29 (16·9%)	22 (13·4%)	60 (20·3%)	33 (14·5%)	46 (23·2%)	43 (20·4%)	45 (19·7%)
Working-class group:							
Artisans, skilled workers	27	20	52	44	36	44	46
Policemen, etc.	-	-	3	3	-	2	2
Labourers, farm servants	4	1	7	3	3	3	4
Miners	1	1	5	1	-	1	3
Domestic servants, gardeners	-	1	3	3	2	-	-
Total working-class	32 (18·6%)	23 (14·0%)	70 (23·7%)	54 (23·8%)	41 (20·7%)	50 (23·7%)	55 (24·0%)
Not given, uncertain, dead	4	26	31	34	4	2	8
TOTAL	172	164	296	227	198	211	229

Table 8.7 (*Contd.*)

Women	1900	1905	1910
Professional group:			
Proprietors, gentlemen	-	-	-
Ministers	2	6	5
Doctors	1	3	2
Lawyers	4	1	3
Teachers	5	5	10
Officers, officials	2	-	1
Other professional	3	5	3
Total professional	17 (20·7%)	20 (25·0%)	24 (27·3%)
Commercial and industrial group:			
Bankers, etc.	2	2	3
Manufacturers, etc.	4	4	7
Large traders	3	13	8
'Merchants'	1	2	1
Managers, agents	2	7	5
Total commercial and industrial	12 (14·6%)	28 (35·0%)	24 (27·3%)
Agricultural group:			
Farmers	2	-	5
Crofters, small farmers	-	-	-
Factors, etc.	-	-	1
Total agricultural	2 (2·4%)	-	6 (6·8%)

Intermediate group:			
Small business	3	4	2
Shopkeepers	10	6	6
Clerks, minor officials	10	7	9
Total intermediate	23 (28·0%)	17 (21·3%)	17 (19·3%)
Working-class group:			
Artisans, skilled workers	18	12	12
Policemen, etc.	1	-	1
Labourers, farm servants	-	-	-
Miners	-	1	1
Domestic servants, gardeners	4	-	2
Total working-class	23 (28·0%)	13 (16·3%)	16 (18·2%)
Not given, uncertain, dead	5	2	1
TOTAL	82	80	88

Table 8.8

University of Aberdeen: parental occupations of students

	Men			Women		
	1900	1905	1910	1900	1905	1910
Professional group:						
Proprietors, gentlemen	1	-	2	-	-	1
Ministers	11	12	4	3	4	6
Doctors	3	4	1	2	1	-
Lawyers	2	3	3	1	1	2
Teachers	9	11	10	3	7	5
Officers, officials	1	1	6	1	3	6
Other professional	1	2	4	1	-	2
Total professional	28	33	30	11	16	22
	(18·9%)	(21·6%)	(19·7%)	(26·2%)	(25·0%)	(23·7%)
Commercial and industrial group:						
Bankers, etc.	2	3	2	1	2	2
Manufacturers, etc.	2	3	2	1	1	1
Large traders	9	4	7	2	1	3
'Merchants'	6	6	-	1	3	3
Managers, agents	4	6	8	-	5	4
Total commercial and industrial	23	22	19	5	12	13
	(15·5%)	(14·4%)	(12·5%)	(11·9%)	(18·8%)	(14·0%)

Agricultural group:						
Farmers	21	27	17	5	6	16
Crofters, small farmers	3	-	1	-	2	2
Factors, etc.	-	2	1	-	-	1
Total agricultural	24 (16·2%)	29 (19·0%)	19 (12·5%)	5 (11·9%)	8 (12·5%)	19 (20·4%)
Intermediate group:						
Small business	5	6	2	-	2	2
Shopkeepers	10	10	11	2	5	6
Clerks, minor officials	5	4	11	2	2	3
Total intermediate	20 (13·5%)	20 (13·1%)	24 (15·8%)	4 (9·5%)	9 (14·1%)	11 (11·8%)
Working-class group:						
Artisans, skilled workers	18	19	14	8	6	11
Policemen, etc.	-	4	1	-	-	-
Labourers, farm servants	4	3	3	-	3	1
Miners	-	-	-	-	-	-
Domestic servants, gardeners	4	2	3	1	-	2
Total working-class	26 (17·6%)	28 (18·3%)	21 (13·8%)	9 (21·4%)	9 (14·1%)	14 (15·1%)
Not given, uncertain, dead	27	21	39	8	10	14
TOTAL	148	153	152	42	64	93

Table 8.9

Parental occupations of new Carnegie beneficiaries, 1908 and 1912 (%)

	Aberdeen		Edinburgh		Glasgow		St. Andrews	
	1908	*1912*	*1908*	*1912*	*1908*	*1912*	*1908*	*1912*
Professions	15·1	14·4	22·7	19·2	15·4	17·5	12·0	27·9
Officials	6·3	9·4	13·6	9·1	9·9	7·6	18·0	10·5
Commerce	17·6	19·4	15·2	16·4	17·3	19·1	24·0	23·3
Agriculture	17·0	16·1	4·5	4·2	4·3	4·7	2·0	1·2
Manual occupations	28·3	30·0	20·5	30·1	35·5	36·6	21·0	23·3
Retired or dead	15·7	10·6	23·5	21·0	17·6	14·6	23·0	14·0
No. of cases	159	180	264	286	324	383	100	86

Table 8.10

Carnegie beneficiaries 1908 and 1912 (all universities): principal occupations

	1908	1912
Professions: total	146	172
included:		
Ministers	50	69
Teachers	53	72
Doctors	15	7
Lawyers	10	8
Others	18	16
Officials: total	96	81
included:		
Clerks & secretaries	38	30
Commerce: total	148	175
included:		
Retail tradesmen	102	121
Commercial travellers	11	27
Others	35	27
Agriculture: total	55	60
included:		
Farmers	42	56
Crofters	8	-
Farm servants	3	4
Farm stewards	2	-
Manual occupations: total	235	300
included:		
Factory & foundry workers	39	55
Engineers	25	24
Blacksmiths	10	5
Patternmakers	4	2
Joiners & cabinetmakers	26	32
Other artisans, misc. skilled	71	86
Miners	6	17
Railwaymen	5	17
Fishermen	10	11
Shepherds	1	3
Labourers	-	9
Domestic servants, gardeners, etc.	22	16
Misc. unskilled	16	23

between the 1860s and the 1900s. The first conclusion must be that the universities did not become less 'democratic' during this period, but rather the reverse. A second is that the Revised Code and the Act of 1872 do not seem to have had the deleterious effects predicted by contemporaries: one would expect those effects to become apparent by the end of the 1870s, yet that was precisely the period when the universities began to expand rapidly, and the figures for working-class students at Glasgow and parish-school entrants at Edinburgh suggest that the expansion widened the social base of the intake. In the past the parochial schools had brought some poor boys to the universities (though few of the very poorest), but their effects had been limited to rural areas, and there were no scholarships in secondary schools. In the 1880s the reform of the endowed schools and the appearance of higher grade ones created more systematic opportunities for the working class in the towns, and probably accounts for the consolidation of their position in Glasgow University. The school pattern in Edinburgh suggests that the working class there was less favourably placed, and Table 8.9 seems to confirm this. A third conclusion is that the introduction of the entrance examination and the consequent raising of the entrance age did not seem to penalize the intermediate and working-class groups, and it was offset in the 1900s by such factors as the Carnegie scheme and Struthers's national bursary policy. And finally one must conclude that there was little improvement over fifty years in the university opportunities of the children of unskilled workers, labourers, miners, or crofters. The 'non-middle-class' element in the universities was not primarily 'working-class', but a stratum which brought together the children of skilled workers, shop-keepers, and small farmers.

It was from this stratum that elementary teachers were drawn, and by the 1900s the class composition of the universities was strongly influenced by the growing number of training-college students.[18] The extension of a full university education to this group opened wider horizons, although under the training regulations they were covenanted to teach for a minimum period in a public school—from two to six years,

[18] See analysis of origins of Aberdeen training-college students in 1911-13 in J. Scotland, 'The Scottish dominie', *Philosophical Journal*, vii (1970), p. 131.

depending on the financial aid received. Schoolteaching, like the ministry, diverted the ambitions of poorer students into an outlet of limited scope, and they were less numerous, as Table 8.11 shows, in the professional faculties of law and medicine; this table also shows the class background of divinity students, calculated from a separate sample.[19] Several points may be made about this table. First, the social gap between the arts and professional faculties seems to have widened after 1880, perhaps because of the increasing numbers of training-college students. Second, the background of divinity students matched that of arts students, but with a higher number being sons of farmers: the ministry was 'democratic' in a traditional way, and it should be remembered that university divinity students belonged to the Established Church, and probably had higher social origins than those of other denominations. Third, law and medicine recruited urban students, and seem to have made a special appeal to the lower middle class and the commercial bourgeoisie. There was less self-recruitment than might be expected, and no more than an eighth of the Glasgow medical students were doctors' sons.

The number of law students at Glasgow was too small to permit reliable generalizations, but fortunately we have details of the social origins of entrants to three of the Scottish legal corporations. These are the Faculty of Advocates, the Writers to the Signet (the most exclusive of the solicitors' bodies), and the Society of Advocates in Aberdeen, where 'advocate' meant 'solicitor'. Table 8.12 refers to entrants in the first three years of each decade between 1820-2 and 1910-12, and reveals some fluctuations which cannot be fully explained in the absence of any history of the Scottish professions.[20] Qualifying as an

---

[19] The table covers men only. Since divinity students as such were not among the 'first entrants', the sample here is of all divinity students at Glasgow in the relevant year; a high proportion of the 'professional' parents were ministers or teachers.

[20] Based on lists in F. J. Grant (ed.), *The Faculty of Advocates in Scotland, 1532-1943* (Edinburgh, 1944); *A History of the Society of Writers to Her Majesty's Signet* (Edinburgh, 1890); *The Society of Writers to His Majesty's Signet* (Edinburgh, 1936); J. A. Henderson, *History of the Society of Advocates in Aberdeen* (Aberdeen, 1912); *Supplemental history of the Society of Advocates in Aberdeen, 1912-1938* (Aberdeen, 1939). Parents having surnames with territorial designations, but with no occupation shown, have been classified as 'proprietors and gentlemen'. For the Advocates in earlier years see N. T. Phillipson, 'The social structure of the Faculty of Advocates in Scotland 1661-1840', in A. Harding (ed.), *Law-making and law-makers in British history* (1980), pp. 146-56.

Table 8.11

Parental occupations of Glasgow students by Faculty (%)

	1860	1870	1880	1890	1900	1905	1910
Arts (& science)							
Professional	30·8	25·0	15·5	18·5	24·3	31·4	22·6
Commercial	22·3	25·8	18·4	11·1	19·8	19·0	18·8
Agricultural	11·5	8·9	11·1	8·1	4·5	3·8	3·8
Intermediate	14·6	14·5	18·4	14·1	25·2	13·3	18·8
Working-class	19·2	13·7	25·6	31·9	25·2	31·4	33·1
Not given	1·5	12·1	11·1	16·3	0·9	0·9	3·0
No. of cases	130	124	207	135	111	105	133

Medicine & law

Professional	21·4	17·5	18·0	20·7	24·1	26·4	30·2
Commercial	21·4	12·5	18·0	32·6	31·0	26·4	32·3
Agricultural	11·9	17·5	11·2	6·5	5·8	2·8	1·0
Intermediate	23·8	10·0	25·8	15·2	20·7	27·4	20·8
Working-class	16·7	15·0	18·0	12·0	14·9	16·0	11·5
Not given	4·8	27·5	9·0	13·0	3·5	0·9	4·2
No. of cases	42	40	89	92	87	106	96

Divinity

Professional	24·7	21·7	15·1	15·9	41·0	27·9	29·2
Commercial	15·1	13·3	15·1	19·5	7·7	18·6	8·3
Agricultural	38·4	10·0	10·5	12·2	12·8	9·3	10·4
Intermediate	6·9	13·3	7·0	7·3	18·0	20·9	14·6
Working-class	13·7	16·7	18·6	20·7	18·0	23·3	31·3
Not given	1·4	25·0	33·7	24·4	2·6	-	6·3
No. of cases	73	60	86	82	39	43	48

Table 8.12

Social origins of entrants to legal profession

	1820-2	1830-2	1840-2	1850-2	1860-2	1870-2	1880-2	1890-2	1900-2	1910-12
Edinburgh: Advocates										
Proprietors, gentlemen	24	13	4	6	10	2	6	4	3	3
Advocates, judges, etc.	5	5	4	4	3	5	2	4	-	4
Other lawyers	8	4	3	5	6	2	7	4	6	4
Other professional	7	7	3	7	6	7	4	12	3	6
Commercial and industrial	4	3	1	1	3	7	5	8	3	12
Agricultural	-	-	-	-	-	2	-	2	2	1
Intermediate	-	1	-	-	-	-	1	-	-	-
Working-class	-	1	-	1	1	-	-	-	-	-
Not given, uncertain	4	7	-	-	2	3	-	5	3	1
TOTAL	52	40	15	24	31	28	25	39	20	31
Edinburgh: Writers to the Signet										
Proprietors, gentlemen	12	8	3	2	2	6	3	7	2	3
W.S.	5	6	4	8	18	10	8	6	8	8
Other lawyers	9	5	2	4	3	8	7	11	8	12
Other professional	20	11	4	2	9	6	4	20	2	16

Commercial and industrial	14	7	-	-	1	2	5	11	4	11
Agricultural	5	2	-	-	-	-	-	3	2	-
Intermediate	2	6	-	-	-	1	-	3	1	1
Working-class	1	4	1	1	-	-	-	-	-	1
Not given, uncertain	7	7	2	1	3	2	3	9	6	1
TOTAL	75	56	16	17	36	35	30	70	33	53
Aberdeen: Advocates										
Proprietors, gentlemen	-	2	1	-	1	-	1	-	-	-
Aberdeen advocates	1	2	1	-	3	3	5	5	2	1
Other lawyers	-	-	-	-	-	1	-	1	1	-
Other professional	-	2	2	1	-	1	1	2	2	-
Commercial and industrial	3	6	4	2	2	1	-	1	2	2
Agricultural	-	4	2	1	-	1	2	1	-	-
Intermediate	4	4	2	1	-	1	-	-	-	-
Working-class	1	4	1	-	1	-	-	-	1	-
Not given, uncertain	-	-	1	-	1	3	-	-	-	-
TOTAL	9	24	14	5	8	11	9	10	8	3

advocate had once been common among the landed élite, but this custom seems to have ended after the 1830s, and over the next few decades entry to all the legal bodies fell off heavily; the response to which, especially clear in the case of the Edinburgh Writers to the Signet, was to limit recruitment more narrowly to legal families. It is obvious that at all periods the two Edinburgh bodies, which relied on an apprenticeship system and exacted heavy entrance fees, drew almost entirely on the wealthy bourgeoisie, although the Aberdeen advocates were less exclusive. What is interesting is that after about 1880 the Edinburgh legal profession was increasingly attractive to the commercial and industrial middle class, and examination of the original lists shows that the leading business families of Glasgow as well as Edinburgh were sending their sons into the law. This suggests a judgement which is tentative because it cannot be easily documented: that the Scottish urban bourgeoisie came of age in the decades around 1880. Early in the century it had been a cliché to describe Edinburgh as 'professional' and Glasgow as 'mercantile'; by its end, a homogeneous class had emerged which brought together professional men, merchants, industrial employers, university professors, senior government officials, and the growing sector of upper management in banking, insurance, and so on. The remodelling of secondary education which began in this period owed much to their needs, and largely satisfied them.

In the 1900s all the universities except St. Andrews set up Appointments Committees, which were essentially concerned not with posts in commerce but with the public service, at home and abroad.[21] The growth of the civil service as a new career for graduates was especially significant because it brought Scottish students into direct competition with English ones; if the universities were to satisfy parents who aimed at the national, 'British' élite, they had to bring their standards into line, and this was a particular incentive for the development of Honours work. The principle of open competition for the Indian and home civil services, with its preference for a general rather than a professional education and its insistence on entry

---

[21] There is the same emphasis in R. N. Gilchrist, *After graduation: what?* (Aberdeen, 1911), a collection of articles giving career advice.

by strict academic merit, seemed to fit in well with Scottish traditions, but in the early years, as we have seen, Scottish candidates did poorly. In the first four years of the Indian examination, which started in 1855, only twenty-four of the 295 candidates came from the Scottish universities, mostly from Aberdeen (13) or Edinburgh (9). But although the examination continued to favour those with an English classical education, the proportion of Scots later rose, and by 1874 eighty-nine of the 741 successful competitors who had gone out to India since 1855 were Scots—more than a fair share, since Scotland had just over a tenth of the United Kingdom population.[22]

The controversial issue proved to be the maximum age of entry rather than the examination. This was at first twenty-three, but was later reduced to twenty-one. This made it difficult for English candidates to complete a university education, and they went instead to crammers, which vitiated the original purpose of the examination as a test of liberal education. The age-limit of twenty-one did allow Scottish graduates to compete, but they were then at a disadvantage compared with the specially crammed southerners, and they too were tempted to abandon their studies early. An inquiry into this question in 1876 preceded a major change of policy by Lord Salisbury, the Secretary of State, which ensured that Indian civil servants got a university education, but worked against the Scottish universities. From 1878 the maximum age was nineteen: once selected, pupils spent two years at a university taking special courses, and the India Office assumed that the university would be a residential one able to provide moral supervision. At first this threatened to exclude the Scottish universities, but after protests they were allowed to satisfy the new conditions by setting up special committees to supervise the ICS students. In 1892, however, the Salisbury system was abandoned and a maximum age of twenty-three restored.[23] In 1895 the Indian examination was merged with that for the higher posts in the home civil service which had been introduced in 1870.

---

[22] *Fourth Report of Her Majesty's Civil Service Commissioners* (PP 1859, viii), pp. 339-40; *The Selection and Training of Candidates for the Indian Civil Service* (PP 1876, lv), p. 35. The latter figures refer to Scottish-born candidates, not Scottish graduates.

[23] J. Roach, *Public examinations in England 1850-1900* (Cambridge, 1971), pp. 195 ff., 218-22.

At Aberdeen, candidates for these examinations could make use of the services of David Rennet, a mathematical coach associated with the university for over forty years. His work was inspired, it was later claimed, by 'a Dramatico-democratic Motive, the startling triumph of poor lads of ability over the best that wealth and other advantages could bring to secure success in the competition. ... He would have it that what they wanted was the Public School type of man ... and that they did not fancy greatly the often socially undeveloped product of the Scottish Universities. Rennet, believing in men before manners, was apparently determined that they should have that product whether they liked it or not.'[24] Aberdeen cultivated a special link with the ICS, but in general the Scots were not greatly attracted by the combined competition after 1895. In the years 1906-10, for example, the Scottish universities provided only thirty of the 473 candidates, and seventeen of them were from Edinburgh. Moreover, a high proportion of the Scottish entrants came from one school, George Watson's: of 1,557 successful candidates between 1896 and 1911, this school provided forty-three, which put it up with the leading English schools interested in the examination and far ahead of other Scottish ones (Fettes, 12; Edinburgh High School, 8; Glasgow High School, 8; Robert Gordon's, 8; Edinburgh Academy, 7; etc.)[25] Between 1896 and 1916, nearly half of the candidates who went forward from Edinburgh University had been to George Watson's; this interest was clearly fostered by school and family tradition as much as by success at the university itself.[26]

In 1912 a Royal Commission on the civil service investigated its relative neglect by Scots students, which witnesses attributed to weak motivation and the greater openness of the other professions in Scotland. According to Dudley Medley, professor of History at Glasgow, most students came to the university with

---

[24] *Aberdeen University Review*, ii (1914/15), p. 26 (obituary by Harrower); cf. pp. 250-3 for details of Aberdeen entrants 1856-1913.

[25] *Royal Commission on the Civil Service. Appendix to First Report* (PP 1912/13, xv), pp. 125-7.

[26] T. A. Joynt, 'Edinburgh civil servants, 1896-1944', *University of Edinburgh Journal*, xiii (1944/5), p. 120. Of 110 entrants, 47 came from George Watson's. Fifty-one were Honours classics graduates, and only one held the B.Sc.

their intentions fixed. 'We save some of the better ones from teaching and draft them into other professions', but in the absence of family precedent the civil service was 'an unknown world to them.' Medley and others rejected the proposal which was then current for an interview to be added to the written examination; this could be very unfair to students who did not have 'the same outward polish and outside manner' as those from the English Public Schools.[27] Despite this, one may perhaps conclude that most Scottish civil servants came from the same middle-class homes as their English equivalents, and that the successes of Scottish day schools reflected national differences in patterns of middle-class education rather than any democratization of the service.

Thus the top tier of secondary schools were successful at preparing the middle class for 'British' as well as local careers. As James Bridie said of his own school, Glasgow Academy, 'One could confidently look forward to a respectable social position in the city of Glasgow; but there was something more remarkable about the place. Field-Marshal's batons seemed to be served out regularly to one in ten of the boys.'[28] And one champion of the Merchant Company schools praised their services to the middle class: 'They have supplied education to a section of the community who are thoroughly alive to the power which education gives in the struggles of life.' He went on to say that 'There was another reason for their success. The schools were built up on the old educational lines which appeal to Scotsmen, and are expressed in so clear and vivid terms in the very advanced educational scheme which the Scottish Reformers put forward in 1560 in the *Book of Discipline*.'[29] For those who used schools like George Watson's or Glasgow Academy liked to think that because these were day schools which did not seek to impose an alien accent and manner, like the local versions of the Public Schools, they were somehow part of the national democratic tradition, and because in some

[27] *Royal Commission on the Civil Service. Appendix to Third Report* (PP 1913, xviii), pp. 207, 210, and cf. evidence of Lodge, pp. 214-15, 217.
[28] J. Bridie, *One way of living* (1939), p. 41.
[29] J. Harrison, *The Company of Merchants of the City of Edinburgh and its schools, 1694-1920* (Edinburgh, n.d.), p. 33.

of them, though not in all, a few scholarship boys sat alongside the middle-class pupils, it was an easy step to suppose that every pupil who made a success of his life had won through by hard work and merit alone. The system thus endowed the Scottish middle class with a certain complacency not available to English parents, who were very well aware that in buying a Public School education they were buying a privileged start in life.

When in 1877 the Scottish universities protested against Salisbury's plan for residence they claimed that they possessed

characteristics which, in some respects, render them peculiarly suitable as places for the education of the responsible administrators of a Dependency. There is a great deal of liberty and independence, and yet a high moral tone, in the student-life of these Universities. The prevailing tone among the students is marked by frugality and honest endeavour to make the most of opportunities. Among the students of a Scotch University there is no luxury; probably hard work is more universal with them even than with German students; and (what is most important), manly, careful, practical qualities are brought out by their mode of life and study.[30]

Forty years later, the emphasis had changed. The Glasgow Appointments Committee, in recommending men for administrative posts, 'is in the habit of considering not only the intellectual record, but the participation of likely applicants in the public work of student life as evinced by presidency in some of the student societies, membership of the Officers Training Corps and other similar tests of administrative capacity and recognition of public duties.'[31] From the 1880s onwards, the development of 'corporate life' had changed the old image of the frugal student buried in his books and working by himself in his austere lodgings. Now he could relax in a Union, cultivate the body as well as the mind, and even live in a hall of residence.

The Scottish universities had not always been non-residential, but the last traces of older customs disappeared at the beginning of the nineteenth century. At King's College, Aberdeen,

---

[30] Joint Memorial of University Courts, Feb. 1877, in GU GC Reports, Apr. 1877.
[31] *R. Comm. on Civil Service. Appendix to 3rd Rep.*, p. 306, and cf. p. 212 (Medley).

the 'Commoners' Table' for the 'sons of gentlemen' living in disappeared only in 1825, after which 'the number of the sons of the northern gentry attending the University was perceptibly diminished'.[32] The desire to tempt back the upper classes was always a motive for the revival of corporate life, and it was part of the plans of Lorimer and his followers in the university endowment movement.[33] In 1862 Lorimer called for the foundation of a Hall at Edinburgh to 'cultivate the social habits of the students, and to reclaim them from the boorish solitude in which too many of them' passed their time. To achieve this aim it was 'quite indispensable that the institution should be presided over by a gentleman', and that it should offer 'economy combined with refinement'—with the emphasis perhaps on the former, since Lorimer thought that the expense might be brought 'much nearer to that in the Sailors' Home at Liverpool, than in a college at Oxford'.[34] The experiment was tried at St. Andrews, where Principal Forbes founded 'College Hall' in 1861 with a Rugby and Oxford man as warden; the hall was enlarged in 1868, but eventually failed and closed in 1874.[35] A new impetus came only with the admission of women, who were thought to need more moral supervision. In 1896 a women's hall of residence was opened at St. Andrews under Louisa Lumsden, the former headmistress of St. Leonards, but it was disapproved of by Principal Donaldson, who thought this 'conventual rule' alien to the Scottish spirit of independence. Personal animosities led to Lumsden's departure a few years later, but the hall survived, and by 1909 Donaldson thought that 'It is a grand institution and doing splendid work. We get a very nice class of girls to come, with great benefit to the whole University.'[36] By this time there were also women's halls at Glasgow and Edinburgh, and at Edinburgh men were

[32] *Rep. R. Comm. Univ. Aberdeen* (1858), p. 91.

[33] e.g. J. Inglis, *Inaugural address delivered to the University of Edinburgh on his installation as Chancellor* (Edinburgh, 1869), p. 29; D. Thorburn, *The endowment of the universities of Scotland an object of national importance* (Edinburgh, 1863), pp. 9-11, 20-1, 35-6.

[34] *The Museum*, ii (1862/3), pp. 70-3.

[35] R. G. Cant, *The University of St. Andrews. A short history* (new edn., Edinburgh, 1970), pp. 118-19; J. C. Shairp & others, *Life and letters of James David Forbes* (1873), pp. 401-3.

[36] L. I. Lumsden, *Yellow leaves. Memories of a long life* (Edinburgh, 1933), pp. 117-19, 140; *Comm. on Scottish Univ. Minutes of Ev.*, p. 9.

provided for in a series of self-governing halls begun in 1887 by the pioneering social thinker Patrick Geddes. All these ventures were administered as private companies rather than by the university authorities.

Athletics developed in the same semi-official way, with money being raised privately to pay for gymnasia and playing-fields. The 1870s seem to have been the formative period, and the various athletics clubs were numerous enough by the 1880s—along with literary, religious and social groups—to form the basis for the SRCs, whose foundation was in turn closely linked with the building of Unions, the founding of student magazines, and similar activities. This movement has not received the serious historical attention which it deserves; it is clear that modern patterns of student life were established within quite a short period, and that they were connected with similar movements towards athleticism and a stronger institutional life in the secondary schools, and with the rise in the average age of students. The students themselves became enthusiastic exponents of 'corporate life', and it was student activists who called periodically for such things as the revival of academic dress or of official religious services.[37] The spirit of the new student movement found its characteristic expression in the *Scottish Students' Song Book* of 1891; this had a preface by Blackie, who had himself published a book of student songs in 1869,[38] and reflected his German-inspired ideal of a student estate within the urban community. Since practically all students continued to live at home or in lodgings, Scottish student culture remained distinct from that of Oxford or Cambridge, and it was not long before the once new student Unions were themselves being regarded as traditional and contrasted favourably with the alien residential ideal.

Glasgow developed a particularly distinctive student life, which had wider literary and political repercussions. In the 1900s it produced James Bridie, whose memoirs, *One way of living,* give a lively picture of the scene, and in the 1890s it had

[37] Gowns, never worn by students at Edinburgh, died out at Glasgow. They survived at Aberdeen and St. Andrews.

[38] *Musa burschicosa. A book of songs for students and university men* (Edinburgh, 1869). The *Song Book* was published jointly by the SRCs: J. M. Bulloch, 'The meaning of the "Scottish Students' Song Book"', *Aberdeen University Review,* xxiv (1936/7), pp. 116-22.

produced John Buchan. Buchan's father was a Free Church minister in a poor parish, and he reached the university through Hutchesons' school; from Glasgow he went on with a scholarship to take a degree at Oxford—a common enough path at this time, and one more or less obligatory for those aiming at academic careers. Buchan's case shows how the Scottish universities could form an escalator to the national élite, though few were absorbed into the British Establishment with his dazzling success. However, it was at Glasgow if anywhere, with its high proportion of working-class students, that one would expect the appearance of those 'organic' intellectuals described by Gramsci, who remain in sympathetic communication with their class of origin. And indeed they were not absent, for there were connections between Socialism and schoolteaching. James Maxton, for example, was a schoolteacher's son, went to Hutchesons' on a bursary, combined teacher training with university attendance, left the university without a degree to begin teaching, and obtained his MA later by part-time study. He was only converted to Socialism after leaving the university, but became involved in Keir Hardie's candidacy for the rectorship in 1908; this campaign was the work of the Socialist Society, led by Thomas Johnston, who had come to the university as an adult student. Maxton's course was also followed by a Socialist of a sterner kind, John Maclean: brought up in poverty, Maclean was educated at Queen's Park, a higher grade school in the Glasgow suburbs, and also entered teaching before completing his degree. Even when standing as a revolutionary parliamentary candidate after the war, he advertised himself proudly as 'John Maclean, M.A.'[39] These cases, incidentally, illustrate the continuing importance of adult and part-time attendance. A. S. Neill, another schoolmaster's son, went to Edinburgh at the age of twenty-five after some years' teaching experience, and after editing the student newspaper he at first thought of a journalist's career before starting his life's work as an educational pioneer.[40]

---

[39] Based on the *Dictionary of National Biography*, and N. Milton, *John Maclean* (1973), pp. 22, 305, and unnumbered illustration.
[40] A. S. Neill, *'Neill! Neill! Orange peel!' A personal view of ninety years* (1972), pp. 80 ff.

While the university authorities looked benevolently on the development of student life, they were also carrying out their own exercises in the invention of tradition. Just as in practical terms they were anxious to assert that their degrees were worth as much as English ones, so symbolically they strove to make clear their part in an ancient European tradition. Ceremony and outward show, much neglected earlier in the century, took on new life, and costly and elaborate halls were built with benefactors' money which were hardly used except for the annual graduations. The first manifestation of this movement was the celebration of Edinburgh's third centenary in 1884, masterminded by Grant as a spectacular piece of public relations, and attended by university figures from all over the world.[41] Similar celebrations at Glasgow in 1901, Aberdeen in 1906, and St. Andrews in 1911, though elaborate enough, did not achieve the same *éclat*. Grant also marked the centenary by writing a very competent history of his university, and here too imitators failed to reach the same standard, though at Aberdeen the university librarian, P. J. Anderson, turned out an abundant collection of source-material. This historical work overlapped with another class of literature, that designed to stimulate the nostalgia of graduates and keep them in touch with their Alma Mater. This spirit seems to have been especially strong at Aberdeen, where individual class-years formed associations and published records of their members' achievements, and Aberdeen started the first alumnus magazine in 1913, the *Aberdeen University Review*. St. Andrews had its own sentimentalizing bard in Andrew Lang,[42] and at both these universities nostalgia seems to have centred as much on the buildings and physical setting as on student life; perhaps this was because so many graduates worked abroad, so that their only memories of adult life in the home country were tied to their university experience. Even at Glasgow, less picturesque and more impersonal, a General Council committee in the 1900s was busy planning an annual Commemora-

---

[41] R. S. Marsden (ed.), *A short account of the tercentenary festival of the University of Edinburgh* (Edinburgh, 1884), *passim*.

[42] J. B. Salmond (ed.), *Andrew Lang and St. Andrews. A centenary anthology* (St. Andrews, 1944). Aberdeen gave rise to a university novel as early as 1874: Neil Maclean, *Life at a northern university*.

tion Day, local graduates' associations, class clubs, halls of residence, and 'the encouragement of University Athletics for the sake of the public spirit and corporate sentiment that they tend to foster.'[43]

The head of this committee was Medley, and the professors of History seem to have taken a special interest in this kind of activity. When new chairs in History were set up in the 1890s they were almost inevitably given to men trained in England, who introduced the kind of concentration on constitutional and diplomatic history which was thought appropriate for the education of a governing élite.[44] The same emphasis was apparent in classical teaching, where the appointment of lecturers in ancient history and philosophy showed the influence of Oxford Greats. In philosophy, the last exponents of the 'common sense' school died in the 1890s, and the Hegelianism introduced at Glasgow by Edward Caird in 1866 carried the day. Preparing young men for the study of theology was no longer an important function of university philosophy, but professors continued to impart an earnest and only half-secularized morality and to preach a gospel of civic duty. The influence of T. H. Green was felt directly through the Balliol connection, but the most characteristic figure of the pre-war years was perhaps Sir Henry Jones, professor of Moral Philosophy at Glasgow from 1894 to 1922. Jones was a Glasgow graduate and a product of the old connection between Glasgow and Welsh Nonconformism, and he combined academic activities with political ones as a friend of Lloyd George.

The message of 'citizenship' and 'service' was also expounded by the historians. Medley at Glasgow, and Richard Lodge at Edinburgh, took a special interest in the Officers' Training Corps which were a feature of university life in the 1900s, while at the same time Lodge was deeply interested in social questions, and was one of the founders of the Edinburgh University Settlement; Glasgow had had such a settlement,

[43] GU GC Reports, Apr. 1906.
[44] On this subject see D. B. Horn. 'The University of Edinburgh and the teaching of history', *University of Edinburgh Journal*, xvii (1953-5) pp. 161-72; B. P. Lenman, 'The teaching of Scottish history in the Scottish universities', *Scottish Historical Review*, lii (1973), pp. 165-90; J. D. Hargreaves, 'Historical study in Scotland', *Aberdeen University Review*, xl (1963/4), pp. 237-50; A. L. Brown, 'History in the making', *College Courant*, xxix, no. 58 (1977), pp. 6-11.

founded by Edward Caird and not only modelled on but actually called Toynbee Hall, since 1886.[45] Lodge was also converted to the cause of national military service, and when the call came in 1914 he was dispatched to lecture to the troops in France. Thus from the 1880s onwards students were being urged from various quarters to see themselves as an élite being prepared to take their places as leaders of the community, and to accept the duty of service as the counterpart of the privileged chances which they had been given.

This reached a climax of a kind in R. B. Haldane's rectorial address at Edinburgh in 1907, 'The Dedicated Life'. Haldane, an Edinburgh graduate, was the leading British exponent of German educational ideas, and this address breathed the pure Hegelian spirit. The state embodied the higher 'ethical' life of the community, and only by serving it could individuals fulfil their duty. 'The University is the handmaid of the State, of which it is the microcosm—a community in which also there are rulers and ruled, and in which the corporate life is a moulding influence.' Only by cultivating the spirit of dedication which the university teaches can students 'make themselves accepted leaders; so only can they aspire to form a part of that priesthood of humanity to whose commands the world will yield obedience'.[46] Haldane was also a witness before the Civil Service Commission, where he praised the democratic educational system of Scotland. 'If you could have that system developed very much you would get the perfect system. You would get an equal opportunity for everybody, which I think is the real foundation of democracy.'[47] Other witnesses, including Struthers, argued that the 'educational ladder' was practically complete in Scotland, and the commission accepted this view, commending the Scottish system for English imitation.[48] Their concern was to secure the best brains of the country for

[45] H. Jones & J. H. Muirhead, *The life and philosophy of Edward Caird* (Glasgow, 1921), pp. 114-16; M. Lodge, *Sir Richard Lodge, a biography* (Edinburgh, 1946), pp. 44, 137 ff.

[46] R. B. Haldane, *Universities and national life. Three addresses to students* (1910), pp. 94, 109.

[47] *R. Comm. on Civil Service. Appendix to 1st Rep.*, p. 79; cf. *Appendix to 3rd Rep.*, pp. 239 (Harrower), 278-80 (Burnet).

[48] *Royal Commission on the Civil Service. Fourth Report* (PP 1914, xvi), pp. 29-30.

the civil service regardless of class, and their report illustrates how the old ideal of providing opportunities for individuals was now being interpreted in terms of recruiting an élite. Democratic élitism of this neo-liberal type linked with concepts of national efficiency formed the ideology which gave a common aim to the educational policies of Struthers, the theories of Darroch, and the preaching of leadership, civic service, and the virtues of corporate life by university professors.

CONCLUSION

Examples have been cited from time to time of those invocations of John Knox and the democratic ideal without which no speech or book on Scottish education was complete. An extensive anthology could easily be compiled, and the development of this discourse, the psychological needs which it met, the social interests which it concealed, and the contribution which it made to the self-deception of the Scottish mind, deserve a study to themselves. The aim of this book, however, has been to examine, as closely and carefully as possible, how the relationship between schools and universities actually worked and how it changed. It has not been my intention to demolish the myth of educational democracy, or to write the lad of parts out of the script. In a European context, the democratic potential of the Scottish system was perhaps less remarkable than it appears when contrasted only with England, but it had remarkable features none the less.

It is the parish school which has traditionally been idealized, but I have argued that in the early nineteenth century the importance of the parochial tradition was limited to certain regions, that it served the convenience of the rural middle class rather than the direct interests of the poor, and that only a minority of university students came from the parish schools. This minority was not identical with the working-class minority in the universities, who more commonly entered as adults, taking advantage of the open structure of the university system and the absence of rigorous entry standards. For the urban working class, indeed, the school system before 1872 offered few formal opportunities for social mobility, since the elementary schools which had multiplied during the earlier part of the century rarely matched the parish school model, and since scholarships to secondary schools hardly existed.

By 1914 Scotland was an urban society, and it is not self-evident that class divisions and class-consciousness were any less marked in its cities and towns than in those of other countries. Social grading in education was a natural product of social differentiation, and was apparent from an early stage. As industrialization proceeded, it produced a middle class whose numbers and influence were constantly increasing, and it is their demands which are the key to the history of secondary and higher education in our period; in the domain of values, both the secularization of educational institutions and the Anglicization of university culture reflected the same social pressures. Most of nineteenth-century Europe had a dual system—secondary schools for the privileged, primary schools for the masses. But the institutions which Scotland inherited from the past were not easily adaptable to this pattern, since there was no clear distinction between primary and secondary schools, and no close articulation between the universities and a privileged school sector. From the 1820s onwards, the main object of middle-class educational reformers was to create schools of a genuinely secondary type, to link them closely with the universities, and to push up the general standard and the age-level through the device of a university entrance examination. This aim linked Chalmers and the 1826 commission, Blackie and Lorimer in the 1850s, the secondary education movement in the 1870s, and the Balfour commission of 1882.

This campaign met various obstacles. One aim of middle-class political spokesmen was to extend their local control of the system. This was satisfactory in the case of privately-founded proprietary schools like Edinburgh Academy, and in the case of the burgh schools under town council control, but to gain influence over the universities demanded a long battle against the Church and the professoriate, which culminated in the creation of Courts and General Councils in 1858. By the 1860s Scottish educationists were thinking in terms of a national system of secondary schools, but here the obstacle was the refusal of Parliament to subsidize middle-class education (an issue of principle which was to recur over the universities in the 1880s). The 1872 Act was unable to satisfy the reformers on this point, but for the following twenty years the reform of endowments allowed progress to be made without calling on state aid.

The greatest obstacle to change was perhaps the position of the parish schools, threats to which stimulated a reassertion and reinterpretation of the tradition which they represented. They might supply a minority of university students, but it was a large minority, and as long as it existed there was strong resistance to introducing an entrance examination or abolishing the junior classes. In the 1860s, when we can first examine the student body in detail, the universities remained open both to those sons of the rural poor who did find their way up through the parish schools and to working-class students who came in adult life. When the entrance examination was finally introduced in 1892, it had little discernible effect on the social composition of the student body. This, I have argued, was because by then the secondary schools had developed to a point where the transition to a new system could be a smooth one, and because there had been a battle over the nature of secondary education itself. In the 1870s and 1880s two distinct ideals were put forward, corresponding partly to the professional interests of primary and secondary teachers, but reflecting also the mediation of social conflicts through the political process at both national and local level. The advance of democracy after 1867 created a body of feeling suspicious of educational élitism. The school boards which took over the burgh schools often lacked sympathy with the cause of secondary education (leading the reformers to prefer independent governing bodies), or, as in Glasgow, had an alternative model of how it should develop. The reform of endowments gave rise to intense local conflicts which made secondary education for a time one of the leading questions in Scottish politics. Much was made of the rights of the 'poor', but the real conflict was perhaps between those who spoke for the professional and upper middle class and those who wished to preserve the rights of the middle class in a broad sense and of its artisan and shopkeeping fringe; it was the latter, an important part of the clientele of Radical Liberalism, who had always made the most practical use of such democratic opportunities as the school system afforded in the towns.

Their spokesmen succeeded in building various restrictions into the Act of 1882 which created the Balfour commission, but on the whole that commission was able to get its way, as over the Heriot's issue, creating schools of a decidedly secondary type and insisting on a narrow definition of 'merit' for the award of scholarships. Under Craik the SED seemed to share this approach. But the dispute over the Equivalent Grant in

1892 was a crucial turning-point. The policies of the county committees in the 1890s, of the urban school boards which created higher grade schools, and of the rural ones which kept something like the parish school tradition alive where demand existed, ensured that secondary education continued to be given in a large number of centres. By the turn of the century, it was possible to identify two tiers of secondary education: an upper tier comprising the larger burgh schools and the leading endowed schools created or reorganized in the 1870s and 1880s, patronized chiefly by the better-off middle class and catering very efficiently for their needs, and a lower tier in which secondary education had originally been built on a primary foundation. This hierarchy of prestige was to prove long-lasting, but in the 1900s the SED under Struthers strove to assimilate the schools to a common pattern, and to encourage the easy transfer of pupils from elementary schools through bursary schemes. Thus by 1914 although the educational system was vertically divided, with a barrier after the age of twelve between the Supplementary Courses and secondary education proper, the secondary sector itself showed considerable diversity, and alongside the more expensive schools there were many which were free or easily accessible. As the nineteenth-century reformers had hoped, the road to the university now lay via the portal of the secondary school. Controversy had long centred on freedom of access to the universities, but in the twentieth century it was equality of access to secondary schools which became the focus of conflict.

In the 1900s as in the 1860s, a large minority of university students were the children of shopkeepers, artisans, small farmers, and skilled workers, and in Glasgow at least workers in such modern industries as shipbuilding and engineering were taking their share in the university tradition. Whatever qualifications one may make—that there were few children of unskilled workers, that only a minority of families was involved even in the favoured groups, that the professional careers open to those without a privileged background were of a limited kind—there can be no doubt that throughout our period the recruitment of the Scottish élite was from a wide social range. In earlier years the system worked in a very haphazard way: there might be a 'ladder from the gutter to the university', but it was left to the individual to climb it, and this was perhaps easier in the countryside than in the towns. By the end of the century, much more attention was being paid to the need for 'capacity catching machinery' (another of Huxley's phrases) to seek out promising children and give them positive help. Both the Balfour commission and the SED under Struthers had a restricted view of 'merit', and were as concerned to exclude the unfit as to help the deserving, but they did insist on effective scholarship arrangements, and succeeded for the first time in constructing a ladder of opportunity in the cities. By the 1900s, it is true, the emphasis was less on the individual, more on the state and its need to recruit the best brains from all classes for the sake of national efficiency; the 'lad of parts' aspect of the democratic myth had been transmuted into a meritocratic élitism which satisfied contemporary notions of equality of opportunity, but which may strike the democrat of today as peculiarly narrow. From the point of view of the schools, the new structure of scholarships, leaving certificates, and university entrance examinations meant that the pupil who was to succeed had to be ruthlessly driven over a series of hurdles, and it is perhaps to this period, and especially to the tradition of the higher grade schools, that one may ascribe the examination-consciousness and fact-grinding often seen as characteristic of the Scottish secondary school.

The nature, teaching, and organization of secondary schools changed profoundly in the course of the nineteenth century. This book has discussed their internal life only incidentally, but we have seen that in the 1860s the burgh schools had a loosely-structured curriculum with much freedom of choice, and that in most schools there was a strong commercial and utilitarian bias. The reform movement, however, wished to tie secondary schools more closely to the university ideal, which meant more emphasis on the classics and on 'academic' subjects. The Balfour commission gave a significant lead by imposing an organized pattern of study laid down by the school authorities in the endowed schools which it reformed, and the SED under Struthers pushed this further by using its control of grants and of the Leaving Certificate to impose what was, in effect, a common national curriculum. This was not narrowly classical, for science was insisted on, but it was academic in the sense that it was designed for a restricted layer of pupils and that open vocationalism was excluded from the secondary school. Secondary education was defined as that which gave general culture, and it was sharply distinguished from the further education given in the Supplementary Courses, where a vocational bias was encouraged. This apparent exclusion of 'liberal' education from the elementary school alarmed traditionalists like Laurie and Ramsay, whose protests echoed the conflicts of the 1880s, when the defenders of Heriot's Hospital in Edinburgh, and the makers of Glasgow's higher grade policy, sought to keep open the road to the professions and the universities, while the Balfour commission thought that the artisan class needed a distinctive type of school which would specialize in practical education. The traditional view was that the classics had an intimate connection with the ideology of opportunity, and were in some sense part of every child's birthright. Scottish education has been periodically criticized for its 'bookishness', but perhaps this was a defect worth tolerating to keep open the paths of social mobility.

The question of whether education encouraged anti-entrepreneurial values and failed to serve the needs of the economy is a complex one which could only be answered by looking, as this book has not, at science teaching in the universities and at the important technical sector. One would also need to examine the attitudes of industrial and commercial employers, who down to 1914 seem to have shown little interest in formal educational qualifications. What can be said, perhaps, is that the values of classical and liberal culture seduced the professional part of the middle class at an early stage, and that the more utilitarian values of the commercial bourgeoisie never succeeded in challenging their dominance. This is shown by the history of the university arts curriculum. From the 1820s until the 1850s, the main aim of reformers was not to introduce new subjects, but to raise the general standard of achievement, to encourage graduation, and to create Honours degrees comparable in their career value to those of the English universities. As the ideas of Lorimer show, these aims were connected very closely with the assertion of a 'professional' ethos. In the 1860s, however, when the establishment of the General Councils had given a voice to a wider range of middle-class opinion, the emphasis shifted to the question of options; more variety should be allowed in the degree so that the universities could serve the needs of the commercial class. National debates on science and culture were reflected in the influence of such spokesmen for utilitarianism as Playfair and Huxley. The Royal Commission report of 1878, which was much concerned with specialized options but hardly at all with Honours, marked the culmination of this tendency. It was resisted by the universities, and the changes made in 1892, linked through the entrance examination with curricular developments in the secondary schools, widened students' choices but retained a strong emphasis on general culture, breadth of study, and the traditional academic subjects. By the turn of the century the arts faculties were again being criticized for neglecting the needs of commerce, but to little effect; their main role had become the training of generalists with Honours degrees for such occupations as the civil service, and (above all, and increasingly) of schoolteachers. Besides, the views of the amateurs on the General Councils became less influential as academic professionalism and university autonomy gained ground—just as, in the school sector, the bureaucratic professionalism of the SED insulated secondary education from the direct parliamentary intervention of earlier years.

In 1892 the universities abandoned the uniform arts curriculum with its strong philosophical emphasis, and from then on Scottish university education lost some of its distinctiveness and moved (though less rapidly than G. E. Davie has suggested) towards a common British pattern of specialized degrees. Anglicizing tendencies always existed in the universities, because of the social prestige of the English university model and the interest of middle-class parents in 'British' careers. But the concept of Anglicization is not in itself an adequate key to the debates on university reform which extended over seventy years before 1892, and which reflected numerous pressures and practical difficulties arising within the universities as well as outside. For the curriculum, and for philosophy in particular, two long-term changes were crucial. First the decline of divinity as the chief outlet of the arts faculties, which removed the original vocational justification for teaching philosophy at a time when in any case intellectual progress was undermining the religious foundations of the Scottish philosophical school. And second, the steady rise in the average age of entry, which was the most fundamental of all the changes affecting the universities. Between the 1860s and the 1890s the commonest age of entry rose from fifteen to seventeen, and by the 1900s it was eighteen. The Leaving Certificate came to be regarded as a test of liberal culture, and the task of giving a general education to adolescents was pushed back into the schools. Older students, and better school preparation, inevitably made the old general curriculum seem obsolete, and opened the way to entirely new levels of specialization. The casualty of the process, however, was philosophy, since unlike languages or science it could not be taught in the schools—at least, no one seems to have suggested following the French example. In the early nineteenth century the universities were teaching students of what would later be regarded as secondary school age, and the fact that they did it through philosophy created an educational ethos which was unique to Scotland. But the secondary syllabus of later years followed a more conventional pattern. Within the universities, philosophy continued to hold a large place after 1892, but the disappearance of a distinctively Scottish school of philosophers made its contribution to the national culture a more marginal one.

After the First World War a myth began to be woven around the old university curriculum, as it had been earlier around the rural school—the figure of John Harrower, indeed, linked the two. The appearance of this type of nostalgic myth was a warning sign which indicated a loss of creative vitality. In the nineteenth century men generally acted first and used the myth afterwards to justify their actions; the democratic myth had played a positive role in helping the Scots to resist some of the crasser educational ideas of the time (e.g. those of Robert Lowe), and in giving a historical sanction to innovations; in particular, as we have seen, it helped to impose a broad and relatively open concept of secondary education. But if what was 'Scottish' was identified with the image of a rural, static society then almost any change was by definition a decline from the national ideal, and this approach became a barrier to historical understanding by obscuring the equally 'Scottish' nature of industrialization and the changes which it brought in its train.

The middle classes of Glasgow and Edinburgh, for example, might favour certain English forms for the educational institutions which they created or adapted, but their way of life and values were by no means identical with those of comparable English groups, and they certainly needed no lessons from England in the techniques of preserving class distinction and social privilege.

The most florid tributes to the egalitarian myth often came from those who enjoyed the fruits of the privilege and inequality which were as much a feature of Scottish education as its democratic potential. This was not necessarily paradoxical, or cynical, for individual opportunity and inequality were two sides of the same coin. The bourgeois society of the nineteenth century chose to stress the 'lad of parts' aspect of the Scottish tradition, the boy from a humble background who used education to escape from his class, rather than (for example) the more communitarian aspect of the tradition represented by the literate village community or the well-read and articulate artisan. The idea of the career open to talents and the marshal's baton was part of that legitimizing ideology by which civil equality and social inequality were reconciled. Down to 1914, and well beyond, 'democracy' seemed to mean above all equality of opportunity and the selection of talented individuals for social promotion. At the end of the twentieth century, however, the demands of egalitarian democracy and of the post-industrial economy may well suggest that this selectivism has ceased to be either just or efficient, and that the time has come to reinterpret the Scottish tradition in a more radical way and to aim at developing the intellectual resources latent in every individual.

In this endeavour, we may learn from the history of the nineteenth-century universities. One of their most notable features was the openness and flexibility of their educational function, and the attendance of men of widely differing ages. By 1914, as a result of the changes which we have examined, a more homogeneous and full-time student body on modern lines had taken over, although even then entrance was not selective: the examination on entry was a qualifying not a competitive one. In resisting the introduction of an entrance examination, traditionalists had put forward a very clear and consistent doctrine of open entry, which was reiterated in each phase of the debate. The view that an entrance examination was 'inconsistent with the hitherto unchallenged rights of his Majesty's subjects' (Edinburgh University, 1829); that universities should be 'available for all grades of society—for all ages—for all intellects—for all attainments' (Kelland, 1854); that 'the Universities are public institutions, and that we have no right to exclude any person who thinks he is able to profit by our instructions' (James Nicol, 1876); or that 'every professor and every subject should be accessible to the general public without reference to graduation' (Laurie, 1893)—such views seem disconcerting, and even perverse, in an age when university education is equated with selection, standards, and 'excellence'. But they deserve to be recalled and pondered, and in the post-Robbins era the Scottish universities may invoke their past traditions to assert that their social mission is not to be defined only by the needs of school leavers, and that they have a duty to place their resources of science and scholarship at the service of the whole community rather than of a specially selected élite.

APPENDIX I
UNIVERSITY ENROLMENT FIGURES

(A) In 1825/6

The Royal Commission of 1826 asked the universities to give details of student numbers for the last fifty years. Most had some difficulty in doing so, and even the figures given for 1825/6 and/or 1826/7 are unreliable. The chief difficulty was that matriculation was either not enforced at all or only recorded when a student first entered, and the only annual figures collected might be for individual classes. The figures for divinity were also unreliable because of the practice of 'irregular attendance', i.e. non-residence.

Aberdeen

In 1826/7 the figures for King's College were 235 (apparently arts students only) and for Marischal College 225 (including some law students). The colleges had joint teaching for medicine (68 students) and divinity (150); but they gave different figures—81/69 and 67/83 respectively—for the proportion of regular and irregular divinity students. These figures suggest a total of about 600 resident students.

Edinburgh

The following figures were given for 1825/6: arts 823, medicine 892, law 298, divinity 223 (regular 131, irregular 92), giving a resident total of 2,144. One suspects that the figures may not have been as reliable as the university suggested.

Glasgow

The university lacked any reliable data, but provided a total of 1,222 students (later adjusted to 1,256) for 1826/7; this was calculated from an existing alphabetical list. The fact that medical students were stated to be 277 in 1825 and 432 in 1826 is sufficient commentary on the accuracy of the Glasgow figures; the number of law students was 21 in 1826/7.

St. Andrews

In 1825/6 there were 223 students in United College (arts) and 89 in St. Mary's (divinity; 57 regular, 32 irregular), giving a total of 280 residents.

Conclusion

If the figures above can be trusted, there were about 4,250 students at this time, though it should be remembered that (as later) many of them were attending single courses or part-time. All the universities reported a large increase in the previous fifty years, and felt that numbers were still rising. By the 1840s, however, contemporaries reported a sharp decline at Edinburgh, and numbers also declined at St. Andrews, where the fame of Chalmers had swollen them temporarily in the 1820s. The only relatively complete series of figures for the 1840s and 1850s is for Aberdeen, where there does not seem to have been any fall: the colleges had over 600 students throughout the 1850s.

Sources

Univ. Comm. Rep., pp. 161, 262-3, 327, 357, 408-9; *Univ. Comm. Ev. Edinburgh*, Appendix, pp. 127-9, 132; *Ev. Glasgow*, pp. 524-8; *Ev. St. Andrews*, pp. 252, 400; *Ev. Aberdeen*, pp. 217-18, 290-1, 293.
Rep. R. Comm. Univ. Aberdeen (1858), pp. 116, 118-20, 138, 143.

(B) 1861/1892

After the 1858 Act annual matriculation became compulsory, and the universities kept records on a comparable basis. The following figures relate to the academic year beginning in the calendar year shown. For 1861-87 they are taken from a parliamentary return printed in PP 1888, lxxviii. From 1889, like those in section (C) below, they are from the annual *Statistical Reports* submitted to Parliament by each university. There is a gap for 1888/9.

Aberdeen

	Arts	Div.	Law	Med.	TOTAL
1861	393	69	12	160	634
1862	375	69	8	164	616
1863	353	54	12	158	577
1864	331	54	8	139	532
1865	324	47	15	136	522
1866	313	35	20	176	544
1867	320	40	12	176	548
1868	321	30	10	166	527
1869	310	40	15	188	553
1870	328	37	12	189	566
1871	331	39	19	216	605
1872	325	54	21	256	656
1873	352	42	13	251	658
1874	336	36	14	250	636
1875	348	38	25	285	696
1876	333	28	21	295	677
1877	334	24	13	334	705
1878	352	19	19	344	734
1879	372	27	23	316	738
1880	382	32	23	335	772
1881	417	25	35	336	813
1882	450	27	23	368	868
1883	439	32	28	360	859
1884	462	31	30	378	901
1885	460	27	27	378	892
1886	440	33	18	378	869
1887	453	32	27	406	918
1888					
1889	403	30	24	457	914
1890	404	28	24	466	922
1891	374	22	46	472	914
1892	392	19	49	452	912

Edinburgh

	Arts	Div.	Law	Med.	TOTAL
1861	623	94	202	543	1,462
1862	613	76	272	549	1,510
1863	616	77	278	509	1,480
1864	637	74	254	475	1,440
1865	660	67	292	458	1,477
1866	708	64	296	457	1,525
1867	665	65	338	445	1,513
1868	661	75	311	517	1,564
1869	702	67	343	586	1,698
1870	687	68	335	678	1,768
1871	729	57	343	725	1,854
1872	737	58	329	782	1,906
1873	711	59	321	839	1,930
1874	793	66	318	899	2,076
1875	774	58	337	896	2,065
1876	894	70	317	1,070	2,351
1877	945	67	363	1,169	2,545
1878	906	70	368	1,323	2,667
1879	965	81	378	1,499	2,923
1880	1,037	79	441	1,603	3,160
1881	1,046	93	461	1,669	3,269
1882	1,020	105	485	1,741	3,351
1883	1,017	102	504	1,748	3,371
1884	1,070	114	503	1,736	3,423
1885	1,147	112	470	1,873	3,602
1886	1,084	107	493	1,872	3,556
1887	996	99	489	1,891	3,475
1888					
1889	979	124	470	2,003	3,576
1890	950	114	473	1,951	3,488
1891	938	90	488	1,852	3,368
1892	959	80	452	1,736	3,227

Glasgow

	Arts	Div.	Law	Med.	TOTAL
1861	691	87	79	283	1,140
1862	784	89	99	294	1,266
1863	789	95	91	267	1,242
1864	748	101	71	259	1,179
1865	780	102	84	272	1,238
1866	739	86	96	283	1,204
1867	754	80	116	323	1,273
1868	754	86	116	324	1,280
1869	734	83	129	336	1,282
1870	772	71	116	320	1,279
1871	817	72	111	349	1,349
1872	742	52	118	346	1,258
1873	805	48	138	342	1,333
1874	904	60	153	367	1,484
1875	942	74	170	415	1,601
1876	1,113	66	159	435	1,773
1877	1,243	60	223	492	2,018
1878	1,327	55	213	501	2,096
1879	1,380	85	210	560	2,235
1880	1,406	99	207	592	2,304
1881	1,331	120	220	649	2,320
1882	1,307	111	213	644	2,275
1883	1,183	118	250	661	2,212
1884	1,196	101	247	717	2,261
1885	1,158	106	245	732	2,241
1886	1,118	112	237	793	2,260
1887	1,097	101	200	790	2,188
1888					
1889	1,097	92	188	779	2,156
1890	1,139	83	193	772	2,187
1891	1,049	85	202	797	2,133
1892	1,099	86	199	783	2,167

St. Andrews				*All universities*
	Arts	Div.	TOTAL	TOTAL
1861	133	30	163	3,399
1862	146	35	181	3,573
1863	143	25	168	3,467
1864	139	27	166	3,317
1865	139	32	171	3,408
1866	141	32	173	3,446
1867	136	31	167	3,501
1868	153	31	184	3,555
1869	146	31	177	3,710
1870	144	28	172	3,785
1871	149	27	176	3,984
1872	133	24	157	3,977
1873	112	28	140	4,061
1874	118	23	141	4,337
1875	120	27	147	4,509
1876	103	27	130	4,931
1877	129	24	153	5,421
1878	139	22	161	5,658
1879	138	20	158	6,054
1880	168	20	188	6,424
1881	169	24	193	6,595
1882	173	22	195	6,689
1883	171	24	195	6,637
1884	175	28	203	6,788
1885	178	34	212	6,947
1886	178	38	216	6,901
1887	176	42	218	6,799
1888				
1889	172	36	208	6,854
1890	177	24	201	6,798
1891	162	27	189	6,604
1892	170	27	197	6,503

Note: a small number of medical students at St. Andrews after 1889 have been added to the Arts figure.

(C) *1893-1913*

A small number of women studied in the law and divinity faculties, but these have not been shown separately.

Aberdeen

	Arts		Science		Div.	Law	Medicine		TOTAL
	Men	Women	Men	Women			Men	Women	
1893	330			13	19	45	405		812
1894	319			23	20	48	379		789
1895	312			27	25	51	367		782
1896	324			28	23	43	337		755
1897	351			38	21	42	324		776
1898	307	84	47	–	15	34	316	9	808
1899	281	95	60	2	16	38	325	11	828
1900	279	98	41	1	11	40	316	14	800
1901	285	117	52	1	14	36	308	18	831
1902	276	120	58	1	15	41	333	20	864
1903	255	131	71	3	14	36	354	20	884
1904	243	147	73	3	14	33	355	11	879
1905	254	168	79	6	22	33	308	10	880
1906	276	190	74	8	21	23	292	6	890
1907	273	235	81	12	21	24	277	9	932
1908	315	239	86	11	20	27	266	6	970
1909	316	253	107	17	18	33	255	8	1,007
1910	292	246	114	16	18	20	249	14	969
1911	301	277	121	16	22	15	265	18	1,035
1912	304	275	122	25	26	16	257	18	1,043
1913	204	275	193	21	25	21	252	21	1,0–

Year	Arts Men	Arts Women	Science Men	Science Women	Div.	Law	Medicine Men	Medicine Women	Music Men	Music Women	TOTAL
1893	798		171		77	458		1,560		-	3,064
1894	750		151		69	446		1,512	11		2,939
1895	705		145		68	443		1,455	9		2,825
1896	575	186	147	2	59	437	1,411	8	5	3	2,833
1897	575	184	144	3	59	394	1,403	2	10	6	2,780
1898	620	195	164	5	64	367	1,405	7	8	11	2,846
1899	639	199	145	4	47	365	1,361	7	5	17	2,789
1900	642	213	164	6	40	358	1,351	13	4	20	2,811
1901	649	250	168	1	33	399	1,389	7	6	18	2,920
1902	605	273	203	3	41	388	1,408	19	6	10	2,956
1903	601	263	225	4	50	344	1,472	15	10	17	3,001
1904	605	296	241	7	46	348	1,479	2	7	12	3,043
1905	627	343	281	9	53	326	1,442	40	7	19	3,147
1906	618	408	277	12	55	307	1,453	40	8	18	3,196
1907	627	501	279	17	64	298	1,433	54	8	11	3,292
1908	645	512	286	14	64	305	1,380	60	8	12	3,286
1909	686	536	309	18	44	276	1,353	24	8	15	3,279
1910	718	569	368	20	45	255	1,347	26	7	11	3,366
1911	724	591	416	20	51	276	1,309	17	4	11	3,419
1912	732	519	409	25	53	276	1,313	6	5	14	3,352
1913	712	507	399	27	63	252	1,302	2	4	15	3,283

Note: women studying medicine at Edinburgh normally did so in extra-mural schools. The fluctuations above seem to reflect changing practice as to official matriculation within the university.

Glasgow

	Arts		Science		Div.	Law	Medicine		SCE		TOTAL
	Men	Women	Men	Women			Men	Women	Men	Women	
1893	799	110	131	-	86	190	680	58	-	-	2,054
1894	698	146	120	4	71	176	668	61	-	-	1,944
1895	626	167	112	3	59	182	615	71	-	-	1,835
1896	584	166	120	5	62	217	613	78	26	-	1,871
1897	609	176	111	7	57	203	592	81	-	-	1,836
1898	652	217	145	6	50	213	595	81	7	-	1,966
1899	663	258	163	6	40	204	611	76	8	1	2,030
1900	686	276	165	7	41	195	593	67	8	-	2,038
1901	670	271	187	7	51	198	611	62	3	8	2,068
1902	682	274	207	8	57	190	650	76	12	2	2,158
1903	693	316	237	11	47	193	636	60	23	3	2,219
1904	697	345	251	10	48	186	648	62	19	1	2,267
1905	687	430	249	9	43	207	636	58	31	6	2,356
1906	708	512	281	9	56	203	632	58	39	7	2,505
1907	688	554	320	13	58	236	624	64	29	-	2,586
1908	692	578	358	15	64	210	626	83	53	19	2,699
1909	739	534	419	24	61	204	627	71	37	12	2,728
1910	761	552	432	33	56	175	651	78	35	17	2,790
1911	753	548	428	39	63	194	643	82	35	9	2,794
1912	799	505	468	45	57	204	630	87	30	10	2,835
1913	776	499	509	39	69	178	712	109	10	15	2,916

Note: SCE = Single Class Enrolment

	Arts		Science		Div.	Medicine		TOTAL
	Men	Women	Men	Women		Men	Women	
1893	157			17	32	8		214
1894	155			11	29	8		203
1895	164			12	24	12		212
1896	172			16	22	26		236
1897	171			24	16	35		246
1898	193			18	14	33		258
1899	128	81	24	1	20	20	6	264
1900	134	87	24	–	29	21	5	275
1901	141	91	33	4	16	16	4	282
1902	155	108	33	8	17	11	8	309
1903	138	93	26	7	18	17	9	292
1904	135	89	31	8	23	22	6	293
1905	143	111	30	6	31	15	3	320
1906	143	109	30	7	21	9	7	310
1907	146	128	35	9	22	11	3	334
1908	132	146	42	9	23	9	10	350
1909	143	146	43	10	17	11	12	354
1910	128	154	43	8	20	16	12	353
1911	115	124	46	11	20	19	12	319
1912	108	117	41	15	21	13	10	307
1913	111	110	35	17	23	17	9	309

Note: from 1899 the faculty figures add up to more than the general total, because of students registering in more than one faculty.

Dundee

	Arts		Science		Law	Medicine		TOTAL
	Men	Women	Men	Women		Men	Women	
1893								
1894								
1895								
1896								
1897								
1898								
1899	8	17	33	2	21	26	7	132*
1900	15	22	36	1	10	51	5	137
1901	25	41	32	3	7	40	9	153
1902	23	59	32	6	8	37	10	174
1903	22	79	42	11	9	42	13	207
1904	17	82	43	15	10	39	8	199
1905	19	60	44	9	16	50	17	198
1906	14	67	32	11	16	56	16	203
1907	15	81	40	6	23	47	8	216
1908	27	95	49	6	12	46	9	235
1909	23	81	49	4	11	49	11	218
1910	30	68	47	8	10	58	15	226
1911	20	51	43	9	13	61	12	203
1912	19	53	34	9	16	61	14	201
1913	25	44	40	9	13	61	16	199

* including 18 summer session students (in medicine) whose sex was not shown

Note: as at St. Andrews, there is overlap between faculty figures. The figures above are taken from the annual

All universities

	Men	Women	TOTAL	Women as %
1893			6,144	
1894			5,875	
1895			5,654	
1896			5,695	
1897			5,638	
1898			5,878	
1899			6,043	
1900	5,227	834	6,061	13·8
1901	5,346	908	6,254	14·5
1902	5,461	1,000	6,461	15·5
1903	5,557	1,046	6,603	15·8
1904	5,584	1,097	6,681	16·4
1905	5,605	1,296	6,901	18·8
1906	5,624	1,480	7,104	20·8
1907	5,657	1,703	7,360	23·1
1908	5,718	1,822	7,540	24·2
1909	5,818	1,768	7,586	23·3
1910	5,863	1,841	7,704	23·9
1911	5,924	1,846	7,770	23·8
1912	5,993	1,745	7,738	22·6
1913	6,025	1,751	7,776	22·5

APPENDIX II
G. E. DAVIE'S
'THE DEMOCRATIC INTELLECT'

G. E. Davie's remarkable book *The democratic intellect. Scotland and her universities in the nineteenth century* is much more than a history of university reform, dealing as it does with science, philosophy and literary studies in the nineteenth century, and relating them to the general cultural history of Scotland. But its first part gives an account of 'university politics' which differs in many respects from that which I have presented, and the aim of this Appendix is to comment on some of these differences of interpretation.

For Davie, 'Anglicization' is the key to understanding this history. He argues that after the Union of 1707, along with its own Church and legal system, Scotland retained a distinctive 'social ethics', the central expression of which was an 'educational system which, combining the democracy of the Kirk-elders with the intellectualism of the advocates, made expertise in metaphysics the condition of the open door of social advancement'. (p. xii) The position of philosophy in the university curriculum was central to the 'liberal educational arrangements which bridged the gap between the disparate sections and sects of Scottish society, allowing the talented to rise without disloyalty to their origins or family convictions, and creating in the process an intellectual culture of unusual balance'. (pp. 292-3.) This social ethic, still relatively intact in the early nineteenth century, disappeared after a sixty-year struggle, partly through a general failure of national self-confidence and the debilitating effects on Scottish culture of barren sectarian struggles, partly because many Scots deliberately adopted assimilation with England as a desirable and progressive policy. These Anglophiles were opposed by a more patriotic party, but in vain, so that by the twentieth century a once vital intellectual tradition was hardly remembered or understood.

'Instead of the steady rhythm of independent institutional life', writes Davie, 'a new pattern emerged of alternation between catastrophe and renaissance, in which the distinctive national inheritance was more than once brought to the very brink of ruin only to be saved at the last minute by a sudden burst of reviving energy'. (p. xvi.) The universities commission of 1826 was a first assault on the tradition; this was repelled, but the real crisis came with the events surrounding the Disruption. Revival from this took the form of 'rallying the dissident factions round the educational system as that item above all others in the inheritance which divided the Scots least … In this way, it was hoped that the universities would assume responsibility for the nation's spiritual leadership in the room of the divided Church, and, in that capacity, achieve the practical reaffirmation of the moral ideals of Scottish life in a form appropriate to the nineteenth century.' (p. xvi.) This patriotic role is allocated to Lorimer and his movement Their plans were 'grudgingly endorsed' by the 1858 Act, and the Inglis commission outlined a 'programme of democratic intellectuality'. This was hampered, however, by the reluctance of Parliament to vote the necessary funds, and above all by the intensification of sectarian strife, which was reflected in contests for the university philosophy chairs. 'In this way, recovery within less than twenty years turned into ruin', (p. xvii) and the 1876 Royal Commission was able to make radical proposals for turning the universities into specialized institutions on English lines. This threat was temporarily averted, but the 1889 Act led to a compromise acceptable to Scottish opinion, after which the defence of national educational traditions was left to the schools rather than the universities. The 1889 settlement 'gave the anglophil party most of what they had fought for since 1826, without at the same time being too offensive to Scottish susceptibilities'. (p. 6.) The old general curriculum survived, but only as an alternative to new specialized degrees. Thus 1889 'constitutes the great dividing-line between past and present in the educational history of Scotland' (p. 8), while the period between 1858 and 1889, when under the Inglis regulations Honours could be pursued only after general study, 'is even now remembered in retrospect as a Silver Age in the history of Scottish Universities, and as a last sunset, before they ceased to shine'. (p. 91.)

In Davie's interpretation, the defence of the Scottish general curriculum was also a defence of the democratic tradition, and the cause of English-style specialization (and its eventual triumph) represented a move towards social exclusivism. This equation, however, is not self-evident: liberal, non-vocational education is commonly associated historically with the needs of a leisured class. For Davie the link lies in the democratic nature of the Scottish philosophical approach. The history of philosophy is his starting-point, and his book projects the crisis of the 'Scottish' philosophy on to a wider screen as a crisis of the universities and university culture. But in reality philosophy did not occupy as central a position in the debates on university reform as Davie suggests, nor indeed did the curriculum itself. Davie sees the importance of the entrance examination question, but he implies that those who defended the Scottish educational ideal were necessarily hostile to the examination, which was not the case.

This especially affects Davie's account of Lorimer, which is central to his story. He is right to say that Lorimer wished to revive the universities as centres of national consciousness, that he favoured the traditional philosophical approach, and that his scheme for building 'postgraduate' specialization on a general foundation forms an attractive historical might-have-been. What is less easy to accept is the 'democratic' nature of Lorimer's proposals. Few men spoke more clearly or more self-consciously for the professional classes and their interests (above, pp. 58-9), and—contrary to Davie's assertion (p. 49) —Lorimer was strongly in favour of an entrance examination: he argued for it in a major article in the *Edinburgh Review* in 1858 (but Davie failed to identify Lorimer's anonymous articles), it was a part of his Association's programme, and it was incorporated into the bill which he drew up for Moncreiff in 1857 (above, p. 65). Like Blackie, Lorimer thought higher standards in the schools vital to university reform; he was critical of the parochial tradition, and in the 1870s he was an active member of the secondary education movement (above, pp. 59, 170).

One weakness of Davie's account of the reform movement in the 1850s is that Blackie is left out, although at the time he was at least as prominent as Lorimer. Another is that in imposing the pattern of Anglophile and patriotic parties Davie greatly exaggerates the significance of Shairp, whose ideas differed only in emphasis from Lorimer's. It is difficult to find any real Anglophile party in Scotland at this time—Shairp himself was still a schoolmaster in England when he published his pamphlet *The wants of the Scottish universities* in 1856; and if there was such a party Lorimer himself might qualify for it, since he was eager to introduce such English ideas as the tutorial system and the corporate ideal (above, pp. 60, 329). It would be more correct to speak of a single reforming party, drawing its inspiration from various sources, native and foreign, and opposed by cautious traditionalists—whose existence is indeed described by Davie (pp. 46, 64). A defence of the 'democratic intellect' might be found, if anywhere, in the criticisms of Lorimer made by Kelland (above, pp. 62-3); but too much should not be made of this, for Kelland gave general support to the reform movement.

I have argued that Lorimer and Blackie were taking up the earlier plans of Chalmers and the 1826 commission, not reacting against them, and that the needs of the professional middle class form one of the linking threads. There was a good deal of continuity between the recommendations of the 1826 commission and the 1858 Act, a point obscured in Davie's account because he largely ignores the questions of university government and finance which preoccupied contemporaries and the national and university politics out of which Royal

Commissions and the Acts of 1858 and 1889 grew. When these are taken into account, the picture becomes both more complex and less dramatic, and a process of evolution in response to changing social and educational demands replaces the scenario of catastrophe and renaissance. Even in the matter of the curriculum, one might point out that the 1858 system of Honours, praised by Davie as 'the most vital and promising development in the Universities' before 1889 (p. 79), was only a watered-down version of what the 1826 commission had proposed (above, p. 71).

The reader of Davie's book would not know this, for it has surprisingly little hard information about what was actually taught or what the various commissions proposed, and what there is is not always correct. This is especially so of the changes made in 1892: according to Davie, the Ordinary degree represented the retention of the Scottish tradition in a 'fossilised, static form' for the 'unadventurous types', while those doing Honours degrees 'were relieved of the burden of doing compulsory philosophy and, instead, were given a narrower type of training which left them intellectually indistinguishable, or almost so, from the Southern product'. (pp. 79-80.) Davie is right in saying that the Ordinary degree pointed to Scottish careers and the Honours degree to British ones. On the other hand, the facts are that the Ordinary degree was itself extensively remodelled, and made more flexible, not more rigid (above, p. 270); that the great majority continued to take this degree (above, p. 284); and that a philosophical subject (usually logic or moral philosophy) was compulsory for Honours students along with a classical language and a science (p. 271). The abolition of 'compulsory philosophy', so central to Davie's thesis, came not in 1892 but with the reforms of 1908-10, which he does not mention.

The reader of the two books will find other episodes where the facts do not support Davie's interpretation or where his over-schematic approach simplifies the issues. His Anglicization hypothesis was a bold and stimulating one, and his book has had much influence. Enough has perhaps been said here to show that it is inadequately anchored in historical evidence, and that it cannot by itself explain the long and complex process by which the Scottish universities were adapted, and adapted themselves, to the changing conditions of the nineteenth century.

SELECT BIBLIOGRAPHY

This bibliography is intended mainly as a guide to further reading, and the emphasis is on secondary works—including recent work on primary and adult education. References to manuscript sources, and to contemporary books and pamphlets, will be found in the footnotes. I have thought it useful, however, to provide a full list of official reports, etc., and to list some other types of printed source-material.

I. OFFICIAL PUBLICATIONS

(A) UNIVERSITIES

Report made to His Majesty by a Royal Commission of Inquiry into the state of the Universities of Scotland (1831) (PP 1831, xii).

Evidence, oral and documentary, taken and received by the Commissioners ... for visiting the Universities of Scotland
  I. University of Edinburgh (1837) (PP 1837, xxxv);
  II. University of Glasgow (1837) (PP 1837, xxxvi);
  III. University of St. Andrews (1837) (PP 1837, xxxvii);
  IV. University of Aberdeen (1837) (PP 1837, xxxviii).

First Report of the Commissioners appointed ... for visiting the Universities of King's College and Marischal College, Aberdeen (1838) (PP 1837/8, xxxiii);
  Second Report (1839) (PP 1839, xxix).

Report by the Commissioners appointed ... for visiting the University of Glasgow (1839) (PP 1839, xxix).

Report of the St. Andrews' University Commissioners (1845) (PP 1846, xxiii).

Report of Her Majesty's Commissioners appointed to inquire into the state of the Universities of Aberdeen, with a view to their union (1858) (PP 1857/8, xx).

Scottish Universities Commission. General Report of the Commissioners under the Universities (Scotland) Act, 1858. With an Appendix (1863) (PP 1863, xvi).

Report of the Royal Commissioners appointed to inquire into the Universities of Scotland, with Evidence and Appendix
  I. Report with Index of Evidence (1878) (PP 1878, xxxii);
  II. Evidence - Part I (1878) (PP 1878, xxxiii);

III. Evidence - Part II (1878) (PP 1878, xxxiv);
IV. Returns and Documents (1878) (PP 1878, xxxv).
Report of the Commissioners under the Universities (Scotland) Act, 1889, as to the Subscription of Tests by Principals, Professors, and other University Officers in the Scottish Universities, Vol. I (n.d.) (PP 1892, xlvii);
Appendix to the Report of the Commissioners under the Universities (Scotland) Act, 1889, as to the Subscription of Tests ..., Vol. II (n.d.) (PP 1892, xlvii).
General Report of the Commissioners under the Universities (Scotland) Act, 1889. With an Appendix (1900) (PP 1900, xxv).
Report of the Committee on Scottish Universities, with Appendices (1910) (PP 1910, xxvi);
Minutes of Evidence taken before the Committee on Scottish Universities, with Index (1910) (PP 1910, xxvi).
Scottish Universities and the Inclusive Fee. Copy of Correspondence between H. M. Treasury and the Scottish University Courts relative to the institution of an Inclusive Fee for graduation courses (1913) (PP 1912/13, lxvi).

(B) SCHOOLS

1. Early returns and statistics

A Digest of Parochial Returns made to the Select Committee appointed to inquire into the Education of the Poor: Session 1818, Vol. III (1819) (PP 1819, ix, part 3).
Parochial Education, Scotland. Returns to an Address of the Honourable House of Commons, dated March 30th, 1825; ... (1826) (PP 1826, xviii).
Education Enquiry. Abstract of the Answers and Returns made pursuant to an Address of the House of Commons, dated 9th July 1834 (1837) (PP 1837, xlvii).
Report from the Select Committee on the State of Education in Scotland (1838) (PP 1837/8, vii).
Answers made by Schoolmasters in Scotland to Queries circulated in 1838, by order of the Select Committee on Education in Scotland (2 vols., 1841) (PP 1841, xix).
Census of Great Britain, 1851. Religious Worship, and Education. Scotland. Report and Tables (1854) (PP 1854, lix).

2. Argyll Commission

Education Commission (Scotland). First Report by Her Majesty's Commissioners appointed to inquire into the Schools in Scotland. With an Appendix (1865) (PP 1865, xvii).

Education Commission (Scotland). Appendix to First Report ... being Answers to Heads of Examination, and Correspondence (1867) (PP 1867, xxv).

Education Commission (Scotland). Second Report by Her Majesty's Commissioners appointed to inquire into the Schools in Scotland. With an Appendix. Elementary Schools (1867) (PP 1867, xxv).

Education Commission (Scotland). Report on the State of Education in the Country Districts of Scotland (1866) (PP 1867, xxv).

Education Commission (Scotland). Statistical Report on the State of Education in the Lowland Country Districts of Scotland (1866) (PP 1867, xxv).

Education Commission (Scotland). Report on the State of Education in Glasgow (1866) (PP 1867, xxv).

Education Commission (Scotland). Report on the State of Education in the Hebrides (1866) (PP 1867, xxv).

Education Commission (Scotland). Statistics relative to Schools in Scotland collected by the Registrars of Births, Deaths, and Marriages (1865) (PP 1867, xxvi).

Education Commission (Scotland). Third Report of Her Majesty's Commissioners ... . Burgh and Middle-Class Schools. Together with the General and Special Reports of the Assistant-Commissioners [cited as *Vol. I*] (1868) (PP 1867/8, xxix).

Education Commission (Scotland). Report on the State of Education in the Burgh and Middle-Class Schools in Scotland. Vol. II. - Special Reports (1868) (PP 1867/8, xxix).

3. Schools Inquiry (Taunton) Commission

Schools Inquiry Commission. Vol. VI. General Reports of Assistant Commissioners. Burgh Schools in Scotland, and Secondary Education in Foreign Countries (1868) (PP 1867/8, xxviii, part 5).

4. Colebrooke Commission

First Report of the Royal Commissioners appointed to inquire into the Endowed Schools and Hospitals (Scotland), with Evidence and Appendix (1873) (PP 1873, xxvii);
Second Report (1874) (PP 1874, xvii);
Third Report (1875) (PP 1875, xxix);
Appendix to Third Report (2 vols., 1875) (PP 1875, xxix).

5. Moncreiff Commission

First Report of the Commissioners on Endowed Institutions in Scotland; with Evidence (1880) (PP 1880, xxiv);

Second Report (1881) (PP 1881, xxxvi);
Third Report (1881) (PP 1881, xxxvi).
Report by the Commissioners on Endowed Institutions in Scotland in terms of the 11th section of the Endowed Institutions (Scotland) Act, 1878 ..., with Evidence and Appendix [cited as *Special Report*] (1881) (PP 1881, xxxvi).

6. Balfour Commission

First Report of the Educational Endowments (Scotland) Commission, with Evidence and Appendix (1884) (PP 1884, xxvii);
Second Report (1885) (PP 1884/5, xxvii);
Third Report (1886) (PP 1886, xxviii);
Fourth Report (1887) (PP 1887, xxxiii);
Fifth Report (1888) (PP 1888, xli);
Sixth Report (1889) (PP 1889, xxxii);
Seventh Report (1890) (PP 1890, xxxi).

7. Parker Committee

First and Second Reports of the Committee appointed to inquire into Certain Questions relating to Education in Scotland; with Appendix (1888) (PP 1888, xli);
Third Report (1888) (PP 1888, xli).

8. Elgin Committee

Education (Scotland). Report of the Committee appointed to inquire as to the best means of distributing the Grant in Aid of Secondary Education in Scotland (1892) (PP 1892, lxii).
Minutes of Evidence taken by the Committee ... with Appendices (1892) (PP 1892, lxii).

(C) ANNUAL REPORTS

1. Education Department

Material relating to Scotland is in *Minutes of the Committee of Council on Education,* 1839/40 - 1857/8, and in *Report of the Committee of Council on Education; with Appendix,* 1858/9-1872/3.
The annual reports of the SED are in *Report of the Committee of Council on Education in Scotland; with Appendix,* 1873/4-1907/8. After 1908, the report was split into sections and only the general report was

published as a Parliamentary Paper. The complete collection of reports was published as *Scotch Education Department. Reports, &c., issued in 1908-9* [etc.]; in 1911 the heading was changed to *Education (Scotland)*.

2. Board of Education for Scotland

First Annual Report of the Board of Education for Scotland (1874) (PP 1874, xx);
Second Annual Report (1875) (PP 1875, xxvi);
Third Annual Report (1876) (PP 1876, xxv);
Fourth Annual Report (1877) (PP 1877, xxxii);
Fifth Annual Report (1878) (PP 1878, xxx);
Sixth and Concluding Report (1879) (PP 1878/9, xxv).

3. Universities

Each university made an annual *Statistical Report* and *Financial Report* for the year 1889/90 onwards. For details see the printed indexes to Parliamentary Papers.

II. OTHER PRINTED SOURCES

1. Dick Bequest Reports

A. Menzies, *Report to the Trustees of the Bequest of the late James Dick, Esq., for the benefit of the country parochial schoolmasters in the counties of Aberdeen, Banff, and Moray* (Edinburgh, 1835).
[A. Menzies], *Report to the Trustees of the Dick Bequest ... after ten years' experience of its application* (Edinburgh, 1844).
A. Menzies, *Report of twenty-one years' experience of the Dick Bequest ...* (Edinburgh, 1854).
S. S. Laurie, *Report on education in the parochial schools of the counties of Aberdeen, Banff and Moray, addressed to the Trustees of the Dick Bequest* (Edinburgh, 1865).
—— *Report to the Trustees of the Dick Bequest on the rural public (formerly parochial) schools of Aberdeen, Banff, and Moray, with special reference to the higher instruction in them* (Edinburgh, 1890).
—— *Dick Bequest Trust. General Report to the Governors 1890-1904* (Edinburgh, 1904).

2. University records and registers

W. I. Addison, *The Matriculation Albums of the University of Glasgow from 1728 to 1858* (Glasgow, 1913).

J. M. Anderson, *The Matriculation Roll of the University of St Andrews 1747-1897* (Edinburgh, 1905).

P. J. Anderson, *Fasti Academiae Mariscallanae Aberdonensis. Selections from the Records of the Marischal College and University, MDXCIII-MDCCCLX* (3 vols., Aberdeen, 1889-98).

—— *Officers and graduates of University and King's College Aberdeen, MVD-MDCCCLX* (Aberdeen, 1893).

—— *Roll of alumni in arts of the University and King's College of Aberdeen 1596-1860* (Aberdeen, 1900).

W. Johnston, *Roll of the graduates of the University of Aberdeen 1860-1900* (Aberdeen, 1906).

A. Morgan, *University of Edinburgh. Charters, Statutes, and Acts of the Town Council and the Senatus, 1583-1858* (Edinburgh, 1937).

The Universities (Scotland) Act, 1858, together with Ordinances of Commissioners under said Act, with relative notes of alterations thereon authorised by Orders in Council of various dates (Glasgow, 1916).

The Universities (Scotland) Act, 1889, together with Ordinances of the Commissioners under the said Act, with relative Regulations & Declarations, and University Court Ordinances made and approved subsequent to the expiry of the powers of the commissioners (Glasgow, 1915).

University of Aberdeen. Minutes of the General Council (3 vols., Aberdeen, 1898-1916).

T. Watt, *Roll of the graduates of the University of Aberdeen 1901-1925. With Supplement 1860-1900* (Aberdeen, 1935).

3. Selected memoirs and biographies

A. Bain, *Autobiography* (1904).

J. S. Blackie, *Notes of a life* (Edinburgh, 1910).

M. R. L. Bryce, *Memoir of John Veitch* (Edinburgh, 1896).

W. L. Calderwood & D. Woodside, *The life of Henry Calderwood* (1900).

[Christison], *The life of Sir Robert Christison, Bart. ... Edited by his sons* (2 vols., Edinburgh, 1885-6).

A. C. Fraser, *Biographia philosophica. A retrospect* (Edinburgh, 1904).

G. A. Gibson, *Life of Sir William Tennant Gairdner* (Glasgow, 1912).

A. E. Gunther, *The life of William Carmichael McIntosh* (Edinburgh, 1977).

H. J. W. Hetherington, *The life and letters of Sir Henry Jones* (1924).

H. Jones & J. H. Muirhead, *The life and philosophy of Edward Caird* (Glasgow, 1921).

W. Knight, *Some nineteenth century Scotsmen* (Edinburgh, 1903).

—— *Principal Shairp and his friends* (1888).

—— *Memoir of John Nichol* (Glasgow, 1896).

M. Lodge, *Sir Richard Lodge, a biography* (Edinburgh, 1946).

[MacAlister], *Sir Donald MacAlister of Tarbert, by his wife* (1935).

D. Macmillan, *The life of Robert Flint* (1914).

Mrs Oliphant, *A memoir of the life of John Tulloch* (3rd edn., Edinburgh, 1889).

W. Reid, *Memoirs and correspondence of Lyon Playfair* (1899).

J. C. Shairp and others, *Life and letters of James David Forbes* (1873).

A. M. Stoddart, *John Stuart Blackie. A biography* (2 vols., 3rd edn., Edinburgh, 1895).

[Story], *Memoir of Robert Herbert Story ... by his daughters* (Glasgow, 1909).

S. P. Thompson, *The life of William Thomson, Baron Kelvin of Largs* (2 vols., 1910).

A. L. Turner, *Sir William Turner ... . A chapter in medical history* (Edinburgh, 1919).

J. Veitch, *Hamilton* (Edinburgh, 1882).

J. C. Smith & W. Wallace, *Robert Wallace. Life and last leaves* (1903).

III. SECONDARY WORKS

1. History of education: general studies

A. J. Belford, *Centenary handbook of the Educational Institute of Scotland* (Edinburgh, 1946).

R. Bell & N. Grant, *A mythology of British education* (1974).

T. R. Bone, *School inspection in Scotland 1840-1966* (1968).

—— (ed.), *Studies in the history of Scottish education 1872-1939* (1967).

C. G. Brown, 'The Sunday-school movement in Scotland, 1780-1914', *Records of the Scottish Church History Society,* xvii (1981), 3-26.

I. R. Carter, 'The mutual improvement movement in North-East Scotland in the nineteenth century', *Aberdeen University Review,* xlvi (1975-6), 383-92.

D. Chambers, 'The Church of Scotland's Highlands and Islands education scheme, 1824-1843', *Journal of Educational Administration and History,* vii, no. 1 (1975), 8-17.

C. M. Cipolla, *Literacy and development in the West* (Harmondsworth, 1969).

M. L. Clarke, *Classical education in Britain 1500-1900* (Cambridge, 1959).

M. Cruickshank, *A history of the training of teachers in Scotland* (1970).

—— 'The Dick bequest: the effect of a famous nineteenth-century endowment on parish schools of North East Scotland', *History of Education Quarterly*, v (1965), 153-65.

S. J. Curtis, *History of education in Great Britain* (7th edn., 1967).

M. B. Dealy, *Catholic schools in Scotland* (Washington, 1945).

J. Grant, *History of the burgh and parish schools of Scotland. ... Vol. I. Burgh schools* (1876).

J. Highet, *A school of one's choice. A sociological study of the fee-paying schools of Scotland* (1969).

W. Humes & H. Paterson (eds), *Scottish culture and Scottish education 1800-1980* (Edinburgh, 1983).

J. Kerr, *Scottish education. School and university. From early times to 1908* (Cambridge, 1910).

H. M. Knox, *Two hundred and fifty years of Scottish education, 1696-1946* (Edinburgh, 1953).

—— 'Simon Somerville Laurie: 1829-1909', *British Journal of Educational Studies*, x (1961/2), 138-52.

M. Mackintosh, *Education in Scotland yesterday and today* (Glasgow, 1962).

A. Morgan, *Rise and progress of Scottish education* (Edinburgh, 1927).

—— *Makers of Scottish education* (1929).

G. S. Osborne, *Scottish and English schools. A comparative survey of the past fifty years* (1966).

D. G. Paz, *The politics of working-class education in Britain, 1830-50* (Manchester, 1980).

J. Scotland, *The history of Scottish education* (2 vols, 1969).

—— 'The Scottish dominie', *Philosophical Journal*, vii (1970), 128-41.

J. M. Simpson, 'Three East Lothian pioneers of adult education', *Transactions of the East Lothian Antiquarian and Field Naturalists' Society*, xiii (1972), 43-60.

L. Stone, 'Literacy and education in England, 1640-1900', *Past & Present*, no. 42 (1969), 69-139.

J. Strong, *A history of secondary education in Scotland. An account of Scottish secondary education from early times to the Education Act of 1908* (Oxford, 1909).

J. Synge, 'The selective function and British rural education', *British Journal of Educational Studies*, xxiii (1975), 135-52.

A. R. Thompson, 'The use of libraries by the working class in Scotland in the early nineteenth century', *Scottish Historical Review*, xlii (1963), 21-9.

J. H. Treble, 'The development of Roman Catholic education in Scotland 1878-1978', *Innes Review*, xxix (1978), 111-39.

A. Tyrrell, 'Political economy, whiggism and the education of working-class adults in Scotland 1817-40', *Scottish Historical Review,* xlviii (1969), 151-65.

N. A. Wade, *Post-primary education in the primary schools of Scotland 1872-1936* (1939).

R. K. Webb, 'Literacy among the working classes in nineteenth century Scotland', *Scottish Historical Review,* xxxiii (1954), 100-14.

E. G. West, *Education and the industrial revolution* (1975).

D. J. Withrington, 'The Free Church Educational Scheme 1843-50', *Records of the Scottish Church History Society,* xv (1963-5), 103-15.

2. History of education: local studies

A. Bain, *Education in Stirlingshire from the Reformation to the Act of 1872* (1965).

W. Barclay, *The schools and schoolmasters of Banffshire* (Banff, 1925).

W. Boyd, *Education in Ayrshire through seven centuries* (1961).

H. Hutchinson, 'Church, state and school in Clackmannanshire: 1803-1872', *Scottish Educational Studies,* iii (1971), 25-38.

J. C. Jessop, *Education in Angus. An historical survey of education up to the Act of 1872* (1931).

J. M. Roxburgh, *The School Board of Glasgow 1873-1919* (1971).

J. A. Russell, *History of education in the Stewartry of Kirkcudbright* (Newton Stewart, 1951).

—— *Education in Wigtownshire 1560-1970* (Newton Stewart, 1971).

I. J. Simpson, *Education in Aberdeenshire before 1872* (1947).

3. General works with relevant sections

R. H. Campbell, *The rise and fall of Scottish industry 1707-1939* (Edinburgh, 1980).

A. L. Drummond & J. Bulloch, *The Scottish Church 1688-1843. The age of the Moderates* (Edinburgh, 1973).

—— *The Church in Victorian Scotland 1843-1874* (Edinburgh, 1975).

—— *The Church in late Victorian Scotland 1874-1900* (Edinburgh, 1978).

W. Ferguson, *Scotland. 1689 to the present* (Edinburgh, 1968).

E. Halévy, *A history of the English people in the nineteenth century. I. England in 1815* (2nd edn., 1949).

J. E. Handley, *The Irish in modern Scotland* (Cork, 1947).

H. J. Hanham, *Scottish nationalism* (1969).

J. G. Kellas, *Modern Scotland* (2nd edn., 1980).

A. A. MacLaren, *Religion and social class. The Disruption years in Aberdeen* (1974).

L. J. Saunders, *Scottish democracy 1815-1840. The social and intellectual background* (Edinburgh, 1950).

T. C. Smout, *A history of the Scottish people 1560-1830* (paperback edn., n.p., 1972).

4. *Before and after the 1872 Act*

W. H. Bain, '"Attacking the citadel"': James Moncreiff's proposals to reform Scottish education, 1851-69', *Scottish Educational Review*, x, no. 2 (1978), 5-14.

M. Cruickshank, 'The Argyll Commission report 1865-8: a landmark in Scottish education', *British Journal of Educational Studies*, xv (1967), 133-47.

B. Lenman & J. Stocks, 'The beginnings of state education in Scotland, 1872-1885', *Scottish Educational Studies*, iv (1972), 93-106.

M. Monies, 'The impact of the 1872 Education (Scotland) Act on Scottish working class education up to 1899', unpublished Ph.D. thesis, Edinburgh, 1974.

J. D. Myers, 'Scottish teachers and educational policy, 1803-1872: attitudes and influence', unpublished Ph.D. thesis, Edinburgh, 1970.

—— 'Scottish nationalism and the antecedents of the 1872 Education Act', *Scottish Educational Studies*, iv (1972), 71-92.

A. H. Peden, 'A Study of some aspects of the Argyll commission of 1864-68', unpublished M.Ed. thesis, Edinburgh, 1972.

J. Scotland, 'The centenary of the Education (Scotland) Act of 1872', *British Journal of Educational Studies*, xx (1972), 121-36.

T. J. Wilson, 'Scotland and the Revised Code 1861-72: some problems of interpretation', unpublished M.Ed. thesis, Glasgow, 1979.

D. J. Withrington, 'Towards a national system, 1867-72: the last years in the struggle for a Scottish Education Act', *Scottish Educational Studies*, iv (1972), 107-24.

—— 'The 1872 Education Act—a centenary retrospect', *Education in the North*, ix (1972), 5-9.

—— 'How the churches defended religion in the Education Act of 1872', *Times Educational Supplement. Scotland*, 7 Jan. 1972, p. 4.

5. *Secondary schools*

Air Academy and Burgh Schule, 1233-1895 (Ayr, n.d. [1895]).

F. W. Bedford, *History of George Heriot's Hospital* (3rd edn., Edinburgh, 1872).

W. Brodie, *Kelvinside Academy 1878-1923* (Glasgow, 1924).

R. Brown, *The history of the Paisley Grammar School, from its foundation in 1576; of the Paisley Grammar School and Academy, and of the other town's schools* (Paisley, 1875).

J. Cleland & T. Muir, *The history of the High School of Glasgow* (Glasgow, 1878).

T. Davidson, *Bathgate Academy 1833-1933* (Bathgate, 1933).

The Glasgow Academy. The first hundred years (Glasgow, 1946).

J. Harrison, *The Company of Merchants of the City of Edinburgh and its schools, 1694-1920* (Edinburgh, n.d. [1920]).

A. Heron, *The rise and progress of the Company of Merchants of the City of Edinburgh 1681-1902* (Edinburgh, 1903).

W. H. Hill, *History of the Hospital and School founded in Glasgow, A. D. 1639-41, by George and Thomas Hutcheson of Lambhill* (Glasgow, 1881).

Hillhead High School 1885-1961 (n.p., 1962).

History of the Hospital and Schools, 1881-1914 [Hutchesons'] (Glasgow, 1914).

A. G. Hogg, 'The Leaving Certificate and the development of secondary education in Edinburgh', unpublished M.Ed. thesis, Edinburgh, 1970.

A. F. Hutchison, *History of the High School of Stirling, with notices of schools and education in the burgh generally* (Stirling, 1904).

Laurel Bank School 1903-1953 (Glasgow, 1953).

Loretto's hundred years, 1827-1927 (1928).

R. J. Mackenzie, *Almond of Loretto* (1905).

D. G. McLean, *The history of Fordyce Academy. Life at a Banffshire school, 1592-1935* (Banff, 1936).

M. Magnusson, *The clacken and the slate. The story of the Edinburgh Academy 1824-1974* (1974).

W. M. Metcalfe, *The John Neilson Institution. Its first fifty years* (Paisley, 1902).

D. Murray, *Merchiston Castle School 1855-58* (Glasgow, 1915).

J. B. Ritchie, *Forres: its schools and schoolmasters. A record of three hundred years* (n.p., 1926).

W. C. A. Ross, *The Royal High School* [Edinburgh] (Edinburgh, 1934).

St. Leonards School 1877-1927 (n.d.).

G. St. Quintin, *The history of Glenalmond. The story of a hundred years* (Edinburgh, 1956).

A. Shewan, *Spirat adhuc amor. The record of the Gym (Chanonry House School), Old Aberdeen* (Aberdeen, 1923).

H. F. M. Simpson, *Bon Record. Records and reminiscences of Aberdeen Grammar School from the earliest times* (Edinburgh, 1906).

E. Smart, *History of Perth Academy* (Perth, 1932).

W. Steven, *The history of the High School of Edinburgh* (Edinburgh, 1849).

J. Thompson, *A history of Daniel Stewart's College 1855-1955* (Edinburgh, 1955).

H. L. Waugh, *George Watson's College. History and record* (Edinburgh, 1970).

J. Williamson, *A history of Morrison's Academy, Crieff* (Auchterarder, 1980).

J. R. S. Young, *Edinburgh Institution, 1832-1932* (Edinburgh, 1933).

6. University history: general themes

E. Ashby, *Technology and the academics. An essay on universities and the scientific revolution* (1959).

A. Collier, 'Social origins of a sample of entrants to Glasgow University', *Sociological Review*, xxx (1938), 161-85, 262-77.

G. E. Davie, *The democratic intellect. Scotland and her universities in the nineteenth century* (2nd edn., Edinburgh, 1964).

—— *The social significance of the Scottish philosophy of common sense* (n.p., 1973).

D. B. Horn, 'The Universities (Scotland) Act of 1858', *University of Edinburgh Journal*, xix (1958-60), 169-99.

I. J. McDonald, 'Untapped reservoirs of talent? Social class and opportunities in Scottish higher education, 1910-1960', *Scottish Educational Studies,* i (1967), 52-8.

D. I. Mackay, *Geographical mobility and the brain drain. A case study of Aberdeen university graduates, 1860-1960* (1969).

A. McPherson, 'The generally educated Scot. An old ideal in a changing university structure', in A. McPherson & others, *Eighteen-plus: the final selection* (Bletchley, 1972).

—— 'Selections and survivals: a sociology of the ancient Scottish universities', in R. Brown (ed.), *Knowledge, education, and cultural change. Papers in the sociology of education* (1973).

W. M. Mathew, 'The origins and occupations of Glasgow students, 1740-1839', *Past & Present*, no. 33 (1966), 74-94.

G. Mercer & D. J. C. Forsyth, 'Some aspects of recruitment to school teaching among university graduates in Scotland, 1860-1955', *British Journal of Educational Studies,* xxiii (1975), 58-77.

L. R. Moore, 'The Aberdeen Ladies' Educational Association, 1877-1883', *Northern Scotland,* iii (1977-80), 123-57.

—— 'Aberdeen and the higher education of women 1868-1877', *Aberdeen University Review,* xlviii (1979/80), 280-303.

A. Morgan, *Scottish university studies* (1933).

A. C. O'Dell & K. Walton, 'A note on the student population of Aberdeen University', *Aberdeen University Review,* xxxiii (1949/50), 125-7.

J. R. Peddie, *The Carnegie Trust for the Universities of Scotland, 1901-1951. The first 50 years* (Edinburgh, 1951).

J. P. Powell, 'Some nineteenth-century views on the university curriculum', *History of Education Quarterly,* v (1965), 97-109.

J. Robb, *The Carnegie Trust for the Universities of Scotland 1901-1926* (Edinburgh, 1927).

P. L. Robertson, 'The finances of the University of Glasgow before 1914', *History of Education Quarterly,* xvi (1976), 449-78.

M. Sanderson, *The universities in the nineteenth century* (1975).

—— *The universities and British industry 1850-1970* (1972).

J. Scotland, 'Battles long ago—Aberdeen University and the training of teachers 1907-08', *Scottish Educational Studies,* vii (1975), 85-95.

N. Shepherd, 'Women in the University. Fifty years: 1892-1942', *Aberdeen University Review,* xxix (1941/2), 171-81.

R. N. Smart, 'Literate ladies—a fifty year experiment', *The Alumnus Chronicle* [St. Andrews], no. 59 (1968), 21-31.

—— 'Some observations on the provinces of the Scottish universities, 1560-1850', in G. W. S. Barrow (ed.), *The Scottish tradition. Essays in honour of Ronald Gordon Cant* (Edinburgh, 1974).

[B. W. Welsh], *After the dawn. A record of the pioneer work in Edinburgh for the higher education of women* (Edinburgh, 1939).

C. J. Wright, 'Academics and their aims: English and Scottish approaches to university education in the nineteenth century', *History of Education,* viii (1979), 91-7.

7. Universities: institutional history

P. J. Anderson (ed.), *Rectorial addresses delivered in the Universities of Aberdeen 1835-1900* (Aberdeen, 1902).

—— *Studies in the history and development of the University of Aberdeen* (Aberdeen, 1906).

The Book of the Jubilee. In commemoration of the Ninth Jubilee of the University of Glasgow 1451-1901 (Glasgow, 1901).

J. M. Bulloch, *The lord rectors of the Universities of Aberdeen* (Aberdeen, 1890).

—— *A history of the University of Aberdeen 1495-1895* (1895).

R. G. Cant, *The University of St Andrews. A short history* (new edn, Edinburgh, 1970).

J. Coutts, *A history of the University of Glasgow. From its foundation in 1451 to 1909* (Glasgow, 1909).

The curious diversity. Glasgow University on Gilmorehill: the first hundred years (Glasgow, 1970).

I. G. S. Ferrier, 'The office of rector in the University of St. Andrews', *The Alumnus Chronicle*, no. 45 (1956), 10-24.

The five-hundred year book. To commemorate the fifth centenary of the University of Glasgow. 1451-1951 (Glasgow, n.d.).

Fortuna domus. A series of lectures delivered in the University of Glasgow in commemoration of the fifth centenary of its foundation (Glasgow, 1952).

G. Foulkes (ed.), *Eighty years on. A chronicle of student activity in the University of Edinburgh during the eighty years of the existence of the Students' Representative Council* (Edinburgh, 1964).

A. Grant, *The story of the University of Edinburgh during its first three hundred years* (2 vols., 1884).

D. B. Horn, *A short history of the University of Edinburgh 1556-1889* (Edinburgh, 1967).

W. Knight (ed.), *Rectorial addresses delivered at the University of St. Andrews. Sir William Stirling-Maxwell, Bart., to the Marquess of Bute, 1863-1893* (1894).

P. R. S. Lang, *Duncan Dewar. A student of St. Andrews 100 years ago. His accounts* (Glasgow, 1926).

J. D. Mackie, *The university of Glasgow 1451-1951. A short history* (Glasgow, 1954).

J. I. Macpherson, *Twenty-one years of corporate life at Edinburgh University. Being a short history of the Students' Representative Council and an account of its majority celebrations* (Edinburgh, n.d.).

A. J. Mill, 'The first ornamental rector at St. Andrews University: John Stuart Mill', *Scottish Historical Review*, xliii (1964), 131-44.

D. Murray, *Memories of the old College of Glasgow. Some chapters in the history of the University* (Glasgow, 1927).

C. A. Oakley, *Union Ygorra. The story of the Glasgow University student over the last sixty years* (Glasgow, 1950-1).

R. S. Rait, *The Universities of Aberdeen. A history* (Aberdeen, 1895).

J. B. Salmond (ed.), *Veterum laudes. Being a tribute to the achievements of the members of St. Salvator's College during five hundred years* [St. Andrews] (Edinburgh, 1950).

W. D. Simpson (ed.), *The fusion of 1860. A record of the centenary celebrations and a history of the united University of Aberdeen 1860-1960* (Edinburgh, 1963).

A. Stodart-Walker (ed.), *Rectorial addresses delivered before the University of Edinburgh 1859-1899* (1900).

K. E. Trail, 'The union of the Universities of Aberdeen', *Aberdeen University Review*, xv (1927/8), 97-110.

A. L. Turner (ed.), *History of the University of Edinburgh, 1883-1933* (Edinburgh, 1933).

Votiva tabella. A memorial volume of St Andrews University in connection with its quincentenary festival. MCCCCXI-MDCCCCXI (n.p., 1911).

8. *Bibliography and methodology*

R. M. W. Cowan, *The newpaper in Scotland. A study of its first expansion 1815-1860* (Glasgow, 1946).

J. Craigie, *A bibliography of Scottish education before 1872* (1970).

—— *A bibliography of Scottish education 1872-1972* (1974).

P. M. Jacobs, 'Registers of the universities, colleges and schools of Great Britain and Ireland', *Bulletin of the Institute of Historical Research,* xxxvii (1964), 185-232.

H. Kaelble, *Historical research on social mobility. Western Europe and the USA in the nineteenth and twentieth centuries* (1981).

A. A. MacLaren (ed.), *Social class in Scotland: past and present* (Edinburgh, n.d.).

F. K. Ringer, *Education and society in modern Europe* (1979).

H. Silver & S. J. Teague, *The history of British universities 1800-1969, excluding Oxford and Cambridge. A bibliography* (1970).

G. Sutherland (ed.), *Education* [Irish University Press, 'Commentaries on British Parliamentary Papers' series] (n.p., 1977).

D. J. Withrington, 'What is and what might be: some reflections on the writing of Scottish educational history', *Scottish Educational Studies,* ii (1970), 110-18.

E. A. Wrigley (ed.), *Nineteenth-century society. Essays in the use of quantitative methods for the study of social data* (Cambridge, 1972).

INDEX

ADDITIONAL BIBLIOGRAPHY (1989)

R. D. Anderson, 'Education and the state in nineteenth-century Scotland', *Economic History Review*, 2nd series, xxxvi (1983), 518-34.
— 'Secondary schools and Scottish society in the nineteenth century', *Past and Present*, no. 109 (1985), 176-203.
— 'Education and society in modern Scotland: a comparative perspective', *History of Education Quarterly*, xxv (1985), 459-81.
— 'In search of the "lad of parts": the mythical history of Scottish education', *History Workshop*, no. 19 (1985), 82-104.
— 'Scottish university professors, 1800-1939: profile of an elite', *Scottish Economic and Social History*, vii (1987), 27-54.
— 'Sport in the Scottish universities, 1860-1939', *International Journal of the History of Sport*, iv (1987), 177-88.
— *The student community at Aberdeen, 1860-1939* (Aberdeen, 1988).
J. M. Beale, *A history of the burgh and parochial schools of Fife* (n.p., 1983).
C. G. Brown, *The social history of religion in Scotland since 1730* (1987).
S. J. Brown, *Thomas Chalmers and the godly commonwealth in Scotland* (Oxford, 1982).
S. & O. Checkland, *Industry and ethos: Scotland 1832-1914* (1984).
G. E. Davie, *The crisis of the democratic intellect: the problem of generalism and specialisation in twentieth-century Scotland* (Edinburgh, 1986).
T. M. Devine & R. Mitchison (eds), *People and society in Scotland. I. 1760-1830* (Edinburgh, 1988).
G. Donaldson (ed.), *Four centuries: Edinburgh University life, 1583-1983* (Edinburgh, 1983).
T. A. Fitzpatrick, *Catholic secondary education in south-west Scotland before 1972* (Aberdeen, 1986).
J. T. D. Hall (ed.), *The tounis college: an anthology of Edinburgh University student journals, 1823-1923* (Edinburgh, 1985).
P. Hillis, 'Education and evangelisation: presbyterian missions in mid-nineteenth century Glasgow', *Scottish Historical Review*, lxvi (1987), 46-62.
R. A. Houston, *Scottish literacy and the Scottish identity: illiteracy and society in Scotland and northern England, 1600-1800* (Cambridge, 1985).
I. G. C. Hutchison, *A political history of Scotland, 1832-1924: parties, elections and issues* (Edinburgh, 1986).
K. H. Jarausch (ed.), *The transformation of higher learning, 1860-1930* (Chicago, 1983).
L. Moore, 'Invisible scholars: girls learning Latin and mathematics in the elementary public schools of Scotland before 1872', *History of Education*, xiii (1984), 121-37.
A. D. Morrison-Low & J. R. R. Christie (eds), *'Martyr of science': Sir David Brewster, 1781-1868* (Edinburgh, 1984).

D. K. Müller, F. Ringer & B. Simon (eds), *The rise of the modern educational system: structural change and social reproduction, 1870-1920* (Cambridge, 1987).

N. T. Phillipson (ed.), *Universities, society, and the future* (Edinburgh, 1983).

K. Robbins, *Nineteenth-century Britain: integration and diversity* (Oxford, 1988).

P. Robertson, 'Scottish universities and Scottish industry, 1860-1914', *Scottish Economic and Social History*, iv (1984), 39-54.

S. Rothblatt, 'Historical and comparative remarks on the federal principle in higher education', *History of Education*, xvi (1987), 151-80.

W. D. Rubinstein, 'Education and the social origins of British elites, 1880-1970', *Past and Present*, no. 112 (1986), 163-207.

N. Shepley, *Women of independent mind: St George's School, Edinburgh, and the campaign for women's education, 1888-1988* (Edinburgh, 1988).

T. C. Smout, *A century of the Scottish people, 1830-1950* (1986).

D. Southgate, *University education in Dundee: a centenary history* (Edinburgh, 1982).

A. Thomson, *Ferrier of St. Andrews: an academic tragedy* (Edinburgh,